CONTENTS

FOREWORD

I FIRST MET Chief Emeka Anyaoku in May 1986 at Pollsmoor prison where, as Commonwealth Deputy Secretary-General, he had accompanied the Eminent Persons Group in their historic mission to South Africa. Since then, we have met on many occasions and in happier times: in Lusaka and later in London shortly after my release from prison; on his many visits to South Africa as Commonwealth Secretary-General beginning immediately after the Harare Commonwealth Heads of Government Meeting in October 1991; and at a variety of international gatherings.

In what has grown to be a warm personal friendship, two qualities of the Chief have consistently struck me: his unwavering commitment to democracy and justice; and his quiet personal style for achieving these objectives.

Never seeking the limelight for himself, Emeka Anyaoku's most enduring strength is his ability to win the trust of different peoples, at different times, and in different places.

Master of quiet diplomacy, the Chief also brings to the international arena that great African tradition of consensus building that has positioned him in a key role as a builder of bridges across peoples and nations.

In South Africa, which had for so many years been a central concern of the Commonwealth, Emeka Anyaoku was quick to grasp during the transition to democracy that the country's problems had first and foremost to be resolved by South Africans.

But he also understood that the international community had an important role to play in lending confidence and strength to these internal processes.

The Commonwealth was represented by a distinguished team chosen by the Secretary-General at the start of the CODESA talks in December 1991. When it became apparent that political violence was proving to be the single greatest impediment to the negotiations, Emeka Anyaoku put forward to the African National Congress and the other political parties the idea of international experts from a variety of relevant backgrounds whose presence in South Africa would help to arrest the growing violence.

This contributed to the adoption of UN Resolution 772 under which the United Nations, the Organization of African Unity, the European Union and the Commonwealth established observer missions in South Africa which played a critical role until the elections in April 1994. Although small in numbers, the Commonwealth teams proved to be especially well qualified and effective in their role.

With the end of apartheid in South Africa many a critic wondered if the Commonwealth would at least lose some of its momentum. On the contrary, with Emeka Anyaoku's driving force, the Commonwealth has seized the initiative in the broader international campaign towards multiparty democracy, respect for human rights and sustainable development.

Over the last five years, the Commonwealth has become increasingly known for its various programmes to promote and consolidate democracy, including in South Africa. At the time of writing, the Secretary-General had made clear his desire that the few remaining military authorities in the Commonwealth give way to democratically elected civilian governments; not least in his home country, Nigeria.

With the thawing of the Cold War, the world has witnessed a frightening upsurge of ethnic and racial tension. The Commonwealth, which includes in its membership countries from north and south, is uniquely placed to take up the challenge of what I have called "making the world safe for diversity".

In South Africa, despite the many problems we still face, we are endeavouring to show that with tolerance, it is possible to live in harmony, regardless of our different shades and beliefs.

This book is about the search for a common humanity — for those uniting qualities which transcend class, colour, time and place — through a unique international organization which has shown itself to be an effective instrument of global peace and understanding.

It is also a book about the profoundly humane man who, from his village in Nigeria, to the bustling metropolis of developed and developing countries, has made this search for a common humanity his life's mission. We, the peoples of the Commonwealth, owe him our support in this crucially important endeavour.

Nelson Mandela

Nelson Mandela and Emeka Anyaoku outside Marlborough House, London, May 1993.   *Photo by Gary Weaser, The Guardian*

DEDICATED

to the dignity of Christopher Okigbo
"For him it was not a matter of choosing between Africa and Europe, but of evolving standards of judgement which could take on the ... achievements of different cultures within a singular critique." (Odia Ofeimun, Africa Forum)

to the courage of Martin Luther King
"Injustice anywhere is a threat to justice everywhere. We are caught in an inescapable network of mutuality, tied in a single garment of destiny. Whatever affects one directly, affects all indirectly." (Letter from Birmingham Jail)

to the devotion of M.K. Gandhi
"My devotion to Truth has drawn me into the field of politics; and I can say without the slightest hesitation ...that those who say that religion has nothing to do with politics do not know what religion means." (Mahatma Gandhi in Shanti Sadiq Ali, Gandhi & South Africa)

to the vision of Ben Okri
"In the beginning there was a river. The river became a road and the road branched out to the whole world. ... A dream can be the highest point of life." (The Famished Road)

to the commitment of Arnold Smith
"To build a global community we must stretch the horizons of knowledge, understanding, and goodwill and develop habits of consultation and cooperation that transcend the limits of race, region, or economic level." (Stitches in Time)

and to the memory of W.E.B. duBois
"Africa is at once the most romantic and the most tragic of continents. ...There are those, nevertheless, who would write universal history and leave out Africa." (The World and Africa)

"I pledge to use all the energy and resources available to me to work towards:

A Commonwealth whose actions will foster its values and serve the needs and interests of its member states, especially in the areas of economic and technological development;

A Commonwealth where member nations and people are demonstrably equal partners, because they are actuated by a genuine sense of equality and interdependence;

A Commonwealth realistic and imaginative enough to be guided in its activities by the knowledge that our proper constituencies are not only the present generation, but also the future unborn of this world;

A Commonwealth determined to contribute to efforts to wipe out the intolerable historical legacy that sustains, sometimes unwittingly, the notion that some human beings are inherently superior or inferior to others;

A Commonwealth striving always to bring, in the words of Jawaharlal Nehru, 'a healing touch' to international and (perhaps some day) even major national conflict situations that are of concern to its members."

Chief Emeka Anyaoku,
Acceptance Statement to Commonwealth
Heads of State and Government,
Kuala Lumpur, 24 October 1989.

PREFACE

THIS IS A remarkable story of international relations and the politics of race, of diplomacy, dedication and tenacious commitment to principle, spanning over 30 years of personal involvement in world events — from independence and civil war in his own country, to global promotion of human dignity and equality, economic and social development, individual liberty and democracy, international peace and order, and a world in which the behaviour of nations would be guided by the acceptance of one common humanity.

And it is the story of an influential international statesman who believes in consensus rather than confrontation, in persuasion rather than force, and in the power of morality over corruption.

Just who is the architect of this strategy for the Commonwealth and beyond? What is the basis for his influence in international affairs, and access to over 50 heads of state and government? Where did he come from, and what moulded his thinking? What was his route to international statesman, and what barriers did he overcome on the way — of race, ethnicity, culture? How did a traditional Nigerian chief emerge as a modern proponent of democracy and human rights, including those of women?

This book is about Chief Emeka Anyaoku, the man and his work. It combines a biographical profile with current themes and statements, professional and personal achievements, and challenges of the approaching millennium. His definition of democracy, and democracy's "enemies within", strikes a particular chord at this time of rising ethnic tension in various parts of the world, as do his concerns for the environment, sustainable development and the role of all people in forging a common humanity, as well as for the future of South Africa and of his home country, Nigeria.

The Commonwealth, unlike the United Nations, has no charter. It has, instead, a series of declarations to which all member countries voluntarily subscribe.

The Harare Declaration agreed in Zimbabwe set the Commonwealth on a new course as an influential global organization, followed by the

Millbrook and Edinburgh declarations from two other Heads of Government meetings in New Zealand and Britain, during Chief Anyaoku's tenure as Secretary-General. These declarations show the extent of his influence, in conceptualizing and negotiating them.

Three of the many declarations that he played a key role in preparing when Deputy Secretary-General are: The Lusaka Declaration of the Commonwealth on Racism and Racial Prejudice (1979), The Okanagan Statement and Programme of Action on Southern Africa (1987) and The Commonwealth Accord on Southern Africa (1985). The latter, known as the Nassau Accord, played a pivotal role in the pressure to end apartheid, through establishment of the Eminent Persons Group and initiating multi-lateral agreement on the imposition of economic sanctions.

The declaration that provides the basis of modern Commonwealth principles, the Singapore Declaration of Commonwealth Principles of 1971, recognizes "racial prejudice as a dangerous sickness threatening the healthy development of the human race." The future SG, then Assistant Director of the International Affairs division, was involved in the development of this declaration, which continues to form the basis of the Commonwealth's shared values.

The contents of this book are based primarily on lengthy interviews with the subject, who patiently endured long hours of questioning, and I would like to thank him for his encouragement and fortitude, as well as his frankness and honesty. Not being a diplomat myself, many of my questions were blunt; his answers on occasion were diplomatic, but he never avoided a question, no matter how searching or sensitive. When I first presented him with the idea of a biography in 1990, after a visit to his home village of Obosi, he took a very long time to consider my request, but with characteristic dedication, he gave it his full attention and support, once his decision was taken.

In a manner which I soon learned was typical, he always looked to the future, seldom dwelt on the past; and while he told me of his plans and vision, he seldom boasted of his achievements. I had to learn about those from others.

I want to thank also his good friend and icon, Nelson Mandela, for agreeing to do the Foreword to this book and doing so with great eagerness and enthusiasm.

Numerous insights were gleaned from discussions with others, many within the Commonwealth Secretariat, and I would like to take this opportunity to thank them for helping me to broaden my understanding on a range of issues over a number of years. My husband and partner,

David Martin, deserves thanks in the same context, for sharing with me his vast personal knowledge of African history and politics, and his worldview. To *Ugoma* Bunmi Anyaoku, a very special thanks for her warmth and patience in allowing me access to her home and family, and sharing details of special family occasions.

I must thank the staff of the Secretary-General's private office, Mary Mackie in particular, who ensured that I had access to current public information and who was always ready to track down missing documents, even while running to keep up with the Secretary-General and very busy with her daily tasks. Marilyn Benjamin worked very hard on collecting and organizing his speeches for me. Chuks Ihekaibeya contributed to my understanding through provision of key bibliographic references and encouragement. Ade Adefuya provided useful historical data and current press clips; and the director of the private office, Stuart Mole, agreed to an interview which turned into a most interesting discussion. Prunella Scarlett of the Commonwealth Business Council, who was active for many years in the Royal Commonwealth Society, provided insights and guidance on the non-governmental and private sectors, and a shared perspective on the subject. Thanks to Steve Godfrey, the Commonwealth Development Adviser (South Africa), for your enthusiasm and support. And John Syson, for Mozambique Special Fund, for documents, and keeping us all on track. My greatest regret is in not contacting Arnold Smith before his death in 1994; thanks to Clyde Sanger for producing Smith's insightful book, *Stitches in Time.*

Several long-time friends and colleagues of the Chief were helpful in various ways, including Prof. Arnold Bradshaw, a Trinity College graduate who was his Greek lecturer at Ibadan University College, and the widow of Prof. John Ferguson, another Classics lecturer at Ibadan; Dr Agbim in London, E.S. Reddy in New York and S.K. Singh in New Delhi deserve special mention.

Thanks Kate Popoola for national insights and for Onyeka Onwenu's music which kept me moving, and Hugh McCullum, for your willing and insightful editorial remarks, always delivered with positive reinforcement. To other colleagues at SARDC, without your capacity, support, patience and fortitude, I would have been unable to complete this work. Finally, but not last, to Paul Wade of Inkspots and Sarah Higgins of Creda for their talent and flexibility, and to the most patient and supportive publisher in the entire world, with steady nerves far beyond a normal publishing deadline, Kassahun Checole of Africa World Press. Thanks for understanding why this story needs to be told.

Broad research was undertaken from written sources too numerous to mention, mostly reports and documents published by the Secretariat since 1990. The historical perspective draws considerable inspiration and content from the work of Elizabeth Isichei, Chinua Achebe and Patrick Manning, and from I.E. Iweka-Nuno's partial translation of the history of Obosi from the Igbo copy. A brief bibliography is appended of books and booklets that were especially important in providing background to my understanding of the Secretary-General, his home country and the modern Commonwealth.

My intention was always to produce an accessible publication, not a scholarly work; and to widen understanding of the person, the institution and the continent of Africa. I have tried to ensure that, while this information is presented in an accessible manner, it is also as accurate as possible. Having said that, I must acknowledge that it is filtered through my lens, presented from the perspective of a Canadian citizen who, like the subject, is at home in another culture in another part of the Commonwealth, as well as being deeply rooted in the soil of her birth.

Phyllis Johnson

The Author

Phyllis Johnson is a Canadian writer, broadcaster and editor who has lived half her life in Africa, and is a long-time student of African history and politics. She has written several books and numerous articles, mainly on southern African issues. She has followed Commonwealth developments since 1973, and covered five summits as a journalist and broadcaster. She is Executive Director of a regional information resource centre, the Southern African Research and Documentation Centre (SARDC) in Harare, Zimbabwe.

There is a saying in Western Samoa:
From the direction of the wind
(To tell a story from the beginning)

1

THE CHANGING TIMES

Tempora mutantur, nos et mutamur in illis.
As the times change, so do we change with them.

THE ATMOSPHERE was electric that day in the Putra World Trade Centre in Kuala Lumpur, hissing and buzzing with anticipation. The Malaysian Prime Minister, the Hon. *Dato' Seri* Dr. Mahathir bin Mohamad, was presiding over a summit of world leaders from 49 countries, and had decided to dispense at once with a most contentious matter. It was an internal issue potentially as divisive for this particular gathering at this time as the main international policy issues they faced together (apartheid, debt, trade, development): that of leadership of their own organization.

Inside the Dewan Tun Hussein Onn B room, on that day in late October 1989, an African vice-president twisted his ballot paper into a tight tube so he could recognize it in order to see which pile it would be assigned to by the Chairman, and therefore whether his candidate's pile of votes was the taller of the two. When he saw that it was, he leaned back in his chair and waited. Only the Chairman knew the exact count, and he never told; but media speculation that it was 34-14 was supported by the piles of ballot papers — one pile was more than twice as high as the other one. The Chairman's announcement was solely the name of the meeting's choice, and the Commonwealth leaders made it unanimous. They had chosen their third Secretary-General in 25 years, and the first from Africa: a distinguished Nigerian chief equally at home with the cultural delicacy of village politics and local government as with the cut-and-thrust of international power politics and conflict resolution.

"It's the Chief," boomed his predecessor, hurrying toward the meeting room. "We've got a new pope," barked another senior official into the telephone.

Chief Emeka Anyaoku was already well-known to Commonwealth leaders, who chose him over a former Australian rugby player and prime minister, Malcolm Fraser; though he remained an enigma to many outside the organization. When he took office, he occupied the most senior position of any black African diplomat on the international stage, with direct personal access to over 50 Heads of State and Government, and Her Majesty, Queen Elizabeth II. He has emerged in the international community as a builder of bridges across ethnic barriers, able mediator in situations of conflict, and activist proponent of democracy.

His first official function, two days after taking office on 1 July 1990, was to receive Nelson Mandela, released a few months earlier from 27 years of detention in South Africa. At a glittering dinner at Commonwealth House in London, the Secretary-General introduced Mandela to top financial and commercial magnates from Britain and South Africa. Before his first term was halfway through, Chief Anyaoku was shuttling to another World Trade Centre — in Kempton Park, Johannesburg — to encourage and cajole and play an important behind-the-scenes role in helping to bring to an end more than four decades of racial "separate development" in South Africa.

Chosen by Commonwealth Heads of Government to succeed a Canadian and a Guyanese, the Chief obviously relished his opportunity to head the multi-racial, multi-cultural secretariat that services the world's most effective North-South meeting place and will guide it into the 21st century.

"Its off the Richter scale for headhunters," said the London _Daily Mail,_ of the job of Secretary-General, "undeniably the most prestigious international job on the market today. It means unlimited jet travel round the world. It means liaising with heads of state. It means representing more than 1,700 million people. It means being completely in charge of an organization which has no block votes and no vetoes."

Within weeks of the decision in far-off Malaysia, the 19 communities of Idemili gathered to honour him in his home area in eastern Nigeria. Eleazar Chukwuemeka Anyaoku, already a traditional _Ndichie_ chief, was invested with an honorific title of _Ugwumba Idemili,_ in a colourful ceremony attended by the rulers of all 19 clans of Idemili, the first time they had collectively bestowed such an honour. His wife, Bunmi, who is a chief in her own right, added Idemili to her title, becoming _Ugoma Obosi and Idemili._

Each _Eze,_ or king, from the 19 communities is resplendent in flowing traditional robes, wearing his crown and bearing symbols of office, and

each has brought his council of *Ndichie* chiefs. It is a glittering, lively, dignified, hot and dusty ceremony of investiture at Ogidi, the local government headquarters, attended by some 15,000 people. Sunlight bounces off
the masquerades — huge eagles, multi-coloured peacocks — from every
community, and these main dancers are fanned constantly by others in
the mid-day heat. The titled female chiefs also dance, though some are
hampered by heavy, ivory casings from ankle to knee, and some of the
music can only be danced to by the kings. The drums rumble and throb,
sharp whistles cut the air, mellowed by the clear, high, delicate piping of
the traditional Igbo reed flute.

This gathering, in the open air under a huge canvas awning, is
presided over by Dr Pius Okigbo, a respected former ambassador, one of
few men wearing a suit. After deep, melodious tones, blown through a
hole in the side of an ivory tusk, to call the ceremony to order, Dr Okigbo
welcomes home our son, Chief Emeka Anyaoku, with a traditional greeting; an Anglican priest offers prayers; and kola nuts are blessed, broken
and distributed. National television is present to record the day's events
with several cameras and reporters, commentating in local languages but
often using a phrase in English for the "extended family system".

Dr Okigbo says it is most appropriate that the Traditional Rulers
Council of Idemili Local Government has chosen to honour *Adazie Obosi*
in this way. He describes the Chief as the most distinguished and successful African diplomat in recent decades, and asks the family to pray
for his continued success. He says it is a remarkable sign of his humility
that, as one of the most outstanding international civil servants of his
generation worldwide, he was willing and proud to come back home and
accept the position of *Ichie Adazie Obosi*. He urges the Chief to continue to
maintain contact with his roots in Idemili local government, "which gives
each of us, wherever we go, pride and honour."

The guest of honour is taken away and clothed by the kings, in a robe
of heavy black velvet, patterned with gold-thread embroidery. Still wearing his round red cap which identifies him as an *Ndichie* chief, he squats
in front of one of the kings who bestows his new title, and replaces his red
cap with a similar one, studded with eagle feathers. Bunmi Anyaoku is
also conferred with her new title, and they are given symbolic gifts,
including, for him, a chair and an ivory tusk, both old and intricately
carved; and for her, a small, carved wooden stool, a black flywhisk and a
small white fan.

The recipient speaks of the quasi-religious significance and spiritual
symbolism of the Idemili river, and of the dynamism and generosity of its

peoples. He speaks of a river which has, for centuries, sustained the life of the many communities who fetched its waters daily for domestic use; and provided a flowing swimming pool to the young and the old who, generation after generation, have learned to swim in its many streams, and have enjoyed the sun on the shores of the river.

The river branches out to the globe, and he speaks of the Commonwealth of Nations as a microcosm of the world, because of its composition and scope. Rich member countries of the north and less wealthy of the south, and major racial groups, are learning to live together in equality and mutual respect, he tells the Traditional Rulers of Idemili Local Government. Some member countries long achieved democracy with stability and with commendable progress in economic development, while others are still searching, in some cases haltingly with unsure steps, toward more assured means to political stability and economic progress, he tells an audience that includes senior representatives of the federal government of Nigeria. The essence of the challenge facing Commonwealth countries, he says, is to find ways to cooperate in resolving the problems facing them.

The leaders of over a quarter of the world's population placed their confidence in this influential African to prepare their organization for the 21st century. The leaders of his local government area, and his home village, have honoured him with the same confidence. Herein follows, in this volume, a brief profile of the man and his work, viewed through the prism of his dual role as a distinguished international diplomat and a titled African chief/local government leader: *Ichie Adazie Obosi, Ugwumba Idemili.*

He moves easily between these local and international roles, and his is a story of achievement in both spheres. Thus it is a positive view of Africa, its people, culture and place in the world, through the life of one person — Chief Emeka Anyaoku. His name, in his native Igbo language, means Eye of Fire (*Anya* = Eye, *Oku* = Fire) or fiery eye, and is associated with ancestral chivalry and courage.

The Chief

His eyes were twinkling and his laughter came from far deep down in his throat as he put down the telephone receiver in his Hill Street study, after a hearty, but respectful conversation in his native Igbo language with an older man from home. The man, several years his senior, had called to congratulate him on his 93rd birthday, Chief Anyaoku said. Anticipating an expression of surprise on the visitor's face, he explained. A chief in his home area in eastern Nigeria is supposed to have reached 80 years on taking office, and since Emeka Anyaoku had been inducted into the society of *Ndichie* chiefs in 1980, simple arithmetic would deduce that, in 1993, he had reached the age of 93! So while the Chief, in London with family and close friends, was celebrating his 60th birthday, in his village of Obosi he had the homage and respect of a man considerably older. In the new millennium, the year 2000 coincides with *Adazie* turning 100!

With the same ease and humour with which he handled the attainment of two quite different ages on the same day, so he handles the many different cultures in which he operates as Commonwealth Secretary-General, reaching for the dream that he shares with Nelson Mandela — of building bridges of understanding and "making the world safe for diversity". He has searched for, and found, similarities in quite different cultures in all the regions of the world, as he visited all but one (Tuvalu) of the 54 Commonwealth member states. These are not only the obvious similarities of a shared political history of colonization resulting in similar legal and governance structures, but are those found in echoes at the heart of local cultures: in the proverbs, the methodology of human interaction, and aspects of royal rule.

When Chief Anyaoku took office as the first African Secretary-General, there were those who viewed him from superior heights and saw a quiet technocrat whom they expected would do their bidding. In the British conservative establishment of the time, their perspective transmogrified from disappointment through frustration and anger to grudging respect; and finally, admiration for a person whom they began to see as a sharp intellect (schooled in the Classics), even visionary, with a diplomatic demeanour that cloaked a rock-steady resolve. The transition was not of himself, though it was of his making, but in attitudes of people who encountered him in all walks of life. However, those who saw only his extensive command of the English language and the art of international diplomacy, overlooked his well-watered roots and his deeply African way of doing things.

"Drawing sustenance from the deep springs of African culture, and deriving inspiration from the riches of western philosophy," said the oration at Trinity College, Dublin conferring an honorary doctor of laws degree, "he is greatly respected as an illustrious citizen of the world who works devotedly for peace and the betterment of humanity."

In the year 2000, when the third Secretary-General vacates his post after two terms, he leaves the international community and the

Commonwealth quite different to what it was when he took office a decade earlier. Perhaps most significant, his own persona and conviction have altered the "image" of Africa in whomever he has encountered. His achievements are numerous, particularly in the people he has touched, attitudes he has changed and leadership he has influenced. Not least of these achievements is the isolation imposed by the Commonwealth on his home country, Nigeria, and, eventually, the bittersweet transition from military to civilian rule. He presided over the Commonwealth's consistent and increasingly engaged approach in support of the negotiations by South Africans that ended *apartheid* rule in their country; and he negotiated technical and diplomatic support for the first majority government. His own personal contribution toward ending *apartheid* (separate development, based on race and ethnicity) and establishing democracy *(demos,* the people; government by the people) in South Africa stretches back over 35 years of active service and ranks him with Lord Pitt and others as "an elder in the cause of freedom in southern Africa".

Known affectionately as "SG" or Chief, more respectfully as Secretary-General or *Adazie,* he has contributed to the restoration of democracy in over a dozen countries and has been involved personally in the mediation of disputes from Anguilla to Bangladesh to Gibraltar to Zanzibar, from Lesotho to Solomon Islands. Of particular concern are what he calls "inter-mestic" issues, which are domestic in character but have international ramifications.

The first African Secretary-General of the Commonwealth has guided the organization into a vision and framework for the next millennium, grasping more firmly than some may realize, the legacy and challenge of Marcus Garvey. As an heir to the vision of the early 20th century political activist from Jamaica, Anyaoku has continued to pursue the tasks of enfranchisement, independence and economic development of the "third world". He, too, has turned his attention to the place of Africa and the African diaspora within the concept of a common humanity, and has refused to submit to false conceptions of Africa and the role of its people and their culture in world history. As Garvey did almost a century earlier, Anyaoku has undertaken an international crusade to promote the concept of a common humanity and defend human rights across the globe, to establish a new framework for human development in Africa and the Caribbean, and the restructuring of global relationships on a more equitable basis. Like Garvey, he believes that racism is rooted in large part in perceptions of African underdevelopment, and that the goal of a common humanity can be reached through strengthening socio-economic development.

Chief Anyaoku has spent all of his adult life in opposition to apartheid, racism and inequality, and in support of common understanding, sustainable development, and respect for diversity and human dignity. He has developed and nurtured a vision of the Commonwealth as a force for democracy, human rights and good governance, an instrument for economic development, and a builder of global consensus. Among his material achievements is the restructured Commonwealth secretariat, leaving a leaner, more efficient engine. Queen Elizabeth II, whose role he has respected and strengthened as Head of the Commonwealth, undoubtedly will miss his counsel.

And when he steps down as Secretary-General in the year 2000, by the traditional linkage between age and wisdom and authority in his village, he has 100 years. ...

Harare, 1991

The venue is Harare, the capital city of Zimbabwe. Its wide, tree-lined streets are purple with the iridescent blossoms of jacaranda trees in early summer. The city, home to about one million people, sparkles in the southern African sunshine as the planes land, one after another, carrying an array of distinguished leaders from 47 English-speaking countries in all regions and time zones of the world.

The modern state of Zimbabwe in October 1991 is more than 11 years old but not quite 12, having emerged in 1980 from a short, bitter colonial interlude that had shattered the lengthy imperial history of African culture and governance. The massive stone structures still standing at Great Zimbabwe, Khami, and many other sites throughout the country are a legacy that yields its secrets sparingly for the period 1100 - 1500 AD. From the 16th century, the documents of explorers from the great seafaring nation of Portugal pick up the tale of encounters with African kings and courtiers, ambassadors, teachers, healers, priests, farmers, cattlemen, traders, hunters, goldsmiths, artists, weavers and iron-mongers. Reports to the metropolis tell of trade with the interior, of Portuguese interest in purchasing gold and ivory, and spreading their religion headed by a man in Rome.

In the last decade of the 19th century, the vast grasslands dotted with rock *kopjes* (hills) and the farmland fertile in soil and minerals were invaded from the south by a pioneer column sent from the British-ruled Cape province of South Africa by its Prime Minister, Cecil John Rhodes, and funded by the British South Africa Company. The column included farmers and miners, investors, hunters and chancers coming to seek their fortune in a land of "darkness" whose culture they did not understand and whose people they regarded as inferior. The Africans who inhabited the land welcomed these white pioneers as their guests and fed them for two years, offering fruit, vegetables and grains from their burgeoning farms. But the conquering weapons were the gun and the hut tax, which forced farmers into salaried employment in order to pay their taxes in foreign funds. Thus began the period of Rhodesia: 75 years of company and colonial rule followed by 15 years of settler rule and a guerrilla war by the original inhabitants — in all, just 90 years.

It was into this historical setting that the leaders of over a quarter of the world's population arrived for the "jacaranda summit", the 28th summit of the Commonwealth, a voluntary grouping of independent states, mostly former British colonies. The "problem" of Rhodesia had preoccupied the Commonwealth for 15 years following a unilateral declaration of independence (UDI) by white residents in 1965 until independence in 1980, and many leaders were coming to see for the first time — and to celebrate the first decade of — modern Zimbabwe.

The occasion is alight with symbolism. It is the first such gathering of world leaders managed by an African Secretary-General, Chief Emeka Anyaoku; in a country whose pre-independence issues almost tore the Commonwealth apart; and just across the Limpopo river lies the current focus for division: South Africa. It is the first world summit of this size since the release of Nelson Mandela from 27 years in prison, and he is a special guest. With his release and with a new British prime minister, John Major, this summit has a more congenial atmosphere than the previous six, which were attended by Margaret Thatcher and were fractious on the subject of sanctions against South Africa. The world leaders welcome the new President of independent Namibia, Sam Nujoma, to his first summit as a Commonwealth member, and express their grief at the loss of Rajiv Gandhi, Prime Minister of India, the world's largest democracy, assassinated the previous May.

The leaders pose in front of a several-metre-high painted backdrop of the Victoria Falls, a "wonder" of the world and Zimbabwe's leading tourist attraction: *mosi-oa-tunya*, the smoke that thunders. There are men in flowing blue or white robes from West Africa, besuited men from Asia, Australia, the Americas and elsewhere in Africa, from the Pacific, the Caribbean and Europe, and the Prime Minister of Bangladesh, a woman dressed in white. There is the diminutive, nonagenarian autocrat from Malawi, Dr Hastings Kamuzu Banda, who stumbles and falls as he enters the conference hall, and is propped up by the Prime Ministers of Canada and Malaysia. There are the hats and colourful dresses and saris of the spouses, especially the First Lady of Zimbabwe, Sally Mugabe, accompanied by the Secretary-General's wife, Bunmi Anyaoku, both stunning in shades of cherry and pink.

These Commonwealth Heads of Government Meetings, known as CHOGM, are the longest and most concentrated regular gatherings of heads of state and government in the world — and the most informal, bringing together the leaders of over 50 countries, both industrialized and developing, to discuss wide-ranging matters of mutual interest in a forum bridging South and North. The Zimbabwe CHOGM is seen as a signpost to the future for an organization that some observers thought had no future, as a loose grouping of former British colonies; and places it firmly in the direction of its new role in extending the benefits of sustainable development within a framework of respect for human rights and democracy.

In his first formal address to Heads of Government as their Secretary-General, Chief Anyaoku notes the significance of the venue, the strength of Commonwealth values, and its current political priorities, an agenda topped by the problem of *apartheid* in neighbouring South Africa. "It is... for me, a very special Heads of Government Meeting — my first as Secretary-General. I am delighted that it is being held in Harare — a great city of the continent from which I come. ...

"First, Harare is a unique venue, symbolizing the bond between the Commonwealth and Zimbabwe; a bond forged in the heat of the epic struggle by the Zimbabwean people against an attempt by a minority to replicate another *apartheid* republic this side of the Limpopo. ... UDI called into question everything for which the Commonwealth stood. To its lasting credit, the Commonwealth resolutely met that challenge. ...

"Second, the Meeting is unique in that it is taking place next door to South Africa at a critical moment in the history of that country. The situation in South Africa has rightly occupied a prominent place in Commonwealth affairs since 1961 and has tested our association to the limit. Fortunately, there have, in the last eighteen months, been substantial and welcome developments. But we are still to attain our ultimate objective — the ending of *apartheid* and the establishment of a non-racial democracy in a united and non-fragmented South Africa. ...

"Lastly, this Meeting is unique because it concerns no less a subject than the future role of our whole association. Two years ago in Kuala Lumpur, Heads of Government, reflecting on the past 40 years, expressed pride and confidence in the Commonwealth. Looking ahead, they decided that the time had come to take stock and chart the Commonwealth's future course in a world of momentous change. ...

"Certainly there is a stronger desire within the Commonwealth to promote the values for which it stands. Those principles, enunciated in the Singapore Declaration almost 20 years ago, set out a commitment to values such as democracy, human rights and the rule of law. ... In the evolving new world order, there will be an increasing need for international consensus if we are to deal effectively with a host of problems with a global reach. These are economic, political, environmental — and even social challenges, like AIDS, drugs and drug-trafficking. ...

"As the world leaves behind the old barriers of the Cold War, we need to progress beyond domination to a world of reconciliation and partnership. That is the central mission of the Commonwealth... which will emerge from Harare invigorated and renewed..."

The President of Zimbabwe, Robert Gabriel Mugabe, is in the Chair, the leader of a liberation movement for independence and majority rule, who spent a decade in prison. "The time has come for us to take a close look at ourselves," he says. "We are members of the Commonwealth in good faith for as long as we continue to uphold the principles we have proclaimed. Indeed, when we ourselves, individually or collectively, betray our own principles, we cannot proclaim ourselves as champions of human rights. ...

"The Commonwealth in the 1990s should be a torch-bearer of principles which so many expect us to uphold. These sacred principles were not conceived and left in Singapore in 1971, but are and should be a living and indestructible weapon whereby the Commonwealth continues to conquer and extend the frontier of freedom and liberty from era to era."

The Torch-bearer

The Secretary-General had prepared the summit thoroughly, leaving little to chance, in the practiced manner of his many years in charge of political affairs and administration, and in his personal style of wide consultation on a number of identified key issues. Ever since his decision to contest the post, at the urging of a number of Commonwealth leaders, and particularly since his election in Kuala Lumpur, he had been contemplating the state of the world, the future of the Commonwealth, and a specific, interventionist approach.

In the short span of two years between the summits of Commonwealth leaders in Malaysia in 1989 and Zimbabwe in 1991, global politics had encountered revolutionary change. The Berlin wall between East and West Germany was torn down, removing the physical symbol of the Cold War. The architect of *perestroika*, economic restructuring in the Soviet Union, Mikhail Gorbachov, lost his job; and there was the uncertainty of a new Hot War, Operation Desert Storm, in the Gulf.

During this period of global turmoil, the future Secretary-General quietly wrapped up his previous duties in London, and returned to his home at Obosi in eastern Nigeria for a period of retreat and contemplation before taking up his new office in mid-1990.

"There, more than most places, I could escape, if I wished, from the immediate concerns of world affairs and reflect on the tasks and responsibilities ahead," he told the Diplomatic and Commonwealth Writers Association in London in July, in one of his first engagements after taking office. "...as a result, I start my duties physically and mentally refreshed."

He said he was acutely conscious of the changes in the world that coincided with the beginning of his tenure, symbolized for him by two dramatic events in recent months: the destruction of the Berlin Wall in Europe, and the unconditional release of Nelson Mandela after 27 years of incarceration in South Africa.

Both events, he said "were about the triumph of the human spirit over the walls of confinement. ...The former represented more than anything else the whole surge towards democracy, whether expressed through bloody revolution, as in Romania, or in more gentle, but no less powerful, assertions of the people's power which have been taking place in many parts of the world. And the second was not only a fulfillment of what many individuals and groups including in particular the Commonwealth had worked and hoped for over recent years, but also an earnest hope that real change could at last begin to take place in South Africa."

He regarded these dramatic changes as both an opportunity and a challenge, as expressed in an Igbo proverb: "If God carves a drum for you, then the act of beating it is your job."

During the six-month retreat in his home village, the future Secretary-General had reflected on the direction of the association during his tenure, and concluded that he should "direct the Commonwealth's attention and resources towards tackling two broad categories of factors:
• the factors that blight the dignity and quality of life in so many developing Commonwealth countries; and

- the factors that still encourage some sections of developed countries to perceive the peoples and problems of the Third World in alien and sometimes disdainful terms. ...

"I plan to see the Commonwealth embark on a crusade for the dignity and fraternity of all human beings no matter where they are from or live," he noted on 24 May 1990.

He took this a step further in early June, when he focused his reflections on the aftermath of the Cold War and the paradox that, "as the Cold War which has been largely responsible for international tension and political polarization recedes, factors that make for division within communities have been on the increase. And some of these factors in turn sever relations between nations.

"There are ethnic and racial loyalties which are threatening the cohesion of societies in Europe, Asia, Africa and the Americas. There is religious fundamentalism creating new divisions and tension in communities in Europe, Africa and Asia, not to mention the Middle East. There are worsening economic conditions in many developing countries, including and especially in Africa, which is giving rise to new levels of instability and insecurity within states.

"I believe that as far as international organizations go, its track record and unique qualities give the Commonwealth comparative advantage in helping its member countries, and indeed the international community as a whole, to make an impact on these problems."

He then settled on a thematic approach devised within the framework of his philosophy of a "common humanity":

"1. Central to my vision of the Commonwealth is the promotion and actualization of the concept of one common humanity.

"2. In seeking to link the effective cooperation and friendship of its diverse member countries and peoples, the Commonwealth is moved by, and operates on the assumption of, the validity of the concept of a common humanity.

"3. Until national domestic and foreign policies are guided by this concept, cooperation within and between nations cannot attain its full potential.

"4. Politicians and policy makers must borrow a leaf from medical science where a great deal of the successes scored in research and curative practice have flowed from the underlying assumption that barring differences influenced by environmental factors, essential human historical attributes are the same for peoples everywhere." (from Reflections at Obosi, notes, May/June 1990)

Beyond Obosi

As the day neared for him to return to London, the Secretary-General-designate had two immediate concerns. The first was the future of the association itself at a time when, because of quarrels over South Africa and sanctions, Britain and some other countries within its sphere of influence were casting their interest elsewhere. There was need to renew interest and confidence in the Commonwealth as a vibrant and influential association.

The second concern, related to the first, was South Africa itself. He concluded that, "if the Commonwealth has any strong claim to mean something different from any other international organizations, it is its role as the champion of multi-racialism and the concept of racial equality. And so there was no way it could ever be indifferent to what was happening in South Africa. For me, it was important; and African countries, my own country Nigeria included, and many others, see that as a test case for continuing Commonwealth relevance."

These were the main themes that dominated his thinking. How could interest and confidence be renewed in the Commonwealth, and in the Commonwealth mechanism, beyond merely technical assistance; and how could the organization continue to have relevance for its members, who encompass almost one-third of the world's population?

"There are those who think the Commonwealth is doing great things in technical assistance and development work. Yes of course. That is so. But I never thought that would guarantee the continued appreciation of the Commonwealth by its members. Because after all, the total budget of the Commonwealth secretariat, including technical and developmental assistance, is about 40 million pounds a year. There are many charitable organizations that spend more than that. There are many development agencies that have departments headed by executive officers who would spend more than that. And so if the Commonwealth, in my thinking, was ever to aspire to remain something that its members would take seriously, it would not just be because of the 40 million pounds that it spends on technical assistance.

"It has to make a mark on the political scene," he reflected. "And what are those marks? I decided, of course, South Africa is a well-beaten track but it must continue to be relevant, relevant in a way that would create less controversy within the Commonwealth, and so be less divisive, while not betraying its commitment. Secondly, relevant in the sense of becoming more directly involved in the political issues of our time.

And thirdly, the riskiest part of my thinking, areas that hitherto were regarded as 'no-go' areas because they were internal affairs. I thought that if the Commonwealth was to be what all its members claim that it is — an informal, close relationship — then it should be able to intervene, even in internal affairs. And the true test would be how it wins the confidence of the parties concerned, particularly the government of the day in such countries, for such intervention. ...

"And then I wanted also to find for the Commonwealth a more strategic role in the pursuit of sustainable development. When I say a more strategic role, I am aware that the organization has had a good record in helping its member countries deal with different projects in the area of socio-economic development, but dealing with a number of projects does not yield as much impact on the thinking and appreciation of the Commonwealth as being part of the national effort to plan policies in strategic areas. So I wanted the Commonwealth to become more involved in macro-economic policy advice to governments. ...And then I also wanted to restore, to some extent, confidence in the structure of the Secretariat."

He reflected further in public to the diplomatic and Commonwealth writers in London on 25 July 1990, just three weeks after taking office: "A central attribute as a worldwide association encompassing nations at all levels of economic development, embracing peoples of many different races, religions and cultures, is surely its ability to bridge racial, ideological and economic divides and inequalities, assisted by its common language and common heritage. I view that sense of 'community in diversity' as the Commonwealth's greatest strength. Its vehicle is the framework for both official and unofficial Commonwealth-wide consultation and co-operation which has been built up, facilitated by traditional friendliness, informality, flexibility and capacity to share skills and experience. The biennial Commonwealth Heads of Government Meeting is simply the most visible manifestation of this multifaceted framework. ..."

He had concluded, therefore, that his main institutional goals were the removal of South Africa as a barrier to relations within the Commonwealth, definition of the future strategic role and renewed confidence in the role of the Commonwealth, and restructuring the Secretariat in order to raise the level and scope of services to member states. In addition, there were three political strands which he explored and settled on: *apartheid* in South Africa; political issues of the day relating to democratization and human rights; and interventionist attempts to help to resolve conflicts or to assist in pursuing democratic development.

Chief too

Obosi is a bustling "village" of a quarter of a million people in eastern Nigeria, near the Niger river and the market city of Onitsha; it is green, with red earth roads. The Anyaoku compound, divided among family members, contains spacious modern dwellings with easy access to out-doors and air-conditioning in the dusty, humid, West African heat.

This compound is the meeting place for residents of the heart of Obosi's Ire quarter, with a large open space in front of the gate for con-sultations and celebrations. Family heads meet within the compound. The plot was larger in the time of Anyaoku's father and grandfather, before it was subdivided among their children and the families who served them. Emeka Anyaoku's plot contains the *iba*, the seat of the chief, in a special meeting room maintained for that purpose, with the symbols of office including a stuffed leopard skin, a fan, flywhisk, an ivory tusk and a wooden stool, both old and beautifully carved.

The flat white fan, made of cowhide with a bold design, was present-ed for ceremonial purposes at his investiture as chief in 1980, together with the round red cap worn by Ndichie chiefs. The tusk and stool were added at the ceremony a decade later, on 27 January 1990, when he was honoured by the Traditional Rulers Council of Idemili for his achieve-ments at home and abroad.

Earlier on the same day, his wife Bunmi had become a chief in her own right, with the title *Ugoma Obosi* conferred by the *Eze*, the traditional ruler of their local government area, His Royal Highness *Igwe* Iweka II.

Local government legislation allowing women to be chiefs in this area was passed only in 1984, on 24 November. Although Chief Anyaoku's maternal grandmother was titled *Nyamala*, and his wife became *Ugodi* in 1980, these were titles for women and not chiefly titles. Bunmi Anyaoku became the third woman chief in the area after 1984, particularly signifi-cant because it was the first time such a title had been conferred on some-one from outside the area. She is not Igbo but Yoruba. For her investiture, Bunmi wore the traditional Igbo coral beads around her neck and heavy ivory rounds on her arms. And she wore a length of Yoruba cloth, a red-and-white fabric called *aso oke*, which her mother brought, to blend with the red sash of office. Another heavy ivory piece for the leg, calf-length, was too heavy to wear.

Igwe Iweka II, wearing an embroidered gold cap and carrying a fly-whisk made from animal hair, blessed and broke kola nuts, and a priest gave Christian prayers to bless the ceremony. *Igwe* described Bunmi as a tower of strength to her husband in their diplomatic life, providing moral support and helpful advice.

"The title *Ugoma Obosi* is a fitting title to bestow on a lady who has represented some of the best qualities we look for in outstanding women, and who has played her own part in promoting international peace and security, as well as peace and progress in Obosi."

She was asked to pledge loyalty to *Igwe* and his "privy council" of *Ndichie* chiefs and, if given an assignment on behalf of the community, to do it faithfully and loyally. In addition to the red sash, she was presented with a staff of office about 1.5 metres in height, a small white fan and a white flywhisk. Later the same day at Ogidi, she was granted her second title, becoming *Ugoma Obosi and Idemili.*

A candidate for chief is first selected by the eligible families and then put forward to *Igwe* and council for approval. Ceremonies are conducted at family and village level before the final investiture, which can be performed only by *Igwe*. The rank of chief carries a ceremonial role in family and community festivities, a leadership role within the extended families, and responsibilities in local governance, including customary courts, now constituted by the civil authority but often on recommendation of the traditional ruler.

It is unusual for a chief to be non-resident or absent for long periods, and a concession was made for *Adazie;* a relative who is a title-holder performs the role in his absence. Since that concession was made, however, the mobility of modern leadership has been accepted and there are two more non-resident chiefs with local representation.

Marlborough House

Rested and refreshed from his sojourn in Obosi, Chief Anyaoku was filled with the enthusiasm and vigour that his private office staff were to find both exhilarating and exhausting. He walked through the front door of Carlton Gardens — around the corner from the Court of St James and off Pall Mall between Buckingham Palace and Trafalgar Square — for the first time as Secretary-General on the morning of Monday, 2 July, 1990. It was to be another three years before he moved to the Commonwealth headquarters adjacent to St James Park at Marlborough House, with its high ceilings and painted murals of European battle scenes. The stately home built by the architect Sir Christopher Wren for the first Duke and Duchess of Marlborough in the early eighteenth century, completed in 1711, was undergoing a major refurbishment.

None of this environment was new to him or the slightest bit strange, it had the familiarity of a favourite woolen muffler which, almost without notice, shielded the occupant from the most difficult days of London's inclement weather. But on this day, it was summer; and as he entered Carlton Gardens, he had an extra spring in his step when he greeted the reception staff and commissionaires, and turned up toward his new office. The junior staff were not surprised that his warm greeting was the same as before, coming as it did from himself and not from his title or status. Some of the senior staff were less certain; and their uncertainty reflected attitudes of the order of things, from a colonial time long past.

As is the Chief's way, he looks to the positive, he seeks the best in people and, confronted as he often was, with a certain superiority, inadvertently or otherwise rooted in the racial perspectives of the beholder, he always radiated charm and correctness, leaving the other individual wrong-footed. This method of dealing with ignorance is a matter of upbringing, a wellspring from early life's experience in a culture confident with its identity, expressed in a local proverb that says, "a kind word has a good reply". This approach was well-honed and consistent through his 30 years at the Commonwealth Secretariat as he occupied increasingly senior positions.

On one occasion in the 1970s, when he was Assistant Secretary-General, the Vice-Chancellor of a British university was to meet him at 3 o'clock and he returned from lunch to find a man in the entrance to Marlborough House looking at the paintings. Expecting that this was his distinguished guest, and as the messengers were away conducting other visitors, he approached him and asked, "Can I help you?" The man looked at him dismissively, and said, "Thank-you very much, I have an appointment with the Assistant Secretary-General." The tone and manner were such that his host returned to his office and told his secretary that she should arrange to bring up his guest. When the man was ushered in for the appointment, he was very uncomfortable. "And I was mischievous enough to say to him, please sit down, I do admire people who feel confident in unfamiliar surroundings. It has happened to me, and to my colleagues, endless times."

During his first months as Secretary-General, he was so often complimented on his speeches by people who then inquired if he wrote them himself, that he resolved to speak from notes for a period, and often did — so there could be no doubt as to who was generating the ideas contained in the address. Even speeches for official occasions, for which notes were provided from elsewhere in the Secretariat, were subject to his judicious rewrite to engage his own ideas. He also added a personal reference to the specific event or location. And always, a joke or a light-hearted story, a quote from the classics or an African proverb.

"We have a saying in my place," he would begin, "We have a proverb that, if you are not grown up enough and strong enough before you inquire into who murdered your father, you will suffer the same fate. So you have to wait until you can deal effectively with the person. ..."

The use of proverbs in African cultures is not exclusive to local language and experience but extends to embrace quotations from other literature and languages. Thus a Classics scholar could make good use of Greek and Latin proverbs, ie *Tempora mutantur, nos et mutamur in illis* (as the times change, so do we change with them), as he did to describe the far-reaching implications of the end of the Cold War.

There is another Igbo dictum that says, "to make a speech without using proverbs is like trying to climb a palm tree without a climbing rope."

In his first official address to the Commonwealth Parliamentary Association (CPA), in Harare in September 1990, he bluntly addressed two themes at the heart of the Commonwealth heritage: racism and democracy. He told the legislators at their 36th CPA meeting that they held the key "to eradicating one and nurturing the other". He chose his words carefully, speaking from a text which he had prepared in advance; and afterwards, when he received more comments on his presentation than on the subject matter, he "formed the uncomfortable impression" that they thought somebody else had written the material.

Addressing the same forum the following year in New Delhi, he spoke from notes. That speech was recorded and transcribed for publication by the editors of *The Roundtable*, a journal founded in 1910 and published by the Institute of Commonwealth Studies at the University of London, without offering the courtesy of an opportunity for polishing by its author.

In 1992, when the CPA met in Nassau, The Bahamas, he returned to a prepared text, speaking more broadly about democracy as a response to some of the world's problems. The comments afterwards were directed to the contents as well as the presentation, and there was clearly no longer a question of whose ideas were being presented.

"Historical conventions and modes of thought have not all been terribly favourable to the easy acceptance of my authority. It's a simple issue of historical attitudes."

Long walk to freedom

Two weeks after the investiture ceremony at Ogidi and across the continent, Nelson Mandela was released from prison and continued his "long
walk to freedom", on 11 February 1990, the 25th birthday of the
Anyaokus' eldest son. A week later, Mandela acknowledged the support
of the international community: "My release from prison was the direct
result of the people inside and outside South Africa. It was as a result of
the immense pressure exerted against the South African government by
the international community."

Chief Anyaoku had intimate knowledge of the informal contacts
among South Africans over the past few years, and advances over the
past few months since FW de Klerk had replaced PW Botha as leader of
the National Party and then as President of South Africa; so he expected
that such an event would occur soon. But the emotional impact of the
announcement itself, as it sped round the world on the airwaves, reached
deep into the heart of the man on retreat in his West African village. "I
expected it was coming. But I was nevertheless taken by surprise. I
remember jumping up, several times, and shouting, for joy. And I must
say it was when I realized how determined FW de Klerk was to pursue
his line of negotiations."

Some imprisoned ANC leaders had been released the previous
October, and certain aspects of "petty *apartheid*" had been dismantled:
segregation of beaches, public facilities and buses. Just nine days before
Mandela's release, De Klerk announced at the opening of Parliament that
bans and restrictions on proscribed organizations and people would be
lifted, and political prisoners and detainees held for non-violent activities
would be freed unconditionally. He announced the suspension of capital
punishment and lifted some restrictions imposed by the State of
Emergency. He stopped short of lifting the state of emergency or removing troops from the townships.

Within days, Chief Anyaoku left for London on his way to southern
Africa to greet Mandela when he walked into free Africa for the first time
on 27 February 1990, to a tumultuous reception organized by exiled colleagues at ANC headquarters in Lusaka, Zambia and by host President
Kenneth Kaunda, then chairman of the Front Line States. The Chief was
at Wembley stadium on 16 April for Mandela's international reception,
and the following month, Mandela was in Nigeria. In Abuja, the capital,
he attended a meeting of Commonwealth foreign ministers on southern
Africa, reinforcing the ANC's appeal for continued isolation of the

apartheid regime: "To lift sanctions now would be to run the risk of abort-
ing the process towards the complete eradication of *apartheid*."

Offered the carrot of loosening sanctions by the British Conservative
government, De Klerk met this part way in the language of the Groote
Schuur minute in May 1990, by undertaking to review security legislation
and reiterating his commitment to work towards the lifting of the state of
emergency. There was progress to report, therefore, after De Klerk's first
nine months in office, but Mandela made it clear that the international
community had played a role, and continued to have a role, in ensuring
that pressure for change was aimed at eradicating *apartheid*, not just
unbanning of the ANC and release of political prisoners. While firm on
the question of maintaining international sanctions, "to my delight, he
was relaxed about contacts with Pretoria," Chief Anyaoku said later. "He
said to me that he thought I could talk some sense to De Klerk, that dealing with De Klerk, providing it was someone like me, would not be
unhelpful."

Mandela, who was anxious to make contact with business groups and
investors (and they with him), and to retain the confidence of national
and international business communities, accepted the Chief's invitation
to travel to London in early July to meet the industrial barons of South
Africa and their biggest investor, Britain. So it was that the Secretary-
General's first official function, on 3 July 1990, just two days after taking
office, was to host a dinner at Commonwealth House for the ex-prisoner
now celebrity, Nelson Rolihlahla ("trouble-maker") Mandela, to meet the
business community and financiers from the City of London and South
Africa.

"If the Commonwealth has a peculiarity which sets it apart," the
Secretary-General said in his first official speech, "it is surely its
inevitable stand on the racial question, wherever and however it may rear
its head. The Commonwealth, as this gathering needs no reminding, has
fought racism, especially in southern Africa, with a tenacity and resolve
unparalleled by any other comparable international organization."

He noted that Mandela's presence was positive proof of the changes
taking place in South Africa — "changes that have brought *apartheid* to its
crossroads. For how else can one describe the fact that the Government
and the ANC have taken the first tentative steps towards negotiations
with the Groote Schuur meeting at the beginning of May?"

He gave a clear analysis, saying the "decisive factors which have
brought us to this point of hope and promise are really two: the unremit-
ting resistance by the black majority inside South Africa and the pressures

by the international community including especially economic sanctions. Internal pressure complemented by external pressure: that has been the winning formula. ...it has taken this combination of pressures to get us this far and we will still need it to take us to our ultimate objective name- ly, negotiations leading to the end of *apartheid* and the establishment of a non-racial, democratic and united South Africa."

Looking forward to post-*apartheid* reconstruction, the Secretary- General highlighted employment creation and training, noting that, "Today, there are some 800 odd management accountants in South Africa. Not one of them is a black South African. There are more than 1,000 white chartered accountants but fewer than 12 black chartered accountants. As for black architects, they are as real as unicorns!" He already had plans in place for an Expert Group on human resource development for post- *apartheid* South Africa, which later recommended an enhanced pro- gramme for training and work experience in a number of priority areas.

To emphasize the enormity of the task ahead, he noted the statement of the British minister for overseas development, in testimony to the House of Commons Foreign Affairs Committee, that "South Africa will need to raise £9 billion [US$14 billion] a year until the end of the century to finance the development programme of its black population."

The host urged his guests to stand ready to join a post-*apartheid* South Africa in a "partnership for development and democracy" — and to con- tribute generously to that cause. "To invest in a post-*apartheid* South Africa will be to invest in stability and democracy. ...There must be few interna- tional financial centres that can compete with the City of London in its knowledge of the South African economy, its ways and bye-ways. In this matter, therefore, you are truly *interlocuteurs valable*, as the French say."

The occasion provided the financiers with an opportunity to interact informally with Mandela. In attendance were 40 guests, including the for- mer British foreign secretary, Geoffrey Howe, eight representatives of governments and six from the diplomatic community. The others were businesspeople, bankers and industrialists with interests in South Africa, including the South African multi-national, Anglo-American with whom ANC had been having contacts for some time.

Mandela was moved to a different table after each course, to interact with different people. For him, it was not an unfamiliar environment. "You must remember I was brought up in a 'British' school and at the time Britain was the home of everything that was best in the world. I have not discarded the influence which Britain and British history and culture exercised on us," he explained to South African journalist, John Carlin. "I

confess to being something of an Anglophile..." he told a London newspaper. "When I thought of Western democracy and freedom, I thought of
the British parliamentary system. In so many ways, the very model of the
gentleman for me was an Englishman. Despite Britain being the home of
parliamentary democracy, it was that democracy that had helped to
inflict a pernicious system of iniquity on my people. While I abhorred the
notion of British imperialism, I never rejected the trappings of British
style and manners."

South Africa advancing

Anyaoku and Mandela had met four years earlier when the
Commonwealth Eminent Persons Group (EPG) visited the latter in
prison, an occasion captured by the inscription handwritten in a 1986
pocket diary: "To Emeka Anyaoku, Compliments to a friend I hold in
high esteem. N.R. Mandela, Pollsmoor Maximum Prison 16.5.86." On the
basis of the EPG's "possible negotiating concept" and the trust established through Anyaoku's long-time personal contacts with the ANC
through President Oliver Tambo and the international affairs director
Thabo Mbeki, and later with Mandela, discussions about the way forward included an active personal and institutional role.

"So, because of this trust and confidence and encouragement, I was
determined that the Harare CHOGM the following year should re-estab-
lish official contact with Pretoria, because that was one way to make some
contribution to the evolving situation. That was why, in Harare, once the
phased sanctions programme was agreed, I again suggested that I should
be mandated to talk with De Klerk." After this was agreed, "I opened up
contacts right there and then, in Harare, by sending for the South African
trade representative..."

Some members of the ANC executive had been preparing for talks
with the Pretoria regime for some time, since before their Kabwe conference in Zambia in June 1985, when a new strategy was drafted by Tambo,
Mbeki and others. International pressure began to be seriously strengthened later the same year, when Commonwealth Heads of Government
meeting in Nassau, The Bahamas, approved the Commonwealth Accord
on Southern Africa drafted by a small international group of senior officials chaired by Chief Anyaoku, then Deputy Secretary-General. The
Accord called for strict enforcement of the mandatory arms embargo and
the ban on sporting links, and agreed to the adoption of a specified list of
voluntary economic sanctions. Later summits in 1987 and 1989, and a

review meeting in 1986 were fractious on the subject of tightening sanctions, with Margaret Thatchers's government refusing to accept the majority position. In an organization that makes decisions by consensus, the leaders of over 50 other countries decided to proceed, "with the exception of Britain".

The summit in Kuala Lumpur, Malaysia in October 1989, at which Chief Anyaoku was elected Secretary-General, had been conflictual over financial sanctions, with Thatcher in open disagreement, though her foreign minister, John Major, was regarded as more conciliatory.

Heads of Government reaffirmed the continuing validity of the EPG's "possible negotiating concept". They said they had recognized in their Nassau Accord "that the constitutional system was a matter for all the people of South Africa to decide. They continued to believe that the Commonwealth's role in this regard was essentially to facilitate the opening of negotiations between the South African authorities and authentic black leaders.

"They agreed that the only justification for sanctions against South Africa was the pressure they created for fundamental political change" and, "other than Britain, also acknowledged that the impact of sanctions had begun to influence the policies of the South African regime."

They took the view that this was not the time to consider any relaxation of existing sanctions and pressures, until there was "evidence of clear and irreversible change". Therefore they agreed, "with the exception of Britain", that such measures should be expanded to include new forms of financial sanctions such as reducing access to trade credit, and the establishment of an independent agency to report on financial links and monitor financial flows and related policies.

This was a subject which occupied the mind of the Secretary-General-designate, both before and after his election, and while he prepared for the Harare CHOGM. Essential to "my perception of my plans for the future were my particular concerns for arresting the division within the Commonwealth over sanctions. I wanted to arrest this division in order to make the Commonwealth more effective, in a united form over South Africa."

In from the Cold

Just three days after the Mandela dinner, the Cold War ended, officially. Signaled by the dismantling of the Berlin Wall the previous year, the termination of the Cold War was certified on 6 July 1990 by the London

Declaration of the North Atlantic Treaty Organization (NATO), which declared that "the walls that once confined people and ideas are collapsing".

The following day, the Secretary-General outlined some of the opportunities inherent in the end of the Cold War that he intended to pursue during his term of office. Addressing a Cumberland conference, he said the absence of the Cold War "will present new opportunities for peaceful resolution of regional and local conflicts — it will now be easier to view these conflicts on their own terms undistorted by the prison of the Cold War. The superpower disengagement will not necessarily mean an end to external involvement, but should make it easier to check escalation."

He predicted that new world relationships would facilitate consensus on such issues as environment, drug abuse and drug trafficking, and AIDS. He said there will be a popular demand for democracy the world over, "no longer a question of popular democracy here, guided democracy there. It is a demand for classical, liberal democracy encompassing freedom of association, freedom of the press, freedom of religion, culminating in free and fair elections."

Pursuing the theme of opportunities emerging through the end of the "armed peace" with its "incalculable waste of resources both human and material", in his first major engagement outside London as Secretary-General, he addressed the 10th anniversary summit of the Southern Africa Development Co-ordination Conference (SADCC) — which later became the Southern African Development Community (SADC) — in Gaborone, Botswana. "There is for all who believe in genuine multilateralism, in international co-operation based on equality and mutual respect, the challenge of thinking of new strategies for ensuring that in the emerging international dispensation, the developing countries of the South do not become, as a North-based commentator has put it, 'the object rather than the subject of post-cold-war history', the problem rather than the solution.

"No less threatening for many a developing country is the prospect of further economic marginalization. Already the debt burden, the continuing fall in commodity prices and protectionism have brought the development process to a standstill in many parts of the developing world generally ...Unless the nature of international co-operation changes and changes radically and soon, the emerging economic trends will only consolidate this stuntification. ...the case for economic co-operation, co-ordination and integration, the need for self-reliance has never been more compelling or pressing."

High Level Appraisal

The Secretary-General later painted this as the global canvas against which he had taken office, "and from which the Commonwealth must construct its agenda of action for the 1990s." At his instigation, a High Level Appraisal Group (HLAG) had been established for this purpose at the Kuala Lumpur summit the previous year, to appraise the Commonwealth's possible role in the 1990s and beyond, and to examine whether its institutions are equipped for the task. Against a backdrop of "dramatic and far-reaching changes on the international scene", it concluded that the Commonwealth had reached "a stage of maturity in its evolution. In looking to the 1990s and beyond, it must therefore set itself a new agenda."

"In the lead-up to the Kuala Lumpur Heads of Government meeting," Chief Anyaoku said later, "as we were getting ready for that meeting in the Secretariat, and as I looked forward more and more confidently to the possibility of winning the election [for Secretary-General], I began to become more concerned with the type of Commonwealth I would be dealing with in the future."

This first ever "examination of the whole Commonwealth by itself", conducted by 10 Heads of Government chaired by Prime Minister Mahathir of Malaysia, was to report to the next meeting of Commonwealth leaders in Zimbabwe in 1991. Their report would form the basis for the Harare Declaration. This decision "gave me, as I began my tenure of office, an unusual opportunity for actively participating in the determination by Heads of Government of the framework for the organization's activities in the 1990s and beyond."

Chief Anyaoku said he hoped the appraisal would enable the Commonwealth to concentrate its efforts on issues where it has a comparative advantage. "A central attribute of the Commonwealth is its ability to bridge racial, ideological and economic divides and inequalities, assisted by its common language and common professional and institutional heritage. This will be of increasing value to a world in which new tensions within racially and culturally mixed communities and new threats to the stability and cohesion of established nation states are appearing, often as a result of the assertion of ethnic, racial and religious loyalties."

In the introduction to his first report to Heads of Government, he envisaged new dimensions for activities in four major areas through "forging a stronger link between dialogue and cooperative action". These were: politics, development, the promotion of good governance, and human resource development.

"I am convinced of the Commonwealth's need for change," the Secretary-General said, "change not for its own sake but in response to changing times — to perceived needs and emerging priorities." The High Level Appraisal "serves to endorse my conviction that there are times when, building on the track record so far, tactics have to change and new strategies have to be adopted and followed. I believe that we stand at such a time."

He noted that this was the first review conducted at such a high level, by Heads of Government. And he stressed the inclusive nature of the appraisal, "which will call for action from the whole Commonwealth, through member countries acting bilaterally and multilaterally, through governmental and non-governmental institutions, and through individuals."

The Commonwealth in the 1990s and beyond

After two postponements that would have shaken the resolve of a less committed Secretary-General, the High Level Appraisal Group finally met on 15 October in Harare, on the eve of CHOGM 1991. The full roster of participants compensated for the delays: The Hon RJL Hawke, Australia; The Rt Hon Sir Lynden Pindling, The Bahamas; The Rt Hon John Major, Britain; The Rt Hon Brian Mulroney, Canada; The Hon PV Narasimha Rao, India; The Rt Hon Michael Manley, Jamaica; The Rt Hon *Dato' Seri* Dr Mahathir bin Mohamad, Malaysia, Chairman of the Group; HE General Ibrahim Babangida, Nigeria; The Hon Mr Goh Chok Tong, Singapore; and HE Dr Kenneth Kaunda, Zambia. The host, President Robert Mugabe, participated in part of the deliberations.

The Chairman's report acknowledged that deliberations were based on the report of a working group of officials set up by the Secretary-General, and were greatly facilitated by the Secretary-General's memorandum proposing a Strategic Action Plan based on the working group's report. This confirmed support for the founding principles enunciated at Singapore, their abiding relevance 20 years later, and belief that the future role rests in application of those principles to the contemporary world situation.

"We are convinced that, in facing the challenges of the future, the Commonwealth will be able to draw upon its unique strength and character, rooted in its common traditions and language, in the embrace of its membership which spans nearly one-third of humanity and every corner of the globe, and in its remarkable ability to fashion a sense of common purpose out of diversity."

The deliberations identified several areas, some old others new, which deserve special emphasis in years to come: economic and social development; environment; the special needs of small states; democracy, human rights and sound administration; human resource development; and enhancing the role of women in society.

"That was where I began to inject the thought that the Commonwealth could begin to think of a more constructive role in South Africa than previously," Chief Anyaoku said later, "and in this I was wanting to build on the positive signals that were coming from Pretoria itself. This strategy would have been impossible if De Klerk had not, in February 1990, made the statement that he made."

The HLAG report reflected continuing concern about the situation in South Africa where recent changes "have raised hopes of achieving a free, non-racial and democratic order" but "violence continues to obstruct progress. ...Now that the goal is closer than ever before, we considered ways in which the Commonwealth should continue to play a significant role in facilitating the negotiation process. *It should aim to bring the main parties together with a view to securing an end to violence and lending momentum to the negotiations.*"

The report also considered the adequacy of Commonwealth institutions in fulfilling the task ahead and proposed further examination by senior officials, "taking into account the Secretariat's need for adequate resources to implement these priorities." The HLAG welcomed the Secretary-General's internal review which identified existing resources which could be released for redeployment to new priorities, and endorsed his proposal to institute a management audit by external consultants, to enhance the cost-effectiveness and efficiency of the Secretariat. The HLAG examined three other matters:

• a standing facility to observe elections, and thus assist member countries in reinforcing democratic processes and institutions, already started by mounting observer missions to several member states on request.

• the criteria for membership: "admission of new members or readmission of old members should be contingent upon the historic links and shared traditions... and on their adhering to Commonwealth values, principles and priorities as set out in the Harare Commonwealth Declaration."

• an information strategy aimed at strengthening the image of the Commonwealth in the eyes of the world.

Three documents were therefore annexed to the report: Guidelines for the Establishment of Commonwealth Groups to Observe Elections in Member Countries; Memorandum on Commonwealth Membership; Sharpening the Commonwealth Image: An Information Strategy.

It was the unanimous view of the 11 Heads of Government who met on the eve of the Harare summit that the Commonwealth has a distinctive contribution to offer, as an institution "which can enrich the lives not only of its own members but also of the wider global community of which they are a part." Characterized later by Chief Anyaoku on a number of public occasions: "The Harare Commonwealth Declaration, issued by that summit, is a key contemporary statement of Commonwealth belief and purpose, and a manifestation of a collective resolve to address a new and compelling global agenda."

A Sense of Place / A Sense of History

"Having been elected to my new post, I naturally was very interested in where my first Commonwealth summit would be held. ...if a place like Harare could do it, that would be very good, for a number of reasons.

"First, Zimbabwe occupies a special place in the history of the evolution of the modern Commonwealth. The crisis in Rhodesia posed the most serious threat to the continued cohesion — indeed at a certain stage, the existence — of the modern Commonwealth. The first Secretary-General, Arnold Smith, had to cope with this.

"And secondly, the final emergence of Zimbabwe as an independent member. It was at the Commonwealth summit in Lusaka in 1979 that the accord was reached which paved the way for the Lancaster House conference, and after the Lancaster House conference, member countries provided the military contingents that monitored the ceasefire between the forces of the illegal regime and the liberation movement. The Commonwealth also provided an official team of observers to monitor and spread confidence at a critical time in the pre-independence elections. ...Their presence was decisive, among other things, in discouraging Lord Soames, the then Governor, from proceeding to nullify elections in one part of Zimbabwe, as was threatened at some point.

"So, Zimbabwe moved to freedom, and did so in a remarkable and continuing act of reconciliation. Zimbabwe itself, in terms of its population mix and social evolution, represents some of the goals that the Commonwealth seeks to pursue. ... And since the birth of Zimbabwe, we have seen a steady increase in what the Commonwealth has been able to

do for Zimbabwe — and a remarkable increase in what Zimbabwe has
been able to do for the Commonwealth, culminating in the government's
generous willingness to host this meeting. ...So the involvement of the
Commonwealth in Zimbabwe was such that I thought if the CHOGM
could take place there, it would be very appropriate.

"And the second reason was the proximity of Zimbabwe to South
Africa. I believed that the CHOGM in Harare — and I'm going back to
1989 — that the next CHOGM would have a lot to do on the South Africa
question. I wanted it to be easier for people like Mandela and others to
come over, and I wanted the atmosphere for the discussion to be both
realistic and involved. So Harare seemed to me a very good place for it.
And third, I saw the next CHOGM as providing an important
opportunity for redefining the role of the Commonwealth in the future.
...it seemed to me that Harare would be an excellent place for doing so.
For all these reasons, I was very keen that whatever chance there was of
getting the meeting to Harare, it should be taken. ...I remember talking
with people like Bernard Chidzero and Nathan Shamuyarira [then
Ministers of Finance and Foreign Affairs respectively] and even at some
point, with President Mugabe himself. So from that moment, when the
decision was taken that the venue would be Harare, I was very keenly
looking forward to it."

Asked if it was that simple, when the decision was taken for Harare,
Chief Anyaoku replied carefully, "It wasn't very simple. In fact, there
were a number of bruises. I think to this day, Margaret Thatcher bears a
grudge against the Commonwealth and the Secretariat for that decision,
which she thought was unfair to Malta. Whether that was out of a sense
of fairness to Malta, or out of disinclination for Harare, that's a matter for
speculation. But the fact was that she wasn't happy about it. ...Well
before the Kuala Lumpur summit, Malta had mounted a fairly effective
campaign for getting it to Valetta. ...Malta had just hosted the summit
between [US President George] Bush and Gorbachev, and thought that
the Commonwealth summit would be a very good thing. They had the
support of a few governments. ...

"I don't think the Zimbabweans came to Kuala Lumpur prepared to
lobby for hosting the CHOGM. In fact, when I talked with them they
were doubtful about it. ...But for the reasons I mentioned, I thought that
if the Zimbabwean government could be persuaded that would be very
good... And I think Michael Manley and Kenneth Kaunda were very keen
that it should be Harare. I don't think I could claim to have initiated it by
myself. ... I asked the question, but I think, in fairness, it was a thought

which both my predecessor, Sonny Ramphal, and Michael Manley, KK, that we all shared."

Returning to the imagery of the venue to chart the way forward, in his Introduction to the *Report of the Commonwealth Secretary-General 1991*, Chief Anyaoku concluded: "The last time Commonwealth leaders went to Southern Africa, to Lusaka in 1979, it proved a historical turning point for Zimbabwe. In 1991, Zimbabwe itself will, I am convinced, be the setting for another turning point... Zimbabwe is an ancient civilization which was born again as a new nation. I can think of no better location for the renewal of the modern Commonwealth."

The long road to Harare

The first Commonwealth Secretary-General (1965-1975) was Arnold Smith, a Canadian, whose accession to office coincided with the unilateral declaration of independence (UDI) by Rhodesia's white minority. He said in his autobiography, *Stitches in Time:* "Above all, the Rhodesia issue became a race between Britain concluding a settlement with Ian Smith and Britain recognizing the growing economic strength of Nigeria. Even before this strength was demonstrated, as it was on the eve of the Lusaka Heads of Government Meeting in [August] 1979 by Nigeria's deliberately ignoring British tenders and their nationalizing BP, the implications should have been plain: Britain had at least as much to lose economically by upsetting Nigeria as by offending South Africa. As the British gradually realized that the financial see-saw was tipping towards independent Africa, the danger of a sell-out receded. But this point was years away in January 1966, when Nigeria first became a major actor in the Rhodesia drama."

Lord Peter Carrington, who was Britain's Foreign and Commonwealth Secretary at the time of the Lusaka summit, told the same story from a different perspective in his memoirs, *Reflect on Things Past.*

Lord Harlech had reported to him that the internal settlement "would not be recognized by any black African state — Nigeria, very hostile to Rhodesia and carrying a lot of weight, was orchestrating this position. ...There would be a likely break-up of the Commonwealth. ...To have recognized the internal settlement at that time would have led to embargoes on British goods around the world, rejection of British counsel and influence 'because of Rhodesia'. ...

"We were dealing with the lives and fortunes of people, many of them in origin British people, at a critical point in this history, and contrary to some impressions we were deeply aware of it and deeply cared. But Rhodesia's importance to British foreign policy was largely negative: it created a problem because it soured our relationship with other states but its own significance in terms of our economic or strategic interests was not large. Its importance, regrettably, was as an irritant — with the Commonwealth, with our European partners and with the United States.

"...Somewhat less helpful was the announcement, to my fury, by the Nigerian Government of their nationalization of BP (Nigeria) [British Petroleum] on the morning the conference started! That said, I am bound to record that the Nigerian Foreign Minister played a full and constructive part in our proceedings and in helping us towards our aim."

The unmistakable signal from the Nigerian government had helped to focus the attention of the British government and its Prime Minister, Margaret Thatcher, on the benefits of concluding negotiations at Lusaka and later at Lancaster House, where Lord Carrington played a critical role, as did his staff on location during the transition to independence in Zimbabwe.

However, Carrington's attitude toward the Commonwealth in general is worth noting: "The cultural sense of unity between Britain and the nations of Western Europe is much more profound, deeper, older, than anything with the Commonwealth *per se*. We and the ancient peoples of Europe have developed our institutions, our philosophy, our arts and our manners in parallel and in close community. We British have always been on the fringe but nevertheless an integral part of the Graeco-Roman world from which European consciousness derives. We can't alter that and it is fundamental — more than the past (but comparatively recent) fact of Empire or the present (and even more recent) fact of Commonwealth."

Another point worth noting is the identity of two key players from Nigeria who were involved in this drama: the Head of State (1976-1979), Gen. Olusegun Obasanjo who approved the action that infuriated the British government, returned to office 20 years later as the popularly elected civilian President of Nigeria in 1999; and the then Deputy Secretary-General of the Commonwealth, Chief Emeka Anyaoku. The latter was involved at all stages of the Commonwealth role in Zimbabwe negotiations including the talks in Geneva, Lusaka and Lancaster House, and the transition to independence within the country.

Chief Anyaoku was determined that the Commonwealth, coming home to Harare in 1991, should achieve two principal goals. First, that the redefinition of the future purposes of the association should be accomplished. "You see, in the Commonwealth there are countries that one thinks of as not having very progressive views. There are others one thinks of as living too much in the past. There are others that one suspects are not as sensitive to the needs of the developing world and the future as they should be. Zimbabwe provides a good balance, where I believed that the most realistic assessment of where the Commonwealth should be going would be made. So I was thinking about how to use Harare CHOGM to achieve that.

"Secondly, I was thinking of how to use Harare CHOGM to deal with the South African question because again, Harare, because of its proximity to South Africa, and its own involvement, would inject both a degree of realism into the discussion and an assurance that we would not depart from the essential goals of the Commonwealth *vis a vis* South Africa.

"Then, in terms of restructuring the Commonwealth Secretariat, which I was very keen on, I felt that Harare, under the chairmanship of Mugabe, would be a good place for getting the sort of endorsement and authority that I was keen to have. ..."

There is an Igbo saying that, "the beginning is the most important part of the work."

The host and chairman of the meeting was emphatic in his support for the proposed strategy, particularly on South Africa. "Since our last meeting in Kuala Lumpur," President Mugabe said, "the struggle for a free and democratic South Africa has attained new heights. South Africans are now talking to each other. A positive start has been made. Our decisions and deliberations on South Africa should bring hope to the oppressed and encouragement to the government of South Africa. We must assist the South Africans to embark without further delay on negotiating a new constitution based on universally shared democratic principles. It is to be hoped that the message which our meeting will send to South Africa will make it clear that there is no credible alternative to dialogue."

The Secretary-General had crafted his debut speech to CHOGM with particular care and attention to detail. "If you look at my speech, what I said, not only in resolving *apartheid* but in helping South Africa to pursue a line that makes nonsense of racism and notions of racial discrimination. ...I wanted, in southern Africa, in Harare, to capture the mood of people who have suffered for generations against racism, and that speech is very assertive of the confidence of the black person. I wrote those words very carefully. ...So, in southern Africa, I wanted to stress a point of racial equality.

"Second, I wanted to make the point that the Commonwealth could be very constructively helpful to resolving *apartheid*. So, while it condemned *apartheid* and what *apartheid* stood for, it was more pointed in the direction of helping all the people of South Africa to resolve it.

"Thirdly, I spoke about the potential of the Commonwealth, which I had thought about, without wanting, in my first meeting, to be didactic. I didn't want to be telling Heads of Government, 'You should do this, you should do that'. I deliberately wanted to tell them that the Commonwealth could do this, could do that, and 'I hope you will decide to so use it'.

"That was a deliberate strategy that I adopted. ...when I was finishing that speech, I could not but recall the whole process of my campaign for election. There were people at that time who thought that an African Secretary-General would mean the Commonwealth would do nothing but concentrate on South Africa. They expected a degree of, almost fanaticism on South Africa, from any African, not just from me — that an African Secretary-General would just put South Africa as the 'all and all' of Commonwealth concerns and interests. And that the method would be driving the Commonwealth to very extreme positions. And I therefore deliberately wanted to give, in Harare, my first summit, a very measured presentation of what the Commonwealth could do. And from the reactions I got, it went quite well. It was deliberately so structured. It was measured, it was a speech that I hoped would not only impress and satisfy the Mugabes, the Kaundas, the Manleys, the Narasimha Raos of this world, but also reassure the John Majors, the Bob Hawkes, the Brian Mulroneys, and this was what I did. ...I was enormously encouraged and cheered by the response. John Major was the first to say to me, that's great. Mugabe thought it was a very good speech. Michael Manley liked it. And of course my own President, Babangida. So I was quite pleased with the reactions I got, from people who just could have been simply polite but went beyond that. ..."

"One of the things that perhaps should be recorded was that, during the Retreat, when we were discussing this declaration for the future, one of the controversial points was the balance that was to be struck in that declaration between those who wanted the Commonwealth to concentrate on development and socio-economic matters, and those who were speaking about promotion of its fundamental political values. And I had to intervene a few times to say that the constituency of the Commonwealth expects us to do both things, and expects us to maintain a balance that would not mean sacrificing one to the other. ..."

The Retreat is a Commonwealth tradition in which Heads of Government spend a mid-summit weekend in isolation at a resort, without officials, and continue their discussions, formally and informally; and make their final decisions, as well as playing sports, relaxing and getting to know each other.

"We actually meet around the table, in short-sleeved shirts. We sit in formal meetings. We had two long formal sessions at Victoria Falls [Zimbabwe]. Then, at dinner, we talk to people individually. ...And the relaxation, the personal friendships that were rekindled in the evenings when we were all performing our different songs and different entertainment. Some of us Africans went and sang. The Australian Prime Minister sang and danced, so did the Canadian Foreign Minister standing in for her Prime Minister. ...It was fun."

The usefulness of the Retreat, however, goes beyond the fun and relaxation; it provides an opportunity for serious direct discussion on thorny issues. There were, for example, "two meetings I had to begin to discuss the basis of a statement on South Africa. Then we had the paragraphs ready, and settled the statement in Victoria Falls. So I became more relaxed."

The three most problematic issues at the Harare summit were: 1 the discussion on the promotion of fundamental Commonwealth political values: democracy, human rights, rule of law, etc; 2 South Africa; and, 3 surprisingly, the venue of the next biennial summit, because the level of interest was so low that no one wanted to host it. "This required quite strong behind-the-scenes intervention by me; it was quite serious, because the venue was eventually settled for Cyprus." A notable indication of the achievement of Chief Anyaoku's goal of rekindling interest in the Commonwealth is the fact that from Cyprus (1993) onwards, there was no difficulty in finding willing hosts for the next CHOGM, although he continued to influence the final selection.

Onward from Harare

In the informality of Commonwealth consultations, the leaders unanimously approved the definition of a new dual agenda that relaunched the Commonwealth as an important, catalytic international organization and prepared it for a strategic role in fostering development and peace toward the year 2000.

The leaders of 51 members states noted the significant progress made in the area of socio-economic development, but highlighted continuing acute problems of poverty, population growth, debt burdens and environmental degradation. They noted the importance of protecting and promoting democracy, the rule of law, good governance; and fundamental human rights including equal rights and opportunities regardless of race, colour, creed or political belief; equality for women; universal access to education; alleviation of poverty and promotion of sustainable development. They strongly supported *"continuing action to bring about the end of apartheid and the establishment of a free, democratic, non-racial and prosperous South Africa."*

In his report to Heads of Government, Chief Anyaoku had said they could take pride in the "tenacity" with which the Commonwealth has fought racism in South Africa, and the leadership it has provided in the international sanctions campaign. The purpose of sanctions "has never been to punish, but to serve as a means of persuading Pretoria to begin and sustain negotiations until the movement to a non-racial and democratic South Africa becomes irreversible." He noted that important changes in the South African political environment "have included real, if sometimes still faltering, steps towards the process of genuine negotiations and the end of apartheid."

As a result of these changes, he said, the Commonwealth Committee of Foreign Ministers on Southern Africa (CFMSA) had recommended the relaxation of sanctions in phases, as concrete objectives are met. This was based on a strategy for "programmed management of sanctions" that he and the Australian Foreign Minister, Senator Gareth Evans, had drafted for a special CFMSA meeting earlier in the year after consultations with ANC's international affairs director Thabo Mbeki and others. Although considerable progress had been made by mid-1991, he warned that "the world must not be blind to the fact that, even as I write, real obstacles still stand in the way of making the end of *apartheid* a reality for South Africans. *Apartheid* will not be truly dead and buried until a new political dispensation gives the majority population of South Africa full voting and constitutional rights. Until this is achieved or at least is clearly in sight, it would be inappropriate to relax all the international pressure without which the universally welcomed process of change could not have been initiated."

He added that the Commonwealth also remains ready to render appropriate assistance to facilitate negotiations as the parties may deem helpful, within the vision of deliberations at the Harare summit to focus on a united approach "not only assisting the final demise of *apartheid* but in building anew a better South Africa."

The legacy of *apartheid* "and the measures adopted in its defense" remain in southern Africa, he said, adding that the devastating structural effects of destabilization on societies in the region will endure unless the international community commits itself to assist in recovery. In this context, he appealed for support for the Special Commonwealth Fund for Mozambique for a full five years as envisaged; and continued support for the Enhanced Commonwealth Programme of Technical Assistance for Namibia, "a substantial portfolio of technical assistance activities in most areas of social and economic development" to meet immediate post-independence needs.

On 15 September 1991, just a few weeks before the Harare summit, Chief Anyaoku had told the sixth regular meeting of the CFMSA in New Delhi that most of the original five steps that the international community called upon Pretoria to take in order to create a climate conducive to negotiations had now been taken. In an interview with *West Africa* magazine, published in its pre-CHOGM issue of 14-20 October 1991, he was asked when sanctions would be lifted.

"The scenario which the foreign ministers have agreed is as follows," he replied. "Now you can ease the 'people-to-people' sanctions in recognition of developments down that line. And as soon as this agreement is reached on transitional arrangements, we could permit all parties to participate effectively and fully in the transition and the negotiations for the new constitution, you release the trade and investment sanctions. And then as soon as the agreement is reached on the text of the constitution for a non-racial democratic South Africa, you relax the financial sanctions which have remained the most effective of all sanctions. Then you leave the arms embargo until the very last stage when the democratic government of South Africa can negotiate that with the rest of the world."

Later, discussing this strategy, he said, "I was convinced before Harare, indeed that was one of the reasons why I had worked very hard to get the package on the phased lifting of sanctions agreed by the Foreign Ministers Committee before Harare. My strategy was to discourage prolonged discussion of that package in Harare, but rather to face Heads with it, as commanding the broadest consensus. ...And in Harare, I was keen that that should be accepted. I was keen that two new dimensions should be introduced into the Commonwealth handling of the South African question:

• One was that the British had opted out of the Committee of Foreign Ministers, they wouldn't join... but I was keen that in Harare they should become part of the consultative group, because, without that, there was always the problem of the Commonwealth moving ahead and Britain not helping the course. The dichotomy was not going to be helpful. So in Harare, I deliberately suggested that the High Level Appraisal Group should continue dealing with the South African question. ...while not disbanding the Committee of Foreign Ministers, I did succeed in getting the meeting to agree that the Secretary-General would be consulting with the Group of 10, now 11 with Zimbabwe, as to initiatives on South Africa.

• And the second thing I was anxious to bring about, was to be officially mandated to contact the South African government. This arose in part from my conversations with Nelson Mandela. You see, before Harare, the Commonwealth had no official dealings with Pretoria. The only official dealings with Pretoria were during the Eminent Persons Group and, as a deliberate policy, once the EPG finished and did not succeed, we cut off dealings with Pretoria. ...

"Then, in the case of South Africa, as mentioned, I organized two meetings of the 11, plus myself, to agree the statement that was issued on South Africa. That was the High Level Appraisal Group, plus Mugabe as Chairman, because that was my way of bringing in the British into the inner circle of consultation on South Africa. At one stage, I went and talked to John Major alone, when he told me that he was uncomfortable at the suggestion that sanctions would just continue, with no reference made to his own position. And I found one or two sentences in the statement that acknowledged, not in the same tone as Margaret Thatcher would have had it, but acknowledged his position that there were some doubts as to the need to continue the sanctions programme."

Therefore, instead of the language of communiques in the Thatcher era where clauses on South Africa often bore the terse phrase, "with the exception of Britain", there was now a more diplomatic presentation of Britain's disagreement with the rest of the Commonwealth and a serious attempt to work together.

The agreement on the way forward for the Commonwealth on South Africa, was reflected as agreed in paragraphs 20 21 of "The Harare Communiquè October 1991", which said the Heads of Government welcomed the important changes made to date and urged all parties to move as quickly as possible to constitutional negotiations:

"20 While the terms of a constitutional settlement were for the people of South Africa themselves to determine, Heads of Government believed that the Commonwealth must remain ready to assist the negotiating process in ways that would be found helpful by the parties concerned. They therefore decided to request the Secretary-General to visit South

Africa at the earliest possible opportunity in order to explore with the principal parties concerned ways in which the Commonwealth could assist in lending momentum to the negotiating process.

"21 On his return, the Secretary-General would report his conclusions to the Ten Heads of Government previously concerned with the High Level Appraisal, and to the President of Zimbabwe, Chairman of the current Commonwealth Heads of Government Meeting. Heads authorized this Group to consider and determine the necessary follow-up action in the light of the Secretary-General's mission."

2

SOUTH AFRICA

*Master of quiet diplomacy, the Chief brings to the international arena
that great African tradition of consensus building that has positioned
him in a key role as a builder of bridges across peoples and nations.
(Nelson Mandela in his Foreword to this book)*

under APARTHEID

CHIEF ANYAOKU watched the inauguration of South Africa's second
democratically elected president with a special interest and satisfaction,
an invited guest as he was at the first occasion five years earlier. Watching
Thabo Mbeki take the oath of office on 16 June 1999 at the Union
Buildings in Pretoria was more with a sense of well-being, less emotional than the inauguration of Nelson Mandela on 10 May 1994. It was a sign
that the new South Africa had made it through the first five years and
reached a maturity to sustain the system of change as it put down roots
into the future. The road would be rough, but the navigators skilled, and
the Commonwealth and its Secretary-General could move on to other
things. As a result, in part, of the firm and supportive stance of the
Commonwealth, South Africa would now be regarded as a member state
in its own right rather than an agenda item and source of political division. South Africa comes of age in the Commonwealth the last summit of
the millennium in Durban, in November 1999 — 38 years after leaving
the organization under pressure to democratize, and five years after its
honourable re-entry.

The Chief was particularly satisfied that Mbeki's inauguration marked
the successful completion of one of the foremost tasks he had set for himself when he took office almost a decade earlier, ie support for South
Africans to end *apartheid* (racial segregation) and replace it with a democratic system of governance, and removal of the issue as a focus for division
within the Commonwealth. He saw it as a victory for equality and common humanity that reinforced the fundamental values of the
Commonwealth, and renewed interest and confidence in the organization.

For the Commonwealth, it had been a long and winding road, and Chief Anyaoku presided over its peregrination. Those who were intimately involved in the process, particularly outside the country, acknowledge the key role played by the Commonwealth; they are rich in their praise of Chief Anyaoku's steady hand and guidance as Deputy Secretary-General from 1978-1989, and his vision and active engagement as the current Secretary-General in the decade 1990-2000. What is mentioned most often is his firm commitment to principle, and his innate sensitivity to the fact that his was a supporting role for a process whose sustainable solution could only be devised by South Africans themselves.

His vision was focused steadily forward. "Neither retreat nor stagnation is an option," he said firmly when negotiations appeared to be faltering into an abyss of violence in late 1992, a perspective that is well-reflected in a proverb: "the end of the journey is reached by moving ahead."

"Chief Anyaoku is regarded as a non-confrontational man," said an article in *Diplomat* magazine halfway through his term of office, "a 'behind the scenes' operator who prefers gentle persuasion to aggressive confrontation. But in this he faces the classic diplomatic quandary — that discreet labours, however productive, often go unacknowledged. Does this frustrate him? 'It is, sometimes a little bit — disappointing, to see that people forget the success stories fairly quickly, and concentrate on where there are gaps. But I put a great deal of emphasis on doing things, on achieving results. Publicising what we do comes second.'

"South Africa is a case in point," the article says. "When apartheid finally crumbled, Chief Anyaoku and his colleagues in the Commonwealth got too little credit for the vital part they had played.

"As early as 1991 the Secretary-General had flown out and become quietly involved in the transition negotiations. That December, six distinguished Commonwealth statesmen were present at the launch of the multi-party talks. Again, in 1992, when violence erupted at Boipatong and was threatening to scupper the negotiation process, the Secretary-General went out to help forge the first framework document. This made it possible subsequently for the UN to send Cyrus Vance, and to have the Security Council resolution adopted which allowed foreign observers into the country." (*Diplomat*, Sept/Oct 95)

Before his first term was halfway through, Chief Anyaoku was shuttling often to Pretoria, discreetly meeting with all parties "behind the scenes"; and he was present at the World Trade Centre in Kempton Park on the night of 17/18 November 1993 when multi-party negotiations endorsed the transitional agreements that led to the first democratic elections the following year.

A common victory

Thirty years after the legendary Rivonia Trial, the "First Accused" had stood outside the Union Buildings in Pretoria and taken the oath of office as President of South Africa. Nelson Mandela had pledged to his country people and assembled world leaders that: "Never, never and never again shall it be, that this beautiful land will again experience the oppression of one by another, and suffer the indignity of being the skunk of the world. ...We, the people of South Africa, feel fulfilled that humanity has taken us back into its bosom, that we, who were outlaws not so long ago, have today been given the rare privilege to be host to the nations of the world on our own soil. ...

"We thank all our distinguished international guests for having come to take possession with the people of our country in what is, after all, a common victory for justice, for peace, for human dignity. We trust that you will continue to stand by us as we tackle the challenges of building peace, prosperity, non-sexism, non-racialism and democracy."

It was a particularly haunting moment when the white service chiefs of the South African army, navy and air force saluted their new Commander-in-Chief, whom they had incarcerated for 27 years; and heart-stopping when the jet fighters, the trainers and the helicopters that had targeted neighbouring countries just a few years earlier, overflew the assembled dignitaries trailing smoke in the colours of the flag of the new South Africa.

The new South Africa, though not yet in control of the levers of power, made certain that assembled world leaders knew they were in Africa, and greeted their new President with praise-singers and praise-songs accorded a traditional ruler, first in Xhosa and Zulu, then in English. "Let me dedicate my poetic praise to the symbol of hope and inspiration," chanted the foremost national praise-poet, Mzwakhe Mbule. "Like diamond and gold you have gone through the pass of time in order to be refined ... Like an oak tree you have survived all kinds of weather..."

It was an emotional moment for all of the international guests, the largest gathering of world leaders since the funeral on another continent of assassinated US President, John F. Kennedy, over 30 years before, in November 1963, the year after Mandela was incarcerated. From Fidel Castro to Hilary Rodham Clinton, Yassar Arafat to Yitzak Rabin to Julius Nyerere, emotions were close to the surface. Even more so for tens of thousands of South Africans who personally witnessed the formal end of institutionalized apartheid with the swearing in of their new President, the first Deputy President, Thabo Mbeki and the second Deputy President, FW de Klerk.

"And then when Mandela appeared," Chief Anyaoku said later, "the symbolism, among the many symbolisms, was to see him flanked and escorted by the white chiefs of the armed services. And I couldn't help feeling ...my mind went back to 1986, when I saw Nelson Mandela at Pollsmoor prison, it went back to all the imagery of those past years, to see those fellows now saluting him and escorting him as their new head of state, it was the first symbolism that hit me.

"And then, during the ceremony itself, when the two African courtiers, one clearly Zulu and the other must have been Xhosa, when they greeted him as they would greet in a traditional African court, it was all very moving. And after the two deputy presidents had taken their oath, when Mandela was taking his oath, Bunmi, I just turned, I saw tears running down from her eyes. I looked and there were many others mopping their faces. It was a very charged and very emotional occasion. And I myself, I just stood, totally dumbfounded. ...then I must say that it was a near overwhelming feeling of satisfaction, but tinged with underlying anxiety, whether it was not all too good to be true. I think one must admit that. It seemed too good to be true. Because the transformation, in terms of projection of the new South Africa was far more comprehensive and quicker than I had dared to expect.

"But I suppose the reason why I was not overwhelmed by it, was because I had been involved in the process since 1991. And after all, I was in South Africa on the night of 17 November to early morning 18, at Kempton Park, when the multi-party final agreement was reached. I had been sensitized to the expectation that there would be a new South Africa... So I was prepared for it, more prepared than most other visitors, but nevertheless, it still hit me that these old symbols and power structures of apartheid should, on that day, be subordinated to the personality and office of Nelson Mandela. This was something that I couldn't easily totally digest. ..."

It was a ceremony which many of the guests found difficult to believe, even as they watched, yet many people in attendance could take satisfaction in their role in bringing about this historical event. None moreso than Chief Anyaoku, who had first seen Mandela, unknown to the latter, 32 years earlier in Ghana, before the South African returned home to arrest and imprisonment. Then a young diplomat in the foreign service of immediate post-independence Nigeria, Emeka Anyaoku was visiting his

High Commissioner, Leslie Harriman, in Accra, when Mandela arrived to confer with President Kwame Nkrumah, through the new African National Congress (ANC) office established by Oliver Tambo. The first time he met Mandela formally, however, was at Pollsmoor Prison, near Cape Town, in May 1986, when the Commonwealth Eminent Persons Group (EPG) visited South Africa, while the rest of the world was still guessing what Mandela looked like after 23 years in prison.

Eminent Persons Group

Mandela and some of his colleagues in the ANC leadership, including Walter Sisulu, had been moved in early 1982 from Robben Island to Pollsmoor, where they were held inside 4-metre-high concrete walls and behind 15 locked metal doors. But inside, the conditions, compared to Robben Island, were like a five-star hotel, Mandela recalled later. Tall, erect and stately, as the world has come to know him now, at that time no one except his warders, fellow prisoners and family knew how his hair had grayed and face wrinkled since the last photographs published in 1962. He had the same slow smile, and the prison warders had measured him up for new clothes, kitting him out in a well-fitting, light gray, pin-striped suit instead of his old prison clothes. The visitors noted that Mandela looked fit and trim, and the suit he was wearing "looked very new". One of the group, Dame Nita Barrow from The Bahamas, noticed that his belt was in ANC colours.

At the insistence of African members of the Commonwealth, notably Tanzania and Nigeria, Chief Anyaoku, then Deputy Secretary-General, headed the team that planned and accompanied the mission, and prepared the report. The seven-person group was co-chaired by Gen. Olusegun Obasanjo, at that time a former Head of State of Nigeria, and Malcolm Fraser, a former Prime Minister of Australia. The EPG recognized the significant role in any political settlement of Mandela, then 67, and insisted on seeking his views, determined to do so in a manner that would neither compromise nor embarrass him, cognizant of his position that: "Only free men can negotiate. Prisoners cannot enter into contracts."

Anyaoku was struck by Mandela's apparent good health and his physical authority, which drew the respect of all around him, even his jailers, thus reflecting his own philosophy of separating people from policy. His attitude was conciliatory, and he pledged himself to work for a multi-racial society in which all would have a place. The group, which had consulted widely with the ANC and other organizations and individuals within and outside South Africa notably President Oliver Tambo, Thabo Mbeki and others at ANC headquarters in Lusaka, attached great importance to the immediate, unconditional release of Mandela and other political prisoners. They concluded that, in dealing with the question of violence, lack of confidence and credibility were major obstacles; that the Government's programme of "reforms" was insufficient; that the initiative for progress rested, in the first instance, with the Government; that a special role devolved upon the ANC; and that if a major conflagration was to be averted, time was running out.

The EPG had to abort its mission three days later, having returned to South Africa after consultations in the region, to hear the government's reply to its proposals. They cancelled both the meeting and the mission after the South African Defence Force launched military attacks on the capitals of three neighbouring countries (Botswana, Zambia and Zimbabwe) on 19 May 1986.

"Negotiations leading to fundamental political change and the erection of democratic structures will only be possible if the South African Government is prepared to deal with leaders of the people's choosing rather than with puppets of its own creation," the EPG report said. "There can be no negotiated settlement in South Africa without the ANC; the breadth of its support is incontestable; and this support is growing. Among the many striking figures whom we met in the course of our work, Nelson Mandela and Oliver Tambo stand out. Their reasonableness, absence of rancour and readiness to find negotiated solutions which, while creating genuine democratic structures would still give the whites a feeling of security and participation, impressed us deeply."

The EPG report, *Mission to South Africa*, placed on record for the first time the idea of a negotiated settlement in South Africa, and recommended a possible negotiating concept:

"On the part of the Government: (a) Removal of the military from the townships, providing for freedom of assembly and discussion, and suspension of detention without trial; (b) The release of Nelson Mandela and other political prisoners and detainees; (c) The unbanning of the ANC and PAC and the permitting of normal political activity.

"On the part of the ANC and others: Entering negotiations and suspending violence."

The report added that a number of elements would have to be encompassed in these proposals if they were to have any chance of acceptance. The first related to the negotiating agenda, what were negotiations designed to achieve? Second, confidence-building measures would be needed "to allay suspicions and fears and to demonstrate Government's good faith". The third element would be "a link between the release of political prisoners and the initiation of a political process," as little would be achieved if the prisoners were released but unable to function. Fourth would be a moratorium on violence by Government and its opponents. The fifth element would be "synchronization" as both the Government and ANC were waiting for the other to make the first move.

The EPG had been constituted under The Commonwealth Accord on Southern Africa — known as the "Nassau Accord" — adopted at the Commonwealth Heads of Government Meeting (CHOGM) in Nassau, The Bahamas the previous October to promote "a process of dialogue involving the true representatives of the black majority population of South Africa." Their mission was almost aborted much earlier, however, even before it had started. *The Observer* newspaper in London, the Sunday after the summit, carried a front-page article saying that Geoffrey Howe (then British Foreign Secretary) would chair the EPG, and that his Prime Minister, Margaret Thatcher was "a decisive voice" in how it would work, none of which was true. "So Nigeria announced that they would have nothing to do with it; Tanzania, Zambia were going to pull out of it. The whole thing was going to collapse," Chief Anyaoku said later. "That was when my predecessor, Sonny Ramphal, asked me to go to Africa to rescue the EPG. And in my discussions in Dar es Salaam, in Lusaka and in Lagos, this was the thing I did. ...

"I remember my most fascinating conversation with *Mwalimu* [Julius Nyerere] in Dar es Salaam. It was his last week in office as President, November 1985, thereabouts. And he said to me, 'but your country has said they would have nothing to do with it'. I said, 'leave my country to me', I would fix that. And then I left him and went to Lusaka, sitting down with KK in his study... Then I went to Zimbabwe, because I was keen to rescue the Accord and get Mugabe and Kaunda to nominate two Africans — Obasanjo and, as it turned out, John Malecela [a former cabinet minister, later Prime Minister of Tanzania]. ...So before I got home I asked Mugabe and Kaunda to send a message to Babangida reiterating their support for the Nassau Accord and the Eminent Persons Group. ...I told Babangida that I had discussed with Kaunda, Mugabe and Nyerere the nominations of Obasanjo and Malacela, and when I got to Lagos, his officials tried to ask me about somebody else. And I said, no, this is it. So, Obasanjo was asked."

The findings of the EPG mission facilitated the imposition of economic sanctions by South Africa's major trading partners in Europe; and when the US Congress passed the Comprehensive Anti-Apartheid (CAA) Act in 1987, it was the EPG report that US Congressmen used as reference, holding copies aloft in the manner of order papers. With the development of what it called simply, a "negotiating concept", the EPG had planted a seed that germinated and grew, with many branches.

The Commonwealth vs apartheid

The Commonwealth had been prominent in the world campaign against apartheid, illuminating the path to the international arms embargo on South Africa as far back as their Singapore summit chaired by Prime Minister Lee Kuan Yew in 1971, which was divided over the British Conservative government's decision to resume arms sales to South Africa. The communiqué said simply that the matter of arms sales had been "discussed fully"; but an agreed Declaration of Commonwealth Principles rejected racial prejudice and intolerance, in favour of equality and liberty.

In Ottawa, Canada in 1973, hosted by Prime Minister Pierre Trudeau, Commonwealth leaders discussing their opposition to apartheid and minority rule in southern Africa "recognized the legitimacy of the struggle to win full human rights and self-determination." They agreed that "Commonwealth members in a position to do so should seek to use their influence to persuade Portugal to grant negotiated independence to its African colonies." Emeka Anyaoku was involved in the design of both declarations, first as Assistant Director and then Director of International Affairs under the first Secretary-General, the Canadian Arnold Smith.

By the time of the Commonwealth Heads of Government Meeting (CHOGM) two years later in Kingston, Jamaica with Prime Minister Michael Manley in the chair, Portugal was finalizing the imminent independence of the last of its African colonies; and Commonwealth leaders "welcomed the British [Labour] Government's decision to comply strictly with the United Nations embargo on the sale of arms to South Africa and to terminate the Simonstown Agreement."

The Commonwealth initiated broader united action to increase pressure on South Africa in 1977, at a summit in London chaired by Prime Minister James Callaghan, when the Gleneagles Agreement effectively isolated South Africa from international sport, leading the way to the UN Declaration against Apartheid in Sport. The Lusaka Declaration of the Commonwealth on Racism and Racial Prejudice followed at CHOGM in 1979, with President Kenneth Kaunda in the chair and drafted by a working group of senior officials chaired by Emeka Anyaoku, who had been elected Deputy Secretary-General the previous year. The declaration recognized "that we share an international responsibility to work together for the total eradication of apartheid and racial discrimination," and included relevant language to facilitate closer co-operation with organizations opposing apartheid, including the ANC and anti-apartheid movement.

Heads of Government in Lusaka confirmed their commitment to genuine black majority rule in Zimbabwe, recognizing that the search for a lasting settlement "must involve all parties to the conflict" — an irreversible commitment by the British government. Meeting in 1981 in Melbourne, Australia under the chairmanship of Prime Minister Malcolm Fraser, Commonwealth leaders welcomed Zimbabwe as a new member, recalling "with particular satisfaction the Commonwealth role in helping to bring Zimbabwe to independence under majority rule." The communiqué, produced by a working group chaired by Chief Anyaoku, condemned apartheid as a crime against humanity, saying it threatened regional stability and endangered international peace and security.

At their New Delhi summit in 1983, hosted by Indian Prime Minister Indira Gandhi, Commonwealth leaders called for the eradication of apartheid, release of Nelson Mandela and establishment of majority rule. Chief Anyaoku had left the Commonwealth briefly to serve his country's civilian administration and attended as Foreign Minister of Nigeria.

The leaders who gathered at Lyford Cay, Nassau, The Bahamas in 1985 at the invitation of Prime Minister Sir Lynden Pindling, took measures a giant step further with a programme of economic and financial sanctions, later strengthened and taken up by other members of the international community.

"We consider that South Africa's continuing refusal to dismantle apartheid, its illegal occupation of Namibia, and its aggression against its neighbours constitute a serious challenge to the values and principles of the Commonwealth, a challenge which Commonwealth countries cannot ignore. At New Delhi we expressed the view that 'only the eradication of apartheid and the establishment of majority rule on the basis of free and fair exercise of universal adult suffrage by all the people in a united and non-fragmented South Africa can lead to a just and lasting solution of the explosive situation prevailing in Southern Africa.' We are united in the belief that reliance on the range of pressures adopted so far has not resulted in the fundamental changes we have sought over many years. The growing crisis and intensified repression in South Africa mean that apartheid must be dismantled now if a greater tragedy is to be averted and that concerted pressure must be brought to bear to achieve that end. We consider that the situation calls for urgent practical steps."

Chief Anyaoku had returned to his post as Deputy Secretary-General and chaired a small international group of five senior officials who prepared the Nassau Accord. This document called on the authorities in Pretoria to urgently take the following steps: declare and take specific action to dismantle apartheid; end the state of emergency; release Mandela and other political prisoners and detainees; establish political freedom and lift the ban on the ANC and other parties; and "initiate, in the context of a suspension of violence on all sides, a process of dialogue across lines of colour, politics and religion, with a view to establishing a non-racial and representative government."

Commonwealth leaders agreed in Nassau on a number of measures designed to impress upon the authorities in Pretoria "the compelling urgency of dismantling apartheid and erecting structures of democracy." They agreed to ban government loans, sale of gold coins called *kruger-rands,* funding for trade missions, computer equipment with military uses, nuclear contracts, the sale and export of oil; to discourage cultural and scientific links, and to place an embargo on arms sales and military cooperation. Some wanted to go further, and so they listed other possible steps, including a ban on air links, tourism promotion and new investment, as well as other financial sanctions.

In a carefully crafted document that drew unanimous approval, they agreed to strict enforcement of the mandatory arms embargo and prosecution of violators, and to actively discourage sporting contacts under the Gleneagles agreement.

They also agreed to establish a group of eminent persons and a review committee of seven Heads of Government: Australia, The Bahamas, Britain, Canada, India, Zambia and Zimbabwe.

At a meeting of the review committee in mid-1986 after the EPG mission reported, divisions began to emerge, with the Commonwealth agreeing to implement the remaining sanctions outlined at Nassau, while Britain would accept only a voluntary ban on new investment and tourism promotion in addition to Europe's decision to ban the import of coal, iron, steel and gold coins. Other members added additional measures banning new bank loans to public and private sectors; the import of uranium; and the withdrawal of consular facilities in South Africa. The British government acknowledged its "different view on the likely impact of economic sanctions".

"In the recent history of the Commonwealth, no single issue has generated so much contrariness or differences within the association as the apartheid system of South Africa. But paradoxically enough, it has also made for greater Commonwealth cohesiveness and unity," the Deputy Secretary-General told the Oxford University Strategic Studies Group a few months before the Vancouver CHOGM in 1987. He added that, "The strategic implications of the continued existence of apartheid in South Africa cannot be much in doubt."

Apartheid vs the Commonwealth

The Union of South Africa had been forced out of the Commonwealth in 1961 over its apartheid policies, at a meeting attended by the "father of apartheid", The Hon Dr HF Verwoerd, despite the historical role of General JC Smuts as a founding member almost 20 years before.

South Africa left the Commonwealth in March 1961, during a meeting in London at which the representatives were no longer entirely white. Half of the 11 Prime Ministers and two Presidents were from recently independent countries in Asia and Africa, including Kwame Nkrumah of Ghana. Their report said, "On 13th March the Prime Minister of South Africa informed the Meeting that, following the plebiscite in October 1960, the appropriate constitutional steps were being taken to introduce a republican form of constitution in the Union, and that it was the desire of the Union Government that South Africa should remain within the Commonwealth as a republic."

The precedent had been set by India's continuing membership after it adopted a republican constitution in 1949. The "Nehru formula" enshrined in the London Declaration at that time came just eight days too late to prevent the withdrawal from the Commonwealth of the new Republic of Ireland, but opened the way for other independent republics to claim their place. However, the application from South Africa was different.

"In connection with this application the meeting also discussed, with the consent of the Prime Minister of South Africa, the racial policy followed by the Union Government. The Prime Minister of South Africa informed the other Prime Ministers this evening that in the light of the views expressed on behalf of other member Governments and the indications of their future intentions regarding the racial policy of the Union Government, he had decided to withdraw his application for South Africa's continuing membership of the Commonwealth as a republic."

On the eve of that meeting in early 1961, *Mwalimu* Julius Nyerere, whose country, then Tanganyika, was not yet independent, had an article published in *The Observer* in London, in which he said: "We believe that the principles of the Commonwealth would be betrayed by an affirmative answer to South Africa's application for readmission as a Republic. Inevitably, therefore, we are forced to say that to vote South Africa in is to vote us out."

Reacting to South Africa's departure, *Pandit* Nehru of India said the Commonwealth would be strengthened by this development, and would be more dynamic and vital in facing future problems. *Tunku* Abdul Rahman of Malaya (now Malaysia) expressed "absolute and complete satisfaction", adding that "the people of Sharpeville had not died in vain." Nkrumah called for increased international pressure, if necessary through economic and political sanctions. And the government of Nigeria placed an immediate and total ban on trade with South Africa, as India had done.

Nelson Mandela was arrested the following year, as Emeka Anyaoku prepared to travel to the United Nations to take up a diplomatic post representing the newly independent Federal Republic of Nigeria.

The UN Committee against Apartheid

The Special Committee against Apartheid, as it was commonly called, had a much longer name in the early 1960s, and Nigeria played a significant and high-profile role, through its Permanent Mission to the United Nations (UN) in New York, represented by the First Secretary, Emeka Anyaoku.

Less than six months after joining the Committee, he was part of a seven-member delegation that went to London to the International Conference on Sanctions against South Africa, in April 1964. The UN delegation held hearings at Church House with leaders of the liberation movement and anti-apartheid movement, and the young diplomat became acquainted with many South Africans and their friends abroad, and heard first-hand about the atrocities of apartheid. One eloquent young speaker, just 21 years of age, appealing for the lives of his leaders who were on trial for treason at Rivonia, and speaking on behalf of his father who was one of the accused, was Thabo Mbeki. He described those on trial for treason as "men of the greatest integrity... who would grace any government in which they served."

Guinea chaired the Special Committee in the mid-1960s, but as a small and radical country, it had little influence with the Western nations on the

Security Council, as relations with its former colonial power, France, were poor, and with Britain, non-existent. Nigeria was a more influential member, whose voice was listened to, and it was often encouraged to take the initiative.

"For instance, in October 1964, when the new Labour Government in Britain announced an arms embargo, but with limitations, Emeka made a strong statement calling on France to follow suit and asking that Britain impose a total arms embargo," says E.S. Reddy, an Indian national who was for many years the senior official of the UN Special Committee against Apartheid.

"Early in 1965, Emeka proposed in the Special Committee that the United Nations should launch a major information campaign on apartheid, since public understanding and support was crucial for the success of its efforts for the elimination of apartheid. That proved to be very important. On no issue did the UN undertake greater information activity; in fact, even critical of influential member states."

The General Assembly had decided in December 1963, on the recommendation of the Special Committee, that humanitarian assistance to victims of apartheid was "necessary and appropriate", and that means should be found to provide such assistance through appropriate international organizations.

The following year, again at the request of the Special Committee, the UN Secretary-General appealed to member states for contributions to the Defence and Aid Fund for Southern Africa established by Canon John Collins, to the World Council of Churches, and to a committee for assistance to refugees in High Commission Territories (Botswana, Lesotho, Swaziland) established by Margaret Legum. The Nordic countries as well as India, Netherlands and Pakistan made contributions; just seven countries in all and less than half a million dollars.

The Special Committee decided that a UN Trust Fund for South Africa would attract more contributions because, at that time, many governments did not contribute to non-governmental organizations. The establishment of the Trust Fund was proposed to the UN General Assembly in 1965, in a resolution presented by Nigeria and prepared by Emeka Anyaoku as his country's representative to the Special Committee.

"That proved to be an important initiative," E.S. Reddy said later. "The Trust Fund provided about a hundred million dollars, received from 40 or more countries, for the legal defence of people charged with political offences in South Africa, assistance to their families, grants for prison education, assistance to refugees (especially in Africa).

"Emeka maintained a keen interest in the South African problem throughout his service in the Commonwealth Secretariat," Reddy said. "I used to visit him often in London. Co-operation between the United Nations and the Commonwealth Secretariat developed on many aspects of our actions. Co-operation on programmes for the education of South Africans, for instance. His role in the transition in South Africa, after he became Secretary-General, is therefore not surprising."

This special moment in history

In 1994, watching Mandela take the oath of office, the deep sense of a historical moment like no other, recalled the words of India's first Prime Minister, Jawaharlal Nehru, in the last minutes before midnight of 14 August 1947 when the bugler would sound the conch shell to signal India's independence: "A moment comes," Nehru said, "which comes but rarely in history, when we step out from the old into the new, when an age ends, and when the soul of a nation long suppressed finds utterance."

Only two days earlier, Chief Anyaoku had shared an emotional meeting with Mandela, still in his party office at Shell House in downtown Johannesburg, when further Commonwealth assistance was requested in training the diplomatic corps and restructuring the public service. He left after offering his best wishes and encouragement, "Well, Madiba, the hour is near." And Madiba replied, in his characteristic manner, "Chief, thank-you, thank-you. You have contributed so much to it."

Just over two weeks later, Chief Anyaoku received a formal request from the South African government to rejoin the Commonwealth. This was accepted and became official on 1 June 1994.

"At this special moment in history," was the message Chief Anyaoku had sent on 1 May, after receiving the election results, "what tremendous excitement and happiness I feel in being able to congratulate you on the resounding victory you and your party have won in the first democratic elections in the history of South Africa. ...There can be little doubt that South Africa, through this historic accomplishment, has made a monumental contribution to the quest for a universal reaffirmation of the reality of a common humanity. ...

"Just as the Commonwealth was proud to have remained in the vanguard of the international campaign against the evils of the past, it is today proud to rejoice with you and all your compatriots as you embark on a new future. Please be assured that as South Africa emerges into a new dawn, the Commonwealth stands ready to contribute in every practicable way to the consolidation of its historic transition. ...Emeka Anyaoku."

The morning after the inauguration, the Secretary-General was back at the Union Buildings before 8 o'clock, the first official visitor to pay a call on the new Foreign Minister, Alfred Nzo. He entered the same imposing building he had by now visited several times, up the steps, past the fountain and across the courtyard. The office, imposing in its own way though not opulent, had dark wood paneling, and colonial style furniture, including a very large desk. This was the same office he had entered in October 1991, during his first visit as Secretary-General, to meet Foreign Minister Roelof "Pik" Botha, in preparation for his first meeting with the then President, FW de Klerk.

On this sunny Tuesday morning, 11 May 1994, the first day that Nelson Mandela woke up as President of South Africa, the Chief entered this office for discussions with Nzo. After some minutes, Pik Botha walked in, sat down and joined in the conversation — as if the office he had occupied for over 15 years was still his own.

Into the lion's den

The Secretary-General's first meeting with FW de Klerk had taken place in the same complex on 31 October 1991, and he had gone to considerable effort to make his nervous host feel at ease in his company; an influential black African diplomat facing apartheid's leader. "The first thing I had to think about was how to deal with him; I knew that the history of Commonwealth relations and attitudes to South Africa was not one that would assure me of a warm reception. And so I had to think especially of how to make it a worthwhile discussion. I decided that the thing to do was to start by accentuating the positive, but not at the risk of being totally frank and blunt.

"I made up my mind that if the Commonwealth could be identified with the negotiation process, in a way that would support the negotiation process realistically, that would be one way of keeping it on track and not allowing it to be hijacked by Pretoria," Chief Anyaoku recalled later. "And I was very glad that the terms of my going there, that the Heads of Government accepted, was that I should talk to ALL the parties, because it would have been less than useful if I had gone to talk only to our friends. And so when I got there, my first formal meeting, deliberately, was with De Klerk. ...a meeting that began frostily."

On that day, the Secretary-General had breakfast with Rev. Frank Chikane, General Secretary of the South African Council of Churches, and then travelled from Johannesburg along the wide multi-lane highway to Pretoria. His thoughts were occupied with the forthcoming encounter as the car drove up the hill to the Union Buildings. A dozen or so steps lead up to the building, and De Klerk's officials were waiting at the top of the stairs. Through the courtyard, past the fountain, along the walkways, and down long corridors, the Commonwealth delegation walked until they reached a waiting room.

After entering Pik Botha's office, the foreign minister offered the local herbal tea, *rooibos* (red-bush). Putting his host at ease, the Secretary-General accepted, saying he had heard of this tea and would like to try it. They discussed the forthcoming De Klerk meeting, characterized as a preliminary contact to explore ways in which the Commonwealth could lend momentum to the negotiating process. Botha was flanked by a high-powered delegation from his ministry, all looking slightly stiff and uncomfortable.

"Before meeting De Klerk, I had met with Pik Botha whom, I must confess, was not particularly helpful because he was the one playing the tune of hostility between the Commonwealth and South Africa. Why should South Africa listen to the Commonwealth? What did the Commonwealth have to offer South Africa? By implication he was casting doubts on the utility of my trip. I took him on, but deliberately did not want to put all my cards on the table because I just felt that, if I did, he would perhaps play them less favourably than I would like to play them with De Klerk.

"To Pik, my main card, which I also played with De Klerk, was that the Commonwealth had been impressed by the reformist statements, the process of repealing the legislative pillars of apartheid and, above all, the publication of the *Manifesto for a New South Africa*. I played that card quite strongly, that the Commonwealth was impressed, and therefore thought that I should come and see how to help South Africa down that path."

The group moved to an anteroom off De Klerk's office. When De Klerk walked in, he went directly to the Chief, shook hands, introduced himself, relaxed and informal, neither hostile nor overly friendly. The delegations took their tea and moved to the cabinet room next door, windowless, containing a big table with 40 places. De Klerk sat at the top, with the Secretary-General on his left, then the rainbow delegation of Commonwealth senior officials from three continents: Moni Malhoutra, Stuart Mole, Moses Anafu and Mary Mackie. Pik Botha and the South African officials sat across from them.

Both sides looked grim, except the Secretary-General who was charming and affable; and participants on both sides of the table noticed the contrast. He remained open and positive, seemingly at ease, in his first meeting with the head of a regime that officially regarded him as "separate".

"De Klerk was welcoming, but I think it would be less than candid to say that he was openly warm. He was proper and correct. He started off and gave me the impression that he was just performing a diplomatic act that needed to be performed and that was it. And so, we began to talk, and I started as I had started with Pik Botha, who was there. But he made some introductory remarks himself, by recalling the history of Commonwealth hostility toward South Africa and asking me why he should listen to me. He said the Commonwealth over the years, was always delighting itself in denouncing South Africa and imposing sanctions, and was generally hostile toward South Africa. And that the Commonwealth did not have many friends in South Africa. Obviously, he meant white South Africa! ...

"De Klerk said, 'why should we talk to the Commonwealth, it was not our friend in past?' "And I said, and I think this was what made some impression on him, I said that, yes, he was quite correct, that was while South Africa persisted in pursuing the apartheid line but that there was significant change in the Commonwealth since he, De Klerk, in February 1990, initiated his reforms and the path that he had chosen. It was in reaction to that, that Heads of Government said I should come, and then on sanctions decided on, not a programme of more sanctions but a programme of sanctions relaxation. This was after the Harare CHOGM in October 1991. So I told him that I was there because of this new mood within the Commonwealth, this new attitude to South Africa, and that I was there to open a new chapter in relations between South Africa and the Commonwealth.

"His first response was sceptical, because he probed me a little more on how widespread that view was, and I had to explain to him that it was unanimous, and the communiqué so recorded it. And he moved on to, but why should South Africa bother about the Commonwealth as against bothering about the European Economic Community or the Organization of African Unity, where they belonged. ...I said to him that the Commonwealth made a virtue of unity in diversity and multi-racialism, that co-operation and understanding across the divides of race, wealth and poverty was the most important attribute of the Commonwealth. And that I believed that in South Africa the greatest challenge they faced was political pluralism and how to cope with it. And that's where the experience of the Commonwealth was unique. ...at that point, he was writing his notes quite seriously. Then, the other point which he raised was the issue of sovereignty, that South Africa would not brook any interference, any abuse of its sovereignty. And I sought to reassure him on that. Then he asked me what news I came with, and I explained to him that I had come with no prescriptions but to listen and learn."

At the end, the President thanked the Secretary-General for coming, and, much to the surprise of officials on both sides, said he hoped there would be time to meet again before he left. De Klerk was clearly relieved by the rapport established at the meeting.

Then, the President of apartheid South Africa and the Secretary-General of the Commonwealth, its implacable opponent, walked out of the room together, along the corridor, and down the stone stairs into an open courtyard in the sunlight, where the moment was captured by the waiting media. Both parties were upbeat but cautious about commitment.

"I was measured in my words because, although the atmosphere had started well, I really couldn't say that there was anything yet to show for that good will. But it was a friendly gesture on both sides. ...

"Then four days after that, my colleagues and I were flying from Johannesburg to Durban on our way to Ulundi to see [Chief Mangosuthu] Buthelezi. ...And this man approached me on the plane and said, 'oh, Mr. Secretary-General, can I speak with you?', in a very heavy Afrikaans accent. And I said 'yes, and who are you?' He told me that he belonged to the right side of South African politics and believed that De Klerk was destroying their country, and he had never voted for De Klerk. But after seeing De Klerk and me on the television the other day, he began to think that De Klerk was talking sense. His children who were at university had said they would very much want to meet me, but he didn't know that he would get into any aircraft and see me. He talked with me for a while about South Africa, and I told him, look, De Klerk is not destroying your country, he is trying to save it. And at the end of our conversation, I asked him who he would next time vote for — 'it might be asking too much for you to vote for Mandela but will you vote for De Klerk?' He said he would. ...

"So, in my second and last meeting with De Klerk, I began by telling him that I had just won him a new vote and that helped the atmosphere of the discussion very much!"

The Committee of Foreign Ministers

The events leading directly to these meetings with apartheid's leaders had begun four years earlier at the Commonwealth summit in 1987 in Vancouver, Canada which issued the Okanagan Statement and Programme of Action on Southern Africa, and established the Committee of Foreign Ministers on Southern Africa (CFMSA). This was a tough statement of intent following South Africa's abrupt ending of the EPG mission the previous year. Chief Anyaoku, several years later, quoted the words of the Indian Prime Minister, Rajiv Gandhi speaking to that Vancouver summit, saying this could stand as the late Gandhi's message to the Commonwealth and the world: "We know from experience in India that the dawn breaks when the night appears at its darkest. Black, brown and white must unite."

The Okanagan Statement gave teeth and timetable to earlier statements, and it recognized for the first time, officially, the role of neighbouring countries and the Front Line States, in particular Mozambique, for which a special fund was established and which became a Commonwealth "cousin" a decade before it joined the Commonwealth as a member in its own right. The document was produced by a committee chaired by the Canadian external affairs minister, Joe Clark, with eight other foreign ministers and Chief Anyaoku, then Deputy Secretary-General. A Committee on Southern Africa had existed previously to monitor the implementation of sanctions, but the decision in Vancouver gave this process seniority at a political level. As part of The Way Forward, the statement issued by Commonwealth Heads of Government from their Retreat at Lake Okanagan, gave a mandate to the CFMSA:

"The unfolding — but often unseen — tragedy of South Africa impels us to ensure that the world continues to focus its attention on apartheid until we meet again in full session. With the exception of Britain, we see great value as a measure of our continuing concern in establishing a Committee of Foreign Ministers able to meet periodically to provide high level impetus and guidance in furtherance of the objectives of this statement." The CFMSA, which the British government of Margaret Thatcher refused to join, comprised the Foreign Ministers of Australia, Canada, Guyana, India, Nigeria, Tanzania, Zambia and Zimbabwe.

Despite the lack of unanimous backing, the CFMSA proved an effective and activist forum in guiding Commonwealth action on South Africa and southern Africa, largely due to the dexterity of Chief Anyaoku and the vast experience, commitment and synergy of the individuals who represented their countries, and their willingness to consult with the ANC and others in the anti-apartheid movement. Chaired by the respected Canadian external affairs minister and former Prime Minister, Rt. Hon. Joe Clark, the other foreign ministers were: Australian Senator Hon. Gareth Evans, Hon. Rashleigh Jackson of Guyana, Hon. P V Narasimha Rao from India (later Prime Minister), Major-Gen. Ike Nwachukwu of Nigeria, Hon. Benjamin Mkapa (now President of Tanzania), Hon. Luke Mwananshiku and later Gen. Benjamin Mibenge of Zamiba, and Hon. Dr. Nathan Shamuyarira of Zimbabwe.

The CFMSA held six regular meetings and one special meeting during the four-year period leading up to the Harare CHOGM in 1991 when Heads of Government agreed to Chief Anyaoku's proposal to open direct contacts with Pretoria. The CFMSA published comprehensive reports on sanctions, financial sanctions and South Africa's destabilization of neighbouring countries; and continued to monitor events in South Africa until after the 1994 elections. When Commonwealth leaders gathered in Auckland, New Zealand for the 1995 CHOGM, they paid glowing tribute to the work of the CFMSA and its contribution to change in South Africa.

Behind the tributes though, there were some fraught moments over the years as the committee of foreign ministers evolved in tandem with events in South Africa, and metamorphosed its approach to remain on the cutting edge. As agreed in Vancouver, the committee focused on four main areas: sanctions; the situation of South Africa's neighbours; reaching into South Africa to support victims and opponents of apartheid, encourage dialogue and counteract censorship; and Namibia. At its first meetings in Zambia and Canada in 1988, there was emphasis on making sanctions more effective, broadening economic and trade sanctions to include direct financial pressure, and creating advanced education and training of black South Africans. In 1989 in Zimbabwe, the focus was on the impact of apartheid on peace and security in the region, and seeking ways to increase pressure on Pretoria which held the region in a vice of military and economic destabilization. A fourth meeting in Canberra, Australia, later the same year began to synthesize a report and proposals for the next CHOGM in Kuala Lumpur, Malaysia.

By late 1989, sanctions were taking their toll on the South African economy; internal opposition to apartheid including mass action was reaching a crescendo with the accompanying crackdown on civil unrest; concerned South Africans across the colour bar were meeting within and outside the country to build confidence in preparing a common future; and the ANC, the Front Line States and the Organisation of African Unity

(OAU) had devised a forward-looking document later adopted by the UN, based on the EPG's negotiating concept, laying out the conditions for opening talks with Pretoria.

On the recommendation of the CFMSA, the Kuala Lumpur summit took a firm line on tightening sanctions, especially financial sanctions, "with the exception of Britain".

The British government felt the need to issue a policy briefing paper explaining its position. The paper said Britain was working to bring about the end of apartheid, to encourage economic development, and "to protect and develop UK interests". These interests included "wide-ranging human and family ties" with the possibility of over one million residents of South Africa having the right of abode in UK; extensive trade, and substantial investments. "In addition, South Africa is the major exporter (and in some cases the sole exporter, apart from the USSR) of such strategic minerals as platinum, manganese, vanadium and chrome." In a blunt admission that acknowledged the importance of the Commonwealth's commitment to financial sanctions, the policy brief noted that, "until apartheid goes, South Africa will not gain the confidence of the international financial markets which it needs to attract capital."

Meanwhile, FW de Klerk had become President of South Africa in September and began releasing political prisoners in October. By December he had reorganized the power structure and wrested control from the "securocrats" by scrapping the National Security Management System and reducing the all-powerful State Security Council to an advisory committee, returning power to the cabinet. It was only a matter of time before he released Nelson Mandela and others in February 1990, and lifted the ban on the ANC and other political organizations. The fifth regular meeting of the CFMSA took place three months later, in Abuja, Nigeria with Mandela in attendance.

The fluid situation of apparently radical change in South Africa while the grip of apartheid remained the same, presented a dilemma for the CFMSA, as some of its members responded to the former while others remained firmly attached to the latter. This breadth of national policy and personal style among the nine foreign ministers made it a dynamic microcosm of the Commonwealth in action, but required skilled guidance by the new Secretary-General to maintain the rhythm and keep it moving in the same direction, ie forward.

In this time of change, he was assisted by Senator Evans from Australia and one or two visionary African foreign ministers, and hampered by a cabinet reshuffle in Canada which installed a less experienced minister in the chair. Always available for consultation formally or behind the scenes, there was the ubiquitous and steady presence of Thabo Mbeki and the ANC representatives in London, Mendi Msimang and Aziz Pahad.

At a particularly fraught moment in early 1991 — after De Klerk had accepted the ANC proposal for an all-party conference and some European governments had begun to lift sanctions — Senator Evans travelled to southern Africa, ostensibly on holiday, to meet, most significantly, Mbeki in Botswana and seek guidance about the way forward. Sharing views on the same trip with other contacts in Zimbabwe who had served on a sanctions review panel and whom he knew to be firmly anti-apartheid, Senator Evans was mildly amused to hear them express support for a phased lifting of sanctions. Well then, he said wryly to his guests, winking at the High Commissioner, Joe Thwaites, who is an implacable foe of racism in any form, "if you and Mbeki both think its okay, that must be the way forward." A few weeks later in London, Senator Evans supported the Secretary-General's plan for the "programmed management of sanctions", and together they drafted a document for presentation to the committee of foreign ministers. This effectively put the brakes on those countries that wanted to lift sanctions before change was irreversible.

The Australian senator and the African chief shared mutual respect for each other's abilities in this exercise, but the Australian harboured no doubts about who was in the driver's seat. Affectionately calling the Chief a "patrician" (aristocrat; of the ancient Roman nobility), the blunt-spoken Senator Evans engaged in friendly sparring. On one occasion when the Secretary-General stalled, saying he wanted to consult his colleagues, the Senator chided that he was in reality buying time to think about it himself "because what you say goes here..." The Chief admits to being a product of old-guard *paterfamilias* but insists that he bows to superior logic. While this banter was regular fare in the CFMSA, it was difficult for some senior officials in the Secretariat who came from the "old" Commonwealth and were not familiar with the behaviour of an African intellectual with a sharp mind of his own.

"I was wanting to build on the positive signals that were coming from Pretoria," the Secretary-General said later. "I wanted, instead of the previous inclination to doubt whatever they said, to adopt the attitude of 'show me'. ...to build on what they said... and so, in doing that, create more common ground within the Commonwealth, because those statements were in accordance with what we had been urging. While you had most of the Commonwealth not believing them, or remaining sceptical, I thought it was a matter to rally everybody around on the basis of: 'okay, let's take what they say at face value and see what the Commonwealth can do to make sure that, whatever they say, they are held to it'. That's the strategy that I began.

"That was why, in the CFMSA, I had begun to put the emphasis on that now well-established phraseology, 'programmed management of sanctions', which we had considered at a special CFMSA meeting in February 1991 in London. It was not an easy meeting. ...This was the meeting at which I put forward the idea, the statement was drafted in my room with the help of others. Gareth Evans joined in the drafting and Gareth was the one who, when I talked about programmed management of sanctions, thought that would save everybody's face. Senator Evans had just been to southern Africa and he knew some of the thinking of ANC. ...I actually challenged one of the ministers as to whether he was doubting my integrity in saying that the ANC agreed with the view I was putting forward. But this was at the time that Thabo Mbeki had left for the airport. I had to get a telephone call to him. ...and in the end the statement was adopted.

"That helped to set the pattern, and so by the time CFMSA got to Delhi in September, it was possible to agree and propose the package that was later adopted at Harare CHOGM. That's the approach: 'South Africa, you have said this; we welcome it. We will now proceed to relax sanctions on the basis of your performance. And we will do so in phases.'

"I think this policy has been effective in two ways. One, it has kept the Commonwealth together in pressuring South Africa. ...At the end of 1989, at the end of Kuala Lumpur CHOGM, the Commonwealth was bitterly divided in its policy toward South Africa, at a time when De Klerk was attaching such importance to scoring diplomatic victories here and there. ...So this had the double advantage of making an impact on South Africa, and healing the wounds within the Commonwealth. ...if you recall, in the Harare communiqué, even the British government's reservation on sanctions was more muted. It was possible for me to go to South Africa at the behest of all Heads of Government and to carry a message which continued to engage the South African government with the Commonwealth in a constructive way."

On 7 May 1991, however, Chief Anyaoku had to issue a blunt warning about the "threatened rupture in relations and the consequent suspension of dialogue" between the government and the ANC. He warned that a breakdown in talks could be "cataclysmic for hopes for the peaceful end to apartheid", and said this was the time for De Klerk to "justify fully" the wide degree of support given to him inside and outside South Africa. He called upon the ANC and the Inkatha Freedom Party (IFP) to "address more vigorously" the role of their supporters in sustaining the violence; and appealed to all concerned to take steps to "arrest the serious threat now posed to the negotiation process by the current violence."

CFMSA New Delhi

On 15 September 1991, opening the sixth regular meeting of CFMSA in New Delhi, the Secretary-General said most of the original five steps that the international community had called upon Pretoria to take in order to create a climate conducive to negotiations have now been taken ...and many of the obstacles that stood in the way of negotiations have been removed or are being overcome, as a result of various meetings and discussions, principally between the government and the ANC.

"The parties have been unbanned; the troops removed from the townships, the state of emergency lifted, many political prisoners released, with many more soon to be released. And the agreement reached between the Government and the UN High Commissioner for Refugees on 16 August 1991 should expedite the repatriation of the estimated 40,000 South African refugees and political exiles. ...The statesmanlike decision by the ANC last year to suspend the armed struggle, and the repeal of the legislative pillars of apartheid by the Government in June of this year, have further consolidated the prospects for negotiations. ...It goes without saying that we would not have been at this pass without the heroic determination of the people of South Africa in the face of almost overwhelming odds, the unwavering commitment and solidarity of the international community, and the courage and realism of President De Klerk and his government."

These achievements had brought the parties to the threshold of negotiations but had not taken them beyond; "what stands between the parties and the negotiating table is the escalating violence."

The source, motivation and instruments of the violence had been revealed, and "no one should be left in any doubt" as to the consequences. First, it gravely damaged the confidence in the government and underscored the point that "the South African government cannot be a player and sole referee at the same time in the transition process." Second, it created an atmosphere of profound insecurity, in which normal political activity is practically impossible, "and in the absence of such normal activity, there can be no advance to peaceful negotiations." Third, "it is the worst violence in the history of South Africa, and if allowed to continue for much longer would sow a legacy of bitterness such as a future non-racial government would find very difficult to eradicate."

Chief Anyaoku noted the important steps taken to try to bring the violence under control, including an all-party meeting in June, and the Peace Accord drawn up by representatives of all major political parties in September. But he said delays in the progress to negotiations were causing a vacuum in which violence could escalate further. ...He drew attention to the expectations of the international community which — especially since the EPG mission — "has come to look to the Commonwealth for a realistic lead."

Acknowledging India's commitment and leadership, Chief Anyaoku said: "in the history of the anti-apartheid campaign, this is no ordinary venue. ...As you all know, shortly after independence India imposed economic and other sanctions against Pretoria. It was not an easy decision and entailed a very substantial price for the newly independent India. Nevertheless the decision was taken, motivated characteristically by a principled stand against a system which trenched on the most hallowed of India's values. What is more, India did not rest the matter there. It went further and took the issue to the United Nations so that the peoples of the world, so recently saved from the horrors of Nazism and Fascism, might unite once more against the resurgent racism embodied in apartheid.

"In this way, India gave a lead to the world in the fight against apartheid, and established a tradition of peaceful and non-violent but most effective campaigning against the inhumanities of apartheid. *We are all heirs to this tradition.* Our meeting here today is therefor an act of renewal."

He paid tribute to a succession of Indian leaders who have "steadfastly upheld and strengthened this tradition" including Mahatma Gandhi, *Pandit* Nehru, Indira Gandhi and the late Rajiv Gandhi, whom he described as "a great Commonwealth statesman. ...In his untimely death, the anti-apartheid cause has lost a fighter of towering stature."

The concluding statement of the group noted that since their meeting in London in February there had been significant developments, including progress on the release of political prisoners and return of exiles. "The government has repealed the Land Acts, the Group Areas Act, the Development of Black Communities Act, the Population Registration Act and substantially amended the Internal Security Act." The CFMSA emphasized the need to continue to use sanctions as an effective form of pressure while retaining"the catalytic role played by the Commonwealth in shaping the international community's response in this context. ..."

The committee had considered the Secretary-General's proposal for the "programmed management of sanctions", and recommended to Heads of Government:

• the arms embargo applied by the UN and supported by specific Commonwealth measures, should not be lifted until "a new post-apartheid South African government is firmly established with full democratic control and accountability."

• financial sanctions, "the most demonstrably effective of all sanctions" including lending by international financial institutions, should be lifted "only when agreement is reached on the text of a new democratic constitution."

• other economic sanctions including trade and investment measures should be lifted when appropriate transitional mechanisms are agreed "which enable all the parties to participate fully and effectively in negotiations."

• people-to-people sanctions, ie consular and visa restrictions, cultural and scientific boycotts, restrictions on tourism promotion and ban on direct airlinks, should be lifted now due to the "substantial progress" made in overcoming the four obstacles to negotiations (repeal of the three "pillars" laws; review and amendment of security legislation, clearing the way for return of exiles and release of political prisoners; the signing into effect of the National Peace Accord on 14 September; and the need to give external support and encouragement to, and to achieve free interaction with, democratic anti-apartheid forces within South Africa). Direct airlinks to be resumed on the basis that South African Airways and other local airlines proceed with appropriate affirmative action.

• the sports boycott continues to be lifted on the selective basis now being implemented in consultation with the democratic anti-apartheid forces.

The concluding statement acknowledged the report of the London School of Economics (LSE) Centre for the Study of the South African Economy and International Finance, established to monitor links with the international financial community. Its ongoing importance was emphasized, "in the context of the continuing need to exert pressure on South Africa, and in the longer term as a means of assisting resource flows for the economic development of post-apartheid South Africa."

President Mbeki of the ANC

Thabo Mbeki was consulted by the CFMSA in its deliberations and was influential in its course of action. Years later, watching him take the oath of office as the second democratically elected President of South Africa, Chief Anyaoku recalled their work together over many years since Mbeki had first contacted him in the late 1970s.

"I first met Thabo Mbeki, at his own request, without knowing who he was; it was a cloak-and-dagger meeting that took place in the lobby of the Kensington Hilton hotel in London, by Shepherd's Bush. He had phoned and said he wanted to see me; the first time he phoned, I was not there, so he left a message to call him back. I called him back. And he told me it would be in the lobby of this hotel. I asked him to describe what he looked like, and he did. So I went there, and I recognized him because of his beard. And we talked. What he wanted really, was my meeting with Oliver Tambo."

Mbeki was political secretary to Oliver Reginald "O.R." Tambo, who had been acting President of ANC since the death of Chief Albert Luthuli in 1967, and he wanted to arrange a meeting between Tambo and Anyaoku, then Assistant Secretary-General. Though presenting himself as an ordinary ANC cadre, Mbeki was already a member of the policy-making body, the National Executive Committee. Within a few months he became director of information, later head of the department of information and publicity, and then international affairs director; one of the next generation prepared by Tambo and others for higher office, in the tradition of the ANC.

Mbeki had returned recently from Nigeria where he served as ANC representative for just over a year through 1977, during the first Obasanjo administration with which he initiated support to South African students in the form of refuge and scholarships; and he led the South African delegation to the Festival of African Culture (FESTAC) in Lagos. The ANC had young students pouring out of South Africa into exile following the Soweto demonstrations of June 1976, and needed to arrange more educational scholarships — in other countries, through the Commonwealth and the UN. The mechanism established in Nigeria was used as a catalyst to facilitate educational support by other countries. Commonwealth leaders meeting in London in June 1977, one year after Soweto, "commended the Government of Nigeria for having established a popularly based national fund for humanitarian purposes in Southern Africa. ...and agreed to examine ways in which similar exercises might be introduced in their own countries."

This Commonwealth commitment was prepared by Emeka Anyaoku who had been active for many years in identifying scholarship mechanisms for African students, since his time at the UN in the early 1960s. After joining the Commonwealth secretariat in 1966, he was involved in establishing a scholarship fund which supported some 4,500 Zimbabwean students over the next 15 years, and in the creation of the UN Institute for Namibia (UNIN) in Lusaka in the early 1970s. The Anyaoku-Mbeki meeting marked the initiation of discussions that led eventually to formalization of a scholarship mechanism for South African students. "It was after Soweto, and Thabo had been to Nigeria and knew that I was well-connected with the Nigerian government. And also that I was in the Commonwealth. And so the dealing with the Commonwealth began in terms of scholarships for some of the South Africans. And then discussions about the diplomatic support for their struggle."

Diplomatic support was facilitated through the declaration on racism and racial prejudice approved by heads of government in Lusaka in 1979, after an all-night meeting of senior officials chaired by Anyaoku, who had been elected Deputy Secretary-General the previous year. The last paragraph of the declaration commits the Commonwealth "as an international organization with a fundamental and deep-rooted attachment to principles of freedom and equality" to co-operation with other organizations in the fulfillment of its principles. "In particular the Commonwealth should seek to enhance the co-ordination of its activities with those of other organizations similarly committed to the promotion and protection of human rights and fundamental freedoms."

The contact with Mbeki led also to a close friendship with Tambo, the softspoken lawyer and intellectual who embodied the principles of the ANC and was its widely respected leader, exiled in London and Lusaka. "I saw a lot more of him, because he was more often in London. By the time of the Lusaka CHOGM in 1979, I had met with Mbeki and Oliver Tambo several times. ...

"So that was the beginning of my contacts with Thabo, and as I saw more and more of him and Oliver Tambo, we became good friends, and worked together. Thabo was a regular along-the-corridors man at Commonwealth Heads of Government Meetings. And when we had the Eminent Persons Group, he was instrumental in making arrangements for the meetings which the group had with the ANC in Lusaka. And then of course, he was in Vancouver in 1987 when the decision to establish CFMSA was taken. And we maintained contact since." That personal contact between two sons of Africa strengthened immeasurably the international campaign to isolate apartheid and later to negotiate a new dispensation.

But for the liberation movement, it wasn't always a peer group. At the Kuala Lumpur summit in 1989, when Chief Anyaoku was elected Secretary-General, representatives of the ANC as usual, were given press credentials as there was no other designation for attendance at CHOGM than Delegate, Official or Press. Among those barred from the meeting rooms at Commonwealth summits, therefore, but much in demand in the corridors were Abdul Minty, now deputy Director-General in the Ministry of Foreign Affairs in charge of multilateral relations including the Commonwealth, at that time he headed the World Campaign Against Military and Nuclear Collaboration with South Africa; Aziz Pahad, now deputy Foreign Minister, who was then deputy ANC Representative in London; and the future President of South Africa, Thabo Mbeki.

On Chief Anyaoku's first mission to South Africa as Secretary-General in late 1991, when he met De Klerk for the first time, he also paid a call on Oliver and Adelaide Tambo, their first meeting on South African soil. He found "O.R." frail but in good physical health after his debilitating stroke two years earlier — and very, very happy to be home. By then, Tambo was ANC Chairman, having relinquished the presidency to Mandela at the Durban conference mid-year, due to his illness. There was also the satisfaction for Chief Anyaoku of meeting Mandela, Mbeki and others on their home turf.

Thus it was not surprising that he was an honoured guest at the second inauguration at the Union Buildings in Pretoria, when Mbeki was sworn in as President — 23 years after Soweto and two weeks after a gruelling election campaign which he led from the front. Mbeki had been elected ANC Chairman after Tambo died in 1993, and deputy ANC President in December 1994, when Walter Sisulu retired. He was elected ANC President three years later. In the June 1999 elections, ANC took two-thirds of the popular vote for the national parliament, but under the Proportional Representation system fell one seat short of two-thirds of Members of Parliament (MPs). Parliament sitting as an electoral college, elected Mbeki as President of South Africa.

A possible negotiating concept

After the ANC conference at Kabwe, Zambia in June 1985, at which Oliver Tambo was confirmed as President and which marked the 30th anniversary of the Freedom Charter, the ANC had broadened its assault at home, both militarily and politically, and in skillfully addressing different audiences; persuaded elements in the white South African establishment that it was a serious and mature contender for power; cemented alliances with other anti-apartheid organizations within and outside the country, raising its profile and widening its political base; and implemented a strategy to influence and advance the pace of international pressure, in collaboration with the Front Line States, the OAU, the Commonwealth and the United Nations.

After Kabwe, Mbeki began to work ever more closely with Chief Anyaoku and the Commonwealth, as the multilateral engine that drove international action on South Africa — through the EPG, the CFMSA, and after 1991, through direct intervention of the Secretary-General as mandated by Heads of Government.

Tambo and Mbeki "were intent on delivering... the mind and soul of the Afrikaner people to the new South Africa," Patti Waldmeir says in her 1997 book *Anatomy of a Miracle*. They were "shrewd enough to understand that behind the facade of the Afrikaner bully dwelt a... yearning to be understood, loved and accepted by Africa. ...What you needed to do — which sometimes wasn't easy — was to start off from where they were." There were few other players of influence who understood that, among them President Samora Machel of Mozambique and Chief Anyaoku, the Commonwealth Secretary-General.

The ANC began to look more formally at conditions under which negotiations could take place, and a dynamic process of political interaction emerged, supported by Tambo and managed by Mbeki. The latter began to engage in discussions outside the country with key white South Africans, notably businessmen such as Gavin Relly, the chairman of Anglo-American, and influential Afrikaner intellectuals, in various places and various ways. Initially, the contacts were a closely guarded secret which evolved from informal to more formal talks as the process entered the public domain in August 1987, at a high-profile meeting in Dakar, Senegal of an ANC delegation led by Mbeki and 50 Afrikaner intellectuals, mass converts to the cause of dialogue.

Sanctions were becoming more effective, and internal revolt more vocal. The Cold War was drawing to a close, and enlightened leadership on both sides of the confrontation in South Africa realized that their external military support would soon evaporate and that it was essential to reach a political settlement. The leadership on the Pretoria side came from intellectuals in the powerful Afrikaner brotherhood, the *broederbond*, who had analyzed a circumstance in which South Africa would no longer be seen as an essential ally by Western countries against the communist Eastern bloc. They presented their radical proposals to their community, not as concessions but as a "prerequisite for survival". In addition, the military rebuke in southern Angola, at Cuito Cuanavale, in late 1988, weakened the power of the securocrats. The *Afrikaner Broederbond* (since renamed the *Afrikanerbond*), more than the National Party, drove the changes within government and cajoled President P W Botha into making concessionary noises including his Rubicon speech. But he could go no further, and was replaced by F W de Klerk, who took over the party leadership in early 1989, becoming President of South Africa in September.

In the same month, a summit of the Non-Aligned Movement in Belgrade was a lively centre of active lobbying for Chief Anyaoku's candidature for Commonwealth Secretary-General, led by a number of key African diplomats, including the redoubtable Robert Ouko, then foreign minister of Kenya. The summit considered and accepted a declaration on South Africa which had been produced in Harare by the ANC and the Front Line States, and adopted by the OAU. A few weeks later, the UN General Assembly adopted the document with few changes. All members of the Security Council signed the declaration on 14 December 1989 which called for the maintenance of "existing measures aimed at encouraging the South African regime to eradicate apartheid, until there is clear evidence of profound and irreversible changes," and stated the terms and conditions to be met by Pretoria before sanctions could be lifted. It contained five points as a minimum for negotiations, drawing on the Commonwealth's Nassau Accord and the EPG's "possible negotiating concept", which had originally emerged from consultations with the ANC and others.

Just six weeks later, on 2 February 1990, De Klerk announced to a restive parliament that the liberation movements would be unbanned, political prisoners released, and other measures taken to remove some of these obstacles to negotiations. On 11 February, Nelson Mandela walked free from Victor Verster prison, where he had stayed for just over one year, at Paarl, in the wine-growing area northeast of Cape Town. In less than three months, Thabo Mbeki and a handful of other exiled ANC leaders flew into Cape Town on a Zambian plane for direct talks.

The first official meeting of ANC leaders with the South African government took place at Groote Schuur in Cape Town on 2 May 1990. This led to the signing of the Groote Schuur Minute, which committed both parties to stability and a peaceful process of negotiation. It was Mbeki's task at the ANC consultative conference in December 1990 and the Durban conference six months later, to present to delegates two controversial decisions from the leadership which the rank-and-file did not yet fully understand: suspension of the armed struggle, and the phased lifting of sanctions.

Chief Anyaoku's long-term vision for the advancement of this process was firmly rooted in the concept of a supporting role at various stages for activities undertaken by South Africans themselves. He had told *West Africa* magazine in mid-1990, "If the negotiation process continues successfully there will be a good chance that by the time of the next Commonwealth Summit we'll be talking about how to help the negotiation process rather than how to persuade the parties to get involved in negotiations. The divergence of view that existed within the Commonwealth, was on how to persuade the parties concerned to go to the negotiations table. Sanctions were intended to persuade the government of South Africa to do so."

Chief Anyaoku shares with Mbeki an attribute noted in the book, *Africa — The Time Has Come*, quoting the Swedish philosopher Søren Kierkegaard: "a passion for the possible".

in TRANSITION

Support for the process

On 9 November 1991, the day after he returned to London from re-opening contacts with Pretoria, Chief Anyaoku sent a written report to Heads of Government. He reported that, during eight days in South Africa, he met all principal parties, including representatives of government and ANC, the Pan Africanist Congress (PAC), Congress of South African Trade Unions (COSATU), IFP, Conservative and Democratic parties, and prominent figures from the academic and business communities and the churches. He said he was received with "a cordiality which I found heartening" but had encountered universal concern about the escalating violence. However, he noted that all sides were determined to commence constitutional negotiations and that he found the mood of hope in the face of escalating violence "particularly encouraging".

He said his discussions had confirmed that the Commonwealth could play a helpful role in lending momentum to the negotiating process, and that his visit had created a climate in which new opportunities may prove possible. He made two specific proposals to Heads of Government.

The first proposal was to send a small group of distinguished Commonwealth citizens to observe the inaugural proceedings of the all-party talks as official guests of the conference. He identified this as a critical stage because it was expected to determine the principles which would underpin a new constitution, mechanisms for negotiating the constitution, and the nature of transitional arrangements. A Commonwealth presence would indicate international support for the process, and help to build mutual trust between the parties.

The second proposal was that, as the negotiations progressed, the Secretary-General himself would be available to observe appropriate stages, accompanied by a team of advisers whose expertise could be useful to the parties and would help to strengthen the professional infrastructure for negotiations.

"My main concern," he said later, "was to involve the Commonwealth in the launching of the CODESA process in a way which would give the process some international credibility but more importantly would give the parties involved in it the benefit of the experience of carefully chosen Commonwealth representatives. And, in the end, it worked... I did receive an invitation from CODESA to send such a team of representatives." It is clear from the sequence of events that this facilitated the issuing of similar invitations to other international organizations.

"One of the underlying currents that was evident to me was that, in seeking to create a new basis for the relationship between the South African government and the Commonwealth — which had hitherto been hostile, very hostile, to South Africa, and this was one of the points I had to iron out with both De Klerk and Pik Botha — I think they were anxious to demonstrate that their attitude towards the Commonwealth would be their attitude to other international organizations. They hadn't begun to trust the Commonwealth enough to single it out for special treatment, so they said to me that they would want to issue similar invitations to the OAU, Non-Aligned Movement and United Nations. And I said to them, 'absolutely'. I was not there to carve out a special niche for the Commonwealth. I was there to see that the Commonwealth potential to help them was made available."

CODESA

The group of distinguished observers to the Convention for a Democratic South Africa (CODESA) was constituted by the Secretary-General to observe its inaugural proceedings. The group comprising six distinguished Commonwealth citizens from Australia, The Bahamas, Britain, India, Malaysia and Zimbabwe, included a former president, a former governor-general, three former foreign ministers, and a former chief justice. They spent four days in South Africa, 18-21 December 1991, and described CODESA as a "milestone" in South Africa's political evolution. "To see so many different political forces working collectively towards a new South Africa was remarkable and impressive by any standard."

They recommended that the next stages should be supported by the international community, including the offer of practical assistance "which the Secretary-General envisaged as the second phase of the Commonwealth's involvement."

In reporting back to the Secretary-General on the results of their mission, they acknowledged his key personal role. "It was clear during our stay that your own visit to South Africa last month had brought about a marked change of attitude to the Commonwealth. To the extent that our presence has been universally welcomed and has served a useful purpose, it has built on your initiative and the bridgehead which you were able to establish."

Chief Anyaoku visited South Africa three more times during the following year. His next visit was mid-May to attend the plenary of CODESA II, and he spoke about this a few weeks later:

"I was there to listen and to advise. I had meetings with De Klerk and Pik Botha and their officials, with Nelson Mandela, with the IFP delegation to CODESA, and I also had a meeting with the PAC who were not part of CODESA, and with the South African Council of Churches. And in these meetings, what I was seeking to do was to stress the importance of building on what I regarded as the common ground. And even at that stage, I realized that the violence, if not checked, would ultimately abort the negotiation process. So I was again talking about violence. ...I sowed the seed of the proposal that I developed on paper during a later visit. ...

"I began by stressing to PAC the importance of their joining the CODESA process. And they stressed to me that they didn't have much faith in it. But I managed to get them to agree that if CODESA II was successful, and the next stage was to involve the election of members of the constitution-making body, that they would join in the elections. ...Inkatha has never supported a strong central government in South Africa. And they were asking me, why don't you bring to these negotiations the experience of the Commonwealth in federations and constitutions with strong devolution of powers to the regions, which is their own interest. But generally they were keen that the Commonwealth should be involved.

...The attitude of the churches remained enthusiastic. Frank Chikane has remained in touch with me, and is very welcoming to the idea of Commonwealth involvement."

"ANC showed interest in principle... I think their belief in De Klerk's sincerity had encouraged their own self-confidence, and they didn't think they needed anybody. But that belief in De Klerk's sincerity has been shattered by violence, and they seem more responsive to third-party mediation. ..."

CODESA II settled a number of issues relating to the transitional arrangements and the interim government; the reports of many of the working groups were adopted. But it floundered over disagreement on a timetable for transition, the issue of power-sharing, and the size of majority required for acceptance of a new constitution. "The concession which one hoped the National Party and Government would make — by coming down to 70 per cent when ANC had crept up to 70 per cent — they weren't prepared to do that." So Working Group Two, dealing with constitutional decision-making, could not reach agreement. The meeting adjourned after delegating the task to the management committee of CODESA, and the conciliatory speeches made on adjournment by De Klerk and Mandela encouraged hope. But meetings of the management committee turned out to be more acrimonious. And, in the meantime, the violence escalated.

"I was hoping to build on this idea of Commonwealth involvement in helping to deal with the violence as a means of setting the stage for resumption of talks. Because it was quite clear to me that as long as the violence escalated the talks might not easily be resumed, particularly after Boipatong."

Boipatong

On 22 June 1992, the Secretary-General was addressing the Commonwealth Press Union (CPU) biennial conference in Edinburgh when he broke from his written text to condemn the tragedy five days earlier at Boipatong, in a strong statement that was sent by fax to the leaders of all main parties in South Africa:

"The latest news of the horrific massacre of more than 39 innocent men, women and children in Boipatong has taken the violence in South Africa to new depths. There must now be the danger that unless effective and impartial measures are taken and taken quickly, by the parties concerned, especially the South Africa Government, to arrest these escalating killings of black South Africans, we will soon be witnessing not only the wrecking of the negotiation process but also a return to the days of full international ostracism of South Africa."

After Boipatong, Mandela had announced that ANC was cutting off both bilateral talks and the multilateral participation in CODESA. Chief Anyaoku, alarmed that this would mark the end of the CODESA process, decided to travel to South Africa again. However, he soon found that in offering Commonwealth mediation and peace-making skills, he had to negotiate a minefield of both internal and external obstacles. This delicate navigation included a divergence of views within the ANC between those in the leadership who had lived outside the country and under-stood the merits and methodology of Commonwealth intervention, and those of the "internal" leadership who had not been exposed to its wide range of multi-cultural expertise, and pinned their hopes solely on the UN. The next weeks were among the most challenging of his diplomatic career, and resulted in a significant contribution to the transition to a sta-ble and democratic South Africa.

"As soon as I heard — I saw Nelson Mandela on the television, dur-ing his visit to Boipatong in which he announced that they were cutting off bilateral talks with the South African government... I telephoned... Nelson told me that they were going to have a meeting of the National Executive the next day, Tuesday, at which they would discuss their poli-cy to CODESA talks.

"I tried to make my point about keeping the CODESA process alive in some form. He said to me, 'Emeka, the people here are very, very angry, very angry'. ...I told him that I was thinking of coming, and he said he thought it would be most productive if I came after the OAU summit," which was to take place in Dakar, Senegal, in July.

When Cyril Ramaphosa, then ANC Secretary-General, called back to confirm this, "I said, fine, but I left him in no doubt that I thought it was a mistake. I was conscious of the fact that the Boipatong massacre had created a new momentum for persuading, not only the South African government, but all of the Commonwealth governments who would pro-vide the resources for doing something on violence. The longer they left it the more the momentum would dissipate. ...

"But when Ramaphosa told me that it was the decision of the execu-tive, I said fine. ...which is why I went to Dakar. I had good discussions there with Nelson and he supported my going to South Africa from Dakar. ...

"At the OAU, I talked also with Boutros Boutros-Ghali, that was where I established an understanding that the UN and the Commonwealth would co-ordinate closely on this subject. I gave him an idea of what I might be proposing to the South Africans. We agreed that we'd be in touch before the Security Council debate, which we were."

While Boutros-Ghali, then UN Secretary-General, supported a Commonwealth role in peace-making in South Africa, he had sharply diverging views on the substance of a settlement and how to move the negotiating process forward.

It was the view of the Commonwealth Secretary-General that the reason negotiations had reached an impasse was because the South African government was not yet ready for movement to full democracy and still believed they could retain a power of veto over key decisions. If they would qualify that approach, he believed there could be negotiations. "But unless and until they were prepared to concede that basic point, I didn't think that third party intervention or negotiations could go too far."

Boutros-Ghali's experience was rooted in the Middle East peace process, and he thought a suitable negotiator should be found who could seek appropriate words. "He told me of their Camp David experience and how finding forms of words could paper over differences in the direction of progress. I told him... it's not a problem of words, it's a problem of stark political realities!"

The UN Secretary-General expressed his view that South Africa was comparable to Israel and the Middle East, and to Cyprus, noting that whites were a minority not only in their own country but surrounded by so many black African countries. "He told me that it might not be fair to ask them to give up control. ...The conclusion I was able to draw from what he was saying was that the Africans should accept a constitutional dispensation which would leave some veto powers in the hands of the whites." Boutros-Ghali was also concerned that the UN and its resources were over stretched, "that he wouldn't be able to do as much as the Africans were expecting of him."

The OAU Secretary-General, Salim Ahmed Salim, a Tanzanian with long diplomatic experience of the struggle against apartheid, had a more informed perspective, also supportive of Commonwealth involvement while trying to define a role for the OAU. At that time, 17 English-speaking African countries belonged to both the OAU and the Commonwealth, and for each organization, that represented one-third of their membership. Salim "recognized that the Commonwealth has long been with the South African issue and that, whatever the Commonwealth did, I should seek to keep him informed and wherever possible to coordinate with him. He also expressed concern over South Africa's continuing diplomatic efforts to divide OAU members..."

From Dakar, Chief Anyaoku went directly to South Africa, where he had "long and quite constructive" discussions with De Klerk and with Buthelezi. The South African ambassador had assured him that he would be taken straight from the airport for a meeting with De Klerk, but to his surprise, he found Buthelezi waiting for him. The order of meetings had been reversed, so that first Buthelezi and then De Klerk emphasized their wish for a tripartite meeting with Mandela.

"In my meeting with Buthelezi, I went over the ground, how terrible the violence was. He, of course, agreed. How clearly violence was obstructing the negotiation process. He agreed with that. How important it was to do something about it. He agreed with that. And how prepared and willing the Commonwealth was to help in doing something about it. He welcomed that. And when I went to talking generally about the nature of Commonwealth involvement, he urged on me that the first thing to do is to bring him and Nelson Mandela together, and De Klerk, to talk about it, and agree what I was proposing. And when I said, what is your agreement to my general idea... is it contingent on that? He said, no, no, that he would welcome Commonwealth help and involvement. But he thought it would be very useful if I could organize a tripartite meeting. ...

"De Klerk, interestingly enough, also suggested that I should encourage Mandela to join in a meeting with him and Buthelezi, and it seemed to me that he was seeking to use my proposal as a basis for resumption of talks at the tripartite level. I listened, but I told him that I did not think it would be an early part of implementation of my proposal, that what I needed was an initial response from his government to my proposal and then I would go to the next stage. ..."

In that meeting, De Klerk "spent more time than I had expected on exonerating his government and himself, and reflecting his anger at the name-callings that ANC were making. For the first time, I heard him being really quite aggressive in his references to Nelson Mandela and the ANC, thereby confirming my worst fears that the breakdown in mutual confidence was near complete. And he was trying to convince me that it was no part of his fault. ..."

Chief Anyaoku told him the Commonwealth could help to address the issue of violence... "it was not crucial at that stage what the facts were, he was seeking to put the blame on the other side. I told him that won't matter, because the reality is that public perception on the other side believes that the police and security forces were either implicated or at least indifferent...

"I was aware that he in his statement had talked about not being opposed to 'fact-finding' missions. I was aware that ANC had called for an international monitoring group. I thought it would be possible to build on that... I wasn't thinking of a group that will come here to find the facts and announce to the world. If I call the Commonwealth group a 'fact-finding' group it will put on them the obligation of telling the world the results of their investigation. And I was not interested in that.

"I was interested in a group that would come and assist the authorities concerned with dealing with this violence, in dealing with it more effectively. They will naturally need to find the facts because they will be in touch with all the parties concerned in unrest areas. They will be a group that will possess the expertise that could enable them to advise the authorities on what needs to be done. The group would be finding out, helping out, and bringing to bear their own individual experience. He said it was an interesting idea, and he would like to look at it more fully. ...

"I did tell him that I would put down on paper my thoughts, the proposal, put it precisely so that he would know what he would be reacting to. ...And I said that I would be leaving South Africa on Sunday, this was Thursday night, and it would help very much if I got the reply by that time."

De Klerk was beginning to see the point that regional organizations representing solely Europe or Africa could not operate alone as they would be viewed as partisan by one side or the other, and the UN was too monolithic to intervene in any meaningful way, whereas the Commonwealth approach was more flexible, practical and multi-cultural, and could be a focus for confidence-building for all of them. The Secretary-General "would personally choose a group that would answer to the sensitivities of all sections of South African opinion."

This was an ongoing process, initiated when Mandela had first raised the issue of Commonwealth observers with Chief Anyaoku, but it was not easy to persuade De Klerk. He had refused an earlier proposal advocating the presence of observers, saying, "South Africa is not Zimbabwe." It was a significant achievement to persuade him, and to create space for collaborative international support in addressing the political violence that threatened the transition to a democratic South Africa.

An African proverb says, "A pilot who sees into the distance will not let the ship capsize."

Persuading the participants

The following day, Chief Anyaoku discussed his proposal with Roelf Meyer, the chief government negotiator, during a long session that marked their first substantive meeting. Meyer emphasized bilateral, rather than trilateral, discussions: "what I could do to bring the government and the ANC together. He didn't stress Inkatha's role as much as De Klerk had... But otherwise, the same positive approach. I think they had briefed each other well. ...Friday night, after meeting with Meyer, I went back and drafted the proposal and put it on paper. That Friday night, it was sent; just before 10 pm, my security driver took it to [foreign affairs director-general] Neil van Heerden's house.

"The next morning, Ramaphosa and Mohamed Valli, who were delegated by ANC, saw me at breakfast and I gave them the document. That was on Saturday morning. ...To ANC, I naturally stressed the point that it was not in their interest to have mass action linked to violence. So they had the greatest interest in having violence issues addressed. And that I thought they were having an exaggerated view of what the UN could do. They didn't appreciate that fully. We had a long discussion. At some point, Cyril Ramaphosa said to me, 'well, Chief, please tell us more about what the Commonwealth can do...

"I discovered subsequently that it is a matter of personalities within the ANC. I discovered, because I kept asking the questions. In my meetings with Mandela in Dakar, Thabo was not there; and in meetings which Mandela had with key leaders in Dakar, with Babangida and others, Thabo was not present. I learned that Thabo had also been speaking to them about the limitations of the UN involvement. And it was clear to me that, when Thabo took the trouble of phoning me in Edinburgh, it was because of his realization of what we could do. But for Cyril Ramaphosa, it was not abundantly clear to him. So he was reflecting his own limited experience."

Another point not well understood was the role of Commonwealth members at the UN and in UN structures, where they can have significant influence in decision-making — not as a block but as influential members of all regional groupings. When Commonwealth governments agree on a course of action, it is accepted by more than 50 countries and that agreement can find its way into the General Assembly through any number of channels, and directly into the Security Council.

After mid-1989 when Oliver Tambo's health was weakened by a stroke, the ANC was made up of at least three loose groupings: those who had been in exile, those who had been in internal leadership, and those who had been in prison. While they all adhered to the party goals and principles, each group had differing perceptions of the country, the world and the way forward, emanating from their different experiences; and the latter two groups had little experience in international relations.

In the tangled web of reasons for some of the differing responses was the close relationship between Ramaphosa — a former head of the mineworkers' union, later secretary-general of COSATU and therefore an obvious choice as ANC's chief negotiator due to his hands-on experience — and Wayne Fredericks, a former US Assistant Secretary of State for African Affairs in the John F Kennedy administration in the early 1960s. More recently, among other things, Fredericks represented liberal US business interests through the Ford motor company and others who supported change in South Africa. Through US Democratic Party politics, Fredericks was also close to Cyrus Vance, the former US Secretary of State in the Jimmy Carter administration, whom he had proposed as the UN envoy to South Africa. Fredericks' contacts dated back many years with Ramphosa, who impressed him deeply as a "moderate" and whom he often said was "the man to watch" in a new South Africa. Fredericks had known Emeka Anyaoku for even longer, from the time of his Nigerian diplomatic posting to the UN in the 1960s, and he contacted him during this period for a briefing on the Commonwealth initiative.

"The Americans want to play a part in bringing about a change in South Africa. So the Commonwealth initiative is one with which they would like to feel involved. Before I left for CODESA II, Hank Cohen [former Assistant Secretary of State for African Affairs] phoned me. I think they want to be in on the act as well, with the UN and Cy Vance."

The ANC response to Chief Anyaoku's proposal was positive. "After talking to Ramaphosa in the morning, he said he was taking it back to their working party, and would come back later. So later in the day he came back, again with Mohamed Vali, and said the working party had agreed to give me the green light. In working out the details of procedures, they had some points they would want to make, and they wanted to toughen up some terms of reference I had proposed. I said, 'you know, at this stage, if you begin to change this or that, the thing may never take off.' They said, yes, they'd thought as much. So then they said I could move on to the next stage. ...

"They rejected a tripartite meeting, and they told me in no uncertain terms that their position on resumption of negotiations was based on eight points. The two most important points were the violence and a concession by De Klerk that he genuinely wants to move to majority rule.

...Whatever terminology you use, they reached the same conclusion that I reached after CODESA II and in my subsequent conversations — that De Klerk had still not contemplated releasing his hold on power. He hoped he could retain the veto powers."

ANC would not consider even a bilateral meeting unless "De Klerk shows that he is prepared to negotiate genuine majority rule. So it was quite clear to me that they wanted to restrict themselves to the violence issues. And when I said, the implementation of this might require just meeting between representatives, they were prepared to contemplate that, even on a tripartite basis — not at the leadership but at the representative level, under the auspices of this Commonwealth proposal, but not otherwise."

Other Commonwealth reaction was swift, public and supportive. The Caribbean community issued a positive statement. The Canadian Foreign Minister, Barbara McDougall issued a politician's statement taking credit for the initiative, telling her media that she had urged the Secretary-General to go to South Africa. The Indian government commended "the work of the Commonwealth Secretariat, and your skilful guidance in particular." The British Prime Minister, John Major, was supportive. "John Major understands that the sanctions debate could still be revived in the context of a continued stalemate in the negotiations and escalation of violence. So he's given me whatever encouragement and help he can. ...he also greatly endorses my actions for the promotion of democracy; the same goes for the Canadians, the Australians, the old Commonwealth as a whole. ...I saw the pursuit of democracy as serving the interests of all Commonwealth countries, including support for democracy in South Africa."

He didn't mention the Igbo proverb that makes reference to the obstacles in his path: "The man who watches a wrestling match imagines many ways to defeat an opponent; but he knows not the difficulties involved."

Arresting violence

The Secretary-General's paper of 3 July 1992 containing a proposal to assist in arresting violence was circulated to Commonwealth Heads of Government 10 days later. In a covering letter, he said that the escalating violence had caused a breakdown of the negotiating process, and that ANC had refused to return to the process until the government addresses certain conditions, including a clear acceptance of non-racial democracy as the objective of a constitutional settlement.

"Mandela has refused to meet De Klerk again until the latter makes an unequivocal commitment to majority rule. In response, De Klerk has written to Mandela denying his government's involvement in the violence and inviting him to return to the negotiations, saying 'in our view, what you are presenting as demands are issues that are being tailored by the ANC to support its programme of mass mobilization to justify the abortion of the negotiation process'."

Chief Anyaoku reminded Commonwealth leaders of their commitment to assist the process in ways identified by the parties as helpful. He enclosed the outline of his proposed initiative which "if assiduously implemented with co-operation from all sides, will not only reduce tension and save lives but, more importantly, will also facilitate the confidence building required for dealing with the other factors currently impeding a return to the negotiating table." He said preliminary indications from the ANC and IFP were positive; government had received the proposal positively but wanted to await the outcome of the Security Council debate before giving a substantive response.

Entitled "Proposed Commonwealth group to assist in arresting violence in South Africa", the Chief's proposal was blunt on the serious threat posed by violence, not only to the negotiating process but to the prospect of a successful transition, having destroyed mutual confidence between the major political leaders. He was therefore proposing that a group "of qualified and experienced persons" be constituted to visit South Africa; their mission would be "to assist the leaders and all concerned in their efforts to bring the violence to an end." In addition, the Group's presence in the country "would make for greater public confidence and help to deter further violence."

Working in quiet, non-public ways and avoiding public statements — and with an emphasis on making a practical contribution to helping to end the violence — the group would:

• assist the agencies and mechanisms set up under the Peace Accord to prevent and combat violence;

• liaise with the authorities, including police, magistrates and Justices of the Peace directly concerned with the maintenance of law and order; strengthen confidence between the law enforcement agencies and communities;

• facilitate communication between the different groups and organizations concerned with the violence; and

• give all concerned the benefit of their own experience and insights.

"It is envisaged that the Group would visit the areas most affected by violence in South Africa; collect and receive information on all aspects of the violence; hold discussions with the relevant authorities, community and religious leaders and representatives of other groups and organizations in a position to assist the team in its work; and generally explore ways of assisting the organizations set up under the terms of the National Peace Accord."

The group of 10-12 people selected on a pan-Commonwealth basis, would comprise distinguished, experienced individuals with a background in security, law enforcement, judiciary/legal, diplomacy or public service, supported by six Secretariat staff. With meticulous attention to detail, Chief Anyaoku outlined the steps to constituting such a group, starting as always with obtaining agreement in principle from the major parties involved and endorsement by Commonwealth governments. He stressed the necessity to discuss details with the major parties, and confirm their willingness to co-operate. Finally, the group would report on its activities to the Secretary-General who would brief Commonwealth governments.

"The ANC, at that time, had great faith in the UN so, while the government was reluctant but not negative, the ANC was positive but not enthusiastic. Buthelezi was both, positive and enthusiastic."

A Commonwealth group to assist

The ANC went to the UN, by way of the OAU, and got a Security Council Resolution — No. 772 on 17 August 1992. Chief Anyaoku went to New York on holiday. "There, ANC came and saw me, the same day as I had my meeting with Boutros-Ghali. And the South African ambassador, on instructions from his government, came to see me too. I had seen Cyrus Vance there, and I decided that, having reached agreement with Boutros-Ghali on co-operation between UN and Commonwealth teams, I would send a planning mission to work out the modalities of such co-operation and behaviour of Commonwealth observers in South Africa. There was, even then, a clear understanding between Boutros-Ghali and myself, because I was determined that the Commonwealth group would not just go there as passive observers but as people who would be active in bringing to bear their skills and experience on the situation. ...

"I had learned that the terms of the Cyrus Vance report and the terms of Security Council Resolution could have been that the UN team in South Africa would be working under the National Peace Secretariat structures. I told them that I would want the Commonwealth to work in close cooperation to strengthen these structures, but not to be subject to South African structures. James Jonah bought that, and eventually the wording of the UN Resolution settled that. The two African members of the Security Council came to speak to me while I was in New York; the Zimbabwean ambassador had me to lunch, and they went and fought the battle. ...

"When I saw Boutros-Ghali, I was interested in finding out the kind of people he had in mind, and it was clear to me that he would be sending low-key bureaucrats. When he told me they would all come from within the UN structures, I said, 'oh but they will not have any room for discretion.' He said, 'no, the UN cannot interfere, South Africa is a sovereign state.' That was his view. ...So I told him that was not the way I was going to approach the Commonwealth contribution. I would get observers from governments because I would want to get people with such skills and experience that they could make some input, their views could command credibility and respect, and so enhance their influence. And Boutros said, 'but how do you think you can get away with that?' I said, well, the Commonwealth operates in a much more informal, much closer manner. And that I deal with heads of government directly, and that the mandate they gave me in Harare gives me enough room to do that. ...

"When I first discussed with him the issue of sending senior experienced Commonwealth policemen to South Africa, he didn't think it would work. He said they would be interfering in the affairs of a sovereign state. I told him I would send people whom I would brief to work in a way that would give the South African structures the benefit of their experience, without being confrontational. And that is exactly what has happened. The South African police greatly value the input from Commonwealth observers. They have written in appreciation of that. ...

"There was no question of his feeling any competition. He is the first UN Secretary-General to take the Commonwealth as seriously as he does. He said he believes in the UN working closely with regional organizations. In fact, he said to James Jonah that he must give me a copy of his report to the Security Council in which he had put forward the idea that the UN must cooperate and use regional organizations in the promotion of international peace and security.

"I told him the Commonwealth was not a regional organization, but a global sub-system. He had no problem in accepting that. ...He said the

Commonwealth had long association with the South Africa issue, that he would see it as having a special interest, special familiarity and knowledge of South Africa. So he had no conceptual problem, and that pleased me very much."

On 27 September 1992, Chief Anyaoku issued a statement applauding a "long-awaited break in the deadlock" — an agreement between De Klerk and Mandela. The agreement "on the release of political prisoners, the prohibition of dangerous weapons at public gatherings throughout the country and the security measures to be taken at identified hostels, removes some of the most intractable obstacles to the resumption of negotiations." But he warned that the "alarming upsurge in the level of violence" points to the need for speedy resumption of negotiations and installation of an interim government to lay the basis for transition to a non-racial, democratic South Africa. He concluded as always, by emphasizing that "ultimately only South Africa's leaders — all of them — can put an end to the violence." And he assured them of the Commonwealth's willingness to assist.

"I then was able to put the team together and to get their governments to pay for them," he said later in the year. "And they have been in South Africa since October, doing a good job, from the reports I get. ...they meet with the heads of the army and police, they meet with Goldstone Commission at senior level, they give ideas and advice. Their ideas are solicited quite often. And they command a degree of respect and credibility... But to ensure that the chances of friction were minimized, I suggested that the Secretariat should establish consultative machinery with the UN and EC. So they meet regularly at technical level... and maintain a liaison which works."

South Africa House/Suid-Afrika Huis

When De Klerk visited London in this period, "we met at the embassy, my first time of entering the South African embassy. ...I regarded it as a sign of the times that I should be there. And since I could go to Union Buildings in Pretoria, well, why not the South African embassy? My concern was that there might be pickets there, which I was not keen to cross, but there were none."

De Klerk's mood "was warm. I think we have established a mutually respectful working relationship. And that's useful. ...I have had occasions where I have said to him that the picture which he was painting was not quite the picture which was reaching me from other sources, naturally. ...I told him that he should appreciate the pressures under which ANC are working, that he has problems among his own supporters as I believe that Nelson must have among his supporters. And it is really for both of them to remain above these pressures, and to help each other in remaining above these pressures.

"He cannot deal with ANC in a way that will strengthen the hands of those who are putting the pressure on Mandela, as I'm sure that one of the most striking things about the way Mandela deals with him is that Mandela has not sought to put him in a position where he'll be worse off with the pressure group within his party. He refuted that. He said that he has not called Mandela any uncharitable names publicly, but that Mandela has been calling him names. He challenged me to give him an instance where he has referred to Mandela publicly in an uncharitable way."

The rapport established by Chief Anyaoku with De Klerk whom he had met for the first time just one year earlier, that enabled them to hold increasingly frank discussions such as this, had a strong foundation in the Chief's philosophy that racial stereotypes could be altered by example. And so he deliberately approached De Klerk in a manner that allowed him to respond positively. Another building block was the perception and perspective of being Nigerian, with the confidence that Nigerians have in their own identity burnished by 30 years of independence; and the full knowledge the South African government had of the power balance between themselves and a proud west African nation of well over double their population. Another foundation stone was the Commonwealth itself, South African history with the Commonwealth and vise versa, and the fact that South Africa would like to play a leading role in the Commonwealth again. Finally, a key factor was the way the Secretary-General played his British card, so there would be positive feedback in private discussions, on his way of doing things.

Following Chief Anyaoku's first meeting with De Klerk in October 1991, the latter had told the British prime minister that he was favourably impressed by the Secretary-General and his approach, and he thought this approach could be of significant assistance to South Africa. John Major, who had been consulted and briefed, as had other Commonwealth leaders, reinforced the South African's positive response and encouraged De Klerk's confidence in the Secretary-General.

According to an Igbo proverb, "Tortoise said that work that has been started is almost finished."

86

EYE OF FIRE

Leadership and vision

Chief Anyaoku, visiting South Africa in late November 1992 for the third time that year, welcomed the agreement for ANC-IFP talks and for a meeting of the signatories to the Peace Accord. He warned of the dangers of a "faltering" negotiation process, and called for "leadership and vision".

"My concern is that there should be significant political shift in the area of resumption of negotiations. I've been anxious that the pace for movement is not going as fast as it should be. And I am concerned that the South African government is in a high position because the ANC, PAC, Buthelezi are all quarrelling among themselves, and De Klerk is now appearing to be the arbiter. ...

"We are considering the possibility of scaling down the Commonwealth observer group, even terminating it... I don't want them to become a permanent feature in a situation that is seeing less and less of major political shifts. I don't want them to become routinized... I told Boutros Ghali that I was anxious that the Commonwealth should not become like the UN, having peace-keepers in a country like Cyprus for 29 years without the problem being solved, that we didn't have the resources within the Commonwealth to do that.

"And we talked about the character of the observer groups, if we were to continue in the future, the sort of observer groups we would be sending. We agreed. ...I suppose at the end of the day, we exert ourselves on issues in accordance with our own philosophical beliefs."

COMSA I, October 1992-January 1993

The Commonwealth Observer Mission to South Africa (COMSA) which arrived on 18 October 1992 included senior police offers from Britain, Canada, Malaysia, New Zealand and Singapore; prominent public personalities from The Bahamas, Ghana and India; a retired Nigerian general, a serving army officer from Botswana and a criminologist from Australia. "And naturally, they have concentrated on those areas where their particular skills could make the most impact. Thus they have provided training and advice on police-community relations; they have negotiated peace agreements between the ANC and the IFP in several communities in Natal, and they have sought to promote socio-economic reconstruction in areas to which they have helped to restore peace. ..."

Chaired by Justice Austin Amissah, a former Attorney-General and Justice of Appeal in Ghana, and supported by a Secretariat team headed by the Director of International Affairs Division Max Gaylard, an Australian career diplomat with a wry sense of humour, the COMSA team deployed in two areas where violence was most pronounced: Pretoria/Witwatersrand/Vaal (PWV) region and Natal. Their behaviour was informed by Chief Anyaoku's pre-deployment briefing and by his three-point guideline, ie, that they should coordinate with others, while maintaining a separate identity, and ensuring above all, impartiality.

He continued to support their work on the ground through his personal intervention with the leadership. "Political contacts made by COMSA in South Africa," their mission report said, "were buttressed by the close personal contact the Commonwealth Secretary-General maintained with all parties and interest groups."

The COMSA mission reported to the Secretary-General that their experience confirmed that the violence could not be resolved as long as the political stalemate continued, and therefore concluded that it was unrealistic to expect a reduction in the level of violence as a precondition for the resumption of multi-party negotiations. "Violence must not be allowed to hold the political process to ransom. Time is of the essence for forces committed to democratic change and any delay will weaken the moderates and fuel the machinations of extremist elements."

The COMSA I report, *Violence in South Africa*, described the National Peace Accord as one of the most successful developments during the transition. "The sight of people from different races and ethnic backgrounds, from different walks of life and with differing political beliefs sitting around a table exchanging views with each other, is one of the most encouraging things that COMSA has seen in South Africa." Their report noted that, because of its long isolation, "South Africa has been secluded from international trends and developments in policing." Therefore, the assistance of the international community in training and facilitating dialogue was essential if the South African Police (SAP) was to move from "a force dedicated to law enforcement to a police providing a full range of services..."

COMSA I concluded that since violence is deeply rooted in South Africa's history and in the current political uncertainty, "a government which is accepted by all peoples of South Africa would be in a better position to deal with the violence." And it recommended, therefore, that initiatives on negotiations and violence should continue in parallel, and with due urgency.

The report concluded that the presence of international observers had played a "visible and widely acknowledged role in helping to calm the political atmosphere", noting particularly the ability of four different international organizations to work harmoniously together despite their differences in approach, and recommending that an international presence be maintained up to and including the first democratic elections.

A survey of the National Peace Accord published by the South African magazine, the *Financial Mail*, a few weeks later, said that the unparalleled level of international scrutiny, together with the range of local observer groups, made South Africa "the most closely watched theatre of national conflict anywhere in the world. ...There's actually little doubt that the ongoing monitoring of political activity is influencing behaviour — in some cases, markedly so. For instance, in southern Natal — the most violent region in South Africa — Commonwealth observer Moses Anafu is attributed with brokering a peace deal between bitterly opposed ANC and IFP factions."

When the COMSA team arrived in Durban at the end of October 1992, "the general perception was that Natal was sliding toward an all-out civil war" and that violence, including the killing of a number of political leaders involved in the peace process, "had gathered a momentum that could no longer be contained". Thus, they decided to concentrate their efforts on helping to form peace committees or strengthening those that existed.

Umbumbulu, a sprawling rural district of some 400,000 people on the upper south coast of Natal, was the area most effected by violence in the entire country and so it was to Umbumbulu that COMSA went to begin their work. Previous efforts to establish as Local Dispute Resolution Committee (LDRC) made up of ANC and IFP had failed, and COMSA agreed to help, realizing they would need the support of the *amakhosi* (chiefs) as well as the political parties if they were to succeed. And succeed they did, in a joint effort that involved COMSA, local business people, ANC, IFP, 40 local amakhosi, and five careful weeks of negotiations.

The *New Nation* newspaper described this achievement as an "unsurpassed feat", but COMSA was quick to deflect the praise and ensure credit went to the local participants. Anafu explained to the media that the ongoing task of the LDRC is "to motivate the community and refugees to put the need for peace above old grievances, and to ensure that structures for security and reconstruction are in place as people return to their damaged homes, to help defuse the tension and keep the spirit of reconciliation alive."

Within days, they held the first of three peace rallies in the Ensimbini Valley of Port Shepstone area, on the Natal lower south coast. The first venue was Nyandezulu primary school on a rainy Sunday afternoon in early December. Leaders of all interest groups shared a platform for the first time, spreading the peace message; and residents who had fled the area, the scene of endemic violence for three years, began to come cautiously home. The South Coast Herald called it a "major breakthrough". Anafu, a thoughtful and widely respected intellectual from Ghana who was Gaylard's deputy, was the guest speaker. His message was that the time had come to work together and face the future, to end divisions and prevent disruption of education.

At the height of the confrontation in Port Shepstone area, "the monthly death rate due to the violence averaged between 25 and 40," COMSA reported at the end of December 1992. "Since the beginning of December, there have only been two confirmed fatalities." Their report noted that Umbumbulu and Port Shepstone were being hailed as the only peaceful areas in the whole of Natal/KwaZulu, and that the committee preparing for a Mandela-Buthelezi meeting had "warmly welcomed the positive developments".

Then, just four months after peace was made at Umbumbulu, the unthinkable happened in Boksburg. Easter 1993, Tembisile Chris Hani gave his bodyguards a day off and planned to stay at home with his family. Returning from a short outing to nearby shops, a car in the vicinity watching his every move, a neighbour heard a shot and noted the car license number. Hani — a classics scholar turned guerrilla leader, the former chief of staff of the ANC liberation army *Umkhonto we Sizwe* — was dead in his driveway, age 50; right-wing extremists were arrested and convicted, the rest is legend. A palpable hush fell over the nation, while 10 April 1993 was engraved on the national psyche. Those who were mourning, and those who were not, held their collective breath to see what would happen next.

Chief Anyaoku sent a message to Nelson Mandela, which said in part: "...There must be few tragedies that could have been calculated to do as much damage as this to the process of achieving the non-racial democracy which Chris Hani and all of you have sought. I join in appealing to all South Africans not to allow this heinous crime to provoke more violence. The challenge now facing your party and all others genuinely devoted to achieving a free and harmonious South Africa is to regard Chris Hani's martyrdom as an inspiration towards a speedy realization of this great objective. Please accept and convey to your party and Chris' associates and family the deepest condolences..."

"When I heard about Chris Hani's assassination," Chief Anyaoku said later, "I thought it was a terrible tragedy for South Africa. ...

"I felt that it was important to support all those calling for moderation. But, at the same time, in order to make such calls effective, the South African leaders needed to act, in the form of quickening the pace of change. So I issued a public statement to that effect, and had it brought to the attention of the South African ambassador in UK, to whom I have spoken a number of times."

This was the point that he stressed to the South African government through its ambassador: "Failure to act, in the wake of Chris Hani's assassination, would result in strengthening the extreme ends of the political spectrum. Those on the left of Nelson Mandela would get more exasperated, more angry and more impatient. Those on the extreme right of De Klerk would get frustrated and be tempted to attempt more assassinations, and the central ground — the sort of consensual views expressed by ANC and NP government — would suffer. So they needed to act quickly, in the interests of the central ground."

Ambassador Kent Durr sent a handwritten note to the Secretary-General on 13 April 1993, thanking him for the wise counsel. "Many thanks for your kind call this morning and for the sentiments expressed — much appreciated. Your sober advice is highly valued."

In a gesture weighty with symbolism — that perhaps more than anything else in this period gave a public signal that all parties had their vision fixed firmly on a new South Africa no matter how much their plans for it differed — the South African embassy in London lowered its flag to half mast. The Secretary-General received a short typed note from his Executive Assistant on 15 April 1993, relating a verbal message received the previous day from the South African embassy with "the Ambassador's regards and to let you know that they were flying their flag at half mast for the day for Mr Chris Hani."

On the same day, the Secretary-General, choosing his words carefully, issued another statement. "The great challenge facing all South Africa's leaders is to take immediate practical steps to divert the natural outburst of despair and anger engendered by Chris Hani's murder.

"At this time when all the friends of South Africa must speak out, I appeal to all South Africa's leaders to proceed urgently to reach agreement on the setting up of the Transitional Executive Council and the naming of a date for the elections that would allow all South Africans to pronounce on the future of their country. They must also meet to send a collective message to their followers that the process of transition is irrevocable and cannot be derailed."

COMSA II, February-May 1993

The first COMSA report had stressed the importance of fixing an election date to give the country "a different sort of battlefield", saying that delaying negotiations would fuel more violence. By the time of the second COMSA report four months later, in May 1993, the multi-party negotiations had resumed. A broader range of 26 political parties and interest groups had gathered at the World Trade Centre in a renewed effort to resolve the political conflict.

"For reasons of resources, and also not wanting the Commonwealth observers to remain there in perpetuity without significant political movement, I raised the possibility of terminating COMSA II on 15 May," Chief Anyaoku said later. "But in reaction to that possibility, I received representations from across the political spectrum — government sources, National Party members of parliament, trade unions, ANC, Inkatha, some NGOs, and Beyers Naude from the church group, from business, and from the peace secretariat itself."

The shortage of resources was, and is, a sharp thorn in the flesh of Commonwealth initiatives such as this one and, despite the obvious and widely acknowledged success of the COMSA initiative, the Secretary-General had to solicit for financial commitments to support it.

"I've had to approach Commonwealth governments who have sent people for COMSA II, asked them to retain as many as possible, until we are able to decide on how COMSA III is to be launched. In doing this, I was very much encouraged by a direct appeal from Nelson Mandela. ...he spoke out publicly, saying that he was appealing to me to make sure that Commonwealth observers remain, according to him, for at least one year. He wants the observers to be there until the elections, because he and others believe that the Commonwealth, which has been gaining experience in elections elsewhere, would have something to contribute to the process. So I have written to Commonwealth governments, telling them that I will be putting forward proposals to them for COMSA III. ...

"In addition, I have been very concerned about how to deal with the potentially serious problems in sustaining progress to the elections, including the issue of relations between the IFP and the ANC, and the perception of Buthelezi's role in all of this. It is commonly said that Buthelezi remains determined not to allow movement forward on elections unless the constitutional future of South Africa is settled now. The last time I was in South Africa, I urged both Mr Mandela and Gatsha Buthelezi, in my separate meetings with them, to try and meet. ...When

Mandela was in London earlier this month, I had a discussion with him ...And he said that, within Natal, the victims of Buthelezi's party's violence would not accept that he should be meeting with him. ...I have sought to urge him that, in the interests of future stability, some form of recognition of his existence must be given by Mandela himself. He promised to think about it.

"In fact, my conversation with Mandela on the morning of 6 May, when he left London, was probably the most difficult discussion he and I have ever had — because we had a short time, and I was clearly irritating him by insisting on my advice that he and Buthelezi should get together. ...I said to him, 'Well, look Madiba, I know I am irritating you. I want you to know it gives me no joy, but I really believe that I would be failing you if I didn't give you the honest advice I feel capable of. You must see Buthelezi.' ...

"Subsequently, I discovered that the same advice had been urged on him strongly by John Major, and by some others. It therefore might have occurred to him that my advice might have been part of a concerted effort. But of course, nothing like that has happened. ...I would like to believe that Mandela knows me well enough now to know that I would not offer him any advice that I am not utterly convinced of its merits. And convinced of its merits in a very independent and honest-to-god way."

Within weeks, Chief Anyaoku was able to welcome the report of an imminent Mandela-Buthelezi meeting arranged by Mandela's close friend Archbishop Desmond Tutu, and the proposed date of 27 April 1994 for the first democratic elections. Delivering the keynote address at the International Conference on Southern Africa at Church House, London, in June 1993 — almost 30 years after his first visit to Church House in April 1964 for hearings of the UN Special Committee Against Apartheid — he used the opportunity to shift the focus of the international community into the middle distance, to support for the next stages of the process.

First, he urged "leveling the playing field", through assistance to the new political parties in selected areas to "allow them to compete on a more equal footing". Second, he stressed the importance of human resource development. "After the polls, having the power and the means to govern in reality will become even more important. ...True democracy can hardly be realized if through lack of the requisite skills, the majority population remains effectively debarred from participating in the running of the new South Africa." And third, socio-economic reconstruction. He urged the international community to respond positively to

Mandela's appeal for massive investment once a representative transitional mechanism for government is established.

True to his commitment to "doing things, achieving results" rather than publicising them, the Secretary-General's prolific collection of public speeches does not include a single one focusing directly on South Africa after the Harare CHOGM when he was mandated to open contacts with Pretoria, for almost two years until that address before an eclectic and influential gathering at Church House. An Igbo proverb says, "when deeds speak, words are nothing."

COMSA III, August-December 1993

In response to appeals to extend the Commonwealth Observer Mission, the Secretary-General constituted a third phase of 11 observers plus skilled advisers who arrived in mid-August 1993 and left in December when, after protracted negotiations, the country was preparing for its first democratic elections. Headed by Hon. Russell Marshall, former foreign minister of New Zealand, this phase of COMSA continued to maintain contact with political parties, strengthen structures set up under the National Peace Accord and work "wherever appropriate" with the SAP and SADF.

Chief Anyaoku envisaged that COMSA III would continue to assist in reducing the level and incidence of violence: through senior police officers sharing their experiences; legal experts assisting with constitution-making; and the observers who, as politicians, would have the ability to exert influence on maintaining dialogue and monitoring incidents which could produce violence. And he added to the mix some expertise in the planning and monitoring of elections.

On 23-24 September, the four pillars of transition agreed at the World Trade Centre were enacted by parliament — the Transitional Executive Council (TEC), the Independent Electoral Commission (IEC), the Independent Media Commission (IMC) and the Independent Broadcasting Authority (IBA). The Secretary-General said the passage of these bills marked the "irreversibility of the end of apartheid", and he announced that the Commonwealth would begin lifting all remaining economic sanctions, including trade, investment and financial sanctions. In a statement from The Bahamas where he was attending the annual meeting of Commonwealth Finance Ministers, Chief Anyaoku said this was a direct response to the adoption of legislation establishing the TEC.

"This legislation and the agreement on the date for the first non-racial elections open a new chapter in the political history of South Africa, a country that is now irreversibly committed to joining the community of democratic nations. ...They also bring to an end the Commonwealth's programme of measures adopted to bring about the end of aparthied." That left only the establishment of the TEC as the major remaining condition before starting to normalize relations between South Africa and the international community.

During COMSA III, as negotiations reached a climax with the agreement on transitional arrangements, the IFP and the Conservative party withdrew in protest, together with delegations from the "homelands" of Bophuthatswana and Ciskei. These groups, together with the Afrikaner Volksfront (AV), formed the Freedom Alliance in October and refused to take part in transitional arrangements.

Commonwealth Heads of Government, meanwhile, went to Limassol, Cyprus for their biennial summit, 21-25 October 1993, where they agreed to welcome a non-racial and democratic South Africa back into the association at the earliest opportunity. They noted in their communiqué the "widely acknowledged contribution" of COMSA in "helping to stem violence, reconcile communities, return refugees and initiate socio-economic reconstruction." And they agreed that "the mission should remain in South Africa until after the election planned for April 1994 when the situation would be reviewed in consultation with the new, democratically elected government."

The leaders welcomed a programme of activities supported by the Commonwealth Fund for Technical Co-operation (CFTC) to assist the transition, including technical assistance to improve police/community relations and to support the electoral, media and broadcasting structures. The Secretary-General had proposed earlier that CFTC set aside half a million pounds (US$800,000) to support the transition to democracy in South Africa, the first time that CFTC funds had been provided to a non-Commonwealth country.

Two projects identified by COMSA were already being funded: mediation training for the National Peace Secretariat and a nationwide project for training marshals. The latter was designed to produce a cadre of well-trained, unarmed marshals to supervise demonstrations organized by their own political parties. A member of COMSA, Chief Supt. Peter Stevens of the police/community relations department at Scotland Yard, initiated the programme that was based on the premise that the marshals' strength and influence lies in their allegiance to the group they are regulating. He and his team proceeded to equip marshals from all parties with technical skills that proved very effective in the months ahead.

As the situation developed, the latter phase of COMSA was reconstituted to add electoral experts from Australia and Malaysia, and a media expert from Canada, supported by Secretariat staff with backgrounds in diplomacy, management and media: Gaylard, Anafu and Colleen Lowe Morna, a journalist from Zimbabwe. They worked closely with a technical assistance component established by a Canadian development adviser, Steve Godfrey, who had played a key role previously in developing educational and skills-sharing opportunities for South Africans through the Southern Africa Education Trust Fund.

Meanwhile, at the World Trade Centre in Kempton Park, Johannesburg, the 22 groups remaining in the negotiations trudged on, after their earlier agreement that none of the legislation would become operational until the entire package was agreed. They continued to work against thoroughly impossible deadlines, to find common ground on an Interim Constitution, an Electoral Act, and removal of the remaining apartheid laws. The Negotiating Council finally delivered its agreed package for endorsement at a plenary in the early morning hours of 18 November 1993.

Chief Anyaoku arrived the previous day from Mauritius to attend the talks as an observer, meeting informally with participants, and he was present when the exhausted but triumphant negotiators met in plenary to endorse the full package of transitional arrangements. Not taking that as a signal to rest but rather as an impetus to move forward, he began consultations the following morning, after few hours sleep, for a fourth phase of support focusing on the preparations for general elections and persuading all parties to participate. He met with Mandela, De Klerk, Buthelezi, the PAC chairman Johnson Mlambo, the Democratic Party leader Zach de Beer, and, for the first time, with the AV leader Gen. Constand Viljoen.

"The next morning, I had a meeting in Durban with De Klerk, at the end of which we both faced the press. He was very forthcoming in his acknowledgement of the Commonwealth contribution, and his government's appreciation of our continuing contribution to the transition process, and was rather generous in his reference to my own personal role. He ended his comments saying that relations between South Africa and the Commonwealth were at an all-time high."

In one of those serendipitous occurrences that sharpen historical perspective, a note was passed to Chief Anyaoku in the early morning of 18 November, during the concluding hours of the milti-party talks at Kempton Park, informing him that Gen. Sani Abacha had seized power in Nigeria. "Inevitably, the next morning during the press conference in Durban, I was asked, if I was doing all that to assist democracy in South Africa, what about my own country? To which I replied that I was sure they all appreciated that it was part of human nature that we could deal with only one problem at a time. ...and that my preoccupation at that time was with theirs. To great laughter."

The Volksfront and the volkstaat

The following day, back in Pretoria, Chief Anyaoku met for the first time with Gen. Constand Viljoen, a former head of the South African Defence Force (SADF), by then retired and leader of the white protectionist Afrikaner Volksfront (Peoplesfront) which, as part of the Freedom Alliance, had remained outside the all-party negotiations. Seeking as usual to set his host at ease, the Chief chose again his appointed safe subject: tea. "When I walked in, he looked very much the soldier in civilian clothes. I wanted him to feel more relaxed, so I talked about his office, and to the lady who offered tea or coffee, I talked about my newly acquired interest in their *rooibos* tea, and so made him a little relaxed. And he became a lot more friendly. We talked... for 1 1/2 hours, an interesting meeting at which he sought to explain to me how very concerned his constituency was that the government which would come into being after the elections would be a communist government. They had to avoid that, by creating a *volkstaat* for themselves, where they could be safe."

Gen. Viljoen, as an experienced military commander, recognized that negotiating for a *volkstaat* would be preferable to fighting a war that his people could not win. He had his first meeting with the ANC leadership three months earlier, establishing a rapport with Thabo Mbeki, practiced proponent of the strategy of inclusion. Mbeki encouraged Chief Anyaoku to contact Gen. Viljoen, who provided pragmatic leadership to a group that could have destabilized the country before, during or after the elections, with all the implications for permanent instability. Instead of trying to protect white privilege as some ANC leaders believed De Klerk was doing, Gen. Viljoen chose to focus on protection of cultural, religious and language rights, which were later enshrined for all ethnic groups in the new constitution.

"After I assured him that the purpose of my visit was to learn and to be of help," Chief Anyaoku said later, "he opened up by telling me how he was called back from retirement to lead his people, what their fears were, and what solutions they were advocating. He presented that in his-

torical terms, that his people, the Afrikaners, were very nationalistic people, committed to maintaining their independence, who saw the recent
developments as threatening all they had built. ...they were now arguing
that they must have their own place of refuge. They should not be subjected, or subordinated, to the emerging communist government. ...He
said to me that the idea of a *volkstaat* is that they should have a place
where, for 20 or 25 years, they would stay and feel safe. They needed a
place of refuge, he said, like Israel for the Jews. ...those who lived outside
could continue living outside, knowing that, if they got fed up, they
could return to the *volkstaat*. ...

"Then, if the rest of South Africa developed along the optimistic lines
that I was saying, that everybody was saying, they would willingly join
in. But at the moment, their reckoning was that it would be a communist
state and they didn't want to have anything to do with a state in which
their cultural identity would be lost. ...It was clear to me that Viljoen and,
from what he told me, his supporters could not reconcile themselves to
living under a government ruled by those who had remained their servants and farmhands, and in their view, not their species. It was clear. ...I
got the impression from him — although he did his best not to give that
impression personally — but from what he was saying about the attitudes and reasoning of his constituents, it was clear to me that that was
part of their problem. ...

"I asked him to show me on the map where this *volkstaat* would be.
He had a big map of South Africa on the wall in his office. He said the
matter was still under negotiation, but he showed me the area of Pretoria,
really the white parts of Pretoria region. Then he showed me what looked
like a shooting star, with fingers reaching out, making the point that the
southern belt, where the concentration of gold was, that they wouldn't
touch that, lest they be accused of being greedy; they were not claiming
that. I said to him, that would be a very strange creation in terms of geographic entities; and he said, but look at the existing homelands and *ban-
tustans*. I said, well, I'm sure you don't want to have what you're advocating to be viewed as a patchwork, and we just laughed about that. But
he was a very serious man. There weren't too many light moments in our
conversation. ...

"He said to me, 'my constituency would not understand some of
these things you are saying. I'm more developed' — it was the first time
I'd heard anyone use the word 'developed' in a personal sense, that he
was more 'developed' than most members of his constituency. He said
the talks which he and his colleagues were conducting with the ANC and

the government were crucial. If they failed to get their *volkstaat*, then he was worried about the future; he said it might be difficult for him to stop his constituency from using violence. I sought to encourage him to reach agreement with the ANC and the government, and so join in the elections. ...When I left him, I didn't think I had convinced him. I have learned since then, of course, that he still needed to be convinced."

Finding Buthelezi

The Secretary-General finished his meeting with Viljoen and went next to see Chief Buthelezi, in a one-to-one meeting that had been difficult to arrange. "It was quite amusing how that appointment was fixed, because my colleagues had tried very hard and he would not return my calls. ...but they were able to tell me his room, and the pseudonym. He was there as Mr, not Hunt, but something similar. So I dialed the hotel myself and asked for the room, and he answered. I used the pseudonym, the name that he was using. 'Mr Hunt?' He said, 'yes, who is it?' Whereupon I burst out, 'oh, my brother Gatsha, it's Emeka calling'. He laughed. I said, look, I'm coming to Pretoria tomorrow morning to see Viljoen and would want to talk to you afterwards. So, we fixed a meeting. It was my first meeting with Buthelezi where he did not have a prepared text to read to me, no second... The first one was in London in September. ...So I had a long conversation with him. Again, it was a question of telling me how IFP had been marginalized, and how determined he was to insist on his points of view, and not join the elections if those points of view were not met.

"He presented four issues. One was regional autonomy; the powers being contemplated in the constitution for the regions were not adequate. Second was the ballot. Third was Kwazulu, it's historical rights which had to be respected. And fourth was that the constitution should be fully settled before elections, he didn't have faith in the sanctity if it was to be reopened in the constituent assembly after elections.

"I talked with him, I sought to persuade him how important it was that he should reach some agreement with ANC and the government, and how difficult it was for some of his friends overseas to understand that he was now in alliance with the advocates and practitioners of apartheid, having for so many years shown himself as being opposed to apartheid. He said to me, well, it was an alliance of convenience... I left him, again feeling that I had not convinced him as to the need to change his stance, and developments since have confirmed that. ...

"His personal relations with me have always been very good. He calls me brother chief, and expects me to appreciate the importance of tradition. But he then fails to respond adequately to my urgings that all traditions have to be modified as times change, and that the modification must respect democratic ideals... He usually reacts very strongly against any suggestion that he should put to test the support he has in Kwazulu. ...The most recent polls rated his support as low as 15 percent. I think the lower his rating has been projected, the more determined it would naturally be for him to resist the elections. ...There was a time I was telling ANC to make him an offer that would be attractive to him, make him an offer that you will have him in your cabinet. ...

"Buthelezi has become a prisoner of his own past. For years, both the government and powerful friends overseas were saying that he was the natural black leader of South Africa, that if the whites ever give up he would be the natural successor. He is bitter that the people who were telling him that have now opted for collaboration with the ANC."

Negotiations continued almost to the eve of elections, and eventually after the adoption of a two-ballot system for national and provincial voting, reference to "Kwazulu/Natal" in the interim constitution, and a council to discuss a *volkstaat*, these two leaders of the Freedom Alliance found themselves campaigning for elections and taking their seats in parliament, with Chief Buthelezi in the post-apartheid cabinet as Minister of Home Affairs.

South Africa in transition

By the time COMSA III produced its report, *South Africa in Transition*, just four months before the elections, South Africans had succeeded in finding a formula for the transition to a non-racial democracy, with the international community playing a supportive role. At its historic last sitting in Cape Town in late 1993, the tri-cameral parliament ended its existence with the repeal of remaining apartheid legislation, adoption of the interim constitution and electoral acts. By year end, the four transition pillars were becoming operational.

The agreed transition was in two stages: the first during which the TEC supervised key arms of government that could level the playing field for free and fair elections; and the second, elections to a Constituent Assembly which would finalize the constitution during its first two years and then serve as the parliament until the next elections in 1999.

In drafting the final constitution, the Assembly was bound by 32 constitutional principles that guarantee a multi-party democracy, three tiers of government and recognition of civil liberties, as well as broad parameters for the devolution of power to the regions. The constitution had to be approved by two-thirds majority of a joint sitting of parliament, ie the 400-member National Assembly and 90-person Senate, with a deadlock-breaking mechanism of a referendum in which 60 percent of voters approve. The final constitution had to be vetted by a Constitutional Court to ensure it adhered to the principles agreed at Kempton Park; the Court has final say on interpretation, protection and enforcement of all provisions.

The COMSA role continued during the transition with its mandate to provide practical assistance in helping to reduce political violence, an assignment that would assume special significance in the pre-election tension. With the addition of electoral and media expertise, COMSA could take closer interest in the preparations for elections, assist in defining areas for technical assistance to the transitional structures, and prepare for the work of the Commonwealth Observer Group to the South African elections (COGSA).

Observing the elections and keeping the peace

With his refined sense of the historical moment, Chief Anyaoku chose the former Prime Minister of Jamaica, The Rt. Hon. Michael Manley to lead a team of Commonwealth observers on their largest ever mission: to monitor the first democratic elections in South Africa, for a national assembly and nine provincial legislatures. COGSA numbered over 100 people from some 30 countries, including 60 "core" observers and 44 "assistants", and was part of a broad international monitoring exercise coordinated by the UN, including teams from the EU and OAU. The Director of the Commonwealth Secretariat's Legal and Constitutional Affairs Division, Prof. Reg Austin, an erudite professor of law from Zimbabwe, was seconded to the UN as Director and Chief Electoral Officer of its UN Observer Mission to South Africa (UNOMSA).

The mission of the Commonwealth group was to observe all relevant aspects of the organization and conduct of elections in accordance with the electoral laws of South Africa, to arrive at an independent judgement on whether the conditions existed for to electorate to express freely its wishes, and whether the result reflected these wishes. They were to act impartially and independently, and submit their final report to Commonwealth Heads of Government through the Secretary-General.

In keeping with the procedure adopted by the Secretary-General, they received a pre-mission briefing from him personally, giving the socio-political context and the Commonwealth methodology based on the elections observation guidelines devised during the high-level appraisal in 1991. The mission was also briefed by officials of the electoral and media commissions, political parties, police, human rights and church organizations. Ten days before the polling they divided into 51 teams deployed to all nine provinces for local briefings before going to urban centres, townships and rural communities.

A Commonwealth Peacekeeping Assistance Group (CPAG) was constituted in February 1994 at the request of the transitional council, to assist in establishing the National Peace-Keeping Force (NPKF). Commanded by a British colonel, deputized by an Indian deputy inspector-general of police, the group of more than 30 army and police officers from eight countries (Australia, Botswana, Britain, Canada, India, Malaysia, Pakistan and Zimbabwe) were assembled to provide training, advice and assistance for NPKF, which was to have a special role in the maintenance of peace and public order during the elections. NPKF was envisaged as a local force comprising elements from armed formations including the SADF and the ANC's *Umkontho we Sizwe*, an ambitious task for the three months remaining. Although it could not be stabilized in time for formal deployment during the elections, the training provided advance preparation for a post-election unification of the armed forces.

Most Commonwealth assistance went to the electoral commission, through provision of 50 electoral experts from 12 countries (Australia, Britain, Ghana, Jamaica, Lesotho, Namibia, Pakistan, Seychelles, Sri Lanka, Trinidad & Tobago, Zambia and Zimbabwe), who worked at national and provincial level, advising on systems and training electoral officials. Among the hurdles the IEC and its advisers had to overcome, in addition to organizing national and provincial elections in just four months, was the political decision mid-way to have separate ballot papers for each, and the late entry by IFP just one week before the polling, after agreement was reached by Mandela, Buthelezi and De Klerk. This eased tension but added to the bureaucratic burden when stickers had to be printed and affixed to the ballot papers. Smooth operations were hampered by the absence of a register of eligible voters and dearth of census information on the size of the electorate, as well as by the decision to allow voters to vote anywhere in the country and cumbersome legal structures put in place to ensure free and fair elections.

"Together with COGSA," the Secretary-General's report said later, "the work of these experts contributed in practical ways to what

President Mandela has described as the Commonwealth's 'crucial role' in ensuring the success of South Africa's first democratic elections."

A joint interim statement was issued with the UN, OAU and EU after four days of voting 26-29 April, and COGSA submitted an independent report in early May. "We salute the statesmanship of South Africa's political leadership," COGSA said. "The transitional structures which they established enabled the people to leave behind centuries of discrimination and to begin anew with a government of national reconciliation. The real and undisputed winners were all the people of South Africa who demonstrated to each other and to the world that they could successfully accomplish this historic and momentous transition. ...the elections represented a free and clear expression of the will of the South African people."

Welcoming their initial report, Chief Anyaoku said, "Seldom in the annals of human history has such a fundamental transformation been accomplished in such a relatively peaceful manner." He added that the enormous turnout was testimony to "the deep commitment of South African voters to the cause of freedom. ...The peaceful conduct of the elections is a tribute to them all."

When South Africa rejoined the Commonwealth on 1 June 1994, after 33 years, President Mandela's said, "The people of South Africa are greatly indebted to the governments and peoples of Commonwealth member states for the sterling contribution they have made in bringing about a non-racial and democratic South Africa. ...The South African Government is looking forward to making a positive contribution in the various fields of endeavour pursued by the Commonwealth."

That they would give back as they had received was no empty promise. The new South Africa began immediately by disbursing voluntary contributions to the Commonwealth technical, scientific and youth programmes. The 1995/96 commitment to the CFTC was increased, and contributions to the Secretariat budget and fund (assessed and voluntary) were paid in full during the first week of the financial year.

Beyond apartheid

Looking firmly forward from the Abuja meeting of the Commonwealth foreign ministers committee that followed Mandela's release from prison in 1990, the ANC had requested a rapid escalation in Commonwealth support for human resource development to prepare South Africans for the massive task of restructuring the economic and social fabric of their society. The Commonwealth agreed to play a significant role, and the

Secretary-General constituted an Expert Group which recommended a programme of training and work experience for black South Africans in a number of priority areas. The study was financed by the government of Canada, with contributions at the Secretary-General's request from Australia, India, Malaysia and Nigeria.

Symbolic of the changing times, the group which he constituted in August 1990 included the first home-based South Africans to serve on an official Expert Group since the departure of South Africa from the Commonwealth in 1961: Papie Moloto and Prof. Francis Wilson. The Secretary-General noted that the group marked a turning point in the Commonwealth's long engagement with South Africa, because it is a project "based on a realistic reckoning of the ending of apartheid".

"This exercise is wholly in keeping with the emerging orientation of Commonwealth policy ...to do all in its power and influence to help ensure that the emerging negotiations truly lead to the ending of apartheid. I am convinced that this orientation in Commonwealth policy is right; but I am equally convinced that it should be pursued with no illusion. ...Your work ...will go a considerable way to ensuring that when the fundamental change does occur, it will be for real."

The expert group's report, *Beyond Apartheid: Human Resources in a New South Africa,* documented the scale of the task of human resource development in South Africa, where over 98 percent of the managerial, professional and technical positions were held by whites, and the magnitude of inequalities in access to education and training. It illustrated the legacy of old apartheid structures which could hamper the transition to a democratic political system, notably public administration, especially economic and fiscal management, and local government structures. Other areas identified for support during the transition were judicial and legal services; the police, army and security services; diplomatic training; transport and communications; non-governmental and community-based organizations; trade unions; teacher training; returning exiles and released political prisoners; and key professional positions in the private sector.

The report advised that post-apartheid human resources development should be "based on an economic strategy to tackle poverty, create new jobs and provide basic services for education, health, housing and welfare," training black professionals and reducing racial and gender imbalances. It offered a framework, including resource mobilization, and was a key planning document in the period leading to majority rule in 1994.

In a Foreword to the report, the Secretary-General said, "Some 30 years ago — in 1961, South Africa left the Commonwealth following uni-

versal condemnation of its racist apartheid policies. It has taken three
decade of suffering and struggle by the people of South Africa and of
neighbouring countries for the prospect of a new, non-racial democratic
South Africa to emerge. During those 30 years, the Commonwealth has
sought to give support and encouragement to the people of South Africa
through vigorous support of the sanctions campaigns, through the promotion of dialogue — for example, the 1986 Eminent Persons Group initiative with which I was intimately associated — and by providing scholarship and educational support to the victims of apartheid.

"Indeed, it can be argued, as Oliver Tambo has done, that the people
of South Africa have always remained a part of the Commonwealth family — it is only the apartheid regime which was effectively expelled from
its ranks."

Mobilizing resources

The report *Beyond Apartheid* provided, as well as a situational analysis
and guide to priorities, a tool for mobilizing financial resources. The
expert group realized that the scale of resources required — 60 million
pounds (about US$100 million) — put this beyond the means of the
Commonwealth alone. They proposed to the Secretary-General that he
should play his well-practiced role of mobilizing others to reach a larger
goal.

Heads of Government endorsed the report, and agreed to assist on a
bilateral and multilateral basis. They requested the Secretary-General to
"bring the Expert Group's Report to the attention of the international community" and to explore the possibility of convening a donors' conference
with the United Nations. However, the UN system was reluctant to become
involved before there was a transitional arrangement in place, preferring to
"wait and see the political developments". When the prospect of a transitional executive loomed in mid-1993, the UN agreed to co-chair with the
Commonwealth a preparatory meeting of donors, including UNDP, OAU,
African Development Bank, World Bank, European Community and
Agence de Cooperation Culturelle et Technique.

The conference itself took place more than a year later, opening on 26
October 1994 at the Civic Centre in Cape Town, hosted by the new South
African government. The International Donor Conference on Human
Resource Development in the Reconstruction and Development
Programme was attended by senior representatives of 47 governments,
22 intergovernmental organizations and 26 international NGOs.

Chief Anyaoku described it as a unique event in international development cooperation: "the first international donor conference in South Africa, the first time that such as conference has been based on dialogue, not pledging, and the first time civil society has played a direct role in human resource development."

As is his practice, while considering the past and reviewing the present, Chief Anyaoku cast his eye forward over the next horizon. The colonial vision of an integrated Africa "from Cape to Cairo," he said, had lacked "a morally validating character", but with the end of apartheid, "the prospect of an economically integrated Africa has become realizable."

The Chief and the Commonwealth were accorded national recognition later the same day, when the Secretary-General visited Parliament for the first time, and spent 45 minutes listening to the debate on restructuring the public service. "It was very interesting, listening to contributions by those who expressed full support for the new government policy and those who voiced concerns," he told journalist Asif Khan. "It was democracy at its most impressive."

When Chief Anyaoku appeared in the Speaker's gallery, at the invitation of the Speaker, Dr Frene Ginwala, the Members of Parliament (MPs) from all parties rose in a standing ovation, clapping and cheering, many waving their order papers. "It was a tribute to the contribution of the Commonwealth to ending apartheid and transforming South Africa into an admirable non-racial democracy." He was deeply touched by the reception, saying that what he saw that day in Parliament, with MPs of all colours and races sitting as equals, could not have been imagined even by the most optimistic person just a few years ago.

Partnership for the new millennium

During the following two years, the Commonwealth technical team continued to provide support to constitutional development and to third-tier, local government elections, for which formal timetables had been established; and initiated a programme of support for public service reform; justice, safety and security; gender equality; diplomatic training; and statutory bodies such as the ombudsman, human rights and public service commissions.

The programme with a Commonwealth identity 1994-96 was valued at 4.34 million pounds (US$7 million), of which a large portion was Britain's contribution to the electoral project designed by the

Secretariat and jointly managed. Twelve percent (335,000 pounds) was
contributed by developing countries, through provision of salary cover
for over 20 experts. The Commonwealth technical team developed an
effective working relationship with Australia, Britain, Ghana, India,
Malaysia and Zimbabwe, the countries which provided a large number
of advisers and experts, notably in elections and policing, and with
Caribbean countries who contributed substantially to the electoral project.

By the second year, the new ministerial apparatus had begun to value
the Commonwealth's multi-ethnic approach, and to request experts for a
specific task, as one key ministry did, "especially from Malaysia and from
Namibia or Zimbabwe."

"The practical value of the Commonwealth has been recognized
through the system of governance," the development adviser reported.
"The CFTC allocation programme is one of the smallest in volume in
South Africa, representing a fraction of one percent of total aid flows. The
effectiveness of this programme depends on the ability to identify 'niche'
activities where the comparative advantage of Commonwealth assistance
is clear, and in which there is a high impact in terms of policy development and the strategic role of the institutions concerned."

"The Commonwealth provides a platform for promoting more effective co-operation with other international organizations," the Minister for
Public Works, Hon. Jeff Radebe said, and has enabled South Africa to
strengthen bilateral commercial, political and cultural relations with
member countries, providing access to important regional and other markets and facilitating trade.

As acting Minister of Foreign Affairs, he was opening a conference on
2 June 1998 on "The Commonwealth and South Africa: Partnership for
the New Millennium", which marked the end of the Commonwealth's
special programme of assistance and the closure of the development
adviser's office in South Africa.

Radebe said South Africa has been able to contribute to the
Commonwealth, notably by offering to host the next CHOGM in 1999
and as a member of the Commonwealth Ministerial Action Group
(CMAG) 1995 — 1997. The Edinburgh summit in 1997 had decided to
establish a Commonwealth Business Council under Lord Cairns of
Britain and Cyril Ramaphosa of South Africa, comprising a small group
of private sector leaders from different regions, to encourage greater
involvement in promotion of trade, investment and economic development.

Constitutional development

A key area for support had been the constitution, including the International Roundtable on Democratic Constitutional Development, a project to bring constitutional experts from around the Commonwealth.

"I had a discussion with Roelf Meyer, the Minister of Provincial Affairs and Constitutional Development... He was concerned that an aspect of their constitution where things were still left very much in abeyance was the separation of powers between the centre and the provinces. And I told him that we have, in the Commonwealth, a number of countries that have had useful experience in the federal structure. That it would be a useful contribution to the debate if we could have a round-table to which we would invite representatives of such countries — Canada, Australia, Nigeria, Malaysia, India — and maybe some non-Commonwealth countries. There would be no prescription, but there would be an exposure of the experiences of these countries, so South Africa could draw on what would be most useful for their circumstances. He was enthusiastic about that."

Meyer's ministry hosted the roundtable in mid-July 1995 in Pretoria, where 120 South Africans, many associated with the Constitutional Assembly, interacted with 17 senior constitutional experts from nine Commonwealth countries.

Chief Anyaoku paid tribute to his hosts with whom he shared the platform, "two people whose names became virtually synonymous with the negotiations; whose perseverance, diplomacy and search for compromise played a critical role in bringing South Africa to where it is today: Cyril Ramaphosa, Chairperson of the Constitutional Assembly, and Roelf Meyer, Minister of Provincial Affairs and Constitutional Development."

He hailed South Africa as a "beacon of hope" in a world witnessing a "chilling resurgence of tensions and conflicts fuelled by ethnic intolerance."

The great absentees of universal history

When the Constitutional Assembly adopted The Republic of South Africa Constitution Bill 1966, in Cape Town on 8 May 1996, the statement on behalf of the ANC was Thabo Mbeki's eloquent, immensely moving and now famous speech, "I am an African".

"On an occasion such as this," Mbeki said, "we should, perhaps, start from the beginning. So let me begin. I am an African...."

"...Whoever we may be, whatever our immediate interest, however much we carry baggage from our past, however much we have been caught by the fashion of cynicism and loss of faith in the capacity of the people, let us say today: Nothing can stop us now!"

Two years later, when Chief Anyaoku returned to address Parliament on the fourth anniversary of South Africa's official return to the Commonwealth, he responded to the same theme with an acute sense of the historical threshold.

He began by paying tribute to the countless South Africans who "worked and waited for this dawn but did not live to see it", invoking in particular the memory of Oliver Tambo "whose courage and determination provided the inspiration and leadership to the struggle against apartheid, especially at a time when the odds appeared overwhelmingly against the struggle. I count it an honour to have known and worked closely with Oliver and Adelaide Tambo in those eventful years."

He chose to speak about "Democracy in Africa: The Challenges and the Opportunities", noting that fostering democracy had become a priority of the Commonwealth since 1991, including in South Africa.

"Franz Fanon once said that the period of foreign rule in Africa was the time when Africans were 'the great absentees of universal history'. That is plainly no longer the case. The success of the anti-colonial struggle has enabled Africa to resume its place in the community of nations and together with the rest of humanity is shaping world history. But if Africa is not to lose its place in world affairs in the coming millennium, it will have to set its house in order."

Chief Anyaoku had crafted the speech carefully, presented it deliberately, and struck a chord that achieved more than the anticipated response. The parliament erupted when he had finished, and a rainbow of MPs crushed round to shake his hand.

"In my career so far," he said a few days later, "very few things moved me as much as the reception I got when I addressed the South African parliament last week on Monday. ...I would regard it as one of the highlights of my career. ...And what Adelaide Tambo said. She recalled the conversation I had with her husband on the night of my election as Secretary-General [almost a decade earlier], when Oliver Tambo called to congratulate me, and how I said, 'that's one thing done, the more important thing now is the liberation of South Africa'."

Former Australian Prime Minister, Malcolm Fraser, confronts his opponent in the battle for Commonwealth Secretary-General, in this cartoon from the *Sydney Morning Herald*, 12 August 1989, by Rollo Fazzari. Fraser may not have known that Anyaoku is an ancestral name earned for courage in battle, and means "eye of fire" or "fiery eye".

The late Robert Ouko, then Kenyan Foreign Minister, was a key campaigner for Chief Anyaoku in 1989, seen here congratulating him after his election in Kuala Lumpur, with Mrs Anyaoku. At right is Judith Sefi Attah, widow of the Nigerian poet, Christopher Okigbo.

Archbishop Desmond Tutu (then Bishop) describing the realities of apartheid to a delegation of the Eminent Persons Group in South Africa in 1986, from left, Chief Anyaoku, then Deputy Secretary-General, with co-chairmen Malcolm Fraser and Olusegun Obasanjo, and another official, Moni Malhoutra.

The Secretary-General at Delhi airport, welcomed on arrival to India for a meeting of the Commonwealth Foreign Ministers on Southern Africa (CFMSA) in September 1991.

Commonwealth leaders attending the summit in Zimbabwe in 1991, pose in front of a painted backdrop of *musi-oa-tunya*, the smoke that thunders, the local name for Victoria Falls where they held their retreat.

The Secretary-General shares a light moment with the Head of the Commonwealth, Her Majesty, Queen Elizabeth II, during celebration of Commonwealth Day 1999.

Chief Anyaoku addresses the biennial Commonwealth Heads of Government Meeting (CHOGM) in Limassol, Cyprus in October 1993.

Photo by David Gadd, Sportsphoto

The Secretary-General in his office at Commonwealth headquarters, Marlborough House, London, near Buckingham Palace and St James. The former stately home, with its high ceilings and painted murals of European battle scenes, was designed by the architect Sir Christopher Wren for the first Duke and Duchess of Marlborough in the early eighteenth century, completed in 1711.

A traditional Ndichie chief with the title *Ichie Adazie Obosi, Ugwumba Idemili*, Chief Anyaoku is seen here in the *iba* (seat of the chief) at his home in the village of Obosi, in eastern Nigeria.

With Nelson Mandela.

With former South African President, FW de Klerk, at their first meeting in October 1991, immediately after Commonwealth leaders approved the Secretary-General's proposal to re-open contacts with Pretoria.

With Thabo Mbeki, who later became South Africa's second democratically elected President, seen here as Deputy President, during a ceremony in London to mark his country's return to the Commonwealth in 1994.

The Secretary-General has direct personal access to over 50 Heads of Government, seen here (clockwise from upper left): with Dato' Seri Dr. Mahathir bin Mohamad, the Malaysian Prime Minister; with UK Prime Minister Tony Blair at the Edinburgh CHOGM 1997; in Fiji, with Prime Minister Sitiveni Rabuka in 1998 launching the multi-million dollar Kula Fund, an investment initiative for the South Pacific; with the President of Zanzibar, Salmin Amour, and Seif Shariff Hamad, leader of the Civic United Front (CUF), parties to a 1999 mediation agreement in Zanzibar, United Republic of Tanzania; and in 1995, with Fidel Castro, President of Cuba, one of few Caribbean countries which is not a Commonwealth member.

With Bunmi, on HMS Oriole off the west
coast of Canada during the Commonwealth
Games in Victoria in 1994. The Secretary-
General is an enthusiastic supporter of
Commonwealth sporting links.

A light-hearted moment in New Delhi; a personal sketch of Chief Anyaoku during his first
visit to India as Secretary-General in
September 1990, by the artist Ranga.

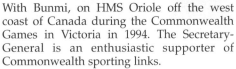

With Whoopi Goldberg and Harry Belafonte at Commonwealth headquarters in 1988, during 75th birthday dinner for Archbishop Trevor
Huddleston.

3

DEMOCRACY

Building on what has already been achieved and reaching
for what we know is possible.
(Emeka Anyaoku, The Task for Auckland, 1995)

ADDRESSING THE South African parliament in 1998, on the fourth
anniversary of the country's return to Commonwealth membership,
Chief Anyaoku chose a French citation:

"Diderot, the great French encyclopaedist of the 18th century, once
said that every age has its dominant idea. Our dominant idea on the eve
of the millennium is democracy. In one version or another, liberty has
been a dominant idea in the world since the turn of the 18th century. But
in all this period it has always had to contend with rivals. Thanks to the
collapse of communism and the end of the Cold War, this is the first time
in 200 years when as far as governance systems are concerned, democracy has been without a credible rival in sight. In that sense, we are all
democrats now."

The selection of this passage for presentation at an occasion that he
regarded as a highlight of his career, and the choice of democracy as the
subject he would address, reflected Chief Anyaoku's major preoccupation during his term of office and the arena of his most significant contributions. As would be expected when dealing with national governance,
there have been successes and setbacks, but the Secretary-General has
tackled both head-on.

British journalist Michael Binyon, writing in *Diplomat* in late 1994,
noted Chief Anyaoku's "diplomatic skills and quiet leverage", crediting
his "charm and resolute optimism" for the gradual move, particularly
within Africa, to pluralist democracies.

"Two qualities of the Chief have consistently struck me," Nelson
Mandela says in his Foreword to this book, "his unwavering commitment

to democracy and justice, and his quiet personal style for achieving these objectives." Both attributes are illustrated and examined in this chapter.

The balance sheet

Chief Anyaoku told the Commonwealth Parliamentary Association (CPA) annual meeting in Banff, Canada in 1994 that the day was not far away "when representatives of military regimes would find no welcome in the councils of the Commonwealth." That day was brought forward the following year with the approval by heads of government of the Millbrook Commonwealth Action Programme. This specified measures to be taken in response to violations of the Harare principles and established a mechanism for implementation, through a Commonwealth Ministerial Action Group (CMAG).

A commitment to democracy and good governance had been implicit in membership of the modern Commonwealth since its inception in 1949, but for most of that period this objective was overshadowed by Cold War considerations and by competition with what Chief Anyaoku called a "more urgent, if not higher, objective", that of ending minority rule in then Rhodesia and eliminating apartheid in South Africa.

The price of diverting Commonwealth effort "was to compel the association to live with a contradiction," the third Secretary-General said in his valedictory report, "professing a democratic vocation but containing within its ranks governments which could not be described by any definition as democratic. Accepting this contradiction, and therefore being vulnerable to the charge of hypocrisy, may not have markedly reduced the Commonwealth's effectiveness, but it did lessen the moral stature of the association."

The Harare declaration, which emerged in 1991 from the capital of the country which had once been called Rhodesia, transformed the Commonwealth "morally and politically", added to credibility among its constituents, and raised its stature and influence in the international community. But it provided no mechanism for implementation. That came four years later at Auckland, New Zealand, after the objective of ending apartheid had also been achieved. Chief Anyaoku attributed the landmark declarations to the "frankness of the discussions" within the Commonwealth family.

When he became Secretary-General in 1990, eleven member countries were counted as military regimes or one-party states; three years later, there were four. By 1995, just three remained. Presidential and parliamentary elections were held in Sierra Leone in 1996 and in The Gambia, though flawed, in 1996/97. The last one, Nigeria, had been suspended from membership in 1995 by the Commonwealth Heads of Government Meeting (CHOGM) in New Zealand under the Millbrook action programme, and eventually had a transition from military rule through multi-party elections to a democratic government in 1999.

The holistic success of the transitions does not suggest that all are perfect or inclusive, stable or entrenched, but the Secretary-General sees it as the beginning of a process. "Democracy has a long gestation period." Having achieved the removal of military regimes in the Commonwealth, a number of problems remain:

- the consolidation of multi-party democracy, so that elections are not "one person, one vote, once" as one southern African politician quipped; and so that change of government is not the measure of a successful democratic process, ie Zambia;
- the strengthening of systems of good governance, so the military do not feel compelled by extensive popular support to seize power, ie Pakistan; and
- the vexed question of "no-party" states which, although they are one-party states by another name, continue to escape the net of the secretary-general and the Millbrook action programme: Tuvalu and Tonga are constitutional monarchies with no political parties; Nauru and Maldives have executive presidents and no political parties; Brunei Darussalam, has a "national executive monarchy" headed by the Sultan and no political parties; Swaziland is an absolute monarchy with no legal political parties; and Uganda is in a situation of civil war under a government which seized power by force over a decade ago and has not yet faced the electorate in competition with other parties. Political parties can register but are not allowed to campaign or contest elections, under Uganda's "no-party" system.

Channels for peaceful competition

In his address that brought members of the South African parliament to their feet on 1 June 1998, Chief Anyaoku touched on a number of related themes including the cultural roots of democracy and the "no-party" states:

"...there can be no genuine or durable democracy without genuine political parties. In saying so, I know that I am putting myself in direct opposition to a surviving school of thought which holds that genuine political parties in the present conditions in Africa are practically impossible and that the foreseeable future ought to lie in a no-party system of government of all the talents. According to this school of thought, in the absence of social and economic conditions of the type which exist in the old democracies in Europe and North America, African political parties are invariably either tribal coalitions or religious groupings or some other partisan formation [which] ...will make for division and national retardation.

"I understand where the advocates of the no-party system are coming from and I respect the sincerity of their convictions; but I do not share the underlying fear and pessimism. ...Nor do I accept that only a no-party government can lead to a government of all the talents as it is always possible to form governments of national unity even if the elections have been contested on the basis of separate party identities. Besides, I believe that it is possible for agreed national constitutions of pluralistic states to proscribe the formation of political parties on the basis of such potentially divisive factors as ethnicity, race or religion."

"A viable democracy has to evolve organically," he said. "It has to evolve through civic education and no institution is better placed to perform the task of civic education than a political party. Inter-party rivalry within the law also contributes to the growth of freedom. Modern political parties provide the channels for peaceful competition between one set of ambitions and another. Political parties then are central to democracy...

"Equally necessary is the fostering of certain habits of mind and a body of understandings between politicians and a general consensus within society at large about the legitimacy and efficacy of the democratic order. ...No institution or set of institutions or arrangements can alone be said to secure freedom and make democracy possible without reference to local conditions. The challenge to African countries is to bring their various traditional cultures into a meaningful working relationship with democracy. "A study of traditional government in any part of Africa would disclose one fact — a healthy hostility against the concentration of power without accompanying checks and balances to control it, beginning with the position of the Chief.

"No chief was a chief except by the will of his people. In many African societies this maxim was impressed upon the chief in the process of his installation and was in addition to the various mechanisms in place to ensure that the chief marched in step with the wishes of his people. It was one way in which traditional African governments founded sovereignty in the people.

"In most cases, the Council of Elders was the Chief's advisory body; but it was more than that. As representatives of the constituent lineages or clans, the Council also doubled up as a parliament. And no chief could continue to disregard the views of the Council without running a real risk of deposition. In many cases, deposition entailed either suicide or exile, depending upon the nature of the misdemeanour.

"Let me illustrate this point with an example from my own community of Obosi. As a senior Chief, I have a uniquely feathered hat, *okpu nkata*, in my house as part of my ceremonial regalia. But it is a hat which I have worn only once and that was on the occasion of my installation. Since then I have not worn it and my fervent prayer is that I should never again have to wear it. To wear it again would mean that I and the other senior Chiefs of the community have come to the conclusion that our king has committed a grievous transgression, as a result of which he is no longer fit to remain king and must either go into exile or commit suicide. The chief in traditional Africa might have appeared an all-powerful despot to the casual observer or passing stranger. In reality he was not, and could not have been, anything of the sort.

"Sir Winston Churchill once said that the best way of governing states is by talking. Indeed government by talking is one of the many definitions of democracy on offer. ...if there is anything which characterized traditional African government, it was this habit of conducting business through discussion. ...This led to the misapprehension that traditional African society had little room for dissent. Nothing could be further from the truth.

"The whole point of the protracted discussions in the councils of elders was to ensure that the resulting action, if action was required, would be based on unanimity, or failing that, consensus, the nearest practical approximation to unanimity. This was important in societies constantly exposed to physical danger and all manner of insecurity, especially during the centuries of slave raids. What was proscribed was not dissent, which had an honoured and guarded place, but the persistent expression of divergent views after a decision had been taken, especially when such divergence could be disruptive or divisive. ...

"Traditional Africa had no separate judiciary; but to its credit, it set the highest premium on justice and fair play. In many societies of the old Africa, the law was for all practical purposes an extension of ethics. That ethical position has been nowhere better formulated than here in South Africa with your concept of *Ubuntu* which teaches that our humanity is possible only because of other human beings."

Harare Commonwealth Declaration, 1991

The Harare Commonwealth Declaration provided a bold framework to convert the Commonwealth into a force for democracy and good governance, defining and using the Commonwealth's "comparative advantage". The document was drafted with Chief Anyaoku's active support, for consideration by 10 heads of government who constituted the High Level Appraisal Group (HLAG). At its heart lay a commitment to the promotion of democracy and human rights, the rule of law, the independence of the judiciary, and just and honest government.

"Different parts of the world have different traditions, different means of establishing a consensus, different institutions and different problems," John Major, then British prime minister, said in support of the declaration at the Harare summit. "Of course each society will strike its own balance between individual rights and the responsibilities of the state. ...But the bedrock of what we do must be the general application of democracy and human rights. ...Universal standards, not western standards. ...Dialogue, negotiation, the peaceful settlement of disputes — that is the way forward and the Commonwealth can set the trend."

This was "an idealism tempered by experience," Chief Anyaoku said later. In committing the Commonwealth to a democratic vocation, its leaders "were only too well aware that circumstances differed from country to country, and that there could be no one standard format of democracy which would be applicable to all the member countries." He noted that the Westminster format for democracy is significantly different to the format adopted in the United States or France, Malaysia or Mauritius. However, he often stressed certain essential ingredients.

"These include the right of a people to choose freely the men and women who govern them; the primacy of the rule of law and the independence of the judiciary; the right to freedom of expression and association; and the continuing transparency and accountability of government."

The singular achievement of the Harare CHOGM was to fashion a consensus document supported by all member governments, emphasizing the practice of Commonwealth principles and their redefinition in the light of the new challenges. The Harare declaration, Chief Anyaoku wrote later, "is a key contemporary statement of Commonwealth belief and purpose, and a manifestation of a collective resolve to address a new and compelling global agenda."

In his first report to governments in 1991, in advance of the Harare meeting, the new Secretary-General noted that the Commonwealth commitment to democracy was "immeasurably strengthened by return of a democratic Pakistan to membership, and by entry into membership of a free and democratic Namibia," as well as the "triumphant return to democracy in Bangladesh. For the first time for many years, there is democratic government throughout the whole Indian sub-continent."

He noted that democracy had "successfully withstood an unlawful challenge" when Trinidad & Tobago "overcame an intolerable threat to its legitimate authority" in mid-1990, when the parliament was stormed and members were held hostage.

He said later that, on taking office he "was very determined to answer those who were increasingly saying that outside South Africa, there was no other political issue in which the Commonwealth had any meaningful role to play. ...that once the South African problem was solved, the Commonwealth would have no further reason to exist and would be confined to the role of technical assistance provider...

"And I was determined that, at a time when there is a clear resurgence of international interest in democracy, the Commonwealth should use its historical connections and quite unique form of relationships to cross the line of nonintervention in internal affairs of member countries by discreetly and sensitively offering its services in a way that would make it possible for member countries to accept and use such offers, without feeling that their sovereignty was being transgressed."

Heads of government at the 1991 CHOGM agreed in principle on the need to move forward with a declaration that would advance the ideals of Singapore 20 years later in a modern context; the main problem was the definition of what "democracy" and "human rights" should mean, and how governments should be behaving in their own countries. "It was a discussion that revealed the cultural differences that exist within the diversity of the Commonwealth."

These discussions took place at Victoria Falls in Zimbabwe, during the traditional weekend retreat of heads of government, and there were some anxious moments, when the Secretary-General had to diffuse tension, both in the meeting and in private discussions with some of the leaders during coffee breaks. One of the participants said it was Chief Anyaoku's carefully laid logic and his sense of humour that eventually helped to bring consensus. Some felt that others were "lecturing" them or that definitions of equality would maintain a position of privilege for those who had preference in colonial times and preclude affirmative action programmes.

"I sympathized with some of these views, because I too have always spoken for democracy requiring to be judged on the basis of essential ingredients rather than common format. The basic requirement should be the capacity of the population to freely elect who should govern them. The people should be free to form associations, provided that they are not destructive associations. There must be rule of law, freedom of expression, a free press, and the government must account to its electorate. ...So they were right in insisting that local circumstances had to be taken into account, and I buttressed that point myself, talking to others, and encouraging them towards a consensus. ...

"Before the Harare CHOGM, the argument that occurred over the draft of what subsequently became the Harare declaration was more in the context of the capacity and the justification of the Commonwealth to do the sort of things I was advocating. The recommendation went to the summit with a consensus having been agreed about what the Commonwealth should be doing. But when the summit discussed these, the emphasis was on definition of the fundamental political values... The Heads were concerned with the definition of those values, because, as Heads, their agreement to those values would imply a commitment on their part to practice them.

"So you had a new form of debate, where some leaders were arguing that the definition of democracy must recognize the differences in local circumstances, that they should not be expected to accept Western definitions and practices. Some were very concerned at the way Western media were treating their countries and expecting their countries to behave, showing no understanding of local circumstances. ...But eventually, having agreed to the definitions, as reflected in the Harare Commonwealth Declaration, there was not much difference of opinion on the role the Commonwealth should play in promoting them."

The declaration reaffirmed the commitment of the then 50 member countries "in the six continents and five oceans" to the declaration of principles espoused at Singapore 20 years earlier and to work with "renewed vigour" for:

- "the protection and promotion of the fundamental political values of the Commonwealth:
  - democracy, democratic processes and institutions which reflect national circumstances, the rule of law and the independence of the judiciary, just and honest government;
  - fundamental human rights, including equal rights and opportunities for all citizens regardless of race, colour, creed or political belief;
- equality for women, so that they may exercise their full and equal rights;"

- as well as, the provision of universal access to education; continuing action to bring about the end of apartheid; promotion of sustainable development and alleviation of poverty; protection of the environment; action to combat drug trafficking and abuse, and communicable diseases; help for small states; and support for the UN and other international organizations in the pursuit of peace and international consensus.

The Harare declaration invited parliaments and non-governmental organizations to play a role in promoting these objectives "in a spirit of cooperation and mutual support." This became a priority for Chief Anyaoku during his term as Secretary-General. He spoke at all annual CPA conferences, offering ideas and encouragement, and he worked assiduously to strengthen the interaction and profile of the non-government sector, which became known as "the people's Commonwealth".

Among the Commonwealth countries represented whose leaders endorsed the Harare declaration were nine still under military rule or one-party governments. When heads of government met two years later in Cyprus in 1993, that number had been reduced to less than half.

Elections observation

The guidelines for Commonwealth election observation were agreed in Harare, including impartiality and transparency, as well as the methodology and norms of behaviour. Election observation missions are mounted at the request of the government, and with the agreement of all significant political parties. The observers are selected by the Secretary-General from member countries, including parliamentarians nominated by the CPA, and are briefed personally by him before they depart on their mission accompanied by a technical team. He does not choose participants from countries with a military regime or a one-party state. For the chair, he defines the ideal choice as a combination of "a good legal mind and political sense".

"I have been extremely scrupulous in ensuring that the people that I send as members of the observer teams have been men and women of impeccable integrity and of undoubted experience relating to elections. They've been public figures whose judgment has usually commanded respect and total credibility. Of course I have had to cope with the problems of some parties who seem to go into elections almost like tossing a coin on the basis of 'head or tail, I win' ...and so when they fail to win they begin to look for reasons to cast aspersions on the electoral process." (interview with Kaye Whiteman, *West Africa*, Nov 93)

The missions are independent and tasked with observing all aspects of the electoral process to determine if the results reflect the will of the people concerned. They prepare a report to the Secretary-General who makes it available to the government of the country, the political parties, and all Commonwealth governments. This eventually becomes a public document.

Chief Anyaoku's analysis of the need for elections observation to strengthen the democratic process was that, in many countries, "democracy has suffered because people lost confidence in the electoral process. Whenever a government was elected on a basis that allowed the losing party to cry foul, the result was erosion of confidence in the democratic process because the emerging government was not regarded as legitimate, and was denied respect by the losing party. ...I began by taking very seriously the role of the Commonwealth in monitoring elections, thereby instilling confidence in the electoral processes, and helping to improve them. ...

"At that time, I relied on voluntary contributions for paying for these election observations. ...I made it quite clear that I hoped it would become a regular item funded through our mandatory assessed budget. ...If the funding does not come from all the Commonwealth, it leaves a loophole for the suspicion that those who paid for it would have some influence over it, which I don't want."

Under the guidance of the Secretary-General, the Commonwealth was associated with democratic elections in 12 member countries during his first term in office, including four former one-party states (Zambia, Kenya, Seychelles, Malawi) and three military regimes which were succeeded by civilian governments (Bangladesh, Ghana, Lesotho). Election observation missions averaged one every five months, and the number of missions increased to 16 during his second term.

Few other organizations can match the quality, integrity and collective experience of the personnel the Commonwealth puts in the field, and the credibility of its observer missions has been widely acknowledged. In addition, the secretariat has often helped to facilitate the electoral process through preparatory missions for confidence-building and the Secretary-General's "good offices" role.

The proposal to strengthen democratic institutions was first mooted at the Kuala Lumpur summit in 1989, when Commonwealth leaders gave their new secretary-general a mandate for mounting election observation missions at the request of member governments. This idea, still nascent, was initiated by Chief Anyaoku, then deputy Secretary-General, in anticipation of a successful bid at the top job; and was identified by him as an area in which Commonwealth countries had plenty of expertise to share, and could strengthen each other's national fabric through this exchange. Other potential areas of assistance identified were constitutional reform, strengthening of election commissions, reviewing electoral laws, and upgrading electoral systems and management, for example by computerization of voter registration.

Commonwealth observation of national elections

1990	Malaysia
1991	Bangladesh, Guyana (voter registration), Zambia
1992	Seychelles (twice), Guyana, Ghana, Kenya
1993	Lesotho, Seychelles, Pakistan
1994	South Africa, Malawi, Namibia
1995	St Kitts and Nevis, Tanzania
1996	Sierra Leone, Bangladesh, Ghana
1997	Pakistan, Cameroon, Papua New Guinea, Guyana
1998	Seychelles, Lesotho
1999	Nigeria, Antigua and Barbuda, South Africa, Malawi, Mozambique

---

Malaysia 1990

The first to benefit from the new mandate was the host country Malaysia, which held national elections less than four months after Chief Anyaoku took office. He sent a group of 10 observers to the elections on 20-21 October 1990, headed by Dudley Thompson, a senior Caribbean statesman and former foreign minister of Jamaica. The group's terms of reference were "to observe every relevant aspect of the organization and conduct of the general elections by the Malaysian Election Commission in accordance with Malaysian law governing elections" and to ascertain whether in the context of that law the federal elections were free and fair.

On 22 October, the mission reported that the voters had been able to freely express their choice of government, that the nomination proceedings were properly organized, and that the polling were properly and impartially carried out. However, they also informed the Secretary-General of their concern about imperfections in the voters' roll and the unequal access of the opposition parties to the mainstream media. Notwithstanding these concerns, they said, "the organization and conduct of the elections were free in accordance with Malaysian law and circumstances."

"There were some anxious moments," the Secretary-General said later, "not only because it was the first but also because of its unique circumstances, it was one of the most trying. I had sent a planning mission and had several telephone conversations with Prime Minister Mahathir. We had our moments of difference of views, but in the end it was a successful exercise."

The Secretary-General's instructions to the planning mission were that they must meet all political parties and local observer groups, as it is the acceptance of the observer mission by all participants in the electoral process that gives them their credibility. Eventually, cabinet agreed to this, and the mission proceeded.

"What happened was that the British press, who were keen to denounce the elections anyway as many of them sympathize with the aristocratic group which had split from the prime minister, were generally critical. And so were the opposition press in Malaysia. The prime minister had told the press of a difference of view between him and me on whether Commonwealth observers should meet a particular group. So the Secretariat's information office [headed by Patsy Robertson] was bombarded with calls saying, 'the Prime Minister has criticized the new SecretaryGeneral, what is his reaction?' And I gave Patsy a written instruction. Her response to the press: 'The Secretary General does not comment publicly on his conversations with Heads of Government'."

Bangladesh

A few months later, in February 1991, he sent a 12-member group chaired by a Malaysian former deputy prime minister to observe elections in Bangladesh, at the invitation of the acting president of an interim government in a country which had come through a civil war, five military takeovers and the assassination of two national leaders in its 20 years as a separate state from Pakistan. Their report concluded that, given criticism of past elections, this one was "as much a celebration of freedom as a political contest", and the electoral process was "palpably" free and peaceful. "It is a sobering fact that no parliament in the history of the nation has been permitted to run its full term," the report said, noting that the essential difference in the 1991 election was the caretaker government. "From this one reality has flowed... a campaign which was open and for the most part even exuberant."

Three years later, concerned by a polarization of positions that had resulted in political violence and splits in some of the main political parties, Chief Anyaoku flew to Dhaka to meet with the key players. It was later announced that the prime minister, Begum Khaleda Zia, and the opposition leader, Sheikh Hasina Wajed, had agreed to a Commonwealth-brokered dialogue following the personal intervention of the Secretary-General.

"I see no real alternative," the Secretary-General said, "to both sides reaching agreement on how to ensure that the people of Bangladesh are able freely and fairly to elect their next government." The process continued, and that eventually occurred, with another Commonwealth observer mission for elections which saw a change of government in mid-1996.

Guyana, 1991

Politics in Guyana had assumed a racial overtone since independence; one party had its base among African Guyanese and the other was supported by Indian Guyanese. "The opposition party had consistently maintained that all elections were rigged, so the outcry to prevent rigging was very strong. But President Desmond Hoyte seemed committed to ensuring that Guyana's elections would be beyond dispute. ...He sent his foreign minister, Rashleigh Jackson with a letter asking me if I would organize Commonwealth observers. ...I sent five planning missions and experts on registration and various aspects of election preparations, because the level of controversy between the opposition and the governing party was the highest of any country that we had dealt with.

"In a remarkable display of statesmanship, President Hoyte agreed to appoint the Chairman of the Electoral Commission from a list of six candidates given him by the opposition party. ...It was his idea. We had discussed the need to win the confidence of everybody in the mechanism for the election; I do not know of any other country where the head of government has chosen the chairman of such a key institution from a list provided by the opposition.

"My office was flooded by petitions from the opposition about what they described as the unreliable and even fraudulent electoral register. Some recalled that years before, in one of Guyana's elections, they had found that the overseas addresses given for voters had no houses on them. We therefore assisted in the preparation of a second register."

A Commonwealth mission headed by a former Canadian provincial premier, David Peterson, QC, observed the elections that resulted in a change of government the following year, and concluded that this was "a reflection of the genuine will of the Guyanese people". The Secretary-General paid tribute to the leadership of President Hoyte and Dr Cheddi Jagan "in seeking a peaceful transition of power," and he remained in telephone contact with both leaders during the handover.

The experience in Guyana highlighted the different approach by the Commonwealth observer missions, and the need to manage relations with other observer groups while ensuring a separate identity. Some US-based observers tended to take a more active role in the electoral process itself and, as one member of the Commonwealth team said, "behaved in a way that sometimes gave the impression that their concept of true democracy is a defeat of the incumbent government."

Of the first six elections observed by a Commonwealth mission after Chief Anyaoku took office, two resulted in a change of government and four re-elected the incumbent. The Commonwealth missions normally issue an interim statement after the polls close but before the results are announced to ensure that their assessment is not influenced, or seen to be influenced, by the final results.

None, one or multi?

Early in the process, between 1991 and 1993, "Seychelles and Kenya and, to some extent, Zambia and Lesotho provided some instructive lessons, especially in how heads of government were willing to change their initial positions after long discussions with me."

In Zambia, President Kenneth Kaunda had taken the view that the people should decide through a referendum whether they wanted a multi-party system, but he came under increasing pressure from within and outside the country. So Chief Anyaoku went to Lusaka in mid-August 1990, six weeks after taking office. He spent two hours in discussion with Kaunda, alone in his study. "And I believe that was the moment when he began to move away from a referendum and to reconcile himself to the fact that Zambia would have a multiparty state."

In Seychelles, President Albert Rene had wanted a referendum. "We spoke for over two hours at the Elephant Hills Hotel, Victoria Falls, during the Harare CHOGM. ...he revised his original position that if a referendum opted for a multi-party state, he would quit." A few weeks later, in December 1991, Rene announced that Seychelles would move from "a single-party popular democracy to a pluralistic democratic system." Seychelles did so, with Commonwealth legal and constitutional support, and Rene emerged victorious from elections the following year.

The argument presented by Chief Anyaoku centred on two points. The first was that, even if 99 percent voted in a referendum in support of a one party state, the fact that one percent voted differently would mean that there was more than one party, that *de facto* there was a multi-party state. "So why go to a referendum, and spend time and resources to establish the point? ...And secondly, given the strength of international support for political pluralism, it would really not be wise to persist in standing against it."

A similar conversation ensued with President Daniel arap Moi in Kenya, with a similar result; but not President Yoweri Museveni in Uganda, who maintains his long-delayed plans to proceed with a referendum on his "no-party" state in the year 2000.

In Malawi, President Hastings Kamuzu Banda went ahead with a referendum on retaining a one-party system, which was overwhelmingly defeated; and his government was also defeated in the first multi-party elections in May 1994, conducted with constitutional, legal and electoral assistance from the Commonwealth and resulting in a peaceful change of government.

One Zambia, one nation

Zambia was the first country in sub-Saharan Africa where the party in government was changed peacefully through the ballot box, in 1991. Kaunda had guided the country to independence from Britain in 1964 and remained in power for 27 years, essentially the entire time Nelson Mandela was in prison. Kaunda's Zambia gave diplomatic and material support to liberation movements fighting for independence in neighbouring countries and provided a rear base for the struggle against apartheid. Elections were held every five years under one party with multiple candidates, and the electorate often changed their representatives and voted cabinet ministers out of office. The economy operated on revenue from the state-owned copper-mines, and the president was expert at wooing support from both eastern and western powers during the Cold War.

Kaunda's leadership and his slogan "one Zamiba, one nation" built a sense of national unity and there was a reluctance among the political elite to test that unity with divisive competition in a multi-party system. However, Zambians had tired of their economic burden, and voted the ruling party out of office in the first multi-party elections in October 1991.

It was the first real test of the declaration approved at the Harare CHOGM, which had closed just days earlier in Zimbabwe.

The Secretary-General was on his first ever visit to South Africa, and had asked to be informed of the results. "If both parties were as confident as they were about victory, then I was concerned that whoever lost might feel that it had been denied a victory." He was lunching at his hotel with Mandela when a telephone call from Lusaka informed him of the trend towards victory by the opposition. They telephoned Kaunda, and both he and Mandela spoke to him. "To my great relief, he himself had made up his mind to accept the verdict of the people."

Chief Anyaoku also telephoned the victor, Frederick Chiluba and "he assured me that he would continue to treat the outgoing president as a respected citizen of Zambia."

Zambia, however, did not prove an enduring model of democracy, and the former president was harassed, his library seized and his premises searched. The constitution was altered, and he was declared ineligible to stand for presidential elections because his parents had come from a neighbouring country although he was born in Zambia. He was disturbed by rumours that he would be arrested, which eventually happened some years later, after he and another opposition leader were grazed by bullets at a rally.

The Secretary-General decided to intervene again because, "if Kaunda, by losing power through the ballot box, were to suffer a fate that would discourage other leaders from subjecting themselves to free elections, it would be a setback."

It took written recommendations from the Secretary-General on how a former president should be treated, including pension rights and protocol, with models from other countries, to facilitate action to improve the situation. "It takes considerably more than the paragraphs of a constitution, however imaginative or flexible," Chief Anyaoku said later, "to secure an effective and lasting democracy."

Ghana, Kenya, 1992: the role of the opposition

Of the first 18 observer missions constituted by Chief Anyaoku, 12 were in Africa, where countries were undertaking extensive democratic restructuring after emerging from the vortex of colonialism and the Cold War: setting up the infrastructure, revising constitutions, forming opposition parties and contesting multi-party elections.

"The duty of the opposition is to oppose," he often said in this period, "but it must be loyal to the interests of the state. ...Mutual confidence and trust must be established between the party in government and parties in opposition, that enables them to agree on what aspects of the national interest transcend party divides and can be withdrawn from inter-party strife."

Both Ghana and Kenya encountered problems with acceptance of the results of their first multi-party elections by the opposition.

Ghana was the first sub-Saharan country to reclaim its independence, in 1957, and join the Commonwealth. The first president, Kwame Nkrumah, was a strong proponent of pan-Africanism, a political innovator and a leader in Africa. He was overthrown in a coup d'etat in 1966. After several changes of government by force, Ghana was engaged in a transition in which the serving head of state became a civilian candidate for president, having retired from the air force. Thus the process not only had to be free and fair, but had to be seen to be so by opposition parties who felt the dice was heavily loaded in favour of the incumbent, Flt Lt. Jerry Rawlings.

The Secretary-General sent a strong observer team headed by a person whose conduct was universally praised: Sir Ellis Clark, the former president of Trinidad & Tobago. The group liaised with all parties, to ensure that they signed a code of conduct pledging to accept the verdict if the election was certified as free and fair by the international observers, and that any criticism of the procedure was established well before the result was received. Notwithstanding all that, the main opposition party, when it heard the final result of the presidential election, refused to accept it.

Chief Anyaoku telephoned the opposition leader to stress the importance of the stability of the country, and made a public statement calling on all parties to respect the will of the electorate, adding that the trend of some political leaders to accept elections as free and fair only if they won, is to be discouraged.

"In the Commonwealth we are able to speak out because we are involved," he said later. "Monitoring and observing elections is not just a quick visit from outsiders, it's a process of engagement. ...

"Those international groups who look to the demise of incumbent governments as proof of the vitality of democracy, and restrict their contacts to urban elites, are a source of strength for disgruntled opposition parties. And that's why in the Commonwealth I think we are right in putting the emphasis on the electoral process, so that we are not vulnerable to easy criticism and it is much more difficult to reject a verdict that emerges through a credible process."

A few weeks later, prior to elections in Kenya, the Commonwealth observers encouraged all parties to go public with their written pledge to accept the results. "The lesson learned from Ghana which I applied to Kenya was that the commitment... should be given wide publicity so the whole population knows. ...to make it more difficult for the losing party to cry foul."

The Kenyan elections in December 1992 were "difficult to evaluate", the observers said, adding however, that it was a turning point in Kenya's history and "a giant step on the road to multi-party democracy." The mission, carefully constituted with broad representation from across the Commonwealth and headed by the Rt Hon Mr Justice Telford Georges from Trinidad & Tobago, who had had the same responsibility in Zambia, concluded: "Despite the fact that the whole electoral process cannot be given an unqualified rating as free and fair... we believe that the results in many instances directly reflect, however imperfectly, the expression of the will of the people."

The process had been arduous, starting with a tête-a-tête the previous year that resumed a rapport between Chief Anyaoku and President Moi which had begun during the Chief's brief service as Nigerian foreign minister almost a decade earlier. Points that emerged from the one-to-one discussions included the need for dialogue with opposition parties, the extension of registration to more than three million new voters who had become eligible in the previous five years, the expansion of the election commission, acceptance of international observers, and the constitutional transition to a multi-party system. At the request of the Attorney-General, the Commonwealth sent a respected Nigerian law professor and constitutional lawyer, and technical experts for training electoral staff. But there were fraught incidents when government and opposition accused each other of inciting violence.

The Secretary-General had a number of meetings with opposition parties, at a time when political meetings were still banned in Kenya. On the occasion of his first meeting, secretariat staff had to calm an irate Nairobi hotel manager who, on seeing Oginga Odinga and half a dozen other opposition politicians arrive, believed that a political meeting was being organized in his lobby.

"So it's not just work in organizing the groups to observe the elections. The more intricate, and perhaps even more important part, is the discussions that help to influence the attitudes and policy of the governments concerned towards the process of a transition to plural democracy."

Cultivation of a democratic culture

Chief Anyaoku's experience in the conduct and observation of Commonwealth elections leads him to support a pragmatic approach to the care and cultivation of a democratic culture.

"The practical aspects of democracy should be borne in mind," he says, "democracy in reality, as it can be practiced, not as it is theoretically defined. It's a point that I have considered as I ruminated over the Kenyan experience of Commonwealth observers and the remarks made by commentators — a number of commentators far removed from the scene seemed inclined to suggest that, because there were some imperfections in the electoral process then the whole thing should be discarded. They were failing to understand that what happened in Kenya, given that the extent of the imperfections did not vitiate the validity of the exercise as a whole, was a very important step forward. And that the challenge is to build on that, in order to make sure that next time round the performance would be less imperfect, and so better.

"Democracy requires some cultivation of the democratic culture and attitudes, by those who want to practice it; for example, tolerance and accommodation of different views which in long democratically established societies are taken for granted. These need time to grow, particularly in places where the history of politics has been that of the winner takes all. ...

"The second point about democracy is my concern that the enemies of this new resurgence of democratic ideals may succeed in destroying, or discrediting, democracy on two grounds. The first is to discredit the ballot box process. The most unhappy experience was in Angola where international observers agreed that the results were a fair reflection of the will of the Angolan people who had enthusiastically embraced the elections, and yet not enough was done by the international community to uphold the verdict. We have seen in Angola a democratic process being shown not to have achieved the peace and reconciliation which many who supported it had hoped for. We have seen in Ghana and to some extent in Kenya, an electoral process generally considered to have produced a result which was a reflection of the will of the people, rejected by opposition parties. If they had succeeded in sustaining that rejection, they would not have helped the cause of democracy. ...

"I want to see the Commonwealth focusing on strategies for upholding the results of certifiable elections. ...to see what strategies we can devise which would make it more difficult for those who are inclined to the view that elections are acceptable only if they win, to discourage such people and instead uphold the near sanctity, in my view, of the results of free and fair elections. ...

"I think we should start off with the political environment which exists before the elections, with the sort of dialogue and understanding that is reached among the political parties. There should be greater involvement of the Commonwealth in the creation and observation of the political environment before the elections."

The observers are given a written brief on the country and its preparations for elections, and a verbal briefing that includes the context and local conditions. "One of the illustrations I used was that, if you had a political rally in London or Ottawa or Canberra, it would be usual for anyone opposed to the prime minister's views to shout such things as 'rubbish, shut up' but if you did that in many developing countries the cultural setting is different, people would not accept that you should be so discourteous to a head of government. ...There are many ways in which countries differ in how they pursue the common belief in freedom and democracy."

Another point is terminology. "I would want to put the emphasis on certifying whether the electoral process can be deemed to have produced a reflection of the will of the electorate. ...I think we should encourage observers to reach a clear judgment on whether the irregularities or the imperfections would justify the cancellation of the entire exercise. I think they should be encouraged to be more precise on that point, and less diplomatic in terms of the pronouncement."

In the case of Kenya, the chairman of the Commonwealth observer mission issued a more specific statement at a press conference before departure, in which he said that the election, in their view, broadly reflected the will of the Kenyan electorate, notwithstanding the imperfections. "And that is the bottom line," Chief Anyaoku said later, "because there is no perfect election anywhere in the world. It is a question of the degree of imperfection, and whether the degree was such as to negate the whole exercise."

Several weeks prior to the election in Kenya, the Secretary-General had told colleagues that, no matter who won, the situation was so polarized that it would be necessary for him to go and speak to all parties about accepting the results. As soon as he received the report of the observer group, he "felt it was my duty to lend the weight of the authority of my office in support of that, before things got out of hand."

With the experiences of Angola, and to a lesser extent Ghana, in mind, and concerned by the ethnic patterns of voting, Chief Anyaoku interrupted his annual leave to go to Kenya in early January 1993, within days of the election. He found the opposition leaders angry and their supporters tense. "It looked to me like a keg of gunpowder and all they needed was a match."

The opposition leaders had polled more votes in total than President Moi but had been unable to agree on a single candidate. The incumbent had the largest number of votes of any individual candidate, 1.9 million and his nearest rival had 1.4 million. The three opposition parties who between them had a total of about 3.3 million votes, rejected the result saying they would not take their seats in parliament. The president accused them of driving the country toward civil war.

The Secretary-General met first with Moi, who had been rapidly sworn in as president in an unpublicized ceremony earlier the same day, to discuss the need for dialogue with the opposition. Then he met the three main opposition leaders and discussed the need to signal to their followers that "they were sufficiently concerned to want to talk about how to keep the country together in peace." They spoke heatedly of serious discrepancies in the electoral process including areas where they were unable to campaign; they were sceptical of the president's sincerity, but in the end they reluctantly agreed to meet him. The next morning Chief Anyaoku met again with the president, who had publicly accused the opposition of rigging the vote in certain areas. Moi too, was sceptical about the sincerity of the opposition leaders, some of whom were former members of his party.

In a statement later that day, the Secretary-General said he had sought "to urge the adoption of a new approach under which dialogue must replace confrontation between the government and the opposition." He said they had all assured him of their willingness to meet. At a press conference before his departure, he spoke about incidents of some electorial discrepancies in other parts of the world, citing the example of goverments elected with minority votes in the UK and in the US, where it was alleged that up to 14 million eligible voters often failed to register for elections. "There is no place where you have a perfect, discrepancy-free election. It is a question of how weighty the discrepancies are. Are they weighty enough to vitiate the outcome?"

Democracy and good governance in Africa

These were some of the issues taken up in late February 1997 in Botswana, at the first Roundtable of Heads of Government of Commonwealth Africa on Democracy and Good Governance. The roundtable was "a wholly new venture," the Secretary-General said at the opening of a preparatory meeting that brought together representatives of parties in government and opposition from 16 Commonwealth countries in Africa. "It has no precedent in Commonwealth history nor indeed in the history of any other comparable organization."

Setting the tone for a lively exchange of views, Chief Anyaoku spent some time explaining what the meeting was not. It was not a platform from which others could preach democracy to Africa, nor a forum to advocate an African brand of democracy. "There is a well-founded suspicion in Africa which borders on hostility to anything smacking of superior wisdom from outside. Like much else in our history, it goes back to the days of slavery when the horrors of the slave trade were presented in Europe and America as positive deliverance of its victims from the scourge of ignorance, superstition and material squalor. When colonialism succeeded slavery, that, too, was presented as a duty of Christianity and civilization. ... No other continent has suffered so much from the solicitude of others. And it is this experience which lies at the root of African suspicion towards any counsel of a political nature emanating from outside the continent."

Some 50 delegates at the preparatory meeting stressed the need for separation of powers between the executive, legislature and judiciary, and for elected local government with "devolved powers" to buttress democracy. They supported an elected assembly with the "resources and capacity to monitor government, exercise financial control, make policy recommendations, as well as to make laws." But the main issue was how to maintain a democratic culture, including tolerance, mutual respect and cooperation. In their submission to heads of state, delegates at the preparatory meeting said: "Democracy and the democratic process must be seen by all — governments, political parties and the citizenry — as much more than periodic elections."

The report went to 16 heads of government who met at a resort in northern Botswana. They acknowledged the constructive role of the opposition, the foundation of elected local government, the participation of women in decision-making, and the importance of responsible media coverage. They stressed that sustainable democracy could only grow from within societies, and referred to "the experience of decolonization and their own national struggles for political freedom inspired by the desire to win democratic rights for their peoples."

The importance of the roundtable was the event itself and the exchange of views, particularly the frank encounter between ruling and opposition parties. A number of participants acknowledged, both publicly and in private, that such a potentially fractious meeting could only have been brokered successfully by a person with the stature and respect of Chief Anyaoku.

As is Commonwealth practice, political linkages are strengthened by technical interaction. The following year, a technical meeting of chief electoral officers and other senior officials from 43 countries was held in Cambridge on "best practices" in election management. "Voting for Democracy" was the largest such meeting to be organized by the Commonwealth Secretariat.

Other options

When asked why Kenya, Guyana and Bangladesh would request Commonwealth assistance while a country like Canada, which has been grappling with a constitutional crisis that threatens the unity of the country, would not make the same request, Chief Anyaoku replied thoughtfully. "This is one of the terrible legacies of history. It wouldn't occur to Canada to ask the Commonwealth for help because, I would imagine that it would not easily occur to Canadian policy makers that they have anything to learn from the Commonwealth."

Many examples within the Commonwealth would be of assistance, ie Malaysia, India, Nigeria and others have federal constitutions; the Namibian experience of constitution-building brought all parties together around the same table; and in South Africa, the experience of not recognizing the need for third party mediation until things went wrong, eventually produced a federal-provincial constitutional mix that is perhaps most relevant to Canada.

In the "old" Commonwealth, is there a feeling that some countries do not have anything to learn, not only Canada but also Australia, Britain and New Zealand?

"There is an intellectual arrogance bred by history. The legacy of the history of colonialism, and slavery, places an inhibition on the capacity to recognize that help in these important areas could come from the developing world, or from the Commonwealth. ...I think one must say that one hopes the citizens of these countries themselves would be the best advocates of such a line of action, for example if you as a Canadian were to write a letter to the press and call for this... I believe that the time will come when it will occur naturally to Canadians or British or Australians or New Zealanders that what exists in other parts of the Commonwealth might have use for themselves.

"One of the greatest potentials of the Commonwealth is to assist in promoting harmony in increasingly cosmopolitan societies. We now have in different parts of the world, including in the "old" Commonwealth, societies that are becoming more culturally mixed, and they are facing problems of how to promote unity within diverse, cosmopolitan communities. I think that what we are doing in the Commonwealth will soon be accepted as having direct relevance for these problems."

This is a point to which *The Economist* in London has also given some thought: "Since Hong Kong, the ultimate colony, was never destined to become an independent Commonwealth nation, there is not much British imperialism left to quarrel about," *The Economist* said on the eve of Chief Anyaoku's assumption of office in mid-1990. "But it was the family quarrels that made the Commonwealth interesting, and sometimes important. To get their word in, all those presidents and prime ministers thought it worth spending a sociable and argumentative week at their summit. With that hard core removed from the debates, Mr Anyaoku must find a way to lure the top people back to the summit next time. How about a panel of eminent persons to examine Canada's federal-provincial relations?"

Early days of observation

Some international initiatives that Emeka Anyaoku was involved in as a senior Commonwealth official in the early days, working with the first Secretary-General, Arnold Smith, were to influence his thinking later on. Among these were the referendum on the island of Gibraltar, and the constitutional crisis in the Caribbean state of St Kitts-Nevis-Anguilla.

Gibraltar had been a British colony since the 18th century. Under pressure from Spain to incorporate the Mediterranean island that lay off its coast, the British government held a referendum for the 27,000 inhabitants to state their preference, and invited the Commonwealth to send observers. Smith sent a team of four eminent persons from New Zealand, Kenya, Jamaica and Pakistan including two ambassadors, a senior civil servant and a lawyer, invited in their personal capacity. They spent 10 days on the island in September 1967 and their unanimous report — drafted by Anyaoku, then Assistant Director of International Affairs, who accompanied them — concluded that the conduct of the referendum allowed free expression of choice. Their report gave international credibility to the dramatic 99 percent vote in favour of remaining with Britain.

Arnold Smith described it as a "modest effort" which "proved to be a useful precedent for urging that a joint Commonwealth group of observers from several countries should cover the elections in Zimbabwe in February 1980 and in Uganda in December 1980."

"I still remember the figures," Chief Anyaoku said, 30 years after that first Commonwealth observation mission, "44 for Spain and 12,138 for UK."

In 1970, the Assistant Director of International Affairs had found himself in a very small country trying to resolve a very big problem: the constitutional crisis in St Kitts-Nevis-Anguilla. The problem was rooted in ancestry and geography. The people of St Kitts-Nevis were primarily descended from plantation workers, while in Anguilla were descendants of fishermen and pirates. Anguilla was separated from the other two islands by 100 km of water and some French and Dutch islands. The St Kitts premier did not consult Anguilla much in policy-making, and in May 1967, Anguilla (pop. 6,000) ejected the St Kitts police and set up a local administration.

A Commonwealth conciliation mission and an all-party ministerial conference had failed to find a solution, and in March 1969, a British commissioner supported by paratroops had landed on a beach to take charge. The British press had great fun with this, especially the cartoonists, but neighbouring islands in the Caribbean took the matter very seriously, considering it a symptom of a wider malaise that could spread to other multi-island states such as Trinidad & Tobago. They also considered the implications for regional security of a number of small islands vulnerable to superpower pressure or mafia persuasion. Among other initiatives, the Commonwealth Secretariat provided senior staff, including Assistant Director Anyaoku, for the Anguilla Commission, which recommended a middle line: autonomy in specific matters while remaining linked to St Kitts-Nevis. The British government later made it a separate, direct dependency.

Almost 30 years later, before the end of Chief Anyaoku's term as Secretary-General, Nevis announced that it would invoke its constitutional right to a referendum on secession, and he issued a very strong statement in support of the Caribbean Community position asking them to reconsider: "While the people of Nevis have the right to determine their own future, in my view secession would have a damaging effect both on the prospects for Nevis and for the region as a whole."

There is an Igbo saying that, "a small despised pot will boil over and put out the fire."

Commonwealth Ministerial Action Group (CMAG)

The Commonwealth Heads of Government Meeting in Auckland, New Zealand in 1995 went much further than ever before in demonstrating the will to enforce adherence to Commonwealth principles among its members, and it established a mechanism to do so.

"We have decided to establish a Commonwealth Ministerial Action Group (CMAG) on the Harare Declaration in order to deal with serious or persistent violations of the principles contained in that Declaration. The Group will be convened by the Secretary-General and will comprise the Foreign Ministers of eight countries, supplemented as appropriate by one or two additional ministerial representatives from the region concerned. It will be the Group's task to assess the nature of the infringement and recommend measures for collective Commonwealth action aimed at the speedy restoration of democracy and constitutional rule."

The Secretary-General had prepared the ground carefully, consulting with key leaders individually and then distilling the consultations into an Aide Memoire for collective consideration at the Auckland meeting, which approved it as the Millbrook Commonwealth Action Programme on the Harare Declaration.

"Auckland was a watershed in the evolution of the Commonwealth," Chief Anyaoku said later, after his well-tilled soil had borne fruit. In public statements earlier in the year, notably in May at the Commonwealth Trust in London when he laid out "The Task for Auckland", he had sought to depict the forthcoming summit as an opportunity for the Commonwealth to show "that it could have the capacity to translate its rhetoric into action. And that it should move away from being an association whose reputation was based on its important declarations to an association that was determined to do something about translating those declarations into action. ...

"Critics of the Commonwealth, in my view, were justified in saying, what was the Commonwealth doing about those members who were not living up to the association's declarations?"

The first CMAG comprised the foreign ministers of Britain, Canada, Ghana, Jamaica, Malaysia, New Zealand, South Africa and Zimbabwe; and elected as its chairman, Zimbabwe's Foreign Minister, Hon. Dr Stan Mudenge, MP, a distinguished historian. The Rt. Hon. Don McKinnon, MP, then deputy Prime Minister and Minister of Foreign Affairs & Trade of New Zealand, was elected vice-chairman.

Inevitable comparisons can be made between the mandate given by Commonwealth leaders to CMAG in 1995, and that given almost a decade earlier to the Committee of Foreign Ministers on Southern Africa (CFMSA).

The CFMSA was established in 1987 solely to deal with South Africa, and it lacked the backing of the British government. Its mandate was weaker, "to meet periodically to provide high level impetus and guidance in furtherance of the objectives of this statement." This contrasted sharply with the CMAG mandate to recommend measures "aimed at the speedy restoration of democracy and constitutional rule."

Nonetheless, the CFMSA had proved an effective forum, largely because of the commitment and synergy of the individuals who represented their countries. CFMSA was instrumental in guiding the Commonwealth course of action on South Africa, and in providing a role model for the much stronger CMAG established in 1995.

The CFMSA was chaired by Canada; the other members were Australia, Guyana, India, Nigeria, Tanzania, Zambia and Zimbabwe. A notable difference between the two groupings was not only the presence of Britain on the CMAG, but the absence of Nigeria.

Heads of Government agreed that they would review the composition, terms of reference and operation of CMAG every two years. This they did in Edinburgh in 1997, where they took another unprecedented step by giving it power to act, in certain circumstances, without reference to heads of government. The composition of members changed slightly, as Jamaica and South Africa were replaced by Barbados and Botswana; and the mandate was extended to cover "member countries deemed to be in serious or persistent violation of the Harare principles." The secretary-general was empowered "acting on his/her own or at the request of a member government" to bring the situation to the attention of CMAG.

While the CFMSA had been a one-issue mechanism, set up to coordinate and advance the Commonwealth position on South Africa, the CMAG was established to deal broadly with effective fulfillment of the Harare declaration, by:

- assisting countries requiring assistance to live up to those principles in the declaration; and
- dealing with countries which seriously or persistently violate those principles.

Military regimes are deemed to be in open conflict with the Harare declaration, and Gambia, Sierra Leone and Nigeria were the military regimes in the Commonwealth when CMAG was established.

Harare to Millbrook and beyond

The three remaining military regimes became the focus for the ministerial group established at Millbrook, adding value to the Harare declaration,

as reflected in a Caribbean proverb, "If words are silver, action is gold."
And there is no better way to describe the road from the Harare
Commonwealth Declaration agreed in 1991, at the first summit managed
by Chief Anyaoku as Secretary-General, to the Millbrook Commonwealth
Action Programme approved in New Zealand in 1995, as he entered his
second term of office. The first document framed the words and made the
commitment, while the latter put the words into action.

The 1994 coup in The Gambia had been a shock. Just a few months
earlier, the elected president, Sir Daudi Jawara, had told him he would
not stand for re-election and sought advice on the method of choosing a
successor. Chief Anyaoku offered Commonwealth examples: in Jamaica,
the retiring head of state, Michael Manley, allowed his party to choose his
successor without intervening in the process; in Singapore, Lee Quan
Yew selected and actively promoted an heir apparent and helped to consolidate his political support. The Gambia was not a place where the
opposition cried foul after elections, and African countries had recognized the country's positive human rights record when they selected
Banjul as host of the African Commission on Human and People's Rights.

Chief Anyaoku roundly condemned the coup, and told Lt. Yaya
Jameh that elections should be held within three to six months because
the longer he stays, "the greater damage he does to the administrative
and democratic structure" of The Gambia. Technical assistance was
offered for organizing elections. In 1995, The Gambia was the only country to object to Commonwealth suspension of the military regime in
Nigeria, and soon thereafter held its elections, which Jameh contested
and won as a civilian candidate for president. However, CMAG confirmed that the activities of some political parties and individuals are still
proscribed, and said it would continue to monitor the situation.

Nigeria preoccupied CMAG until the swearing in of an elected government in 1999 (see chapter 7), and Sierra Leone is far too long and complex a tale to relate here. Whole books will be written. After successfully
brokering a commitment to democratic governance and coaxing an electoral timetable from the military regime of Capt. Valentine Strasser, the
Secretary-General had to express "dismay and disapproval" at another
military coup in Sierra Leone on 16 January 1996, just two months after
CMAG was established. The message was stronger but the statement
similar to that he had delivered almost four years earlier, on 1 May 1992,
when Strasser seized power:

"Any military coup d'etat is a setback to the cause of democracy, particularly at a time when all Commonwealth governments have pledged

themselves to promote democratic rule in their countries; in the few cases where this is not yet a reality, significant steps are being taken towards that objective. I therefore urge the new authorities in Freetown to make the realization of multiparty democracy, to which they have committed themselves in their first announcement, among their highest priorities. The Commonwealth... stands ready to assist Sierra Leone in this task."

Although coated with the sugar of an offer of assistance, this 1992 statement was the first time a Commonwealth Secretary-General had made a bold, public criticism of a military seizure of power, and it reflected his commitment to a more interventionist role.

His statement had unsettled the new military rulers who did not want to be ostracized, and they let it be known that they would welcome a dialogue. A meeting was arranged with Capt. Strasser during an OAU summit in Dakar, Senegal. In private conversation with a young man of the same age as his eldest son, Yemi, Chief Anyaoku offered fatherly advice. "I found a young man who was striving to be a confident young man, not arrogant, still very much wanting to impress me. But beneath all that effort to impress was a basic insecurity. ...The advisers were much older.

"I was able to tell him, as a much older man who had seen the world, that first, I felt very sympathetic to him, with all the responsibility he had taken on. And he should know that many of those who sing 'hosanna' today will sing 'crucify him' tomorrow. I've lived through coups, and so on. I advised him to proceed to lay the foundation for the next civilian administration to come in and spare the country from repeating the mistakes of the past. You can best do it by having a clear, quick programme of democratization, and go back to the barracks. ...

"Once there is a commitment to a democratization process, I would offer technical assistance, to go and advise them on how to reconstruct and refashion some of their economic policies and projects. For example, Sierra Leone is not unendowed with precious minerals, but has had the misfortune of not being able to stop the corrupt practices in exploiting those minerals and exporting them illegally."

Brig. Julius Maada Bio, who seized power from Strasser just before the 1996 elections, was persuaded in private conversations to adhere to the process established by the independent electoral commission, headed by a respected former UN senior official, James Jonah, whom Chief Anyaoku had encouraged to return home for this purpose. With Commonwealth legal and logistics assistance, the elections were held and the candidate of the Sierra Leone People's Party, Ahmad Tejan Kabbah, emerged the victor in the March 1996 presidential run-off.

President Kabbah was overthrown the following year in a violent coup-d'etat that destroyed parts of the capital, Freetown, and he went into exile as the country deteriorated into an even bloodier civil war. The Commonwealth continued to recognize Kabbah as the legitimate head of state, and backed the military intervention by neighbouring countries of the Economic Community of West African States (ECOWAS) that facilitated his return. The rebels returned to the bush and the Secretary-General and his special envoy, Moses Anafu, remained in contact with all parties to encourage dialogue until the ceasefire and peace agreement in 1999, for which the Commonwealth was a moral guarantor. The Commonwealth Action Plan was developed to support the restoration of peace and security, and provide technical assistance for national reconstruction.

When heads of government met again in Durban in late 1999, one Commonwealth member, Pakistan, had returned to direct military rule; and another, Uganda, continued to be governed by a party which had seized power by force and had not implemented a democratic system of multiparty elections. The former was not invited to attend.

Looking back over the past decade of his tenure, Chief Anyaoku says "the difficulty of democratic efforts in Sierra Leone, the military coup d'etat in The Gambia in 1994 and the military takeover in Pakistan in 1999 are by far my greatest disappointments."

A senior official who participated in CMAG, said the Chief's manner and methodology were essential factors in the progress made. It is interesting to see the process he uses, starting with his 'good offices' role, making his own analysis then consulting, lobbying, refining; eventually, the protagonists coalesce around his point of view through sheer force of logic. He has the capacity to deal with reality, to analyse what is possible this year, and what may be possible next year, and how far he can go at a summit, while making the right statements to keep the protagonists on board. He gets results because of his complete integrity."

Chief Anyaoku recognized this as an asset and early in his tenure, when he spoke at Essex University in 1991, he quoted an eminent alumnus and Nobel Peace Prize winner, Dr Oscar Arias, the former president of Costa Rica, who said: "A person's most important feature is not wisdom, or beauty, or knowledge; but integrity; translating words into actions and actions into deeds."

4

SUSTAINABLE DEVELOPMENT

Perhaps the single greatest enemy of freedom is poverty.
(Emeka Anyaoku, Trinity College, Dublin, 1992)

A COMMON THEME that runs through his tenure, and which Chief Anyaoku returns to often, is the symbiosis of democracy and development.

"I have been guilty," he has said on more than one occasion, "of corrupting a well-known Napoleonic maxim in saying that democracies cannot march on empty stomachs. Nor can democracy in itself fill hungry stomachs. ...Development has always been central to Commonwealth concerns. It cannot be otherwise in an association where all but five of the 54 member states are officially classified as developing countries."

Political intervention and functional cooperation were, therefore, the dual pursuits of the modern Commonwealth that the Secretary-General envisioned for the 1990s and beyond. The addition of global consensus-building strengthened the agenda into a tripod — like a three-legged African cooking pot:

- promotion of good governance and fundamental principles;
- pursuit of socio-economic development; and
- building international consensus on issues such as environment, gender, peace and security.

Democracy and development in an inter-connected world. These were the tools that Chief Anyaoku used in shaping the framework for rekindling a Commonwealth agenda. His third report to heads of government, in 1995, was entitled *Development and Good Governance: Local Action, Global Reach.*

"I wanted to find for the Commonwealth a more strategic role in the pursuit of sustainable development," he said later. "When I say a more strategic role, I am aware that the Commonwealth has had a good record in helping member countries deal with different projects in the area of socio-economic development, but dealing with a number of projects does not yield as much impact on the thinking and appreciation of the Commonwealth as being part of the national effort to plan policies in strategic areas. I wanted the Commonwealth to become more involved in macro-economic policy advice to governments, because that is one of the ways in which governments can derive greater value."

Debt and underdevelopment

An early consideration was the debt burden which, speaking in late 1992 at Trinity College, Dublin, he noted had grown more onerous, "with more funds now flowing out of developing countries by way of debt repayments than are flowing into them as resource transfers of all kinds, including official development assistance. ...

"There was an appropriate echo of the biblical rich man and the poor man Lazarus who lay at his gate, in the recent remark of the Director of Oxfam that, 'the poor are not just living off the crumbs of the rich man's table, they are being asked to put the crumbs back'."

Many developing countries start from a disadvantageous position, he noted, of a heavy debt burden, lack of institutional and human capacities to implement change, inadequate physical infrastructure and shortages of essential skills for economic expansion. There are practical local solutions, and others which require international action.

To address the weakness in capacity to record and manage debts and negotiate rescheduling in many countries, a software package was developed in-house, called the Commonwealth Secretariat Debt Recording and Management System (CS-DRMS). Launched in 1985, the participants a decade later numbered 40 Commonwealth countries and nine non-members, such as Thailand and the East European "countries in transition", which pay for access. The development of expertise on debt management within the Secretariat is recognized by member governments as a valuable resource, and has helped to facilitate long-term cooperative relationships with the World Bank and other international organizations, which have been institutionalized during Chief Anyaoku's term. The emphasis is on national capacity-building through joint projects with, for example, the Asian Development Bank and the Eastern Caribbean Central Bank.

There is "some hope for believing that there is a growing readiness to rethink the debt issue," the Secretary-General says, adding that the Commonwealth has made an important contribution to this growing readiness. "The extent of debt is one of the biggest impediments to economic recovery and growth in many developing countries."

The main forum for building pan-Commonwealth consensus on economic policy and debt relief is the finance ministers' meeting held each year just before the annual meeting of the World Bank and the International Monetary Fund (IMF). The Secretary-General maintains close contact with the finance ministers' deliberations, and addresses their opening session. British initiatives at the Commonwealth finance ministers' meeting in 1987 resulting in the Toronto terms, and in 1990, the Trinidad & Tobago terms, have assisted in influencing the Paris Club to increase debt relief. However, the Secretary-General notes that, for many countries even full implementation of the Trinidad & Tobago terms would not be sufficient to ease the debt burden and do not go to the heart of the problem — multilateral debt, which is the highest proportion of external debt for many countries.

The initiative on multilateral debt relief which led to agreement by the World Bank and IMF on the Highly Indebted Poor Countries (HIPC) scheme, was first discussed by Commonwealth finance ministers in Malta in 1994. The British Chancellor of the Exchequer initiated the proposal to address the multilateral debt burden of the severely indebted low income countries through offering easier repayment terms on concessional loans from the IMF Enhanced Structural Adjustment Facility. This included the controversial proposal to finance this by the returns on investment from the phased sales of a small part of the IMF's gold reserves. A Commonwealth member country, Uganda, became the first beneficiary of the HIPC initiative.

The analytical work and sustained advocacy to reduce the debt burden of heavily indebted poor countries, is an example of the consensus-building role on international economic and social issues which Chief Anyaoku has helped to strategize and monitor, and has keenly supported.

The decisions of the Malta meeting, for example, were fed into the World Summit for Social Development in Copenhagen in March 1995, and the Secretary-General formally asked the Halifax summit of the Group of 7 (now G-8) industrialized countries in June 1995 to consider the proposals. For the G-7 meeting in Lyon the following year, he wrote to the French president urging a comprehensive solution and listing five main areas in which existing proposals could be strengthened:

• that the year 2000 be set as the deadline for as many eligible countries as possible to escape unsustainable debt levels;

• that action by multilateral creditors such as the World Bank, IMF and

African Development Bank to make substantial contributions from their resources be carefully coordinated;
- that the reduction of bilateral debt should not be made a condition for delaying action by the international financing institutions;
- that criteria for eligibility be sufficiently wide to include all poor developing countries; and
- that debtor countries be fully involved in drawing up the programme of action.

When ministers of finance met in 1999 in Cayman Islands, they said targets should be set for debt sustainability to ensure a permanent exit from the debt problem with a view to reducing poverty by half by 2015, and with the aim of translating debt relief into social spending. They reviewed the HIPC framework and considered ways of linking debt relief with aid and poverty reduction. The Secretary-General recommended their proposals to the G-8 summit in Cologne, Germany, and discussed them with the heads of the international financial institutions.

Paths out of poverty

The Secretary-General's report to heads of government in 1995, at the end of his first term of office, placed emphasis on poverty and the "paths out of poverty":

"Commonwealth concern over global poverty is rooted in its recognition that about 1.3 billion people in developing countries are poor and that half of them live in seven Commonwealth countries alone. Eighteen of the Commonwealth's countries are classed by the World Bank as being low income (with a GNP per capita of under US$700) and a further 10 as being middle income (US$700 to $2,500). Fifty percent of the world's poor children live in three Commonwealth countries. ...

"The commitment to assist members to eradicate poverty is reflected in all activities of the Secretariat", broadly assisting member countries to develop and implement "sound sustainable development policies that are beneficial to all their people."

These include, as well as practical assistance and advocacy for debt relief, consideration of the impact of economic reform policies on the poor, the social costs of economic structural adjustment programmes, social safety nets for vulnerable groups such as women and children, and advice on trade policy matters. "We also provide assistance in mining and petroleum exploitation where many of our member countries need help in dealing with multinational companies. They rely on us in the secretariat to provide important technical advice, both in formulation of mining policies and in negotiations with multinational companies," the Secretary-General told Ashraf Abdullah of *New Straits Times* in Malaysia.

"We have provided such assistance to Namibia, Zimbabwe, Pakistan, Botswana and Papua New Guinea. We really do want to stress to member countries that unless they get policies right and negotiate well with multinational companies, they will be unfairly exploited." (*NST*, 16 Feb 95)

Setting the tone for the Commonwealth Heads of Government Meeting (CHOGM) in Edinburgh, the Secretary-General's 1997 report prioritized financial management and capital flows. "An enabling environment for the private sector and an ability to attract capital flows from abroad, are now widely recognized to be important elements of a successful development strategy." He reported that the secretariat has expanded its work on the development of the private sector and the domestic capital markets, and in promoting access to world capital markets.

The Commonwealth Private Investment Initiative (CPII) launched in 1995 is a collaborative commercial venture which envisages the launching of investment funds in all developing regions of the Commonwealth, capitalized by regional development banks and others.

First was the Africa Fund (COMAFIN), launched in July 1996 with total commitments of US$63.5 million. Three years later, investments had been made in agribusiness, aquaculture, commercial property and shopping centre developments, tourism and telecommunications. The Kula Fund for the South Pacific was established in 1997 with commitments of $16.9 million; its first investments were in a palmwood furniture business, a fisheries company and a regional retailing network. The South Asia Regional Fund has a total commitment of $108.3 million and operates in all member countries of the South Asian Association for Regional Cooperation (SAARC), with investments in cellular telecommunication, cement and other manufacturing, information technology, tea production and tourism. The Tiona Fund for the Commonwealth Caribbean region, was established in March 1999 with $20.5 million; 12 percent of the capital base was contributed by the private sector in the Caribbean.

The purpose of these funds is to channel commercial investments, establish partnerships between local business and the foreign investor, and encourage larger, more cautious investors to follow. There are plans to launch successor funds for Africa and the Pacific in 2000.

The Secretary-General continued to highlight the major economic decline or stagnation in many countries, and the need to pursue an agenda that could help member countries to improve their economic performance through access to equity capital. "He helped to create a Commonwealth Equity Fund which raised US$56 million for portfolio investment in emerging stock markets," designed to mobilize private capital for development. (*Leadership*, Feb/March 92) CEF made early investments in Bangladesh, Pakistan and Sri Lanka and generated good returns for its shareholders, at 20 percent per annum in the first four years, while helping to develop capital markets.

The practical arrangements put in place to assist development efforts of member countries have pointed to what could be achieved with a more concerted global approach within the framework of what Chief Anyaoku calls "creative internationalism".

These include the four regional investment funds established under CPII; the programmes for poverty alleviation and for capacity-building, including training of civil servants to manage economic reform; support under the Trade and Investment Access Facility (TIAF); the contribution of expert groups such as the one that produced the report on *Protecting Countries Against the Destabilising Effects of Capital Flows;* and the economic policy advice offered to member countries.

The agenda for economic development in the last decade of the 20th century, under the stewardship of the first African secretary-general, has been a practical and realistic assessment based on action, and increasingly accommodating the reality of globalization and its impact on the Commonwealth community.

The terminology at the biennial summits of Commonwealth leaders metamorphosed from the "global change and economic development" identified at Harare in 1991 through "world economic issues" considered at Limassol two years later; to the "expansion of world trade and multilateral debt initiatives" at Auckland and the "globalized world" of the Edinburgh 1997 economic declaration; to full recognition in Durban's Fancourt declaration of "globalization and people-centred development".

There is a saying in eastern Nigeria, "Know your problems first before tackling them."

Edinburgh: action to promote prosperity

The centrepiece of the advance toward economic development during Chief Anyaoku's tenure was the 1997 CHOGM in Edinburgh, the first meeting of Commonwealth heads of government hosted by the British government in 20 years, at a summit billed as "back in Britain". This marked progress toward the Secretary-General's goal of restoring British interest in the

Commonwealth, which had been floundering on the reef of the European Union; and it crossed party lines, having been agreed to by a Conservative government, it was then hosted by a Labour prime minister, Tony Blair.

Chief Anyaoku had reached the conclusion that "the Commonwealth was doing solid work in terms of technical assistance through the Commonwealth Fund for Technical Cooperation (CFTC) and in terms of its ministerial meetings — whether education or law ministers or youth or health ministers, contributing in a significant way to dialogue and to practical programmes." But he believed there was potential for "a more meaningful role in the development and economic recovery of its member states. So I wanted the Edinburgh CHOGM to focus on that."

At the Auckland summit in 1995, Prime Minister Goh Chok Tong of Singapore spoke eloquently of his concern that the meeting had been dominated by Nigerian political subjects. He "expressed the hope that the Commonwealth should be equally concerned with economic issues. So I built on that suggestion that the theme for Edinburgh should be an economic theme."

In his report in preparation for the Edinburgh summit, the Secretary-General said, "The change in our understanding of what drives economic growth, and the increased opportunities for trade and investment, have opened up prospects for the improvement of living standards in many countries." But he cautioned that development remains a serious challenge.

Commonwealth heads of government adopted the Edinburgh Commonwealth Economic Declaration on Promoting Shared Prosperity, a programme of action aimed at enhancing trade, investment, development and the environment. They said in their final communique that the Edinburgh economic declaration was "a fitting complement to" the Harare declaration of 1991 on democracy, governance and fundamental values.

The emphasis on "action" and the focus on positive development inherent in goals such as "prosperity", bear the mark of a Secretary-General who is both practical and visionary, and an experienced communicator who selects keywords for their message and clarity, much as a jeweller considers gemstones.

The Edinburgh declaration of 25 October 1997 stresses the need for globalization to be carefully managed to minimize the risks, such as those exposed by the financial crisis in East Asia and its spread to other parts of the world.

"We believe that world peace, security and social stability cannot be achieved in conditions of deep poverty and growing inequality. Special measures are needed to correct this, and in particular to help the integra-

tion of countries, especially small states and the Least Developed Countries, in the global economy and address the uneven development that threatens many countries. To redress these problems, we believe the following broad principled approaches should be pursued:
- the world economy should be geared towards promoting universal growth and prosperity for all;
- there must be effective participation by all countries in economic decision-making in key international fora;
- the removal of obstacles that prevent developing countries playing their full part in shaping the evolution of the global economy; and
- international regimes affecting economic relations among nations should provide symmetrical benefits for all.

"We also believe that commitment to market principles, openness to international trade and investment, the development of human and physical resources, gender equality, and good governance and political stability remain major components of economic and social progress; and that wealth creation requires partnerships between governments and the private sector.

"The Commonwealth, with its shared traditions and global reach, is uniquely placed to play a key role in promoting shared prosperity amongst its members."

Commonwealth leaders welcomed the progress in dismantling trade barriers but said the benefits are unevenly shared. To this end they pledged to work for a successor arrangement to the Lomé Convention that contains adequate transitional arrangements, and to encourage the European Union and the World Trade Organization (WTO) to accommodate the interests of the African-Caribbean-Pacific (ACP) banana producers and facilitate the diversification of their economies.

They said the multilateral trading system should be strengthened within the framework of the WTO; and opposed the introduction of new non-tariff barriers and the use of unilateral actions and bilateral pressures which run counter to the spirit of the WTO.

The Edinburgh summit decided to establish a Trade and Investment Access Facility to assist developing countries to take advantages of the opportunities of globalization, and to launch an action programme to remove administrative obstacles to trade by, for example, simplifying customs procedures and eliminating bureaucratic hurdles. Commonwealth leaders also agreed to examine the growing importance of "electronic commerce" and the developmental implications of the use of cyberspace for commercial and financial transactions.

The leaders said they recognized that volatility in capital flows can "greatly complicate economic management," and agreed on a number of specific actions including a Code of Good Practice for national policies that can attract and sustain private capital flows, and an investment promotion programme. They agreed to encourage "smart partnerships" involving the public and private sectors.

On the eve of the Edinburgh meeting, the first ever Commonwealth Business Forum was held in London, to facilitate public-private sectors links. Heads of government agreed to set up a Business Council chaired by Lord Cairns of the United Kingdom and Cyril Ramaphosa of South Africa, and made up of a small group of major private sector leaders from different regions, "as well as other mechanisms, in consultation with the Commonwealth Secretary-General, to encourage greater private sector involvement in the promotion of trade and investment."

In pursuing these commitments, heads of government agreed to "enhance the Commonwealth's role in building consensus on global economic issues and on an equitable structuring of international economic relations."

Economic realities

Asked about his own economic perspective, Chief Anyaoku replied without hesitation. "I think it would be fair to say that, over the years, I have come to accept what some would describe — and I would perhaps now describe — as the economic realities."

"I always believed that, for most developing countries, capital — especially investment capital — was not in private hands. The only source of investment funds was the government. So for that practical reason, plus the reason of economic nationalism, I could always understand the fact that national governments — as the possessors of most investment capital — would wish to control the economic activities of the country in the key areas, which in Nigeria we call the 'commanding heights' of the economy. Because otherwise, the countries in Africa would go down the road of the Latin American states where countries could become no more than plantations for absentee landlords and absentee farmers and absentee investors.

"I was, in my earlier days, very much in support of a fair amount of economic nationalism. But over the years, I think one of the practical lessons that we have learned is that economic nationalism, which is best expressed in the form of interventionist policies by the state, has not enabled the countries concerned to develop efficient industries and efficient economic activities, because the state is not the best manager or investor. I therefore have come round to the view that a larger dose of free market economic approach is unavoidable. I have come to accept that if a country really has to attract investment, a much larger dose of free market economic policy is necessary.

"However, I am not sold to the complete *laissez-faire* approach. I think that while it is desirable to get to a stage where international trade, international investment and movement of capital will be free, I still think that national governments have a responsibility to their electorate not only to provide a necessary infrastructure for economic growth but to provide the environment that would empower the nationals to participate as fully as possible in economic activities of the land, through the private sector. So I believe there is still need for checks and balances in the management of external involvement in national economies.

"I think that the management of national economies should not deter external or foreign investors from coming in; it should instead encourage them, but not to the point where the national government totally forfeits control over the economic destiny of the nation."

Channelling the forces of globalization

Commonwealth leaders meeting in Durban, South Africa two years after Edinburgh, spoke of the challenge of channelling the forces of globalization for the elimination of poverty and the empowerment of people. "In today's world, no country is untouched by the forces of globalization. Our destinies are linked together as never before. The challenge is to seize the opportunities opened up by globalization while minimizing its risks. ...We believe the elimination of poverty is achievable — but only if we take determined and concerted action at national and international levels."

In his valedictory report prepared for the Durban summit, Chief Anyaoku said that member countries of the Commonwealth, in the main, have got "the democratic processes and institutions which reflect their respective national circumstances. What they now ask for, to borrow the language of Sir Winston Churchill's Romanes Lecture of 1930 at Oxford, is 'more money, better times, regular employment, expanding comfort and material prosperity'. Will they get it? For the 1.3 billion in the Third World who subsist on a dollar a day in the shadows, the issue is not even one of expanding prosperity but of mere survival."

The Secretary-General returned to this theme often, notably after the Durban summit when he spoke in Cameroon to a joint colloquium of the

Commonwealth and its French-speaking counterpart, the International Organization of La Francophonie (OIF), about globalization:

"We now live in a world economy where enormous volumes of capital ebb and flow seemingly arbitrarily; where 'boutique industries' and 'silicon valleys' are increasingly replacing old methods of production and manufacture; and where the growth in telecommunication on the one hand gives us access to knowledge and information while, on the other, leads us to face the reality of inequality on a daily basis.

"Globalization has led to heightened perceptions of the chasm that separates the rich and the poor; of the few who are able to be part of the 'knowledge economy' and the billions who are not; of the fact that the turnover of corporations is several times the annual product of many countries; and of glaring injustices such as where a refugee child in Sierra Leone sees that the cost of a life in his or her village is worth less than the cost of a life in Kosovo."

Fifty years hence

Chief Anyaoku's ability to exert influence (he would say a modest influence) on development policy, lies in his convictions, his intellect and the clear curve of his philosophy for human development, drawing from the deep rivers of past experience. Part of his strength lies in his ability to look back and to see forward, and to set the present in the context of both perspectives.

"When, 50 years hence, our children look back on the last decades of the 20th century they will, I think, recognize these fundamental trends more clearly than we today can hope to do. They will see that technological change is offering the world hitherto undreamed-of opportunities for economic growth which, properly directed, brings prosperity and well-being.

"Our children will note too the rate at which world trade has grown in recent decades and the world-wide production on which so much of it is based. They will write learned theses about the debate between the advocates of regional trade groupings and those who strive to preserve the benefits of the post-war global trading system. My own position in that debate is simple. Regional trade groupings can bring economic and political benefits to their members. But they must be managed properly, with restraint and, above all, respect for the needs of other groupings so that they can enhance the global system.

"I hope that our children, looking back, will be able to conclude that, after a long cliff-hanger in 1990 and 1991, our generation saved the

Uruguay Round and strengthened a system in which all, whether members of regional groupings or not, could trade freely and to mutual advantage."

On looking back now through the prism of the 20th century, the philosophy and influence of Marcus Garvey is evident in Chief Anyaoku's vision of the 21st. A few months before his election as secretary-general, Chief Anyaoku paid tribute to the "legacy and challenge" of the political activist from Jamaica who made a "monumental contribution to developing a new political agenda for the 20th century. ...

"Marcus Garvey developed a philosophy of internationalism that gave an original and driving impetus to ideas of self-determination, nationhood, independence, self-reliant economic growth, and international partnership for development, which are the very currency of modern thought and contemporary global action.

"The need to strive to create a more just international economic and political order was at the very root of Garvey's philosophy just as it is today a central feature of the Commonwealth's determination to contribute to the global effort to restructure more equitably North-South relations. He looked through the telescope of time with an astonishing clarity. He understood very clearly the emerging interrelatedness and interdependence of global society and stressed time and again the importance of erecting in the developing world self-sustaining economic growth to underpin political independence."

True internationalism, Chief Anyaoku said later, "is based on co-operation between nations on the basis of full mutual respect ...I'm realistic enough not to think for a moment that we will ever reach a stage at which all countries will be on the same level of development of wealth. ...What I am arguing for is ensuring that the bottom line for sustaining an acceptable quality of life is achieved in all countries. I don't accept an approach to respect that is based on material considerations.

"In my part of the world, at Obosi, and generally in my part of the world, we start from the simply philosophy that: "All your five fingers are not equal and should never be equal. If they were all equal, they would be less serviceable. But what is important is that you recognize and accept the reality that each finger, in terms of its serviceability to you, is equal to the other one. In length and size, they are not equal, but in usefulness and in the conceptual approach to those five fingers, they are all equal. I want respect for fellow human beings to be based on the fact that difference in colour, differences in wealth, difference in religion, difference in gender, does not mean or imply either inherent inequality or inherent superiority or inferiority."

5

ANYA = Eye *OKU* = Fire

Africa is at once the most romantic and the most tragic of continents. ...
There are those, nevertheless, who would write universal history and leave out Africa.
W.E.B. duBois.

OBOSI WAS A very large village, in the time of Anyaoku's grandfather, but a son's allocation of farmland could still be determined by throwing a stick as far as he could throw it, from where he stood. From Obosi, it was a few sticks' throw to the river Niger, and later to the main land route to Lagos. The river was the centre of commerce, long before there was a road, before the expansion of the nearby market city of Onitsha into a trading centre that became one of the greatest marketplaces in the world. The popular story has it that you can buy anything at Onitsha, big or small, except a jet engine, and they just may be able to find you one of those...

But Onitsha people, in days gone by, were regarded by the residents of Obosi as intruders, migrants who had crossed the river from the neighbouring kingdom of Benin in the early 16th century.

The Obosi people prided themselves on their length of stay on the land just east of the river, and their direct descent from the historic nearby towns of Ora-Eshi and Nri, the founders of which left Aro-Chukwu at the same time. Nri was the capital and the oldest of all the towns of Igboland; and it was related in local history that the founders of several other towns later left Ora-Eshi and Nri at the same time. Some stopped at Aro, others journeyed to Ihiala, while the rest continued to a place now called Ojoto, where they resided for some time before one of them set off again, with his family, and settled at another place.

This man was a hunter and, in pursuit of his profession, he left Ojoto and travelled some 10 kilometres away, where he found a more suitable place to settle his family, and chose a plot of ground on which to erect his house. Though it was on a hill, the chosen plot was at a lower level than the adjoining land, and, when the rains came, it filled with sandy earth. He found it difficult to get the walls of his residence to stand straight, without leaning, and he therefore called the earth of that place "mbosisi", which means "frequent partly falling". "Abosi" is also a popular ritual plant in Igboland, and "Obasi" is another name for Supreme God. From these, the name Obosi was derived, by which both the inhabitants as well as the town are called, instead of by the name of the founder, Adike [Ah-dee'-keh], the hunter who first settled there and whose family increased the population until it became a town.

Adike's family

After some time, Obosi had been populated, and some people left to settle at another place, called Ibuzo, and later still, at Umuru-Ukpo. Until today, however, the people of Obosi remember their connections with the towns of Nri and Ojoto, since the brothers of Adike and their father had remained there. Obosi people still uphold the usual practice that when anyone is to take an *ozo* title, which is said to have originated at Nri, he must go to Ojoto and get a certain ceremonial stick, known as *ofo*, a symbol of authority and justice, possessed by heads of families. Even the Onitsha migrants adopted *ozo* title-taking, though they came later and, it is said, cared little for the traditions and ceremonies of Nri.

The traditional home of the Igbo people of south-eastern Nigeria lies between the Niger and Cross rivers, though a substantial minority lives west of the river, and its limits are not defined by obvious natural boundaries. Many local traditions recall frequent movements of people within the area, in a general pattern moving anti-clockwise around Igbo-land. This geographic mobility enabled sustainable development through a balance of the population pressures and the resources of the natural environment, and provided a means of conflict prevention. When population pressures became too great, or towns were divided by serious disputes, a section would migrate and establish a new home, preserving memory of its origins.

This founding father of Obosi was Adike-Okpala — Adike the son of Okpala — and as the town became populated with his children and his children's children, the land was divided among the grandsons of his son, Okodu, until there were five quarters bearing their names. These were Uru-owulu, Makum, Ugamuma and Ire (ee'-reh). The fifth, Ota, took in also the families of an uncle, Uru, and of the grandfather's brother, Oba, and later some immigrants from Onitsha, and became known as

Umu-ota, the children of Ota. In any divisible ceremonial rites, it was usual practice to apportion it into equal parts, to enable the Umuota quarter to get their full share, according to the number of families. The quarters of Umuota and Ire occupied the lower part of town, known as Ime-Obosi, while the other three quarters occupied the upper part, Ugwu-Obosi.

The right of official power to govern the town of Obosi was later left to the descendants of Ota's great-grandson, Agu, whose father, Shime [Shee'-meh], was the first man known to be proclaimed an *eze* (e'-zeh), or king, of Obosi: Eze-Shime. By virtue of his being a king, his descendants and those of his brothers, Ozezim and Okwasala, were all known as *Umu-Eze-Shime,* King Shime's children.

The children of Ire

There are three main sources of information on the history of this part of Nigeria prior to the twentieth century — the findings of archaeology, the local traditions handed down from one family generation to the next, and the written observations of foreigners who visited areas nearby. Each has different parameters for factual judgement and deals with a different time-scale, providing different information, often difficult to synthesize.

Archaeological findings indicate a long history of human habitation and some sites have yielded tools and pottery 5,000 years old, with evidence of cultivation at least 3,000 years ago. The nearest major archaeological find to Obosi was at Igbo-Ukwu in 1938, when a man digging a hole for a water cistern near his home came upon a number of bronze objects. These later found their way into various museums, and the tap slag from the foundry work was carbon-dated to the 10th century AD — between 865 and 1005. The beautifully sculpted pieces were linked to the ancient religious and cultural centre of Nri, and its divine kings, the *Eze* Nri. Studies over the next 30 years, based on the excavation of this extensive site, revealed the wealth of the economy and the antiquity of institutions in the society in which the bronzes were crafted. Their artists used highly sophisticated techniques, of which a 20th-century expert observed: "Many of these finely cast works show an extreme addiction to virtuosity..."

Bronze was the most durable means of cultural and artistic expression, but it was not the only one, and durability was not the main consideration for art directed at transcendental ends. Wood was the most usual sculptural medium, and unbaked clay the most ephemeral, in sym-

bolic honour of Ani, the divine Earth. Other characteristic art forms —
oral literature, rhetoric, dance, drama, music — were by their nature the
media of change. Archaeological, linguistic and botanical evidence (as
well as population densities among the highest in the world) suggest
ancient and continuous settlement in an area honeycombed with productive farms and abandoned farm-sites.

Oral tradition normally goes back about twelve generations, often up
to 16 leaders, with more than one from the same generation. Historians of
the area count a generation as 30 years, suggesting these particular towns
were founded during the 17th century. However, story-telling from one
generation to the next often telescopes chronological data into a manage-
able time-frame, giving inaccurately recent dates, though accompanied
with rich detail about the formation of villages and towns, and the relationships between them. Traditions of origin are many and varied due to
the nature of Igbo political life, since the evidence reveals not a single cen-
tralized state, but a very large number of independent, small polities,
with complex and democratic systems of governance.

Shime, grandson of Ota, was the first known King of Obosi, this being
about thirteen generations past, around the time when the Onitshas emi-
grated from Benin, according to *The History of Obosi and of Ibo-Land in
Brief*, partially translated from the Igbo copy by Mr I.E. Iweka-Nuno, and
published in hard cover in 1923. This small volume contains the above
story of Adike and his descendants, after whom the five quarters of Obosi
are named. It goes on to relate that Shime, after the refusal of his two
brothers to assist him, acquired his title independently, was proclaimed
King of Obosi, and reigned long. During his reign, Shime headed the first
civil war against the Onitsha immigrants, and drove them out of Obosi.
The King was still alive when peace was declared, and the driven immigrants were allowed to turn back and live at nearby places. This King also
headed the second civil war against Umu-Oji.

It was perhaps during one of these confrontations with neighbouring
towns that the name Anyaoku was bestowed upon a descendent of Ota's
brother Ire, meaning literally the Eye of Fire, the fiery eye. *Anya* = Eye
Oku = Fire. The history of the name derives from the ancient battle scenes:
it is a name earned in battle, associated with chivalry and courage. When
people went to war, in those days, they took their shields and fought arm-
to-arm combat. Commanders led from the front, not the rear. The warrior's appearance and demeanour was part of his strength; a determined
and well-prepared opponent could win over his adversary, even before
the blows began.

Few people died in these clashes, and warfare was regulated by a number of conventions. In conflicts between related towns, the use of firearms and killing of women and children were forbidden. The killing of clansmen was punishable by temporary or permanent exile, depending on whether the action was inadvertent or not. Some local skirmishes were essentially a form of sport, which gave young men a chance to prove their courage to themselves and others. Since yam cultivation requires short periods of very intensive labour, and long slack periods, conflicts usually took place during the agricultural off-season. A special week of peace was always observed before planting, when no harsh words were spoken and neighbours visited each other and drank palm wine. Even when unrelated groups fought, the loss of life was usually limited. Attacks from outside the extended family were more destructive, causing bloodshed; and towns evolved various forms of protection. These ranged from simple defences — such as moats with removable bridges, high earthen walls or concealed pits containing snakes — to more complex military federations, formed by groups of unrelated towns for mutual defence against a common enemy.

Details of government and social customs differed from place to place, but there were broad similarities. The Igbo "village" or town was often the size of a small city, with an intricate system of participatory political institutions based on kinship, where the voice of the male elders predominated, and with scope for individual mobility. Certain tasks were reserved for the oldest inhabitants, representing the first arrivals: "those who had cleared the forest"; but society had no clear division between work and recreation, or between art and utility.

Attendance at markets, or participation in political meetings, had (and continue to have) a marked recreational element. Stories told to children in the evenings had a moral purpose, to instil in the young the values of their society. There were many opportunities in childhood for work and creative play, including a local version of chess, often played by moonlight. Many of the most attractive products of the society, such as pottery, were utilitarian in purpose. Music and dance, and some of the finest art, were often religious, or spiritual, in intention. Many crimes were considered abhorrent because they were *nso-Ani*, offences against Ani, the divine Earth. Religion was a powerful component of the social order, not a separate entity; and each individual was believed to have a personal spirit known as *chi*, the same word used in Chinese tradition for personal energy.

Justice was dispensed by titled elders, who were members of the ruling society or class, and through the institution of the oracle, as a final

court of appeal. Despite its aura of divine infallibility, the credibility and
reputation of the oracle depended, in the long run, on the justice of decisions taken. The oracle fulfilled psychological and social needs, and was
present in large numbers in a relatively small area. Visitors and oral traditions noted the willingness of people to submit disputes to the arbitra-
tion of the oracle — and to accept the outcome.

When King Shime died, his name was as famous as that of his grandfather, Ota; and it extended to the descendants of his two brothers. King
Shime left two sons, Agu and Dike, and another who was adopted. The
king, before his death, willed his crown to his direct heir and successor,
Agu; to Dike he granted the title of *Ndichie*, being the most senior rank of
life peerage; and the third he made an *Idemiri* priest, whenever coming in
the turn of his descendants. The king's son, Eze-Agu I, followed, as did
his three sons, on whose names and descendants are known as the three
"Royal Houses" of Obosi.

The Royal Family of Obosi, therefore, can be traced down the generations from Eze-Shime. At the time of Iweka-Nuno's translation in 1923,
the last king was the late Eze-Anene. This King reigned from 1878 to 7
July 1915. He, like his predecessors, was a military man as well as a
skilled hunter. He led the battles between Obosi and the towns of Oba
and Abo; and lastly, and jointly with Eze-Analora of the line of Okwasala,
led the people of Obosi against the Royal Niger Company Expedition of
November 1899 to March 1900. "The brave and other noble acts of the
King, Eze-Anene, are not recorded herein," says Iweka-Nuno. "Closing
the history of the original Kings of Obosi, the reader will evidently see
that the natives of Obosi in their government from the older days, were
not ignorant of the words 'Royal Lineage'."

Before 1850, there were six towns in the whole of Igbo-land that had
traditional kingship and chieftaincies. Other towns functioned more like
the ancient Greek city-states, without these hierarchies where elders
emerged from the community and assumed responsibility for leadership.
The six places in Igbo-land which had traditional kingship and chieftaincies were Nri, which to many Igbos is their spiritual home; Aro-Chukwu,
very much nearer the Atlantic Ocean towards Calabar; Onitsha; Obosi;
Oguta; and later, Ogidi. Nri remained a religious and cultural centre and,
alone in the area, had traditions describing the invention of agriculture,
and of iron working, and priests who specialized in purifying towns from
offences against the divine Earth.

The first Europeans reached the course of the lower Niger in 1830, and
discovered that it was already a major artery of local and international

trade in which relations between naval states were governed by diplomatic and marketing conventions. Successive European visitors to the Igbo interior wrote of the well-designed towns, the volume of internal trade, and productivity of the farms. The landscape, by that time, was already much modified by human presence, and was almost covered with orderly and fertile farms, where the yam was the central crop, with cassava, maize, beans and pumpkins. Visitors described extensive farms, as well as small garden plots around each home, and were impressed by the comfort and beauty of the towns. The layout varied from town to town, but certain factors were universal. House construction was adapted to the climate, using thatched roofs and clay walls, which acquired, through daily polishing, the gloss and hardness of marble, often painted with brightly coloured patterns. Typically, the houses were surrounded by vegetable gardens, and shaded by mature trees.

European traders and missionaries in the 19th century also described the quality of manufactured goods, including elaborately woven cloth, made from cotton and worked with intricate patterns. Metallurgy, especially iron working, was another highly skilled industry. The famous blacksmiths of Awka, who worked raw iron, were specialists who plied their trade from town to town throughout the land. The clay pottery combined utility with beauty but, like other manufacturing, was later weakened by the importation of more durable European substitutes.

Here was, as described by visitors from overseas, a centuries-old, self-sufficient society with a thriving international trade — importing salt and fish from the Delta, and luxury goods, including copper, from further afield within Africa. There were thriving value-added exports of textile manufacture and iron production. There were primary exports of plentiful ivory and kola nuts; and, from the prolific farms, which had so impressed their first European visitors, they continued to export food throughout the colonial era and beyond.

The most crucial economic institution was not the trade route, but the market. Some items on display were imported luxuries, and there was fish and salt from the Delta, but the vast bulk of goods which changed hands were produced locally, including maize, palm oil and wine, game meat, chickens, yams, eggs, spices, cloth, pipes, and fruits such as pineapple, bananas and plantains. The activity of economic life, and the vast number of markets, carefully timed to avoid clashing with each other, was the most striking characteristic. Density of population made this possible, and markets served multiple purposes, fulfilling social and political functions as well as economic. Days of the week bore the names of main market days: Nkwo, Eke, Oye and Afo. The four days made one week, seven weeks made one month, and 13 months made one year.

An overseas visitor in the late 19th century, enchanted by a town near Obosi and the beauty of its urban landscape, paid tribute to the quality of life: "one feels...he is in the midst of a free people in a free country." A French visitor noted a few years later, at the turn of the 20th century, that he had found true liberty in *Ani Ndi Igbo* (Igbo-land) — "although its name is not inscribed on any monument".

The trade in slaves

The nature of European commerce in the Americas — facilitated by voyages in search of India in the late 15th century — soon become apparent on the west coast of Africa, although the scope of its international impact emerged decades, even centuries, later. The value of the Americas to European commerce lay in bullion and other mineral resources, and later in the production of tropical crops. The exploitation of both needed a cheap, abundant source of labour, able to work in tropical conditions. Thus, from about 1530, the infamous triangular trade developed, which sent countless numbers of West Africans into slavery in the New World — several hundreds of thousands, estimated at well over a million, from the Bight of Biafra.

People were exported from this area throughout the entire period of the trade — from the first woman taken to Sao Tomé by Portuguese traders in the early 16th century until the trade came to an end in the mid-19th century, over 300 years later. The number purchased by European slavers varied at different periods, quite low to start with, expanding considerably after 1640 when sugar was introduced to the Caribbean.

The years 1730-1810 marked the period of the trans-Atlantic slave trade's most serious impact on Igbo areas, when the numbers taken into slavery were sufficient to reduce the population, though not as sharply as in neighbouring Benin, where population declined without interruption from 1690 to 1850. The slave population may have risen to as much as 20 percent of the total population, and the sex ratio in both societies dropped below 70 men per 100 women, although more women were taken from these areas than from elsewhere due to the shorter distance of walking required to reach the river transport, less than 100 km. Captain John Adams, who made 10 slaving voyages to Africa, recorded that, between 1786 and 1800, 16,000 Igbo people were sold into bondage every year. He estimated that 370,000 slaves were taken from *Ani Ndi Igbo* over a 20-year period. But the social impact could not be measured in numbers alone.

This trade in marketable human beings reached its peak in the 18th century, disrupting the social fabric in areas that lost large numbers of the strongest citizens, in their prime. The homeland was deprived of their labour — which was expended instead on far-off plantations to facilitate the capital accumulation in Europe for subsequent industrialization — and lost new skills they might have developed, as well as the children they would have had. There was also the colossal debit of the countless numbers of people who died before their time, during capture, during Middle Passage, or in exile. The centuries of the slave trade had many grave effects on the quality of life for those left behind, and had a corrupting and brutalizing effect both in the Delta, which developed a wealthy class of middlemen/traders, and in the Igbo interior.

The dense population and small independent city-states made Igboland susceptible, and by far the majority of slaves who recounted their ordeal said they were taken by kidnapping. Others were captured in battle, or were outcasts punished for a crime in their community. The timing and extent of the role of the Aro clan and its oracle in slave exports remains unsettled, as this role was later embellished to justify the colonial military expedition that attacked and destroyed Aro-Chukwu at the turn of the 20th century. Specialists who have studied the origins of Igbo slaves which can be traced have shown that they came from all over the area in roughly equal numbers, not disproportionately through Aro-Chukwu.

Individuals and some polities benefited from the trade, turning it into a business opportunity which made them very wealthy, as did the entrepreneurial class of the Delta ports, who were so protective of their source of wealth and power that they prevented direct trade with the interior for 300 years, the entire period of the slave trade. Their huge trading canoes, with a maximum capacity of 80 people, plied the Niger river, carrying imported goods from overseas and fish from the coast, returning with slaves and elephant tusks for European traders, who came in search of African labour, supplemented by ivory as an insurance policy.

Social changes brought on by the trans-Altantic slave trade included the changes in the gender ratio, which put pressures on institutions of marriage, child rearing, and the division of labour. In the context of traditional Igbo society, it put pressure also on the assigning of tasks to age groups, since certain age groups were particularly disrupted by the slave trade.

The process of state formation continued during the centuries of the trans-Atlantic slave trade, but political institutions were often altered in the process. Most Igbo communities continued in practice to be governed by titled men of mature age, who were successful in their professional life and able to commit sufficient means for bonding in the society of title-holders, much as they did when uniting families in marriage. The recipient had to satisfy other conditions, and be of good character, as well as from the appropriate family line for that position. The decision to confer a title and admit a new member was taken collectively by the ruling society. After the selection of a candidate who, by virtue of right, was to become a lawful title-holder, it was his duty to give to the people whose responsibility it was to install him in that office, a certain amount, as also to the titled elders and other classes of people according to their grades — and also a general feast for the people of the whole town.

An exact quantification can never be made of precisely to what extent the economic develop-ment was hindered by losing the local capacities and energies of exiled sons and daughters, and their descendants, and by the economic consequences of the insecurity it engendered. But the productive results of slave labour can still be seen in the farms and cities of Europe, the Americas, and the Orient.

Prior density and continuing fertility of the Igbo population, and the resilience and adaptability which history has repeatedly required of them, prevented the society from destruction, but the losses were evident in the texture of everyday life. Parents were deprived of their children, women of their husbands, brothers, sisters or fathers, leaving the population in a state of tension and fear. Fields were neglected; houses left without inhabitants. There is an Igbo proverb that says, "A wound heals and a scar remains".

Slavery is an institution common to many, probably most, societies in recorded history. In ancient times, slavery was best documented for the Mediterranean societies of Greece and Rome. Greek slavery was predominantly urban and artisanal, and slaves were mostly non-Greeks, captured in war or purchased. Slaves came to represent as much as one-third of the population in the leading Greek city-states. In Rome, while urban slave artisans were of great importance in the economy, they were outnumbered by a rural population of slave agricultural labourers; as much as one-third of the entire population of Roman Italy was in slave status. As in later days, the exploitation of slaves produced a substantial surplus wealth in the hands of an elite, which was a significant factor in the achievements of those ancient Mediterranean societies. Slavery was eventually replaced with the serfdom of the feudal order, not unlike the plantation labour system that replaced modern slavery in the Caribbean and southern United States. Similarly, the association between sugar and slavery originated in medieval Mediterranean societies and spread slowly from east to west.

The palm oil trade

The trade in slaves from the Bight of Biafra was eventually replaced by palm oil, which traders began purchasing in the late 18th century. This was now more acceptable for commercial activity in Britain, which prohibited its citizens from trading in slaves after 1807 — and became active in trying to prevent other nations from doing so. For the first three decades of the 19th century, the export of slaves and palm oil was simultaneous, but a British naval blockade became an effective barrier in the late 1830s, and most Delta ports stopped exporting slaves. The trans-Atlantic slave trade ceased entirely by the mid-1850s, but internal trade continued overland; slaves sometimes worked in agriculture, or in the labour-intensive task of making palm oil, the new export commodity used as a lubricant or fuel in Europe.

This change in commodities introduced a fundamentally new kind of economic relationship with Europe, which was to last through the colonial period, and beyond. Like many other areas which were later colonized, Igbo-land became an economic satellite of the European industrial economy, providing one of the many raw materials required by Europe's expanding industries, and becoming a sizeable market for exports.

The new economic relationships brought lasting disadvantages that were to govern economic life throughout the colonial period. These disadvantages were masked in the 19th century; when palm-oil prices remained high, *Ani Ndi Igbo* retained political independence, and external trade was valued only as a source of non-essential goods. But from the 1860s, prices fell, and the 1880s saw the beginning of a brutal process of establishing colonial rule.

Many European firms made a successful transition from the trade in slaves to palm oil, which utilized their shipping capacity and commercial knowledge of West Africa. But it was a bulky product, and the limitations of transport and geography meant that only a small area could participate. Economic rivalry was a characteristic of the relationship with Delta polities that sought to protect their middleman status; the reliance on limited palm-oil markets in the 19th century imbued it with a new bitterness, which often led to open warfare. The use of firearms had become generalized in the Delta, for reasons of consolidating economic power.

Many goods brought by foreign traders were already produced in the area, such as textiles, which came first from India, then from Manchester, thus rivalling local industry. Imported spirits displaced local products of palm wine and gin. Iron cooking pots replaced clay, other imported manufactured products were trinkets of little benefit.

By the early 19th century, economic links with Europe were centuries old, and Igbo society was profoundly affected by the direct and indirect consequences of external trade. Yet the entire trading relationship still took place through intermediaries — the Delta traders. No European had set foot in the interior, and they did not realize that the many rivers with which they were familiar on the coast formed the delta of the river Niger. By the late 19th century, control of the area and the trade had been usurped by the Royal Niger Company, precursor to the British government which already had Lagos island as a colony, ostensibly to stop the trade in slaves, but also to regulate foreign trade with local merchants.

Traders and missionaries

The reign of Eze-Anene (1878-1915), the last King recorded in the 1923 publication *The History of Obosi*, coincided with this radical change in trading relations. It was also the generation of Anyaoku Nwora, father of Emmanuel Chukwuemeka Anyaoku and grandfather of Eleazar Chukwuemeka Anyaoku. Anyaoku Nwora was descended through his father Mmabia and grandfather Ifebilo, from Nzekam, the grandson of Ezuge, son of Ire — after whom the Obosi quarter was named — who was a grandson of Okodu, son of Adike, the founder of Obosi. According to family history, Anyaoku Nwora was born about 1850; during his generation, the slave trade ended and the short period of colonial rule began, after a very brief interval of company rule.

The land where his father lived was a large plot bounded by the sandy streets of Okpuno-Ire, the "heart" or innermost part of Ire, in Ime-Obosi. It was about the time when the family in Okpuno-Ire was celebrating the birth of Anyaoku Nwora, first son of Mmabia, midway through the 19th century, that the pattern of external trade relations changed abruptly. European penetration of the course of the lower Niger had been sporadic since 1830, but the period after 1860 saw the steady expansion of European and Sierra Leonian commercial activity on the river. The first mission and trading posts were established in the interior, as well as the first British political representation on the Niger. By this time, substantial numbers of slaves had escaped from ships, or been released, and had settled in Sierra Leone, where they formed a flourishing community with a strong sense of Igbo identity. Some were originally from the Igbo interior or their parents were, and they understood the language and culture. These Igbo sons (not many daughters were traders) of the new diaspora played an active and direct role in trade with the interior.

Trading ventures on a river that was navigable only four months a year and presented health hazards to Europeans, and which were pursued in the face of hostility from the Delta middlemen and their European trading partners, were not particularly attractive. But a faltering trading post established near Onitsha in 1857 was soon saved by the American Civil War. British textile manufacturers were suddenly cut off from supplies of raw cotton from the southern states of the United States of America, and forced to look elsewhere. Trade on the Niger promised economic advantage while satisfying the humanitarian perspective of the Victorian middle class who believed they were making a contribution to development of the underprivileged. Churches, trying to establish missions, encouraged this view, while praying for peasants to convert to Christianity and engage in cash-crop agriculture.

Up to the mid-1880s, the Church Missionary Society (CMS) had a monopoly on missionary activity in Igbo-land. CMS was an Anglican body founded in 1799 and administered by a combination of lay and clerical agents. It had established the earliest and most successful mission in Sierra Leone, where it found a fertile field for work among liberated slaves. These Igbo exiles mastered the language and culture of England so successfully in a single generation that they became a prosperous pro-fes-sional and merchant elite, despite their status as former slaves. The Niger mission was in a very real sense the spiritual child of Sierra Leone, and ultimately of its own extended family. The first mission post, established at Onitsha in 1857, was run entirely by Africans, mainly men of Igbo origin, under an African bishop from Sierra Leone, and, as a result, acquired considerable symbolic significance.

Onitsha's political leaders offered a warm welcome to the missionaries, hoping they would bring trade and prosperity, a supply of weapons, and a solution to the town's diplomatic isolation. Missions and trade were seen as inseparable, thus missionaries were often encouraged by local leaders so they would bring merchants with them. Some leaders also wanted literacy for their communities, and a western education "to insure their ability of gauging the oil casks, square up their accounts, read and write their letters and ... prevent their being made the best of by the merchants and traders of the river." Traditional leaders soon saw, however, that Christianity was undermining their customs and authority. In some places they had to request that converts should avoid gratuitous attacks on traditional religion — such as catching the sacred fish of a local stream — and should eschew European attire.

A story is told by the noted Nigerian writer, Chinua Achebe, of "one of the earliest converts in Onitsha at the turn of the century who did so well in the new faith that the CMS decided to send him to England for higher studies and ordination. While in England he quickly lost the faith that took him there and returned to Onitsha" where he began to make comparisons between the two cultures. Why did the church preach so vehemently against traditional titles, he asked. "What were all those knights and barons and dukes if not hierarchies of *ozo*?"

Just as Onitsha had profited most from European trade, it was also to suffer most severely from European violence. The sacking of Onitsha in 1879, and the subsequent blockade, followed a familiar pattern, in which the British government gave military support to its traders. A Foreign Office official later explained, roughly as follows: where there is money to be made our merchants will go, and if they establish a lucrative trade, public opinion compels us to protect them. Onitsha was sacked and destroyed by a British gunboat with a Gatling gun (a large mounted weapon that fired multiple rounds, used in colonial conflict in many countries in this period) and rocket-launchers; the town was razed, including the king's palace, and most property was destroyed, including produce.

The object of the attack was explicitly stated: to coerce the people of the town with "salutary displays of superior force". This was intended to coerce other states, too, by showing them the irresistible nature of European military technology, and the futility of resistance.

British military expeditions had visited the Niger basin every year between 1871 and 1879, alternating war and trade with the seasons, after realizing that sea power was of little use hundreds of miles inland and that successful trade was intertwined with political frontiers.

In 1877, an officer in the Royal Engineers, a keen explorer who had financial interests in the area, took up the ambition of adding the Niger region to the British Empire "to colour the map red". By 1879, Taubman Goldie had welded the rival British trading interests into the United African Company (UAC), chaired by Lord Aberdare, a former British cabinet minister. When UAC applied to the British government for a charter in 1881, however, to add political control to their economic supremacy, this was refused on the grounds that the company's capital investment was too small.

In order to overcome, and later purchase, the interests of French competitors and re-apply for a charter, the UAC (later the National African Company) raised its subscribed capital to one million pounds and established over 100 trading posts on the banks of the Niger and Benue rivers, employing more than 1,500 men — and then initiated treaty-making with the local city-states. By 1884, the Company had concluded 37 treaties with African polities in the area, one of them with the people of Obosi, whom it called "Abutchi". That treaty was concluded in 1882 between the king, Eze-Anene, and his chiefs, and the Company, in the presence of the British Consul and his interpreter. One of those who signed with his thumb-print was Anyaoku Nwora's father.

On 5 June 1885, Britain declared a Protectorate over the Niger districts, including both banks of the river. Control of this important trading area enabled the British representative at the Berlin Conference in 1885 to claim successfully that British interests were supreme in the Niger basin. This assertion was used in turn to justify its claim to the Niger territories during that conference, at which European powers divided Africa and distributed its parts in what became known as the "scramble for Africa". Rivalry among the European powers threatened to engulf the entire continent in their aggressive politics and expanding economies.

After 1885, British policy in the region became gradually more coherent and consistent. The vague sovereignty bestowed by the Berlin Conference was based almost entirely on treaty rights, and the paper protectorate still had to be converted into effective occupation. By 1886, the number of treaties in the area had risen to 237.

These unequal treaties, which were against the customary law of the land, proved inadequate for the purpose of effective occupation, but became instruments of pressure and coercion on local government leaders. The treaties enabled the competing European powers to demarcate their spheres of activity in the scramble for African territory, but it was force that finally determined the spoils. Local government authority was gradually supplanted by British commercial, military and then consular power, and the pace of transition from an informal trading network to a formal empire was dictated by the needs of a rapidly expanding hinterland trade.

This formative period of missionary and trading activity in the lower Niger ended in 1886 with the granting of a Royal Charter to the

Company, which then became the Royal Niger Company (RNC) — an extension of political authority through Charter Company rule. The RNC was given power to administer justice and maintain order and "good governance" over its area of jurisdiction; and raised an armed police force, commanded by British officers, called the Royal Niger Constabulary, run by a purely commercial organization.

The gradual penetration of Igbo-land beyond the eastern bank of the river began a few years later, in the 1890s, after Anyaoku Nwora had married and was planning for the birth of his own sons and daughters. The state of hostility already created, with intermittent blockades, was to last through the end of the Royal Niger Company's rule in 1900.

So began Igbo-land's gradual confrontation with various forms of foreign culture, and the revolutionary experience of alien conquest and rule. There is a saying in Igbo that,"he whose father was struck on the head by a bullet, uses iron pot as a hat."

Charter company rule

From 1886 until the turn of the century, the Niger region was subjected to Charter Company rule by British merchants, with the protection of their government — a system which the economic philosopher Adam Smith, commenting on the experience of another continent, called "the worst of all governments for any country whatever". Charter officials combined commercial and political functions, and Company rule revealed the economic merits of imperialism, as commercial rivals could be excluded, tariffs manipulated and people forced to trade on unfavourable terms, through an effective monopoly. Charter rule enabled the exclusion of other European colonizing powers; and it created a facade of effective administration, with minimum responsibility and cost for taxpayers in Europe.

Company rule by the RNC survived over a period of 13 years, during which time skilled labour was mostly imported; administrators came from Europe and manual labour from neighbouring countries. The Charter Company offered almost no local employment, except for servants and support staff, and did nothing to develop areas which it ruled. No schools or hospitals were built, no railways or roads, although an attempt was made to establish botanical gardens to extend the range of products available for export. This was sabotaged by local residents, who believed the development of new cash crops would create a plantation economy in which they would become labourers, and they succeeded in blocking it.

The Company's paramilitary police force played a key role in maintaining the authority of an increasingly unpopular regime, through dependence on African rank-and-file drawn from other ethnic groups, further north. Despite this apparently all-encompassing political, commercial and military might, and numerous personnel, the limits of power were confined to the borders of the river, and the influence of the RNC was practically nil a few kilometres away from its banks.

When the Company had started its second blockade of Onitsha in 1885, it had shifted its installations a little further south, creating a commercial headquarters on the banks of the Niger, near the inland town of Obosi. The change brought little profit to the area. In 1889, the town, which had been described by an Englishman several months earlier as "the most lovely paradise I have ever seen", was sacked and its farms destroyed. The yams in the ground — necessary for food and seed — were dug up. The Obosi were offered peace, but refused the concessions demanded of them, and continued to resist, causing a missionary to write that they were "brave but ignorant". The RNC attack on Obosi was clearly intended to protect commercial installations, strengthen power and further economic interests.

In 1897, the year that Anyaoku Nwora's eldest surviving son, Chukwuemeka Anyaoku (later christened Emmanuel) was born, the Liverpool Chamber of Commerce reported that, "there is no competition amongst buyers for export on the river. The Company is the only such buyer, and pays its own price for produce." Local producers reacted to the monopoly by delivering less for export and devoting themselves to agricultural production for their own needs.

The CMS mission at Obosi had been initiated by Onitsha Christians in the 1880s, but attracted only a handful of untitled men and women, perhaps because the well-established and holistic nature of traditional society satisfied the spiritual needs of most of its members. In the 1880s-1890s, support for traditional structures of governance strengthened, a usual response in a time of insecurity and rapid change, and doubtless connected with the great unpopularity of the Royal Niger Company.

Anyaoku Nwora was among those who felt the order of his society slipping away, disrupted by new economic and social influences, and saw the need to adhere to, and strengthen, local institutions. He was by then a titled elder, *Abumadu*, the rank in seniority next to *Ndichie*, and above the *Obo-Isi*, who were selected headmen from six different age-classes of the untitled, between 40 and 60 years.

"Before the English Government took over," says *The History of Obosi*,
"the King and these three sections of societies held in their hands the government of their town, and it was their duty to make the laws and
bylaws... It was their duty to settle any serious matters within the town
or with other neighbouring towns, which was usually done halfway
between Obosi and that particular town... In the assemblies of Court, the
King usually occupies the chair as president, and after the hearing of any
case it is his duty to give out the verdict. And if, however, the members
of the Council fail to come to a decision, but are divided into two opinions, it is then his duty to give a judgement of satisfaction to the merit of
right in the case, which is a final one."

An *Ndichie* chief described the local government role of his society at
that time, in a similar fashion: "In the days before colonialism, the
Ndichie chief was the head of the area where his street ran. He would
adjudicate, he would hear cases, and he would settle cases — both civil
and criminal. If there was a land dispute, for example, or a marriage dispute. If there was some kind of conflict, this would go to his court, where
he, together with the elders of the community, would hear the case. He
would pronounce judgement, and it would be an enforceable judgement.
...And then, generally, matters pertaining to the governance of the community, maintenance of the community, collection of levies for common
purposes, and so on. These are the things that the Ndichie would normally preside over. But all the Ndichies are answerable to the King
because they form the Privy Council, the Igwe's Privy Council.

"During harvest season, the Ndichie, in his area, and then the Igwe,
for the entire community, perform the harvest festival. Traditionally,
when the first yam harvest came out, the people would not normally par-
take of, or begin to consume, food without this ceremony having been
performed. It was a ceremony of thanksgiving to the ancestors and to the
gods — Igba Ofala, the welcoming of new yam. Each community does it,
virtually throughout Igbo-land."

The Ndichie chief "held the land on behalf of the community, and
apportioned farming land to male members of the society as they came of
age. Land was communally held; there was no individual freehold. ...We
had different ways of apportioning farming land, and also of apportioning land where you built your home.

"For farming land, depending on the size of the land that the particular family or community had, the most common way of apportioning it
in the old days was that, when a young man came of age and he was to
establish his own farm — the age would normally be 21 — he would be

taken to the land or area being apportioned. He would be given a stick,
the same stick would be given to all of the eligible young men, and they
would throw. If the land of the community was big enough, the Ndichie
chief would say 'three throws'. If it wasn't big enough, he could say 'two
throws'. And wherever the young man threw — from where he was
standing to where the stick fell — it would be marked and that would be
given to him. So the chap with the longer throw would get more land. It
was thought a fair means of establishing the strength and prowess of the
individual. There was no point in giving land to somebody who didn't
have the strength to farm. ...And if the community had enough land to
justify two or three throws, then he goes to where he threw it and throws
again from that area, farther inside, and so on. The number of throws
would be common to all. The stick would be common to all. But the ultimate area would depend on the individual throw. The Ndichie supervised. He was not physically present, but the elders or his representatives
would go there and give a report. So he presided over all that."

When *Abumadu* Anyaoku's son was three years old, just after the turn
of the 20th century, the child was initiated into the *ozo* title, which can be
conferred on the first son (or other sons) of titled families in Obosi. *Ozo*
title-holders have no power in the government of the town, but are members of a society who may be considered for leadership later on; and they
can govern themselves within the various societies for matters regarding
title-taking.

As the child grew older, however, the father realized that his son
would have to compete in a different world from the one he knew, and
reluctantly agreed that the boy should have an education so different from
his own that it was conducted entirely in a foreign language and culture.

During this period, *Abumadu* Anyaoku was also preoccupied with
external relations, as the titled elders were under pressure from within
and outside the town to sign an agreement with the RNC. It was a matter of considerable anxiety and debate within the society, as many local
government leaders had confidence in the readiness of the Company and
the British government to abide by their own legal forms, which were
signed in the presence of the British consul and his interpreter. The pattern, repeated elsewhere, was that the Charter Company would induce
some of the local government leaders to sign a treaty, the meaning of
which was not fully explained, and then seize their territory. Treaties
signed by local rulers were thought to confer legal justification for colonial power in an area, but a recurring reality of Charter Company rule
was that this "legal justification" was based on duplicity and deceit.

The worst of the Company's atrocities have few parallels in neighbouring administrations, and there was no doubt about the views of local
residents. Their unrest and discontent are recurring themes in the records
of those years. There is a local proverb that reflects this: "Whenever you
see a toad jumping in broad daylight, then know that something is after
its life."

Colonial conquest

Colonization began to take on a more direct governmental approach at
the turn of the 20th century, when the British government took the area
as a protectorate, following the short interlude of company rule. The only
real colony was Lagos and its immediate environs; the many other areas
that now make up Nigeria were protectorates. The explanation given to
one local ruler of the term "Protectorate", often used in Treaties, was that
Queen Victoria "does not want to take your country or your markets; but
at the same time she undertakes to extend her gracious power and protection, which will leave your country still under your Government."

The protectorates in the south-east were transferred from the Foreign
Office to Colonial Office in 1899, amalgamated and renamed: Protectorate
of Southern Nigeria. In the first weeks of the 20th century, the RNC
Charter was revoked, and the territories south of Idah were incorporated
into the Protectorate.

The eminent Nigerian historian, Y Bala Usman (in a 1994 paper) questions the reasons for this amalgamation, "when clearly by 1898 there was
no serious French or German threat to the British control of these territories. Why didn't the British leave the various colonial entities on their
own, even after taking some of them over from the Royal Niger
Company?"

His response has to do with the local factors of migration, trade, war
and diplomacy that already tied this area into one entity. "They found
that the ecological, economic, political, military, cultural and ideological
networks which had developed in this corner of West Africa made it more
efficient and secure for them to amalgamate the various colonial entities
than to leave them separate. The efficient utilization of Lagos was not
possible without the control of its hinterland, which by the end of the
19th century clearly extended to the Lower Niger. ...

"The area that came to form Nigeria stood out from the rest of West
Africa by virtue of its relative densities of population, its compactness
and the pull of its arteries of communication along and from the River

Niger, Benue and their tributaries. The contemporary situation in which the Federation of Nigeria occupies less than four percent of Africa's territory but has 25 percent of its population [a sizeable market with potential for capital generation] and a significant proportion of its usable natural resources, did not start in the 20th century; and the British had come to realise this before the beginning of this century."

The small polities of the eastern area offered particular tactical difficulties for colonialism because, while they could be overthrown with relative ease, their conquest did not have a lasting effect. A town was defeated and sacked; the local leaders signed a treaty, sometimes paid a fine; then they rebuilt their houses, replanted their crops, and continued life as before. There were another 20 similar towns to conquer within a 30-km radius. Britons who came to join the public service in this period were drawn largely from the military, and came in search of situations that suited their skills. Reports such as that on the Aro oracle and network had to be dramatic enough to elicit Foreign Office support for an expensive military expedition. In that case, a force of 3,500 men in four converging columns attacked Aro-Chukwu and destroyed the oracle in early December 1901. But the town, for all its ritual significance, was of no real strategic importance, situated on the outer edge of Igbo-land. T h e r e were no direct taxes as there were in other colonies further south, but forced labour in road construction or carrying equipment on military expeditions had the same effect, and was often justified by the colonial public servants in terms of the Igbo traditional practice of entrusting public works to certain age groups. But there was a great difference between carrying out projects discussed and approved by the community, in traditional ways, and the often arbitrary and excessive demands of the new regime.

Local resistance occurred when colonial rule was experienced directly, rather than as a dimly comprehended possibility, and it took many forms. Sometimes there was immediate resistance, and sometimes it was postponed to a more propitious time, or when the real nature of foreign rule was more clearly understood. Resistance was often undertaken through secret societies which created guerrilla groups to harass the administration. A missionary wrote in 1910 of almost continuous military expeditions in the interior of Igbo-land.

The conquest of *Ani Ndi Igbo* was not completed with the Aro expedition of 1901-2, but became a long and continuing process of colonial advance and local resistance, still incomplete a decade later at the time of unification of the Colony [Lagos] and Protectorate of Southern Nigeria with the Protectorate of Northern Nigeria in 1914, and when *Abumadu Anyaoku Nwora* died, in 1918. The time of his passing is remembered as near the end of the First World War, because, before he died, he witnessed the first international atmospheric virus resulting from germ warfare — the influenza epidemic carried south from the battlefields of Europe. The people of *Ani Ndi Igbo* resisted colonial conquest with courage, and sometimes with temporary success, but the disparity of arm-aments and state resources meant the contest was unequal, and the colonial presence became a source of bewilderment and despair. The conquest showed clearly that small states are no match in war for large opponents. There is an Igbo proverb: "When a fish is larger than another fish, it swallows it."

A Christian education

A Christian education was the main means of effecting social and political transformation, but this had made little progress by the last years of the 19th century, mainly because the people of the interior had no incentive to welcome a Christian education for their children. Their society provided amply for the moral and vocational training of the young, and they saw little reason to seek European-type skills for themselves or their children until these skills had a value. This value was added with the onset of colonial rule and its opportunities for salaried employment for people with skills that could be used in European commercial or bureaucratic administration — as clerks, missionaries or trading elites.

The only viable local schools attended by Igbo pupils in the 1880s were at Bonny and Onitsha. Local and foreign activists criticized the use of English as the medium of instruction at these schools, and the concentration on English themes. This was the first generation of local children to establish a literary acquaintance with Shakespeare, autumn, snow and daffodils. Eighty years later, a young Igbo writer, Chinua Achebe, derived the title and inscription for his first two novels, about the colonial experience in his country, from the imagery of English poets:

W.B. Yeats, *The Second Coming:*
> "*Things falls apart; the centre cannot hold;*
> *Mere anarchy is loosed upon the world.*"

and T.S. Eliot, *The Journey of the Magi:*
> "*We returned to our places, these Kingdoms,*
> *But no longer at ease here, in the old dispensation,*
> *With an alien people clutching their gods.*
> *I should be glad of another death.*"

In Obosi, a disillusioned missionary gave a summary which can stand for the whole history of CMS endeavour on the Niger in the 19th century. He reported that progress was painfully slow and the people indifferent or hostile. "At first they receive us gladly" but as soon as there are any converts, the inevitable collision occurs with local customs and traditions, and "this cordiality is replaced by coldness and suspicion." The new circumstance had created a spiritual and intellectual crisis for individuals and families over how best to respond. The most common solution was a kind of eclecticism — a personal synthesis of elements of the old and the new.

The CMS mission at Onitsha had a period of reconstruction in the 1890s, with the presence of some European missionaries, including a few women, but primarily local people. And by 1907, there were 70 CMS agents who were Igbo, including the first two ordained Igbo clergymen, George Nicholas Anyegbunam and David Okparabietoa Pepple.

The spread of colonial rule gave missions a new prestige and authority, for now towns invited them, in the hope of obtaining friends and advocates among the new rulers. A rumour that British troops were in the vicinity often helped to persuade local leaders to declare themselves as friends of the church. But the main change that occurred at the onset of colonial rule was that Christian education began to have a commercial value, and there was a real incentive for parents to seek this for their children.

Under Company rule, when local residents had been offered employment only as servants, there was little incentive. Now there were at least two good reasons to seek this type of education: to communicate directly with the new administrators, since intermediaries, recognizing their power, were often corrupted by it; and to seek employment with the colonial government or with commercial firms, as both needed local staff who were educated (preferably to a low level) to fill posts in lower echelons which otherwise had to be filled by people imported from elsewhere — expatriates.

Formal education began to be viewed as a gateway to economic opportunity, even though the range of occupations was limited to policemen, clerks or teachers. They rapidly created a new elite. British officials did not speak Igbo, and few Igbos spoke English, so those who controlled the channels of communication wielded great power, largely as government interpreters and court clerks, policemen and court messengers. Frequent changes of posting, and the intrinsic difficulty of mastering a complex tonal language, continued to dissuade all Europeans except missionaries from learning Igbo. The response of Igbo people to this impasse was to learn English, in the persons of some, at least, of their children.

The educational system expanded, therefore, as a marriage of convenience. Government was eager to use mission personnel and expertise in running schools, and provided subsidies accordingly. For missions, this offered a solution to financial problems and an opportunity to exercise real influence, which they had sought previously in vain. Opportunities increased with the competition among churches for converts, subsidies and students, but the quantitative impact was limited. By 1906, an estimated 6,000 Igbo children were in school. While this seemed a large number when compared with the previous decade, it was a tiny minority of the area's children. In order to attend school and be baptized, they had to accept a foreign name to replace, or add to, the local one, which often had deep cultural significance, identifying unique circumstances about the individual, the family and in a more general sense "the values of the society in which the individual is born." One of the students at the CMS Central School in Onitsha was Anyaoku Nwora's son, Chukwuemeka Anyaoku, who was baptized, and christened Emmanuel (which means in the original Hebrew, "God with us") — even though part of his traditional name, *chukwu*, means "god".

The exact relationship between the Supreme God (Chi Ukwu, or simply Chukwu), the sun and *chi* (personal spirit) in Igbo cosmology will probably never be unravelled, writes Achebe. "But if Chukwu means literally Great Chi, one is almost tempted to borrow the words of Christian dogma and speak of chi as being of the same 'substance' as and 'proceeding' from Chukwu. Or is *chi* an infinitesimal manifestation of Chukwu's infinite essence given to each of us separately and uniquely, as a single ray from the sun's boundless radiance? Or does Chukwu have a separate existence as ruler of a community of *chi*, countless as the stars and as endless in their disparate identities, holding anarchy at bay with His will? ...Chi is [however] more concerned with success or failure than with righteousness and wickedness."

The characteristics of the educational system in the colonial period remained fixed in the pattern formed by 1906. This was a near monopoly of mission societies and inadequate involvement of the colonial government, which ran a few schools and gave insufficient subsidies to mission schools, due to inadequate funds. Nonetheless, education became the new highway to wealth, security and influence — and the random patterns of the colonial era have remained an enduring problem for independent Nigeria as countless individuals, and whole regions, lacked educational opportunities and were condemned to poverty.

Colonial rule was not simply an experience imposed from outside, which Africans accepted. Most towns and most individuals were at times resisters, and at times collaborators. Often the young responded eagerly to change, while the old remained indifferent or hostile. Often it was the students who recognized the opportunities in these new developments, triggering a conflict of generations, such as that between *Abumadu* Anyaoku Nwora and his son, Emmanuel, who inhabited a different world from that of his father. To the missionaries, it appeared, quite simply, that education, Christianity and European culture were aspects of the same phenomenon.

Yet in Igbo philosophy, nothing is absolute; central place is given to "the notion of duality," Achebe says. "Wherever Something stands, Something Else will stand beside it. ...nothing is *totally* anything in Igbo thinking; everything is a question of measure and degree."

Anyaoku Nwora had arranged reluctantly for his son to have a Christian education — to go to school at CMS in Onitsha and be looked after by missionaries.

After primary level, Emmanuel C. Anyaoku went to what was then called Middle School, where his guardian and mentor was a missionary from the Caribbean island of Barbados, Rev. William Blacket. So fond was Blacket of his exceptionally bright young student that he later named his own son, Emeka.

The very process of studying western education at a mission school carried with it the concomitant of adopting the Christian religion, with varying degrees of sincerity and zeal, and inevitably involved some divorce from traditional society. The students were compelled to adopt European dress, as well as baptismal names. Later, the passage of time made both education and Christianity into a secure inheritance, amid new possibilities of creative synthesis with traditional customs. But the beginning was a time of great cultural estrangement, when values were wrenched and dislocated. Traditional values continued to flourish, particularly in the personal commitment to the welfare of the extended family/town, which financed the education of many children, and underpinned the activity of many community development associations.

The combined needs of government, missionaries and local interests led to growth of the mission-run education system, though still geographically limited. The number of schools and scholars grew rapidly later, but throughout the colonial period it remained a minority of Igbo children who attended school.

Emmanuel

The locations chosen for government administration, or by commercial firms for factories, represented the new economic opportunities; and one of the truly revolutionary changes lay in the improvement of communications, which rewrote the economic geography of southern Nigeria. A new governor in 1904 added to his predecessor's passion for military campaigns an equally expensive passion for communications, in the form of roads, railways and telegraphs. He complained to the foreign office that districts were too large, necessitating the sending of military forces repeatedly to the same place. He argued that law and order could not be maintained — and trade extended — in the absence of roads. And he argued that the route of a planned new railway should link Lagos with eastern Nigeria.

Construction of the railway running north from Lagos to Kaduna had already started, and the colonial government was committed to its further extension, to development of Lagos harbour, and to the eventual choice of Lagos as the political and commercial capital. During World War I, the need to exploit the Enugu coalfields gave Igbo-land its railway, to Port Harcourt; and in 1927, this eastern line was extended northward to meet the western line at Kaduna. But road-making was the activity beloved of governors and district officers, because it offered a greater measure of political and military control, expansion in trade, and maintenance of law and order. The advantage to Igbo-land was in expansion of the volume of internal trade.

In addition to railways, the colonial government built roads, bridges, dykes, ports and dams, and installed telephones, telegraph, and radio stations; all locally financed, at no cost to the British taxpayer. The dean of imperial studies at Oxford University noted that southern Nigeria was one of few agricultural colonies which "paid its way almost from the start, and which even stood the cost of its own prolonged and expensive occupation." Government revenue, which was one million pounds in 1906, had almost trebled by 1913; the volume of trade doubled in the same period, to exports of seven million pounds and imports from Britain valued at six million pounds.

In traditional Igbo society, there had been a high degree of geographical mobility, and internal migrations had the effect of maintaining the ecological balance between population and resources; but the imposition of colonial rule froze settlements into the patterns which existed at the time, creating pockets of discontent and hardship. Intense population pressures in some areas could no longer be relieved by internal migration, so many people had to leave the land and settle in urban areas. This was one of the causes of the Igbo diaspora — the move to other parts of Nigeria or to other African countries — that is so striking a feature of their 20th century history.

One of those who moved away in his youth was Emmanuel C. Anyaoku, who took a job as a clerk with the railways, after finishing his studies, and went to Kaduna, where he later worked in the hospital. He encountered some difficulties there, however, when he was arrested and locked up after an incident in which the doctor, an expatriate named Drinkwater, called him a bastard. The greatest insult for anybody of his comparable background is to say he has no father. So Emmanuel became indignant and punched Drinkwater. He was locked up in a police cell until the information got to the Resident, who had him released, but he lost his job. So he returned to eastern Nigeria, and became a teacher at a mission school for a number of years. After that, he went home to farm. He rejected many of his traditional customs, choosing others inspired by his Christian education, but he retained deep family connections.

Unlike his father Anyaoku Nwora, Emmanuel became deeply converted to Christianity and accepted the wisdom of the age, spread by missionaries, that traditional customs, rituals and titles were expressions of paganism. Because he was a very serious Christian, he refused to take the chieftaincy to which he was entitled. In the titled families, someone is chosen to succeed to a title that the family possesses. These titles belong to family groups; and the elders of the family, the titled people, decide who will succeed, whenever a title becomes vacant. Emmanuel C. Anyaoku turned his back on this. Henceforth, he was known as *Ononukpo*, "he who perches on the throne but does not sit inside it." The people of Okpuno-Ire continued to regard him as the man who should be *Abumadu*, even though his beliefs inclined him not to take up the responsibility.

The 1920s were a time of great turmoil in Obosi, particularly for the titled elders and the ruling societies. Indirect colonial rule had initiated new institutions which had no equivalent in traditional society, such as Native Courts and their personnel, the Warrant Chiefs. These were not usually the traditional elders of a town, but were often junior members of the community. Abuse of office became legendary, and the position was often used for personal gain and aggrandizement. In traditional society, such a position of responsibility was surrounded by a network of duties, expectations and obligations, known to the incumbent and to society as a whole. If he failed to fulfil them, he would feel the weight of popular dis-approval. There were no such checks and balances on a Warrant Chief, who was responsible only to the colonial authority, which alone had power to dismiss him. This time of uncertainty merits an explanation in Iweka-Nuno's book on *The History of Obosi,* under the subtitle, The Present Condition of Ruling at Obosi:

"Since the end of 1915 to the present year, 1923, there was existing a strong agitation in the town of Obosi. This was due to the vindictive and litigious feelings of the people because of the dissension between the pre-sent Head Chief and Elders (consisting of Ndichies, etc.) of the town, in the choice of a Warrant Ruling Chief, which, after all, was termed as an 'Eze'."

The Elders and Ndichies had declined to nominate the Warrant Chief as their head, "as that particular family, according to the ancient customs of nomination at Obosi, are out of the lineage. ...[but] Government have over-ruled. ...Thus the town of Obosi became divided, as in the case of Charles I. And Parliament."

Therefore, "the General Systems, Laws and Customs of, and Methods of Ruling the Town of Obosi — those which are right in the sight of God as well as the English Government — were hidden to the eyes of the pub-lic by misapprehensions of the people and some occasional wavering, because of many misleading representations by the people of the neigh-bouring Towns, as well as by some of the inhabitants of the town them-selves, who, in order to benefit themselves and their affairs, are altering the customs and good systems of Obosi. ...For which state of affairs it is considered advisable and highly necessary to bring before the public a history of Obosi. ..."

Emmanuel C. Anyaoku, at this time, was the eldest of three surviving children, with a brother, Geoffrey Egwuenu, and a sister, Christiana Afulenu. His first wife had died in childbirth, and their daughter, Elizabeth, did not survive. Despite, or perhaps because of, his Christian education, he took a keen interest in his ancestry and he prepared the Ezuge Genealogical Table "as written down by E.C. Anyaoku, June 1934". He was the first to enter a woman's name on the table — that of his sis-ter, Afulenu.

Cecilia Adiba

After returning from Kaduna in 1930, Emmanuel Anyaoku had married again — to Cecilia Adiba Ogbogu. Her father was a traditionalist and her mother wore heavy ivory bands around her legs and arms, but had her own title, *Nyamala*. She came from Ugamuma quarter of Obosi. Her family was very meticulous, and never married into any family remotely related, as far back as five generations, through a detailed study of the family origins of the prospective spouse.

Cecilia Adiba Ogbogu lived at the home of Rev. Ekpunobi, her guardian, who was the first Obosi to be ordained as an Anglican priest, having been baptized, at the age of 12 or 14, in 1884. In terms of enlightenment, he was the educated man of the community. So some families were eager to send their children to live with him and his family in their formative years.

Cecilia Adiba's birthday is not known, exactly, but she was born just before the first World War. She was known as Influenza Child because, during that war in Europe, toxic atmospheric contaminants, such as influenza, travelled to Africa. Cecilia Adiba studied domestic science and lived with the Ekpunobi family until she finished school. When Ekpunobi learned that Emmanuel's wife had died, he wrote, asking him to come. And marriage was arranged to Cecilia, according to traditional customs and Christian rites, but with little ceremony since Emmanuel had been married before. Their first-born child, a daughter, did not survive. The next, a son, born on 18 January 1933, was given almost the same name as his father: Eleazar Chukwuemeka Anyaoku. Five more children followed. Bertram Ogugua Anyaoku became a respected engineer after taking degrees in London, Netherlands, and Australia (although his father did not approve of him travelling so far away from home). After Bertram came a sister, Adaora, who later married Ekpunobi's son, Christian, a lawyer. After Adaora, there was another sister who died, named Elizabeth after the first daughter from the first marriage who did not live — like the spirit-children, *abiku* or *ogbanje*, who make a pact not to remain in this world but to return to their own. Elizabeth survived to her teens, but died just before her 16th birthday, of tetanus, after stepping on a rusty nail. Then came Timothy, who also died, and after him, the twins. One was Fanny, who became headmistress of a girls' secondary school at Obosi; the other, Mabel Uzona, was educated in Obosi, but later married and moved to Owerri. Their mother, *Asilugo* Cecilia Adiba Anyaoku, died in childbirth, when her eldest son was just 15 years old.

Emmanuel Anyaoku married again, for the third time, and produced another son, Onochie, who also became an engineer and, at a very young age, production manager in one of the oil refineries. Emmanuel, the father, died in 1962. He saw independence, and the engagement of his eldest son, but he never saw the bridge over the river Niger at Asaba, completed two years after his death. The river crossing had continued by ferry, as there was no bridge, long after the road was built from Onitsha to Lagos in the early 20th century. Although the road spanned much of his lifetime, the river remained an essential part of his life.

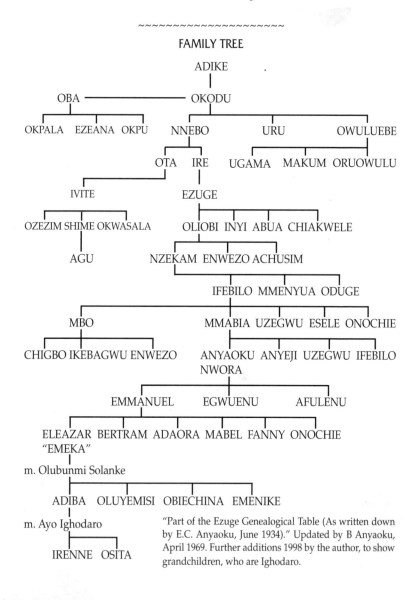

~~~~~~~~~~~~~~~~~~~~

FAMILY TREE

ADIKE
|
OBA ———————————— OKODU

OKPALA   EZEANA   OKPU   NNEBO   URU   OWULUEBE

OTA   IRE   UGAMA   MAKUM   ORUOWULU

IVITE   EZUGE

OZEZIM   SHIME   OKWASALA   OLIOBI   INYI   ABUA   CHIAKWELE

AGU   NZEKAM   ENWEZO   ACHUSIM

IFEBILO   MMENYUA   ODUGE

MBO   MMABIA   UZEGWU   ESELE   ONOCHIE

CHIGBO   IKEBAGWU   ENWEZO   ANYAOKU   ANYEJI   UZEGWU   IFEBILO
NWORA

EMMANUEL   EGWUENU   AFULENU

ELEAZAR   BERTRAM   ADAORA   MABEL   FANNY   ONOCHIE
"EMEKA"
|
m. Olubunmi Solanke

ADIBA   OLUYEMISI   OBIECHINA   EMENIKE
|
m. Ayo Ighodaro

IRENNE   OSITA

"Part of the Ezuge Genealogical Table (As written down by E.C. Anyaoku, June 1934)." Updated by B Anyaoku, April 1969. Further additions 1998 by the author, to show grandchildren, who are Ighodaro.

6

TOWARD A COMMON HUMANITY

Let us not go over the old ground; let us rather prepare for what is to come.
Cicero, "one of my favourite advocates"
(Anyaoku, The Task for Auckland, Commonwealth Trust, 1995)

DURING THE COLONIAL period in Nigeria, which covered just over
half of the 20th century and into which Eleazar Chukwuemeka "Emeka"
Anyaoku was born in 1933, Igboland remained essentially a self-sufficient agricultural economy. The basis of production was still the peasant,
engaged in subsistence agriculture, and collecting or processing palm
products for export. The area's inaccessible geography, hot climate and
dense population continued to discourage European settlement. The
interlude of colonial rule was short, less than 80 years from the first protectorate to independence — and the inhabitants did not become tres-
passers on their own land, as did Kikuyu villagers in Kenya, or Shona
farmers in Zimbabwe.

The Anyaoku compound in Okpuno-Ire was the meeting place for
residents of the heart of Obosi's Ire quarter, and there was a large open
space in front of the gate for that purpose. It remains a meeting place
today — for public discussions, announcements and celebrations. The
plot was larger when grandfather Anyaoku Nwora lived there, before it
was subdivided among his three children and the families who served
him. In great-grandfather's time, it was bigger still. Obosi — now a "village" of 250,000 people — was more wooded then, and rural, with fewer
people and fewer homes. Leopards and other wild animals were sighted
occasionally, and one old Obosi man still living, killed a leopard there,
earning himself the Igbo title, *Ogbuagu.*

By the time Eleazar Anyaoku started school, his father was a crop
farmer who produced yams and cassava, and had a number of large
farms. At home, there were goats, a few cows and a lot of chickens. His

father continued to refuse installation into his chieftancy title, although he had begun to perform a number of traditional duties, and he continued to be known as *Ononukpo* of Okpuno-Ire, "he who perches on the throne but does not sit in it".

The eldest son did not go to school in Obosi, though he returned regularly for the holidays. At the age of seven, he was sent to board with a guardian, as had been his mother and father before him. In the same tradition, he went to live with his father's only brother, Egwuenu Anyaoku, at Umuahia, for purposes of education. One of his friends in pre-primary school, Godfrey Eneli (who died as a Chief in 1998), recalled that "it was a very rural school, the highest class was standard four. ...with the colonial situation in those days, they really didn't encourage pupils to go beyond standard four or standard six."

Godfrey Eneli's father was a catechist in the church at Umuahia, when Eleazar Anyaoku was living with his uncle at the Nigeria Railways station. Eneli said that he, too, "lived beside the rail line, but the preoccupation that was uppermost in my mind was that he [my father] had to wait every Monday or Tuesday by the rail line to receive the *West African Pilot*, Dr Azikiwe's newspaper. ...It was a sign of respect for Zik that even to deliver his newspaper, the railway would pass where my father was living, and it would slow down to drop the papers."

Chief Eneli later recalled his friend Anyaoku as a very active young man. "I had the idea that he would become a leader, which he exhibited every time we all went home on holidays. My recollection of him is that of a very young, active person who despite the idea which we all resented in those days, of serving people whom our parents felt we should go and live with, so that we could learn from them, we nevertheless tried to show that we could do something purposeful for the future. At Obosi, in the village, during holidays, especially Easter time and more particularly at Christmas time, when students came home, we used to have debates, and all kinds of student activities, under the auspices of the Obosi Students Association. At that time, he showed a particular amount of leadership qualities. We used to call him 'lawyer', because he was always arguing, and logical in what he approached. We would be persuaded by his intellect and by his argument, and his approach to whatever discussions we had."

At the age of 10, in 1943, the young Anyaoku moved on to stay with his father's cousin, Nathaniel O. Enwezo, who was headmaster at CMS Central School at Agbor, 75 km from Obosi.

Merchants of Light

For secondary level, there was a new boarding school at Oba called Merchants of Light (MoL), founded by a friend of his father's, Dr Enoch Oli, a Nigerian educationalist trained in London and Oxford. Mr Oli liked to teach his students to speak with a proper English accent by encouraging them to read out aloud the words from the Oxford English Dictionary, until they were tired. There were some 60 boys in the second intake, and when they sat the Cambridge School Certificate examination, young Anyaoku sat 10 subjects and earned the school's first grade one pass, the highest level. Only once, in the first end-of-year exam, he was bested by a classmate who later became a top banker and civil servant, S.I. Metu.

"Mr Anyaoku we all met in 1947, as young men around the age of 14. He appeared to me as a smart, brilliant young man," Metu said later. "These facts were further established when we started living together in the dormitory. In the first year of our stay in the school, we enjoyed his company. And I'm glad to state that in the first end-of-the-year exam of that year, I beat Anyaoku. ... But little did we know that, in that first year, Anyaoku was just reconnoitering the position, and was assessing all of us. After that first year, nobody saw his back again. He set the pace — in Latin, English, he was an all-rounder. And in the School Certificate examination, he came out in the first place, which was no mean achievement, for a new school, which was only six years old. One of his popularities was that he was a very good mixer, he virtually had no enemies because of his general friendliness. ...

"From all we now know of Mr Anyaoku, it is obvious that he was destined to be a diplomat, because he had all the makings — intelligence, friendliness, the ability to get things without offending anybody. So we were not surprised that, soon after Anyaoku left us, he was able to make the entrance to Ibadan university, which was no mean achievement in those days. Even at Ibadan university, he kept maintaining high records. And he left that university as one of the best students. From there, he moved into a diplomatic career, where he has risen to a very eminent position in the world.

"Anyaoku cannot spare any moment for play — he was always reading or working on something. Or occasionally, when he was tired and wanted to relax, he would crack some very serious jokes and everybody would be laughing.

"I remember one incident in the class, when our teacher made a rule forbidding everyone from speaking the vernacular in the class. This was an attempt to make us improve our English. We all kept to these rules, because the punishment was serious. It happened that one of the days, Mr Okoroafor [the teacher] laughed, after an incident in the class. Mr Anyaoku raised his hand to the teacher, and said, I have something to say. ...Mr Okoroafor is laughing in Igbo. The class burst into laughter. The teacher then asked, but how else could he have laughed? The reply was that, he could have laughed in English. Then he was asked to tell us how someone could laugh in English. He said, Mr Okoroafor could have laughed, 'haw, haw, haw' ...And the class burst into roaring laughter...

"These are some of Anyaoku's jokes. There was one incident when we had our history master, the late D.I. Aneto. Aneto had a senior teacher's in English and History, which was no small consideration in those days. He taught us history in such a way that we all enjoyed his lectures. Aneto was fond of weaving some bombastic words. As he used them, it was correct to speak this Oxonian English, but Mr Aneto could be a taskmaster in his art, and we all enjoyed it. It happened that particular day, when he was teaching us about the American war of independence, he spoke such beautiful English that, at one point, the whole class was silent as a grave, in attention. When he continued speaking like that, Mr Anyaoku got up, packed his books, and left the class. Everybody was surprised. The teacher sent for him, and asked him, 'Why have you left?' Anyaoku said, 'The volume of English I have heard in this class today is higher than the school fees I have paid.' And so he had decided to leave. And the whole class roared into laughter. ..."

The same teacher, Aneto, to make a point, once gave him 105% in a history exam.

It was in early 1951 when Benny Asomba entered MoL school, in the sixth intake. When the previous year's results came out, they were posted on the notice board. "One morning, I think it was about noon, I saw every person rushing to the notice board, and shouting Emeka Anyaoku, Emeka Anyaoku, and I discovered that he had As in almost all subjects, which he offered at every school certificate examination. In fact, that was so much that even those who didn't know him became so much interested, and caused all of us to say, I must be like Emeka Anyaoku in my own time."

Young Emeka was a lively boy who occasionally skipped out of school to join the masquerades. In that area of Nigeria, the masquerades — elaborate disguises made from wood and paper and cloth — are represented by huge birds called *ugo*, such as eagles and peacocks, never as human beings. For every young Obosi male, it was something to look forward to, the process of production of masquerades which, in their traditional sense, represented the ancestors, and were regarded as spiritual beings, not as normal human beings wearing masks. These would not normally speak, or make noise, but when they had to speak, the sound was disfigured, so the voice could not be recognized. Some masquerades — for ancestors who died happily with no grudges against the society — would reappear in fine form, beautifully crafted, dancing happily and entertaining. The spirits of those who died unhappily, bearing a grudge against society, would appear in the form of masquerades that looked ugly and were often equipped with whips; people would run away from these *ayaka*, particularly young people and women, other than elderly women. Women were not supposed to have anything to do with the masquerades, and only young boys got initiated — through learning what the masquerades were and how they came about, and gaining the qualification to participate in the production of masquerades.

The initiation into masquerades, called *ima-muo*, was a ceremony performed by the older members, who told the history and mythology of the masquerades. *Ima-muo* means, to understand what the masquerades are all about. Induction was by age group, between the ages of 10 - 14, and after initiation a boy could play the masquerades. The boys considered brave were inducted first, at a younger age. Eleazar, as he still was, was 10 years old when he was initiated into the masquerades in Obosi with a number of his age-mates.

Even when he transferred to MoL, a boys' boarding school, he would slip out, instead of playing games or sports at the school, to play the masquerades at Eke market day, like a carnival or fair, held every month at the marketplace. (*Eke* is a shrine, usually in a marketplace.) When he was caught, he was punished; but the headmaster, Dr Oli, made it clear that the punishment was not for playing *ayaka*, but for slipping out of school, flouting regulations and not taking part in conventional sports. Anyaoku's father, though not happy about his son missing school, tolerated this behaviour, because he, too, considered the masquerades as a sport.

Family traditions, values and beliefs were learned, not from his father — who refused to perform the rituals to have the *ofo* (the symbol of ancestry possessed by heads of families) in the house — but from other sources: his grandmother, and his second uncle at Okpuno-Ire, the father of Mbidebe Ogalanya (who is now his representative in local government and village matters). The *ofo*, named for the tree from whose branch it is taken and consecrated, remains at Mbidebe's house until today, due to the ceremony associated with its return. *Ofo* is "a male symbol that primarily represents ancestral power and authority, and the key values of truth and justice, values believed to be fundamental to the building up of human society." (Ejizu, 1987; Aguwa, 1995) The force of *ofo* is the ruthless avenger against those who perpetrate dishonesty, injustice and deceit.

In the time of nationalism

Emeka Anyaoku's generation was the first outside of Lagos to grow up with the sense of national identity inherent in common usage of the name "Nigeria", and the sense of country fostered by the relatively unified administration of the later colonial period with its legal and bureaucratic system, currency, and spread of communications infrastructure. The nationalist movement that emerged, and the form of the state at independence, however, was the sum of the social traditions of the many and varied local cultures, fused with those of the colonial administration, which left its imprint writ large on the nation lurching towards independence within boundaries created by the jostling of European powers.

The colonial authority was preparing to withdraw, physically at least, from the politics of the area and to leave the people who were caught within those boundaries and systems to create a nation. It would be a multi-nation, born and bred in diversity and duality, fired by civil war and *coups d'etat*, but one nation nonetheless — inspiring fierce loyalty in its citizens.

The world slump of the 1930s had done severe damage to international trade, and therefore government revenue and education programmes; but the protectorate was already in a constant state of change. Communications networks spread; export commodities were diversified; expatriate trading firms expanded; the demand and supply of clerical skills increased for administration and trade; schools spread further into the southern interior; and African entrepreneurs grew in number. Many Nigerians flourished outside the traditional structures, with marketable skills and access to income, and could communicate across linguistic barriers, both colonial and local. It was only a matter of time before they would demand political power to accompany their growing economic power.

As war descended again on Europe in the 1940s and spread to Asia, the economic life of the country was effectively controlled, not by officials in Lagos or London, but by a huge international combine, with financial resources greater than the typical colonial government. Demand for Nigerian raw materials increased, as did the prices, though local sensibilities were offended when big British firms benefited from wartime trade to the detriment of Nigerian enterprise. This power could divert the supply of cotton from the Nigerian looms to the power-looms of Britain; but the war effort depended on its ability to mobilize materials and manpower from the colonies. This gave foreign exposure to large numbers of Nigerians who fought with the Allied forces in Europe, including Anyaoku's future father-in-law who served in the Royal Air Force. An uncle saw action in Burma. "That brought the Second World War more vividly to me and has a special place in my childhood memories."

Within this crucible of war in Europe bubbled feelings of nationalism that returned home to foment change, and strengthened the efforts of those already in the field. The first political party had been founded in 1923 by Herbert Macaulay, a civil engineer, and was an expression of grievances of the educated intelligentsia of Lagos, but it established links with similar movements in other nearby colonies, and played a role in awakening national consciousness, while irritating colonial administrators. Twenty years later, in 1944, Macaulay joined Nnamdi Azikiwe in establishing the National Council of Nigeria and the Cameroons (NCNC), a new congress-type party with affiliation by groups rather than individuals (later renamed National Convention of Nigerian Citizens).

Emeka Anyaoku was still in CMS Central School at Agbor when Azikiwe was touring that year, but he recalls the inspiration he generated as a symbol of Nigerian nationalism. Azikiwe was an Igbo born in 1904 in the North, outside his own ethnic region, where his father was already working in the civil service; and he was one of the first Nigerians to study in the United States, where he acquired his degrees and his nickname — Zik. A formidable athlete, he shed his Christian name Benjamin for Nnamdi in protest after being excluded from the 1934 British Empire Games because the South African team objected to his participation. He served a journalistic apprenticeship in the Gold Coast (Ghana) before returning home in 1937 to establish a string of influential newspapers, including the *West African Pilot*, published in Lagos, and *The Comet*, in Kano. The motto of his flagship newspaper was, "Show the light and the people will find the way." Zik was at home in all three regions of the country, and he was fluent in the three main languages — Hausa, Igbo and Yoruba. His newspapers, pamphlets and speeches set the tone for the nationalist movement for the next 15 years.

The first proposals for constitutional change were drawn up in the British Colonial Office during war-time, and a widespread general strike in 1945, backed by Azikiwe, helped to convince local colonial officials that Nigerians now had the power to disrupt the formal economy if political reform was not forthcoming. Although the post-war policy of the Colonial Office was to initiate steps toward eventual "self-government", the timeframe they envisaged was 30 years — double the eventual transition.

Nationalists now began to feel that power lay within their reach, while others who had been more passive began to realize that the alternative to an active role would be governance by the activists. Not only did the ranks of the nationalist movement split, but new political leaders, particularly in the North, moved in to fill the vacuum of regional leadership created by British notice of withdrawal. Ahmadu Bello, the *Sardauna* of Sokoto — by sheer force of personality as well as belonging to the foremost Fulani family of Sokoto — emerged as the leader who reconciled tradition, modernity and defense of the North. He was assisted by Abubakar Tafawa Balewa, who had come up through the ranks of teacher training and local government service. At a national conference at Ibadan in 1950, the Northern delegates lobbied strongly for a federal — and against a unitary — system of government, arguing that their part of the country lagged behind in educational progress and other social amenities, and they needed time to catch up. Balewa summarized the Northern position:

"The Regions of Nigeria as you are aware have reached different stages in their development. Some of them seem to have advanced very much more than the others and they are therefore now naturally asking to be given the opportunity to make very rapid political advance ... the North is very anxious, not because the North does not like to go at the speed which the other regions are now asking to be allowed to go, but because, honestly speaking, gentlemen, the North is afraid of making this rapid, and if I may call it, artificial advance at this stage."

However, the experience at the Ibadan conference of 1950 had persuaded the *Sardauna* that "we in the North would have to take politics seriously before very long." The primary stages of the 1951 elections in the North had already been held when this combination of modernists and traditionalists transformed a cultural organization into a political party, the Northern People's Congress (NPC). Ahmadu Bello became leader of the new political party and, after the elections, first premier of the Northern Region.

Another man who recognized the political opportunities in this situation of competitive modernity was Obafemi Awolowo, an Ijebu Yoruba who had been active in the Nigeria Youth Movement and opposed to Azikiwe in the dispute that caused the latter to withdraw. Awolowo studied law in London and founded a Yoruba cultural association there in 1945, with a branch in Ibadan in 1947. Through these contacts he launched a political party, the Action Group, just in time for the 1951 elections.

Owerri to Ibadan

These were the predominant national issues and personalities that fed lively discussions at the time Emeka Anyaoku went to teach at Emmanuel College, Owerri, Eastern Region, in 1952, where he lectured until mid-1954, in mathematics, Latin and English. He prepared his lessons with a care unusual in one so young and, with humour as one of his teaching aides, earnestly tried to give back to the students what he had gained from MoL. His own thoughts, however, were in a world outside his time and borders. One of his secondary school teachers had ignited an interest in the Classics, and he had set his sights on continuing his studies at the new University College of Ibadan, the first one in the country, which had opened in 1948.

In the meantime, he and his friends discussed events closer to home, argued and planned, with growing impatience over the slow pace towards independence. They listened to radio broadcasts, avidly read the newspapers, and followed the campaign for the December elections, although they could not yet express their own choice through the ballot box. In these "indirect" elections, organized around a complex preliminary system of pre-election "primaries", communities in each of the three regions sent representatives to their new Regional Assembly in Enugu, Ibadan or Kaduna. These Assemblies then functioned as electoral colleges, deciding whom they would send to the House of Representatives in Lagos.

The divisions in Southern politics, personalized in the irreconcilable rivalry of the two leading figures, Azikiwe and Awolowo, which would span four decades, were entrenched by the 1951 elections. Azikiwe's NCNC, comprising representation from most parts of the country and many ethnic groups, apparently won a majority in both the Eastern and Western Houses of Assembly. But when the Western House convened in Ibadan in early January 1952, there was a period of confusion during which both parties sought the allegiance of elected members and several crossed over to the Action Group, having been persuaded by various means that leadership of the province should not be held by a "foreigner" — although many Yoruba communities were opposed to Ijebu leadership and stayed with the NCNC, including Akure, Ibadan and Oyo. The desire to avoid "stranger" domination was one of the strongest elements in organizing political support in this period, and party support depended on social class and recent history as well as ethnicity, especially at a national level. Later on, concern for amenities such as water supplies, hospitals and schools became a consideration.

Awolowo became premier of the Western Region; Azikiwe returned to his roots in Eastern Region and regained the office of premier; and the Hausa-Fulani/Kanuri joined forces to do the same in the North, under the premiership of Ahmadu Bello, *Sardauna* of Sokoto. Regional legislatures were empowered to legislate on education, agriculture, health and local government. The centre could legislate on all sectors, including those on the regional list. The parties that dominated the new national legislature were also regionally based, and the prospect of independence, however distant, sharpened rivalries for power and position. Though independence was still almost a decade away, Nigerian politics had already assumed many of the characteristics it would endure for the next 15 years, and which would lead to the breakdown of post-independence civilian government in 1966.

There was a certain pride in Owerri and other eastern cities in the leadership of Azikiwe, and in the NCNC, which continued to be the main nationalist movement, putting all of its energies into the constitutional process, yet unable to organize itself into a cohesive national political party and actively opposed by the colonial authorities.

"For me as a young lad, as a student at university, and in my early working years, Zik was an icon," Anyaoku recalls. "He inspired, I believe, most young Nigerians, irrespective of tribe, or region of origin. We saw him as the archetypal Nigerian, far above tribal prejudices and tribal divisions. And I suppose that if I am to speak briefly about my assessment of him, I must begin with the period up to about 1951, when he was an undoubted Nigerian nationalist. And then in 1951, he suffered a rude shock, which I believe left a mark on him; but still a mark that in his last years, he struggled to overcome."

Just before the Easter break of 1953, Anyaoku and his fellow teachers at Emmanuel College, Owerri, read in the newspapers of 1 April, a lively account of a private member's bill introduced the previous day in the

House of Representatives by Anthony Enahoro of the Action Group —
that the House pray ask the British government to grant independence to
Nigeria in 1956. The front pages of the newspapers were taken up with
descriptions of the melée that followed, after the *Sardauna* of Sokoto had
first demanded withdrawal of the motion, due to lack of prior consultation, and then proposed that the date be removed. His real concern was
time — for social change and higher levels of formal education in the
North to "level the playing field" with the Southern intelligentsia. The
motion for independence, as amended, was passed by NPC members
constituting a majority, but only after the Southern parties had left the
House, in a walk-out led by Zik, Awolowo and their supporters. There
was mayhem among the crowds outside the House, shouting slogans and
abusing the NPC, whose 10 members had to be escorted to the safety of
their cars. They left immediately by train for Kaduna, seat of the
Northern Regional Assembly.

The following week, the newspapers carried further stories, datelined
Kano, about the attacks on Igbo houses, shops and schools; at least 70
people were dead and hundreds wounded. Despite the fact that the bill
was introduced by a Yoruba and the riots sparked by an Action Group
decision to send a Hausa-speaking Yoruba, S.L. Akintola, to campaign in
the North, the Igbo residents of Kano were an easy target: they controlled
the markets and the informal trade, they had separate schools for their
children, different religious beliefs (Christians in the predominantly
Muslim North), and lived apart.

Since formal education was closely linked to missionary work, which
had developed little in the North, the colonial bureaucracy looked to the
South for clerks to administer the technical and commercial functioning
of infrastructure such as railways. Those who came were mainly Igbos
from the south-east and almost all Christians, and they retained a social
identification with their place of origin. They lived in *sabon gari* (new
parts of old towns), married within their own religious and ethnic group,
and retained administrative power, even over educated Northerners,
who found it difficult initially to break the Southern monopoly Igbo
clerks and officials made a substantial contribution to the modernization
of the North, but sometimes exercised a tyranny typical of petty official-
dom. Some Northerners blamed Azikiwe, with his chain of newspapers.

Many Igbo families packed up and returned home to the East. In
Owerri and other towns, there was much commotion as relatives returned
from the North; and there was angry debate about the make-up of the
Federation and the Eastern Region's role in it, especially among chiefs and

the educated elite. When Zik had lost the Western premiership the previous year, some members of the Eastern Regional Assembly had suggested breaking away, leaving the Federation. But now it was the North that was determined to go it alone, a position strongly discouraged by the British administrators — mindful of the very large and influential, but landlocked, territory in the North and reminding its rulers of their reliance on southern seaports. After unsuccessfully investigating the possibility of finding outlets to the sea that bypassed southern Nigeria, the contradictions of this period left the Northern political leaders determined to use every political and constitutional mechanism at their disposal to avoid Southern control over matters that touched on Northern interests.

So it was, that on a very cool summer day at the end of July 1953, five representatives of each political party assembled under the chandeliers in an ornate hall at Lancaster House, London, for constitutional talks, chaired by Prime Minister Winston Churchill's Secretary of State for the Colonies. These talks concerned the third constitution in seven years. The pattern had been established that each formula that emerged would be tried for some time, until a breakdown, then more constitutional talks would be held — characterized by sustained bargaining with British colonial officials who insisted they had nothing at stake except survival of the Federation of Nigeria.

The threat of Northern secession cast a long shadow over the deliberations, a chill factor in keeping with the unseasonably cool London summer, especially for the Southern representatives more accustomed to the coastal heat. This was punctured periodically by the enlightenment of the chairman who assured the delegates that British presence was the only thing holding the country together. *Malam* (teacher) Abubakar Tafawa Balewa spoke for the NPC and the North, presenting a proposal for three separate entities (or nations), each with their own defense, customs, external affairs, etc. loosely grouped in a customs union with no central legislative body. The Action Group wanted independence now, with constitutional details to be settled afterwards, and Zik spoke on behalf of the NCNC about the principles of democracy and equality.

By the end of the constitutional talks, Nigeria had the loosest federal arrangement it was ever to have, with a national legislature and police force, defense, external affairs, and revenue collection, but almost all other responsibilities devolved to the regions. The North's claim to half of the seats in the national legislature had been reinforced by a 1952 census, aimed at confirmation of the comparative regional breakdown, which put the national population at just under 30.5 million and the population of the North at just under 17 million. Lagos was excised from the Western Region into a federal territory at the insistence of Northern representatives, acutely concerned about guaranteeing their access to the sea.

All of this was reported in the press and read avidly by the teachers at Emmanuel College, Owerri, including Anyaoku, as he prepared to pack his belongings and travel to Ibadan, seat of the Western House of Assembly and of the University College, to resume his studies. He had been preoccupied in recent months with family matters as he and his father, both determined individuals, disagreed over the course of his future studies.

His heart was set on the Classics, but his father saw no practical career path in this and insisted that his son should read law. So strong were Emmanuel Anyaoku's views that, when his son first told him of his intention to read Classics, he flatly refused him permission to do so. So strong was the loyalty of the son that he now says, "Had he sustained that position to the very end, my life would have been different for me. In the end, he relented when he saw how determined I was — not so much determined as absolutely devoted to the idea."

Influenced to Classics by his Latin teacher at MoL, who inspired a keen interest in the language, laws and culture of the ancient Greeks and Romans, and the classical roots of the English language, he obtained a London University Honours Degree in 1959, as a college scholar. "I belong to the group of people who hold the view that the Classics train you in the art of thinking precisely, and humanely," he says. "Mathematics trains your mind to think precisely but not necessarily humanely. Classics does both."

Professor Arnold von Salis Bradshaw, who taught Greek at Ibadan University College, still recalls the deep voice, the wit and the ready laugh of the young student with a voracious appetite for learning, who, in his university days had already developed the charm that would propel him into a distinguished diplomatic career.

Over 30 years later, at the height of a public debate in Britain on the value of a classical education, which had produced many of the top echelon of British civil servants and financiers, another Classics professor who had taught at Ibadan wrote a letter to the *Daily Telegraph* — in defense of the Classics. That letter, written by the late Professor John Ferguson, said if anyone doubted the value of a classical education, particularly in the Third World, they should look at the careers of Emeka Anyaoku and Gamaliel Onosode, both Ibadan alumni and Classics scholars.

Independence

The debate on federalism was sharply defined during the mid-1950s when Anyaoku was at University College, and Ibadan was one of the main epicentres of debate, bringing together students and politicians from different parts of the country, primarily from the South. The College was the first such institution in the country, attracting some of the best minds of their generation, and it became a centre of "radical national-ism", with debates, discussions and demonstrations focusing on how and when Nigeria would become independent, and in what form.

Anyaoku was one of the student union leaders who campaigned against federalism, in favour of a unitary state, and sent petitions and del-egations to the three most prominent political leaders — Zik, Awolowo, and the *Sardauna* — opposing the creation of three regions in a federal Nigeria. A firm supporter of a strong central government in a unitary nation, he believed that, if it was to be administered in regions or provinces, there should be 22 (as there would be over two decades later), and that a federation in which one region was considerably larger and more powerful than the others was non-functional.

The bargaining and political interaction that took place in the decade of the 1950s was hotly debated by the students at Ibadan. The debate, which set the stage for the politics of independence, dealt with five main issues: the timing of independence; the status of Lagos; the division of powers between the centre and the regions; revenue allocation; and the provisions for minorities.

In many ways, Nigeria is a country of minorities, and during this period, they made their views known, often collaborating within an area to amplify their voices. Most vocal were the Middle Belt people in Northern Region, the Mid-Westerners in Western Region, and in Eastern Region, the Calabar-Ogoja-Rivers (COR) peoples; but only the Mid-Westerners were homogeneous enough to make a difference. They voted consistently against Awolowo's Action Group, the Western Region's majority party, in all pre-independence elections. In the federal election of 1954, the first direct constituency election at national level, they gave enough support to Azikiwe's NCNC to win a majority of Western Region seats in the national assembly; while Action Group remained the majori-ty at regional level, and regional premiers remained the same "big three". These elections were fought largely on local matters; the voters cared lit-tle about regional or national affairs. Women could not yet vote in the North.

The Mid-Westerners failed in their bid to have more regions established before independence. No governing party would agree to reduce its territory and population, and there was no sympathy from the colonial authorities who thought the minority areas neither capable of being administered as single units in a federation nor economically viable, and wanted to maintain the hegemony of the North as one unit. None of the players wanted to be blamed for prolonging colonial rule, so this was left for solution after independence. When the new post of Federal Prime Minister was created in 1957, the *Sardauna* chose to remain in the North as premier, and sent *Malam* Tafawa Balewa to take up the post. Both were given British knighthoods in 1960, with the honorific title, *Sir*.

The results of the federal election of 12 December 1959 were predictable, with the party in power in each of the three regions winning by a handsome majority. Less predictable was that, despite the discriminatory allocation of amenities and patronage, and considerable use of intimidation against communities and leaders, many minority groups continued to vote against the parties in power. After the election, Azikiwe's NCNC decided to carry out a pre-election understanding with Bello's NPC and formed a national coalition government, in the belief that they could prevent the polarization of federal politics along North-South lines which could lead to the break-up of the country. The constant threat of the North during constitutional negotiations to withdraw from the country still echoed. It was not yet foreseen how monolithic would become the voting in the North, which was allocated 55 percent of federal seats for the 1959 election on the basis of the 1952 census.

Balewa remained Prime Minister, with Azikiwe elected President of the Senate in January 1960 and becoming Governor-General at Independence on 1 October 1960 — a date chosen, it is said, to ensure that rain would not mar the ceremony. However, on the day that the red-white-and-blue British flag, the Union Jack, was run down the flagpole for the last time and replaced by the green-and-white flag of independent, federal Nigeria, it rained in Lagos.

Emeka Anyaoku missed the ceremony, and the rain. The previous year, he had joined the Commonwealth Development Corporation (CDC) in Lagos, which sent him on a course to the Royal Institute for Public Administration in London, his first visit to Europe. He was still in London on 1 October 1960, where he joined the formal celebration at Royal Festival Hall, and then adjourned to a lively, noisy, exuberant, coming out party of the already sizeable Nigerian community in London. "The achievement of colonial freedom in Africa," he said later, "brought such joy as can only be measured by those who experienced it." This recalled Kwame Nkrumah's expression of joy at Ghana's independence four years earlier, when he quoted William Wordsworth's immortal lines about the French Revolution of 1789: "Bliss was it in that dawn to be alive, But to be young was very heaven!"

Years later, Chief Anyaoku characterized his generation in the same context as the writer Salmon Rushdie had defined for the independence generation in India, as "midnight's children". Delivering an alumni lecture at Ibadan, he said, "Those of us whose own arrival at maturity coincided with national independence have been accorded the rare gift of growing up with our country and of dedicating ourselves to its service. ... It has been our great privilege but also our weighty responsibility to be the heirs of independence."

Olubunmi

Although the post-independence leadership of government was drawn from different ethnic groups, the high-profile Head of State was Azikiwe, an Igbo, at a time when educated Igbos were moving into the job market in Lagos and elsewhere, in professions which had been exclusively Yoruba, and when the colonial authority was intent on Africanizing the civil service. A spate of books, pamphlets and lectures on Yoruba history, social structures and religion sprang up in Lagos, in a situation of "aggressive ethnicity" between the two main Southern groups of eastern and western Nigeria.

Ethnic identities and loyalties, working through organized groupings and informal contacts, had the positive function of enabling urban migrants to be integrated more easily into the city environment and cushioned against rapid social change. But there was a negative impact of emphasizing social and cultural differences, creating stereotypes by which rival groups were cast in an unfavourable mould, and sharpening individual competition through appeals to group loyalty.

It was during this emotionally polarized period in Lagos that Emeka Anyaoku met a tall, attractive and well-educated, young Yoruba woman at a party, and promised to help her find a job. On that night in December 1961, he and his flat-mate were hosting a bachelor's eve party for a well-known musician friend, Akin Euba, and one of the guests was Ebunola Olubunmi Solanke. Ms Solanke had turned 20 earlier that year, and had just returned from England where she had gone for education, in the tradition of her family, in the fashion of her mother and grandmother before her, the latter educated first in Sierra Leone. It was fashionable at that time, among upper middle-class Yoruba Christian families settled at the coast, to send their children of both sexes to school overseas, to fulfill the perception of a better education and to provide all possible career opportunities for the next generation.

Bunmi Solanke attended a Christian girls' boarding school, then St Mary's School at Hastings and the Pitman College, London. Back home in Lagos and looking for work, her cousin took her to the party hosted by the young CDC trainee manager. As good as his word, he found her a job, first as secretary at an insurance company, and later, as wife and mother, diplomatic partner, hostess, and community leader.

By the time of their wedding at Cathedral Church in Lagos the following year, on 10 November 1962, the bridegroom had been persuaded to join his country's diplomatic service. The notice in the *Sunday Times*, Lagos, on 25 November, announcing the marriage, said "Miss Solanke is a secretary in a Lagos insurance company and her bridegroom is an official of the Ministry of Foreign Affairs in Lagos." Best man at the wedding was the bridegroom's former classmate in Classics at Ibadan, Gamaliel Onosode.

For his new wife, the strangest part of being married to an Igbo man was a culture with a different socio-political role for women. In Yoruba custom, a woman can be head of the family, according to seniority. Even the church wedding between two Christian families faced a cultural gulf when the minister asked who would "give away" the bride. It was a woman who replied, an aunt who gave the bride away, although an uncle had escorted her down the aisle. For her in-laws-to-be, this was very strange indeed. In their culture, women sat together and men sat together, but this new wife was always sitting next to her husband. In significant family discussions, wives are not brought in, as in Yoruba culture, only male members of the family. If in-laws were coastal Yorubas, they would approach the wife if they needed anything, but in Igbo tradition, the man is head of the home and the relatives go to him. The Yoruba belief that the woman makes the home, so the woman is the home, is different to the Igbo belief that it is the man's home.

Diplomatic service

Bunmi's husband had joined the Nigerian foreign service a few months earlier at the urging of his Prime Minister. Relating the story more than 30 years later, when delivering the first "Sir Abubakar Tafawa Balewa

Annual Memorial Lecture" in Abuja, Emeka Anyaoku paid tribute to the founding Prime Minister and acknowledged "a personal debt of gratitude to my respected careers adviser":

"In early 1962, I accompanied my then boss, Lord Howick, Chairman of the Commonwealth Development Corporation, to a meeting with Sir Abubakar. I was at the time an executive in the West African Regional Office of the CDC. The meeting was about the Corporation's work in Nigeria and the region; but after it, the Prime Minister took an interest in my future and persuaded me to consider joining the Nigerian Foreign Service. In hindsight, I could have had no better guidance."

Sir Abubakar, he said later, "brought a transparent integrity to bear in public service; and in keeping with his own character he stood for a gentle, tolerant and humane Nigeria. ...What Sir Abubakar sought to uphold at all times was the pluralistic Nigeria which we inherited at independence. He saw the strength of the nation deriving from this very diversity and sought to build on it."

Joining the foreign service, however, was not as easy as he had imagined, and his letter of application for a post at the rank of first secretary was forwarded to the Public Service Commission after eight contemporaries who were second secretaries made a joint petition of disapproval at the prospect of a newcomer being offered a higher rank. The Commission chairman asked the applicant if he would accept a lower rank; he said no, and the chairman wanted to know why not.

"I told him, when I was in final year at university, the CDC had interviewed over 100 candidates from Sierra Leone, Ghana, Nigeria and southern Cameroon. They wanted only one candidate as a management trainee. They chose me. I had been trained in London, had experience and salary, and could not accept a secondary rank." The runner-up for the CDC job had been Nzo Ekengaki from Cameroon, who later became Secretary-General of the Organisation of African Unity (OAU).

During the lengthy interview, the prospective foreign service officer was grilled on a number of issues. The permanent secretary of the ministry for external affairs, Francis Nwokedi, asked for his views on the Cuban missile crisis, which was current at that time. When he replied that Fidel Castro's arrangements for the defense of Cuba were very much within Cuba's rights and exercise of its sovereignty, provided it was not an offensive system, the permanent secretary asked if he read the British newspapers. Yes, Anyaoku replied, he did. Did he realize that *The Times* editorial was different to what he had said? "I replied that I presumed the Times editorial was written from the perspective of the British government, while I was giving my own view." *The Times* had questioned the right of Castro to have a defensive missile system.

The interview was very long, with some hostile questions, and the candidate concluded that he would not get the job. The next day, however, he met the acting secretary of the Public Service Commission at a reception given by the Egyptian ambassador and, much to his surprise, was told to expect a letter. One of the hostile questioners had said afterwards, "We haven't interviewed this type for a long while."

Anyaoku joined the foreign service in April 1962, and within a month was appointed personal assistant, then Director, in the Permanent Secretary's Office of the Ministry for External Affairs. In the busy year that followed, he was involved with India and Ghana, and the process leading to formation of the OAU ñ and he met Jawaharlal Nehru.

"I was very much an Nkrumah-ist. So much so that, at the time when Nkrumah was at loggerheads with my own country, I was one of those constantly embarrassed by that conflict between Ghana and Nigeria. I was one of those who worked assiduously for the amalgamation of the Casablanca group and the Monrovia group, that facilitated the creation of the OAU on 25 May, 1963. The reconciliation of the Casablanca group of the more radical African governments (Nkrumah, Nassar, Nyerere, and, believe it or not, Morocco) and the Monrovia group gave birth to the OAU, and I worked for that enthusiastically, as *chef de cabinet* of the permanent secretary of the Ministry for External Affairs in Lagos. Then after that, I always saw great merit in Nkrumah's pan-Africanist approach. I ended up being one of those who most admired his foreign policies but didn't care very much for his domestic policies."

It was in Accra, that he first saw Nelson Mandela, in the brief period that the South African lawyer-activist was outside his country in 1962 before returning in August to arrest, the Rivonia trial and 27 years in prison.

His great fascination for India was also fired in 1962, when the first Indian Prime Minister visited Nigeria in September, with his daughter, Indira. "And so it was that when Jawaharlal Nehru visited Nigeria, I was detailed to be the officer who was attached to him. And I was with him when he viewed Nigeria from the air. It was quite wonderful because, I think he discovered my classical education, and so we talked... among other things, we talked about the non-aligned movement. I accompanied him on a number of his official engagements and so had free moments when he would talk. He was a man who was always asking me about this or that, and encouraging me to ask him.

"We talked about the Congo, we talked about Lumumba's death. I was very encouraged when I discovered that he, too, had been as unhappy as many of us were with how the United Nations really betrayed Patrice Lumumba. That's the view I took at the time. And I remember, his saying to me, you must go to India before long. And I said I would. ...he was such a lovable man, so I got very, very enamoured of him. And then I developed great interest in India. ...

"But before that, the first Indian High Commissioner in Lagos, a Mr. P.N. Haksar, was a very special friend and a diplomat whom I admired very much. Of the Third World Heads of Mission, P.N. Haksar was the brightest, he was brilliant, he was very experienced, and he was very much a non-aligned movement devotee. And I found myself always contriving to encourage him to have appointments with the Prime Minister, to be sure that the non-aligned perspective was fed into the Prime Minister's thinking. We struck a special friendship because of that."

The first British High Commissioner to Nigeria, by contrast, was Lord Head, a former cabinet minister in Harold Macmillan's government who was offered a diplomatic assignment of his choice. In Lagos, he saw himself as being well above other ambassadors and high commissioners. He lived not far from the Prime Minister's residence and external affairs officials often received instructions from the Prime Minister's office following his meetings with Head, which were never arranged through them. The director of the permanent secretary's office always tried to see that the African perspective was injected into the Prime Minister's discussions, for balance.

In 1963, the young foreign service officer, at the age of 30, was posted to Nigeria's Permanent Mission to the United Nations in New York, where, among other things, he drafted the resolution — presented to the General Assembly by Nigeria in 1965 — that established a trust fund to enable governments to contribute to the defense of political detainees in South Africa.

United Nations, New York

New York was exuberant in the early 1960s, a frontier town of the new age at the height of the Kennedy era, and the United Nations was expanding, seemingly, every month, with the membership of a newly independent nation. It was a creative and heady time for the representatives of African and other developing countries, and the possibilities seemed endless. The young Classics scholar from Nigeria never lost his wonder on entering the awesome General Assembly of the United Nations, and the power that could be harnessed there, to good ends and bad.

Soon after the young couple settled down in New York, their first child was born, in New York City Hospital, on 20 November 1963. Just two days later, the US President, John F. Kennedy, was assassinated in Texas, and gloom settled like a fog over the UN diplomatic community. Mother and daughter returned home from the hospital on the day of Kennedy's funeral, in a country that had lost its way and a decade that became ever more violent. Nigeria had become a Republic a few weeks earlier, with Azikiwe as its first President.

The Federal Republic of Nigeria quickly established itself at the UN as a vocal and influential opponent of apartheid in South Africa, and against racism in general, through its Permanent Representative, Chief Simeon Adebo, and his young First Secretary, Emeka Anyaoku, whose talent he recognized and encouraged. The Special Committee Against Apartheid was perhaps the most significant committee for Nigeria, and the First Secretary always attended the meetings and spoke for his country. He was Chairman of the Sub-Committee on Petitions, to which letters and telegrams were forwarded for recommendation on action, including requests for hearings before the Committee, which were always accepted.

In December 1963, on the recommendation of the Special Committee, the General Assembly decided that humanitarian assistance to victims of apartheid was both necessary and appropriate, but an appeal to member states the following year, to contribute through appropriate non-governmental organizations, drew very little response. So the Special Committee decided to recommend the establishment of a Trust Fund for South Africa to which governments could contribute directly. This proposal was made to the General Assembly by the Federal Republic of Nigeria, in a high-profile presentation by a senior government minister sent from Lagos, at the urging of Anyaoku and based on a presentation which he had drafted.

The trust fund proved very successful over the years in attracting sizeable contributions from member states for the legal defense of people charged with political offences in South Africa, assistance to their families, grants for prison education, and assistance to South African refugees, especially in Africa.

As Anyaoku and Nigeria became known in New York, with his advocacy of a non-racial agenda, he was invited for speaking engagements to various parts of the United States. On one occasion, at the University of Wisconsin in Milwaukee, he appeared on a platform with the US Assistant Secretary of State for African Affairs, J. Wayne Fredericks. The

Milwaukee Journal of Sunday, 26 April 1964 carried a report on the young diplomat from Nigeria who argued that Africans wanted to stay out of the Cold War, and wanted to present their own perspective, particularly through the new Organisation of African Unity (OAU).

"All that African states ask of their friends abroad is to be judged objectively, not by comparison with attitudes and events in a different part of the world with entirely different problems and background," he said, a theme he was to return to many times in the years to come. Fredericks, a Kennedy appointee, spoke in favour of this perspective.

"The challenge to be understood" is first among the African challenges to the United States, Fredericks said. "Americans must search behind the headlines of revolts in Zanzibar and Gabon, anti-American demonstrations in Ghana ... and uprisings in the Congo and Rwanda. These are disturbing developments but they do not represent the complete picture." To put developments into perspective, Fredericks said, Americans must look at the underlying causes of unrest, including poverty, "squabbles over boundaries, once arbitrarily drawn by the colonial powers", and the desire for self-determination.

The meeting with Nehru that had fostered a keen interest in the Indian sub-continent, was partly responsible for the friendships that developed with two prominent Indian diplomats in New York. E.S. Reddy was a well-respected official who devoted his career to the Special Committee Against Apartheid, and S.K. Singh, later Foreign Secretary, was in the Indian permanent mission to the UN.

A highlight of that era at the UN, in which they were all actively involved, was the adoption in 1963 of the UN Declaration on the Elimination of All Forms of Racial Discrimination, followed two years later by an International Convention.

In 1964 and early 1965, three diplomats posted to the UN from developing countries — S.K. Singh, Anyaoku and a Brazilian diplomat called Figueiredo, decided to host, in their respective apartments, every six to eight weeks, a get-together of selected diplomats, not to socialize but to exchange views on current issues. They called themselves the "Serious Thinkers Club", and they discussed issues topical in the General Assembly or the Security Council, or international events.

A lively and satisfying stint in New York was capped with the birth of the second Anyaoku child and first son, on 11 February 1965 at New York City Hospital. Later that year, in November, in southern Africa, Ian Smith ignited the fuse on a long-running diplomatic and moral time-bomb that eventually led to almost a decade of war and the deaths of 30,000 people, when he announced Rhodesia's Unilateral Declaration of Independence (UDI) from Britain. Among the many fora which debated this event was one in Philadelphia, in which the Nigerian mission was invited to participate. And so, several weeks later, early in the new year of 1966, the First Secretary went to Philadelphia. And it was there that he heard of what seemed at the time a most unlikely occurrence: a *coup d'etat* in Nigeria.

He takes up the story in his Balewa Lecture, many years later:

"I still remember vividly the deep shock and embarrassment with which I heard the news of Nigeria's first military *coup d'etat* on 15 January 1966. I had flown that morning from New York, where I was serving in our Permanent Mission to the United Nations, to Philadelphia to a debate organized by the local Institute for International Affairs. I was debating against a colleague from the British Mission about the unilateral declaration of independence by the racist minority regime of Ian Smith in the then Rhodesia. My task as a diplomatic representative of a thriving democratic Nigeria was to condemn the UDI and chastise the then British Government of Harold Wilson for not using force to bring the illegal regime to book.

"The question put to me immediately after my presentation by a member of the audience was that I should tell them more about the news of a *coup d'etat* in Nigeria. Finding the thought quite inconceivable at that time, I thanked the questioner for his interest in my country but proceeded to suggest that he might have mistaken Nigeria for Niger where there had been some internal trouble, or perhaps for Algeria, where President Ben Bella had recently been overthrown in a *coup d'etat*. When he persisted by telling that he had on his way to the debate heard on his car radio a report of a military coup in Lagos and that the Prime Minister was reported missing, I immediately excused myself from the hall and rushed to the nearest telephone to call my Ambassador in New York. I was then informed by my Ambassador, the late Chief Adebo, that there was indeed news of some trouble at home and that I should return speedily to New York."

The first meeting of Commonwealth leaders ever convened outside the United Kingdom had just ended in Nigeria, hosted in Lagos by the Prime Minister, The Right Hon. Sir Abubakar Tafawa Balewa, from 10-12 January 1966. The leaders agreed that "to assemble from time to time in a different Commonwealth capital would underline the essential character of the Commonwealth as a free association of equal nations, spanning all races and continents." There were a number of other firsts: it was the first meeting after establishment of the Secretariat; they welcomed the new

Secretary-General, a Canadian; and it was the first meeting called to deal with a single political issue, devoted entirely to the question of Rhodesia.

The leaders of the 19 governments represented expressed their concern at the danger to all multi-racial communities in the Commonwealth, and to the future of the Commonwealth itself, if the situation in Rhodesia were to continue. They recalled that the "principle of one man one vote" was the basis for democracy; and declared that, "The Commonwealth should be able to exercise constructive leadership in the application of democratic principles in a manner which will enable the people of each country of different racial and cultural groups to exist and develop as free and equal citizens."

They agreed that the rebellion must be brought to an end, and accepted that the use of force "could not be precluded if this proved necessary to restore law and order". They noted the statement by the British Prime Minister, Harold Wilson, "that on the expert advice available to him the cumulative effects of economic and financial sanctions might well bring the rebellion to an end within a matter of weeks rather than months. While some Prime Ministers had misgivings in this regard, all expressed the hope that these measures would result in the overthrow of the illegal regime in Southern Rhodesia within the period mentioned by the British Prime Minister."

A number of measures were recommended, including the establishment of two committees: one to regularly review the effect of sanctions, including special needs required to support neighbouring Zambia, such as the emergency transport of oil and vital supplies; and the other to coordinate a special Commonwealth programme to accelerate the training of Africans in Rhodesia. The Sanctions Committee would report back to the Prime Ministers by July at the latest if the rebellion had not ended by then; and the Committee would advise if there was need for action by the UN. Some Prime Ministers reserved the right "if the need arises", to propose mandatory action under Chapter VII of the UN Charter, which deals with threats to international security.

As they met, coup planning was in the final stages. Two days after Commonwealth leaders finished their discussions on Rhodesia and left Nigeria, and just hours after Secretary-General Arnold Smith took his leave, their host Prime Minister Sir Abubakar Tafawa Balewa, the powerful premier of the Northern Region Sir Ahmadu Bello, and a number of other leaders of the post-independence state were killed in the 15 January *coup d'etat*, with the resultant setback to the well-being of both countries. A few weeks later, Kwame Nkrumah was overthrown in a *coup d'etat* in nearby Ghana.

Arnold Smith

The new Commonwealth Secretary-General had begun to assemble a multi-national, multi-cultural team at the core of the new Secretariat. He scrutinized the diplomatic corridors carefully in choosing his staff, and identified a mix of experienced officials and promising young candidates from developing countries who could help him to break down racial stereotypes and superior notions still evident, and change the face and function of the then British-led institution. He was looking for "high flyers" and he wanted a young African diplomat who could join the staff at a senior level, little realizing that he was head-hunting a future Secretary-General who would continue the task of changing racial perspectives long after his own departure.

The proposal for a Commonwealth Secretariat had been approved by heads of government in 1964, over the resistance of some of the original stakeholders, and it was established formally in 1965. Canada's Nobel Peace Prize-winning Prime Minister, Lester B. (Mike) Pearson, was persuaded to send a close friend and colleague as a candidate for Secretary-General. He was a seasoned diplomat in the Pearson mould, Arnold Cantwell Smith, from whom Emeka Anyaoku drew inspiration and guidance over the next decade.

The idea of a Commonwealth Secretariat had been raised by Ghana's first President, Kwame Nkrumah. "Just as he believed that small and isolated African countries could only develop by forging unity among themselves, so he argued that the Commonwealth had to have a higher concept of its future role if it were to survive in world affairs," Smith wrote. "It was no longer an association of like-minded countries deriving their institutions from Britain; the main bond was respect for each other's independence, and if it was to have any future strength its members needed to accept new obligations."

While the proposal for a Secretariat was still being debated, the Queen offered Marlborough House as its headquarters, and when the announcement of her support reached the meeting through the British Prime Minister, it swung the more hesitant leaders. Arnold Smith's own insightful description of the Commonwealth was: "an internal pressure group" in which "the different sections of humanity were pressing each other to adjust to the others' needs."

"Smith was an indefatigable and far-sighted diplomat," Anyaoku wrote many years later, saying he was "in complete tune" with the three worlds of his time: the world of the superpowers still locked in the Cold

War, the industrialized world to which Canada belonged, and the developing world of the Group of 77. "Arnold Smith's passion for the Commonwealth and its immense potential for service to humanity was infectious," Anyaoku recalled, "and happily infected those of us who worked closely with him."

Smith shared the credit for the successes during his tenure, writing later that, "The Commonwealth was fortunate in the staff recruited to the Secretariat in those early years. They provided qualities different from those expected in traditional civil servants." He mentioned a top Indian civil servant, Nirmal Sen Gupta; another Canadian, Gordon Goundrey, with wide-ranging international experience; and Emeka Anyaoku, "whose diplomatic skills were most useful, notably among nationalist leaders in southern Africa and with all the African, Caribbean and Pacific members in the negotiations before the Lomé Convention [signed 1975]."

The other African who occupied a more senior, elected position was Amishadai (Yaw) Adu, the deputy secretary-general for political affairs, who had been the first head of Ghana's foreign service, then secretary to Nkrumah's Cabinet and head of the civil service. Smith later wrote that the Secretariat could not have had a better person "to help give it steadiness and direction in the troubled politics of that time," and it was Adu who travelled to New York to brief Anyaoku.

"When instructions came to New York, towards the end of my stay, that I was being posted to the Commonwealth Secretariat, my first reaction was to protest. I said it was neo-colonialist, what had I done to deserve this? ...I was expecting to go as number two to an important position, given my background. And then this instruction came. The Secretariat had been in existence for barely a few months. So I went to my ambassador and I said I wasn't going. He said I should go and sleep over it. I went and slept over it. The next day, I went to him and still said I wasn't going, and told Lagos. Then, within 10 days, back came two replies. A formal reply that reminded me of the foreign service regulation that you do not refuse a posting without tendering your resignation. But Nwokedi, who was still permanent secretary, knew I would resign. He knew me.

"He wrote me a handwritten letter saying that this man, Arnold Smith, came and saw the Prime Minister — the foreign minister and Nwokedi were there too — and said that he was looking for a Nigerian who would help him to make nonsense of racist myths. The Prime Minister, when he left, asked the foreign minister and the permanent secretary to give him three names, which they did. I was the most junior, of the three names. But I had been secretary to the national security committee at the time of the first coup in West Africa, when Olympio was killed [in Togo], with implications for our national security. On the night of the coup, the committee met until 3 a.m., and the Prime Minister had to have the report by 7 a.m. So I went and prepared the report. At a quarter to 7, I was at the Prime Minister's residence with the report. He said, 'you haven't slept, I'm sure'. And I said, 'I'm hoping to do so later today, sir'. He never forgot that. He had seen me during my days at CDC. He was instrumental in my going into the Nigerian foreign service. He said: 'that young man, send him'. After I was told that background, I was so flattered that I went. ...

"There was an African Deputy Secretary-General, Yaw Adu, who came to New York after that to seek me out. He invited me to lunch in the UN General Assembly, and told me about the Secretariat. I began to like the idea. When I got to London and met Arnold Smith, I took an instant liking to him. When he talked about UDI, it was evident that he meant what he was saying. He really dealt with Rhodesia, and this had been one of my main concerns in New York. I was there during UDI, and so on, and Arnold Smith was talking about the Commonwealth doing this and doing that. And I thought, ah, if that's his view of the Commonwealth, then that's the place for me. So I stayed."

Two small bits of advice often repeated by Smith, were imparted immediately after his own election by Commonwealth Heads of Government. One was given by him and the other was offered by the Ugandan President, Milton Obote, a consummate politician whom Smith described as "one of the most delightful of them all". These anecdotes are told in Smith's autobiography, *Stitches in Time*: "In the sunny courtyard of Marlborough House, at the end of that morning session, I was surrounded by a group of cameramen and journalists, who had just heard of my election. 'What do countries as diverse as Sierra Leone, India and Canada have in common?' one asked sceptically. 'We all need to learn to share a planet,' I replied, 'and we believe that using the Commonwealth can help.'

"I had lunch with Mike Pearson and a small group of other heads of government. After some joking, Milton Obote proceeded to offer some serious advice. 'You will find in due course that you will need a flag and a symbol. When you do, don't ask heads of government to approve a design. We have enough to divide us, and problems enough on which we must think out an agreed solution. Decide what you can for yourself, and do it." Good advice, Smith said, that he never forgot. Nor, he could have added, did his successors.

Early days and attitudes

Emeka Anyaoku's first major assignment, within two months of joining
the Secretariat in April 1966 as Assistant Director of International Affairs,
was secretary to the Review Committee. This committee was set up by
the Secretary-General with the approval of Heads of Government to
review all existing inter-governmental institutions to determine which
should be integrated into the newly established Secretariat. The
Chairman was Lord Sheffield, a former British ambassador to
Washington who had been a senior treasury financial secretary, "one of
the best brains of his time," Anyaoku said later. But their first encounter
showed the scepticism on both sides.

"I wrote my first brief for my Chairman. Clearly he had never worked
closely with people from Africa, his career had not brought him in such
close quarters. I wrote my first brief for him and, after reading it, the next
morning he strolled into my office and said, with evident sincerity and
clear delight and kindness of thought, but unbelievably patronizing,
'Anyaoku, did you really write this?' And I said, 'well my Lord
Chairman, the Secretary-General said he would give me an assistant, but
he hasn't yet.' He understood what I meant. ...Then, a typical British civil
servant, he went and called for my file, my CV; and next day when I
came, he walked in and he said, 'I didn't realize you're a classical scholar. No wonder!'

And that was the beginning of friendship and respect that endured so
much so that... at that time, among his other preoccupations, Lord
Sheffield was Chairman of Hill Samuel, the finance house, which had
established a branch in Nigeria involved in setting up a financial institution. They were keen, under pressure from the Nigerian government, to
find a Nigerian to groom to take over the company. And one day, Lord
Sheffield called me to his desk and told me that two Nigerian names had
been recommended from Lagos to the head office here, for eventual
appointment as Chief Executive in Nigeria. He asked me if by any chance
I knew the people. I looked and I said, 'my Lord Chairman, I must declare
immediately an interest'. He said 'why?' and I said, 'that name was my
best man when I got married. You could do no better'. He said, 'is he anywhere like you?' I said, 'he's better'. He laughed and said, 'you're being
too modest'. And Gamaliel Onosode got the job. It was a measure of the
respect that he had built up for my judgement."

There were a good many incidents with Heads of State that were not
so statesmanlike, and one of those was the hurried mission to Pakistan on

30 January 1972, organized on a few hours' notice, for a meeting with President Zulfikar Ali Bhutto. Soon after Smith arrived in Rawalpindi, his Director of International Affairs, Emeka Anyaoku, listening as ever to the radio news, heard that Bhutto, without waiting for their meeting, had announced Pakistan's withdrawal from the Commonwealth over its members' recognition of the new state of Bangladesh, a country of 75 million people. Seventeen years later, in 1989, Bhutto's daughter, Benazir, returned Pakistan to the Commonwealth at the same summit in Malaysia that elected Anyaoku as its next Secretary-General.

Earlier, when travelling with Arnold Smith to the Caribbean in 1968, the young Nigerian diplomat was surprised to encounter his namesake. In Barbados, where they were guests of the Governor-General, Anyaoku was told of a Barbadian called Emeka ...Emeka Blacket. "I very nearly leapt off my seat, because all that my father recorded in his diary and told me, was that his guardian at school was Rev. William Blacket, a West Indian. He didn't know which island he came from. And I never was able to locate his family. But when the Chief Justice, Sir William Douglas told me, I asked him where was Emeka Blacket then. And Emeka Blacket was headmaster of Bishop's High School in Tobago, in Trinidad & Tobago. So immediately after dinner, the ADC to the Governor-General got him on the telephone and I spoke with him." The two Emekas finally met over 20 years later, in October 1990, at the airport in Tobago when one was visiting as Commonwealth Secretary-General. It made a good human interest story for the local press.

Arms sales and principles: Singapore

The Singapore summit of January 1971, presided over by Prime Minister Lee Kuan Yew, was the first to be called a Commonwealth Heads of Government Meeting (CHOGM), and it was "a real crisis summit," Chief Anyaoku said later. "It was a crisis summit because it was the climax of a very damaging internal debate within the Commonwealth on whether the British government should supply arms to South Africa or not. While the Rhodesian debate was still raging on, to add to it, this debate or controversy over arms supply to South Africa really brought the Commonwealth to the very edge of disintegration."

In preparation for the meeting, and to help to reduce tension over this subject, the idea of a Singapore Declaration of Commonwealth Principles was mooted, carefully prepared with full backing of the Secretary-General, by Emeka Anyaoku and Ivan Head, a senior advisor to the

Canadian Prime Minister, Pierre Trudeau. "The debate over arms supply raised the temperature on the future of the Commonwealth, and the definition of the Commonwealth. We were anxious to discourage those who continued to see the Commonwealth in Anglo-centric terms, and so seemed inclined to quit, or visit on the Commonwealth their anger against Britain. We had seen it happen in 1965-66, when Ghana and Tanzania broke off diplomatic relations with Britain over Rhodesia and we worked very hard to make the point that this did not mean severing their links with the Commonwealth. We had a situation where, at the Law Ministers meeting in London in May 1966, the Ghanaian and Tanzanian law ministers came, on the same principle which we argued that Cuba and Fidel Castro attended the UN even though he had no diplomatic relations with the United States: that Marlborough House was an international centre.

"So we were anxious to underscore the point that the Commonwealth was not the British Commonwealth so you could not, if you were that angry with Britain, visit it on the Commonwealth. We thought that one way of doing this was to have a declaration for the first time, which would not only define authoritatively what the Commonwealth is, but also what it believes in. That's why it starts by saying the Commonwealth is a voluntary association of independent, sovereign nations, each responsible for its own policies. Those words were deliberately chosen. And then went on to speak about the beliefs, racism and all that."

At the height of the crisis over arms supply to South Africa, in October 1970, the Tanzanian President Julius Nyerere visited London, and Anyaoku accompanied the Secretary-General to a meeting with him at Chequers, where he was guest of the British Prime Minister, Ted Heath. "Nyerere had a strong view on the matter. We had a good discussion with him, and not long after that, there was a meeting with Ted Heath at Downing Street on the same issue. This incident left a very longstanding impression on me as evidence of Arnold Smith's total colour-blindness, even when a little bit of colour vision might be useful, but in Commonwealth terms very admirable. Since I was handling it in the International Affairs division, as Assistant-Director — my Director was a British diplomat, Bill Peters — Arnold Smith called me to see him, and said that he wanted me to go with him to the Downing Street meeting with Ted Heath.

Whereupon, I said to him, 'Secretary-General, thank-you very much for the honour but might I suggest that you should take somebody else if you really want a very full and frank expression of views by Prime

Minister Heath'. I just thought it would be a bit inhibiting for him, to be discussing such a burning African issue, with me there. And Arnold Smith said, oh yes, he hadn't thought of it and he took David McDowell. Otherwise, his first inclination was to take me, which, as I said, is a most admirable evidence of his total colour-blindness."

Evolution of the Commonwealth

"In Lusaka, for example," says the Chief, when prodded for descriptive detail, "I chaired the Committee of the Whole, in fact it was after the Lusaka summit in 1979 that we began to organize the business of Committee of the Whole in two committees. Because in Lusaka there was one night that the Committee drafting the communique sat from half-past seven in the evening until half-past six in the morning without adjournment, other than a few tea and coffee breaks. And I was in the chair throughout. I seem to recall that only six senior officials, leaders of delegation, kept awake all the time. A good many others either had a relay, being relieved by some of their colleagues, or dosed off. Those who kept awake throughout, if I remember correctly, included Geoffrey Yiend, then cabinet secretary of Australia; Michael Palliser, who was then permanent secretary of the British Foreign & Commonwealth Office; Mark Chona, who was special assistant to the host President Kaunda; and the Tanzanian who was their permanent secretary. It was a marathon session. And the declaration adopted in Lusaka [on Racism and Racial Prejudice], and subsequent declarations, helped to reinforce this evolution of the Commonwealth from what it used to be perceived as — as the British Commonwealth — to the Commonwealth of Nations, accepted as such by most people. ...

"I think the evolution of the Commonwealth is one of the important aspects of my Commonwealth experience," Chief Anyaoku says now. "I recall that, when I was told of my secondment to the Commonwealth secretariat, my first reaction was to object, because at that time my perception — I think this was the general perception — was that the Commonwealth was an extrapolation of the British empire, and so a heavily Anglo-centric organization. And I did not think, given my radical inclinations at the time, such as my support for the non-aligned movement and my rather passionate OAU inclinations, that it was the right place for me. In any case, I came. ...I have therefore, not only witnessed but participated in, the process of the evolution of the Commowealth to the international association that it has become today.

"And in this evolution, the establishment of the Commonwealth secretariat was a key factor. Indeed, those leaders like Kwame Nkrumah of
Ghana, Eric Williams of Trinidad & Tobago, Tafawa Belewa of Nigeria,
Julius Nyerere ...those leaders who wanted a Commonwealth secretariat,
wanted an independent machinery that would underscore the notion that
it was no longer the British Commonwealth. ...The crisis of Rhodesia only
months after the establishment of the secretariat, and the protracted
debate and disagreement caused by British reaction — or non-reaction, as
some thought — to the UDI, continued to jeopardize the association. The
Commonwealth continued to give the impression that it could only act if
the British government wished it to act. ...

"But by and large, the character of Commonwealth activities, the
character of summit meetings, have all aided to reinforce the perception
that the Commonwealth is indeed an international association of sovereign nations, each responsible for its own policies, as was clearly stated
in the Singapore Declaration of 1971. ...from then on to other
Commonwealth declarations, all have underscored the independence of
the Commonwealth. ...

"I suppose I would say that my own contribution to this evolution has
been in the areas of specific activities in which I have played some part.
The whole history of the Rhodesian crisis and the emergence of independent Zimbabwe was one thing that helped to disabuse people's minds of
the Anglo-centric character of the Commonwealth. And more recently,
the whole question of South Africa. I think the fact that the
Commonwealth could pursue a policy and programme of activity on
South Africa which at times did not have British government support,
more than perhaps anything else in recent times, demonstrated the independence of the Commonwealth as an international organization. ..."

The "high flyer" who had joined the Secretariat reluctantly in 1966, as
Assistant Director of International Affairs, was promoted by Arnold
Smith in 1971 to Director, as a result of his work before and during the
Singapore summit, including his involvement in producing the declara-
tion of Commonwealth principles and the draft agreement on technical
co-operation,. He was appointed Assistant Secretary-General in 1975.
Two years later, he was elected by Commonwealth Governments as
Deputy Secretary-General, with responsibility for political affairs and
administration. Among other things, he chaired the Planning Committee
which advised on planning and monitoring of the activities of all
Secretariat divisions. He took up the post in 1978, and was renewed for a
second term in 1984, until his election by Heads of Government as

Secretary-General taking office in 1990. He was re-elected for a second five-year term, 1995-2000. He has participated at a senior level in all 16 Commonwealth Heads of Government Meetings (CHOGM) over the past 32 years, since September 1966.

Emeka's children

The next generation born to the Anyaoku and Solanke families arrived in different parts of the world, but thanks to modern communication and transportation, all were soon informed and in a matter of months the children were taken home to eager celebrations. Their firstborn, a daughter, arrived in November 1963, soon after they had settled into diplomatic life at the United Nations in New York, and was christened Adiba, for her father's mother, the "first daughter, *Ada*, of the seat or throne, *Iba*"; and Folashade, her mother's grandmother. Her second name was chosen by her maternal grandmother, who gave the name of her own mother.

Her brother arrived, just as she was learning to walk, in February 1965, in New York. His name, Oluyemisi, was chosen by his Yoruba grandmother; and he was given two more names, that of his father and grandfather, Chukwuemeka; and Akanbi, the name of his maternal grandfather, a Barrister.

Three years later, in July 1968, Obiechina Omololu Anyaoku was born at University College Hospital, London, at the height of the civil war in Nigeria. He was given his first name, which means "let the line continue", by the late Dr Kenneth Dike because he was born during the civil war; and his second name from his Yoruba ancestry.

He was sick in hospital, still a baby, when his father left on a special Commonwealth mission to eastern Nigeria, to meet the rebel leaders of Biafra. When the baby's mother protested about the father travelling under the circumstances, his rejoinder was that there were many other children he had to help, who were dying in Biafra.

A good many years later, when Nigeria was at peace and Zimbabwe was in transition between elections and independence, came the birth of Emens at West London Hospital, at the end of March 1980. Much had changed by the time of the birth of Emenike Chukwuma Anyaoku, but not the method of choosing his names, because he was also granted one Igbo name and one Yoruba name, to make the initials EC. In keeping with the traditions of the time, father and mother were together in the delivery room to share in the birth of their child; and the baby was registered at birth for a place at Harrow, the school of his two older brothers.

The Federal Republic of Nigeria

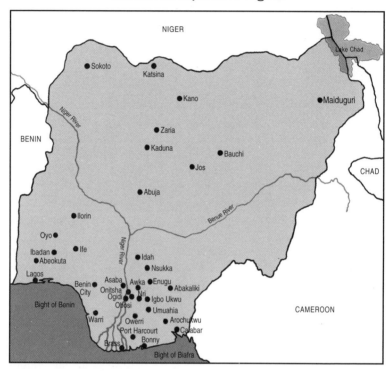

Celebrating Bunmi's birthday at the official residence of the Secretary-General in Mayfair, London, with the family: Adiba, Yemi, Obi and Emens. Emeka Anyaoku had met Bunmi Solanke some 30 years earlier at a party, just before the young classics scholar joined the Ministry of Foreign Affairs in Lagos, and he promised to help her to find a job, which he did; first as a secretary and then as wife, mother, diplomatic partner and community leader.

Eze Igwe Iweka II puts the red sash of office on *Ugoma* at her investiture as chief in 1991. Inset, Olubunmi Solanke and Emeka Anyaoku, almost 30 years earlier, on the day they announced their engagement, 6 May 1962.

Adazie Emeka Anyaoku in Obosi, in the regalia of Ndichie chief; standing with the *Eze* or King, *Igwe* Iweka II.

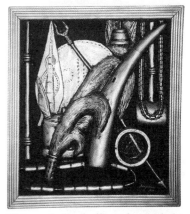

The symbols of office of an Ndichie chief, shown here in bronze relief, and comprising, from left, the staff of office, leather fans, eagle feather and round red hat; fly whisk and a string of coral beads at bottom; an ivory tusk, an arrow, a heavy ivory bangle; a bell, and gavel with beads. The inscription says "Anyaoku 1980", the year of his investiture as chief.

With Bunmi at her investiture as chief, *Ugoma* Obosi in 1991, dressed in traditional Yoruba *asa oke* cloth. At that time she was only the third woman chief in Obosi, and the first to come from another part of Nigeria.

The former Nigerian Head of State (1976-79) and now its democratically elected civilian president since 29 May 1999, Olusegun Obasanjo, races to greet Chief Anyaoku who went to call on him at his farm at Ota near Abeokuta, shortly after his release from prison in 1998.

The Commonwealth Ministerial Action Group (CMAG) of foreign ministers, established by Heads of Government meeting in New Zealand in 1995, to deal with serious or persistent violations of the principles of democracy and good governance contained in the Harare declaration.

The Secretary-General's visit to Chief Mashood Abiola, under house arrest in Abuja, in July 1998, during mediation for his release. This is the last photo of the late Abiola, seen here with the Chief of General Staff, Admiral Mike Akhigbe.

With the interim Head of State, Gen. Abdusalami Abubakar.

229

The Secretary-General with Gen. Abubakar who took office after the death of Sani Abacha and guided Nigeria back to civilian rule.

This cartoon by Gale in *The House magazine,* the parliamentary weekly, on 20 October 1997 shows Chief Anyaoku steering the Commonwealth toward the Edinburgh summit a few days later. Notable names missing from the bus at that time were Fiji whose membership lapsed and Nigeria which was suspended. Both have since returned to democratic governance and re-joined.

Chief Anyaoku in a cartoon by Mwara of *The East African* newspaper in 1995, shown sitting on a ballot box, an appropriate symbol of his achievement at putting into words and then into action the Commonwealth's commitment to democratic governance, in the Harare Commonwealth Declaration 1991 and the Millbrook Commonwealth Action Programme on the Harare Declaration 1995. One of the main beneficiaries of this action during his term of office was his own country, Nigeria, which was suspended from the Commonwealth from 1995 until after democratic elections in 1999.

That famous signature on memos and letters, and official reports to Commonwealth Heads of Government.

7

THE QUESTION OF NIGERIA

*I am deeply in love with my country... the fact that I work
outside the country has not detached me from Nigeria, I belong to Nigeria.
(Chief Anyaoku in Africa Today, Nov/Dec 1995)*

NIGERIA IN THE 1990s became a significant challenge to the
Commonwealth, not of the magnitude of Rhodesia and South Africa con-
fronting as they did the fundamental ethic of non-racism and equality,
but in implementation of the principles of democracy and governance
elaborated in the Harare Declaration in 1991, the year after Chief
Anyaoku took office as the first African Secretary-General. The question
of ending military rule in favour of democracy in his home country was
a nagging ache through almost all of his tenure.

He regarded it as, not as big a challenge as apartheid South Africa or
Rhodesia had been but, "the most dangerous, because it has the greatest
potential for dividing the Commonwealth." And he handled the challenge with the same diplomacy and determination that marked his role
in the transition in South Africa, and with no less dedication.

Midnight's children

"Those of us whose own arrival at maturity coincided with national independence have been accorded the rare gift of growing up with our country and of dedicating ourselves to its service. The generation which
laboured so long to achieve independence, and has lived to enjoy its
results, and also the post-independence generation of new Nigerians,
have experienced a period of boundless hopes, and rising expectations, of
crises and revolution, of tragic strife between brothers, and of hope once
more renewed. It has been our great privilege but also our weighty
responsibility to be the heirs of independence; and what in India's context have been called 'midnight's children'. ...

"It is in that spirit that I wish to consider whether we children of the Nigerian midnight of 1 October 1960 are indeed keeping faith with the fatherland."

Delivering the alumni lecture at Ibadan University in 1983, Chief Anyaoku noted that the university has a special significance "which we acknowledge, in the Latin phrase, as our *alma mater*, our bountiful mother. ...The reference to mother and father underlines the family relationship between our institutions of higher education and the nation state. ...

"This function of the university encourages me, as someone whose working concerns lie in that wider world, but whose heart has never left Nigeria, to speak to you about our country, placing my remarks in the context of my experience of international affairs. It permits me to view our national affairs in the perspective of developments in the many countries whose affairs have constituted my preoccupation over the last two decades."

Wherever he went in the world during the 40 years after Nigeria's independence, Chief Anyaoku was always at home, rooted as he is so strongly in the soil of his birth that he always has someplace to go back to. There is an Igbo proverb that says, "Staying in a place and living there are different."

Despite staying in London for 35 of those years, he has returned for home leave once or twice a year to the place where he lives, Obosi, except for his reluctant absence during a period in the mid-1990s when he was eventually persuaded that his personal security was under threat from the Sani Abacha regime.

The story of Nigeria and the Commonwealth inevitably involves Chief Anyaoku throughout the high points and low, from the outbreak of civil war in 1967 and Commonwealth attempts to mediate; through Nigeria's weighty persuasion of the British government to adhere to genuine negotiations over Zimbabwe in 1979 by refusing British tenders and nationalizing a British petroleum subsidiary; through support for the elected civilian government in the period 1979-1983.

Only two of the 16 biennial Commonwealth Heads of Government Meetings (CHOGM) over the past 32 years since late 1966, were attended by a representative of a civilian government in Nigeria: 1981 and 1983. And it was Chief Anyaoku who attended the New Delhi CHOGM in 1983 as foreign minister of the last civilian government in Nigeria for over 15 years.

The question of Nigeria has shadowed the Secretary-General and the Commonwealth throughout his tenure, drawing at the same time both praise and castigation for doing too much and recrimination for doing too little, as events in his home country taunted and challenged him. He spoke out strongly when necessary, and worked assiduously behind the scenes to return Nigeria to civilian, democratic rule, even as this reached a showdown between the Commonwealth and Nigeria in the mid-1990s.

Gen. Sani Abacha waited until just after the Commonwealth Heads of Government Meeting in Cyprus to seize power in Nigeria in late 1993 but, feeling more confident by the time of the next CHOGM in 1995, he allowed the execution of the political activist Ken Saro-Wiwa and others at a prison in Port Harcourt while Commonwealth leaders were meeting in New Zealand, where his foreign minister, Chief Tom Ikimi, had to make awkward explanations.

That was the final trigger for the suspension of Nigeria from participation in Commonwealth events and activities, making it difficult for any government to lobby against it, no matter how important their trade with Nigeria, particularly in petroleum. This suspension remained in place through the 1997 summit of Commonwealth leaders in Edinburgh, and full membership returned to the Federal Republic of Nigeria only after the swearing in of an elected civilian government headed by President Olusegun Obasanjo at the end of May 1999.

This marked the fifth civilian government since independence in 1960 for Africa's most populous country and one of its wealthiest nations. Since 1 October 1960, there have been four general elections, seven coups d'etat or changes of government by force, two short transitional periods, and two handovers from military to civilian rule after elections, both of them involving Olusegun Obasanjo. The first handover was by Gen. Obasanjo as head of state to an elected civilian government in 1979 and the second was to him as elected civilian president, 20 years later.

Nigeria's face

Nigeria has become widely known as an oil-producing giant that is struggling to meet the aspirations of its people and to find an appropriate system of national governance and leadership. A major supplier of petroleum to the United States and Europe, a major world market for the United Kingdom, the superpower of West Africa, a wealthy country that is deeply in debt. But it has another face, as one of Africa's most influential countries, built on a lengthy history of, in some cases, no less than two thousand years of technically advanced societies renowned for their achievements in artistic, athletic, commercial and intellectual spheres, from which has emerged globally respected authors, artists, academics, athletes and musicians.

Nigeria's "vast oil reserves and unique human resources create the capacity for enormous prosperity and regional leadership. The fate of its struggle for democracy and national unity will have profound implications for the entire continent. Both the potential and the obstacles are on the giant scale of the country itself. British conquest brought together within Nigeria's borders a wide range of cultures and ethnic groups. The colonial 'unity', however, was a top-down authoritarian creation. ...building a nation based on popular participation remains a work in progress." (Apic)

Solid foundations of democratic culture built on traditional systems of local governance have maintained the country's soul irrespective of changes at the head, and a diverse civil society has stimulated the organs of state: dynamic entrepreneurs in the private sector, energetic and irrepressible communications media, active labour unions, vibrant professional associations and vocal human rights groups contribute to national pride. Ethnic tolerance and unity are not the only challenges; the colonial legacy remains a dichotomy to be woven into the fabric of the nation.

"The functional value of European legal and administrative forms, and the unifying impact of the English language in both Nigeria and the wider world, have been fully and gladly acknowledged," Chief Anyaoku says, "it is English, after all, which enables Commonwealth countries and others to communicate readily with each other on many different levels. At the same time, however, Nigeria has sought to restore the correct balance by emphasizing the rich history and continuing value of our own Nigerian cultural heritage, as an important part of the wider African achievement.

"Hence the truly international significance of FESTAC 77 when Nigeria startled the world by organizing a dramatic explosion of continent-wide African arts stressing the significance of black culture in a global context.

"More recently, new audiences outside Africa have been persuaded of the depth and wealth of Nigeria's past by the exhibition of Treasures of Ancient Nigeria. ...For the first time, the full glory of over 2,000 years of Nigerian art were displayed outside Nigeria. I well remember my own pride attending the exhibition in London's Royal Academy, when I saw the mesmeric effect created by these Nigerian masterpieces: Nok terracottas 2,000 or more years old and the later Owo terracottas, 9th or 10th century bronzes from Igbo-Ukwu, and most justly famous of all, the bronzes of Ife and Benin which date to the late Middle Ages and the Renaissance in European chronology.

"For the first time outside Nigeria, such objects were comprehensively demonstrating that Nigerian history did not begin with European colonialism and that Nigerian technology at its highest achievement brought forth artifacts in a distinctly African style which rank equal to the greatest masterpieces of European art. ...

"The Nok Culture, the Igbo-Ukwu tradition, the Ife and the Benin traditions — which span a thousand years and more from as far back as 500 BC — all testify to a society which was highly organized and highly cultured well before its contact with the outside world. In our time these ancient traditions co-exist side by side with contemporary art which reflects our modern life and culture. In their entirety both ancient and modern Nigerian art share the central perspectives of African Art as a celebration of life past, present and indeed the future. ...

"Such treasures still have their place in the living Nigerian culture, not just in museums, and we should also not overlook that other living culture of our theatres, cinemas, and above all perhaps our popular music and dance. Music expresses the energy and vitality which are among our country's national resources."

Writing over a decade ago about the life of a military colleague, Olusegun Obasanjo narrated the colonial roots of the Nigerian army entwined in the stages of European contact for over a century before independence. "When the Queen visited Nigeria in January 1956, she was received by the Nigeria Regiment as their colonel-in-chief. At the end of the visit, she conferred on the Nigeria Regiment the title 'Queen's Own.'...The Nigerian Army which was an offshoot of the British colonial army, was supposed to be completely subordinated to the civil order. It was meant to be an apolitical army, taking orders from the government of the day... This was the legacy bequeathed to the Nigerian army by the British, and it was felt that it was a legacy worth keeping and defending. ...

"In 1960, no Nigerian army officer, in his wildest dreams, could have imagined the army playing any part in political governance."

Nineteen-sixty-six

On 15 January 1966, just two days after a summit of Commonwealth leaders in Lagos, a group of army majors tried to seize power. Their motives were largely idealistic, and their action was a response to widespread popular grievances and protests which had erupted, causing a break-down in law and order in the region around the capital. The stated reasons were similar to those that justified later attempts on power, ie division of authority between the central government and the regions, the power balance between the regions, the deteriorating economic situation, unemployment and escalating corruption.

Unlike later military seizures of power, this first attempt was bloody and left the prime minister dead in its wake, as well as premiers of the North and West, the minister of finance, and many senior army officers. However, the army commander, Maj Gen. Johnson Aguiyi-Ironsi was able to mobilize a military response, and the coup plotters were detained. In a state of shock, the remaining cabinet ministers handed over power to Ironsi.

The response by Commonwealth leaders of that time to the overthrow and murder of their colleague and host of a few days earlier was passive, and the bloodshed was characterized as an "internal affair". Thirty years later, in late 1995, when Nigeria was again under military rule and elections had been annulled, the Commonwealth responded differently. Nigeria was suspended from the activities of a Commonwealth whose leadership, guided by an African Secretary-General, had designed an implementation mechanism for its commitment to good governance and rule of law, advised by a Commonwealth Ministerial Action Group (CMAG).

The military takeover in Nigeria in early 1966, however, was greeted with widespread support and expectation in many parts of the country, as the population had lost faith in the ability of its civilian leadership. This popular enthusiasm for removal of civilian governments by the military amid charges of rampant corruption became the norm for later seizures of power. The military leaders who seized power thereafter, with the exception of Gen. Sani Abacha in 1993, did so on the basis of combating corruption, and were popularly received.

Gen. Ironsi's accession to power had arisen out of preventive reaction and not from an agenda for action, and he had no blueprint for stability and prosperity. His stay in office was soon characterized as "politically clumsy".

In the ethnic tension that marked the nation-state in 1966, the north seethed with anger over the murder of its regal premier, Sir Ahmadu Bello, and its popular prime minister, Sir Abubakar Tafawa Balewa, and began to regard the first military government and its head of state, an Igbo, as a takeover by the east. They began to express their resentment over the educated Igbo middle class which ran commercial ventures and occupied public service positions in the north.

Ironically, Sir Abubakar's last official function outside Lagos, on 4 January 1966, was the official opening of the first ever road bridge across the Niger river, linking eastern and western Nigeria at Asaba by completing the main highway to Lagos. Less than two years later, the bridge was one of the first casualties of the civil war.

Ironsi drew northern resentment over suspicion that his actions were ethnically motivated, and when he announced on 24 May that he was centralizing the public services, he produced a spark of fear in the north over southern domination that eventually ignited a civil war that had been smouldering for over a decade. Since civil servants from any region could now work anywhere in the country, there was fear that the better educated southerners, particularly Igbos from the east, would move into influential positions in the north.

Northern resentment ran deep enough to rekindle the option of secession, and anti-Igbo riots occurred in the north, with vicious attacks on artisans and entrepreneurs. A group of northern officers mutinied and shot some Igbo officers including Ironsi in July; they seized power and handed it to the army Chief of Staff, Lt Col. Yakubu Gowon, a Christian officer from a minority group in the north.

The response in the east of the country, where the military governor was Lt Col. Chukwuemeka Odumegwu-Ojukwu, was one of shock and disbelief, and he refused to recognize Gowon as head of state. Col. Ojukwu, himself an easterner who was born in the north, urged the Igbo population of the north which had fled in large numbers to their ethnic home, to return to their homes in the north. Many thousands lost their lives in a second wave of ethnic violence in the north in September, and over a million people fled their jobs, homes and belongings, desperately trying to keep families together on the dark trek back to their ethnic home in the east. Non-easterners were soon expelled or fled.

"There were three ways in which the North's hold on the political power of the country could be broken: through a popular revolution that could politicize the social problems of the many; through someone who was a member of the existing system working deliberately to change it from within; or through a military coup d'etat. The decade after independence was to see Nigeria go through social upheavals with all three methods of change, but none was sufficient to avoid civil war." (Omotoso)

Civil war

"The war came reluctantly," Ojukwu wrote long after it had ended. "That a conservative estimate of 50,000 unarmed people from a specific area of the nation were massacred is a fact. That I urged them back to the north and they were subjected to an even greater massacre was also a fact. ...And so, chased back to their homes, the alternative as perceived by the Igbos was to resist and I stood at their head to resist. ...I firmly believe I did my best to protect a people threatened with genocide. ...The territorial delimitation of Biafra was like a series of beacons, searchlights, if you will, to help a brutalized and persecuted people identify a safe haven and to inspire them into making the final dash to safety. The philosophy that gave birth to Biafra was that of self-defense. ...

"The memories of the war are still in the minds of people. A lot of Nigerians harbour sad memories of that period. So do I. Yet, it is a period we just can't abolish or erase because it has become part of our history, something we have to live with. ...Nigeria as a result of the war has learnt a lot. ...Any leader of any group of Nigerians today should be seeking greater integration among all Nigerians."

In an attempt to resolve the problem of what was then a stand-off, senior military officers from various parts of Nigeria met in Aburi, Ghana, in January 1967, where agreement was reached for regional autonomy within a loose federal structure. But Gen. Gowon changed his interpretation on return to Lagos after being advised by senior civil servants that this could dismember the country. After that, it was only a matter of time.

On 27 May 1967, Gowon announced a retooling of the national structure into 12 states, aimed a removing the structural basis for regional strife that arose from three powerful regions with unequal access to central power. On 30 May, Ojukwu proclaimed the independent Republic of Biafra.

The Biafran poet Christopher Okigbo, who died in action in Nsukka early in the conflict, wrote lines that were prophetic, considering his tragic fate as a casualty of the civil war.

"When you have finished
And done up my stitches
Wake me near the altar —
And this poem will be finished."

Biafra

The young, upwardly mobile, Nigerian diplomat at the United Nations in New York had been caught off guard by the improbability of the first coup d'etat in his home country; and Emeka Anyaoku was even more astonished by the second, in July 1966, just three months after he joined the Commonwealth Secretariat in London as Assistant Director of International Affairs. Less than a year later, his country was at war with itself, and his home village of Obosi, just across the Niger river bridge south-east of Onitsha, was in a place called Biafra.

At the Commonwealth Secretariat, which was then only two years old and grappling with its own independence from British bureaucrats as well as the rebellion in Rhodesia, there were a number of considerations about Biafra. One was "the pogrom in the north," wrote the then Secretary-General, Arnold Smith, a Canadian. In addition, "two-thirds of the oil was being produced in 1966-67 in Eastern region" which became Biafra and the other one-third produced in the Mid-West region had to transit the east through the refinery in Port Harcourt. "Shell-BP had some 150 million pounds (about US$250 million at current exchange) invested in the East. ...For three years Nigerian affairs took up a considerable proportion of my time... The returns were often meagre, but it seemed to me a necessary investment in the future of one of the Commonwealth's most important members."

The UN was preoccupied with the Middle East and Asia, and the OAU apparently immobilized by the fate of one of its largest, wealthiest members. "...the UN traditionally finds it difficult to deal with domestic crises or problems, except for the issue of apartheid," Smith wrote later. "The OAU set up a Consultative Committee of six heads of state led by the Emperor of Ethiopia who tried intermittently to end the war. But the OAU's basic principle, of unquestioning respect for national boundaries of member states, put the committee on a narrow course when trying to deal with the problem of a secessionist force. In contrast, the Commonwealth secretariat had a flexibility that others lacked. ...Our approach was the lighter one, of simply bringing the Nigerian and the Biafran leaders or their deputies together to reason with each other. This involved a series of secret meetings in my London office or apartment, scores of telephone calls, visits to Enugu and Lagos by Secretariat staff in the course of (or under the cover of) other Commonwealth events."

It also involved many meetings with Biafran emissaries such as Dr Kenneth Dike, Sir Louis Mbanefo, Ozumba Mbadiwe and others who vis-

ited Emeka Anyaoku in London. The widow of one of his former lectur-
ers at Ibadan University College, John Ferguson, later recalled visits to
the Anyaoku household where "the Igbos were downstairs and the
Yorubas upstairs; it was one of few houses in London in that period
where both could go at the same time."

Smith's determination to help both sides to negotiate an end to the
conflict resulted in him sending his Assistant Director of International
Affairs on "home leave" in the middle of the civil war. "At that time,"
Anyaoku told the story later, "the flights into and from Biafra were
dependent on either the Red Cross flights or the arms ferrying flights. I
chose to go on the Red Cross flight which left Amsterdam, either once a
week or once every two weeks, on a Wednesday. By some unfortunate
coincidence, my third child, Obi, was very ill in hospital and the doctors
were very concerned that we might lose him. Bunmi and I went to the
hospital with him, sitting by his bedside, and it was agonizing for me to
leave Bunmi and Obi, who seemed to be dying. And I remember, when I
told Bunmi, I said, 'well I will travel'. And she said, 'with your son in this
state?' And I said, 'yes, because there are many more in worse state, dying
every day, in Biafra.' And she didn't say a word more.

"And I left. When I got into Biafra, by then Ojukwu had moved his
headquarters to Umuahia and one of the first persons I saw was M.T.
Mbu, who was then Foreign Minister of Biafra [and 25 years later Foreign
Minister of Nigeria]. I saw him, I saw Professor Dike. And the permanent
secretary of Biafra's ministry of external affairs, Godwin Onyegbula.
Within two hours of my arrival, a bombing raid occurred and I had to
dive with everybody under the table. It was a frightening experience. But
soon after that, I was taken to Ojukwu's headquarters, and at that time,
he was operating from a bunker.

"Emeka Ojukwu and I had been friends for a long time, and so it was
a personal thing. I remember going there — this was after Arnold Smith
had got the two sides to initial an agreement in London for negotiations,
and we had signs that Biafra was not going to accept their agreement.
Ojukwu was going to do what Gowon had done over Aburi; when they
had reached agreement at Aburi, and Gowon reneged on that. And that
was really what made the civil war, sustained the civil war.

"On this occasion, Arnold Smith was very keen that the agreements
initialed in London by the two sides — three representing Biafra, three
representing Nigeria — should be accepted. But I knew that there were
elements in it which were unpalatable to Ojukwu.

"And I remember my dramatic meeting with him, because his wife,

Njide, at the time, brought us some sandwiches for lunch, just Emeka
Ojukwu and myself. Before she left us, I said, 'Njide, before you leave
there is something I want to say to Emeka. I will be telling Emeka in the
course of our conversations things I know he would not like to hear. And
given the pressure he's under, it would be very natural for him to pull a
gun and shoot me. All I ask you, Njide, to do is to tell Bunmi how I died.'

"And Emeka retorted and said, 'Emeka, that's very dramatic.' I said,
'I intended it to be.' And Njide then laughed and said, 'I don't think
there's anything the two Emekas cannot sort out.' And she left us. ...

"It was partly a Commonwealth mission and partly family, because
by then my only maternal uncle, to whom I was greatly attached, had
been killed, in Port Harcourt. He disappeared from a hospital bed. He
had relocated from the village where he had lived since he returned from
Burma — he fought in Burma during the Second World War. He worked
for the United Africa Company and, because of the civil war, he was evacuated back home to Obosi. But when Obosi was under attack and the
senior citizens were evacuated, he was taken to Port Harcourt. And
another uncle, was also living in Kano before the civil war, during the
massacres, real massacres — the Biafrans called it a pogrom — of Igbos in
the north. My uncle and his family had to evacuate Kano, went first to
Obosi and then left Obosi to go and live somewhere near Uli. And I was
getting letters of their suffering and death, and so the Commonwealth
mission provided me with an opportunity to see them.

"My exit from Biafra was the most hair-raising and most dramatic
experience I have ever had, because I went on a flight that was evacuat-
ing children. It was a flight, no seats in the plane. It was a flight from Uli
airport to Gabon, and it was hair-raising."

Later, near the end of the war, the Anyaoku home in Obosi, just across
the Niger river bridge in one of the main areas of conflict, was bombed,
causing considerable damage including destruction of some of his
father's papers.

"Arnold Smith, at the time of the civil war, behaved with a very
touching degree of concern. He felt — for Nigerians and Biafrans, all of
them — he felt that the war was unnecessary, as I felt. But for him, feeling the way he did, he worked very hard to see that it was brought to an
end." And Emeka Anyaoku saw the methods and possibilities of a "good
offices" role played by a concerned and committed Commonwealth
Secretary-General.

Smith also looked after his staff. "During the civil war, the Nigerian
government wrote two petitions calling for my removal from the

Secretariat on grounds that I had not taken the oath of allegiance to the federal government. I went on secondment, and they required all their foreign service officers to take the oath of allegiance to the federal course, and I said, No, I would not resign. So they petitioned that I should be removed, since I no longer was their secondee and no longer had their confidence. But Arnold Smith recalled that a similar thing had happened at the United Nations after the change of government in Czechoslovakia. The new communist government in Czechoslovakia wanted Trygve Lie, the first UN Secretary-General, to remove Czech nationals who had been seconded or nominated by the former government. Trygve Lie said, No, once a government makes a nomination or gives its blessing, and that nomination is accepted, that the whole ethic of international service would be destroyed if the officer concerned has constantly to look over his shoulder. And so Arnold Smith said that he did not see my being in the Secretariat as inimical to Nigerian government interest.

"Eventually, I resolved the matter, because the late Yaw Adu, who was Deputy Secretary-General, encouraged me, and I went and had a meeting with Okoi Arikpo, who was then foreign minister, during the Commonwealth Heads of Government Meeting in 1969. And it was resolved. But otherwise, they had petitioned twice that I should be removed. ..."

While most of the world and both superpowers supported the federal government in its blockade of Biafra, the people within the blockade sustained their resistance with well-targeted information, clandestine contacts and remarkable ingenuity, constructing everything from rifles and bombs to guns and generators. But the odds were on the other side. The Nigerian army officer who received the surrender in the field was the officer commanding the Third Marine Commandos, Lt Col. Olusegun Obasanjo, whom a subordinate later described as "one of few officers who inspired his men by example; never shirked a challenge, never declined a responsibility, and never deliberately let his fellows down."

Nigeria recovered its equilibrium swiftly and without retribution soon after Col. Ojukwu slipped into exile in early January 1970, leaving close colleagues to negotiate the peace, and Gen. Gowon made his famous statement that there would be "no victors, no vanquished". It seemed that the entire nation had taken up the Igbo proverb that says, "You cannot point an accusing finger without leaving four directed at yourself."

Almost 20 years later, several years after his return from exile, Ojukwu wrote: "The Biafran aim was not to secede *per se*. It was the exercise of the inalienable right of a people to self-determination. When it appeared to the then Eastern region that the basis of the Nigerian understanding was no longer valid, the stigmatized people sought safety from within their own ability. The Biafrans sought to demonstrate once and for all the innate ability of a black people to establish true independence within a polity. The proclamation of the Biafran Republic was at best, the delimitation of the people's last defensive position. ...

"Biafra was not a separatist movement as propaganda made it appear; it was rather a reflex for self-preservation. It is today an attitude of mind rather than a territorial entity and within that attitude of mind exist seeds that will save this country for posterity. All over Nigeria there is Biafra but that Biafra of today is 'the Biafra of the Nigerians and not the Biafra of the Igbo'; the Biafra of the mind not Biafra of the fields."

"All the world's a stage..."

A presidential aide clad in *agbada*, the traditional Nigerian *danshiki* suit with flowing robes over top, slipped through a side door into the Nile Mansions conference centre in Kampala, Uganda where a number of African presidents and foreign ministers were listening to their host, Idi Amin Dada, the new Chairman of the Organisation of African Unity (OAU) on the second day of the annual summit, 29 July 1975.

The aide walked quickly through the rows of seats until he reached his Head of State, then leaned over and whispered in his ear. His former Head of State. There had been another coup d'etat in Nigeria. General Yakubu Gowon slowly rose from his seat, nodded acknowledgement to the chairman, and left the conference room. By evening, the British Broadcasting Corporation (BBC) had mentioned a name, which rippled through the delegates at a sumptuous outdoor reception in the Ugandan capital: Brig. Murtala Muhammad.

Mid-afternoon of the following day, Gen. Gowon appeared before a packed press conference at Nile Mansions, in a bright white *agbada* and cap, to make a statement on the events in his country. "All the world's a stage," he said, quoting the 17th century English author William Shakespeare, "the men and women merely players." Identifying himself as one of the players, he said he would be leaving the stage, but not returning home, although he released his entourage to do so and wished his successors well. "A new Government has been established in Nigeria. I wish to say that I have accepted the change and pledge my full loyalty to my country and the new Government. Therefore, in the overall interest of our nation, I appeal to all concerned to co-operate fully with the new Government to ensure the preservation of peace, unity and stability in our dear Motherland."

The coup d'etat had taken place just before dawn — nine years to the day since Gowon himself had come to power — and was announced on national radio by the Commander of the Brigade of Guards, who had pledged loyalty to his head of state immediately prior to his departure. "Fellow countrymen and women. I, Colonel Joe Maven Garba, in consultation with my colleagues do hereby declare that in view of what has been happening in our country in the past few months, the Nigerian Armed Forces have decided to effect a change of the leadership of the Federal Military Government. ...."

On the following day, 30 July, the new head of state, Brig. Murtala Muhammad, said in a speech to the nation, "Fellow Nigerians, Events of the past few years have indicated that despite our great human and material resources, the Government has not been able to fulfill the legitimate expectations of our people. Nigeria has been left to drift. This situation, if not arrested would inevitably have resulted in chaos and even bloodshed. In the endeavour to build a strong, united and virile nation Nigerians have shed much blood; the thought of further bloodshed, for whatever reasons, must, I am sure, be revolting to our people. The armed forces, having examined the situation, came to the conclusion that certain changes were inevitable. ...

"After the civil war, the affairs of State, hitherto a collective responsibility, became characterized by lack of consultation, indecision, indiscipline and even neglect. Indeed, the public at large became disillusioned and disappointed by these developments. ...Things got to a stage where the head of the administration became virtually inaccessible even to official advisers; and when advice was tendered, it was often ignored. Responsible opinion, including advice by eminent Nigerians, traditional rulers, intellectuals etc., was similarly discarded. The leadership, either by design or default, had become too insensitive to the true feelings and yearnings of the people. The nation was thus being plunged inexorably into chaos. ...

"Fellow countrymen, the task ahead of us calls for sacrifice and self-discipline at all levels of our society. This Government will not tolerate indiscipline. This Government will not condone abuse of office. I appeal to you all to cooperate with the Government in our endeavour to give this nation a new lease of life. This change in Government has been accomplished without shedding any blood; and we intend to keep it so. Long live the Federal Republic of Nigeria. ..."

This was the third military coup d'etat since Nigeria's independence in 1960, and there would be four more interventions by the military in the next 20 years, before the country reached the age of 35 — on average, one every four years.

The military ruled Nigeria for a total of 30 years of the first 39 years of independence. Civilians have governed in total for less than a decade.

From the first abortive coup in January 1966 up to Gen. Sani Abacha's takeover on 18 November 1993, shortly after the Commonwealth Heads of Government meeting in Limassol, Cyprus, they were not all handled with the same aplomb as the long-distance handover from Gowon to Murtala in 1975. Murtala himself was assassinated just over six months later, but order was maintained and the reigns of power were taken up reluctantly by Murtala's deputy and close associate, Gen. Olusegun Obasanjo, who would be the last southern head of state for the next 20 years, and his deputy, Maj Gen. Shehu Musa Yar'Adua, a young officer from Yar'Adua village near Katsina in the north, who won a presidential primary nomination in 1992 and died in Abacha's prison in 1997.

Method of change of Government	Head of Government
1959: pre-independence general elections	Sir A Tafawa Balewa
1964: post-independence general elections	Sir A Tafawa Balewa
1966 Jan 15: coup attempt Maj Ifeajuna/ Maj Nzeogwu	Gen. J Aguiyi-Ironsi,
1966 July 29: coup d'etat , Lt Col. Gowon	Gen. Y Gowon
1975 July 29: coup d'etat, Brig Gen. Muhammad	Gen. M Muhammad
1976 February 13: assassination of Muhammad	Gen. O Obasanjo,
1979 July/August: national and state elections	(handover by Obasanjo to Shagari)
1979 October 1: return to civilian government	S Shagari, President
1983 August/Sept: national and state elections	S Shagari, President
1983 December 31: coup d'etat, Maj Gen. Buhari	Gen. M Buhari
1985 August 27: coup d'etat, Gen. Babangida	Gen. I Babangida
1993 June 12: presidential elections, results not announced	
1993 June 23: election annulled by Babangida	Gen. I Babangida
1993 Aug 26: Babangida resigned, appointed E Shonekan	Chief E Shonekan
1993 November 17: coup d'etat, Gen. Abacha	Gen. S Abacha
1998 June 8: death of Abacha,	Gen. A Abubakar
1999 Jan/Feb: state, national, presidential elections	
1999 May 29: Obasanjo sworn in as President	O Obasanjo, Gen. (rtd), President

Preparing for the civilians

The Obasanjo administration spent the next three years adhering to a meticulous timetable, rigorously observed, in preparation for the elections and handover to civilian rule at home; and pursuing an activist, pan-Africanist foreign policy that was particularly influential in international bodies such as the UN, the OAU and the Commonwealth. Nigeria used its commercial muscle to encourage Britain to move toward majority rule in Zimbabwe and British companies to withdraw from South Africa, to lobby for the Angolan government caught in a post-independence conflict, and to provide diplomatic and material support for the struggle against apartheid in South Africa. During this period, the Front Line States (FLS) opposing apartheid in southern Africa often issued statements as the "FLS and Nigeria".

Emeka Anyaoku was elected Deputy Secretary-General in this period, and encouraged active participation by Nigeria, including scholarships and support for South African exiles. But Gen. Obasanjo did not attend Commonwealth Heads of Government Meetings, apparently due to his own inhibitions as a military leader; he was represented instead by his deputy or the commissioner for external affairs.

A new constitution was drafted, considered by a largely elected Constituent Assembly, an electoral register was prepared and constituencies delimited for national and state elections. The state boundaries were examined and an additional seven states were created, bringing the total to 19. A provision was adopted ruling that the successful presidential candidate would have to lead the polls nationally and win one-quarter of the votes in at least two-thirds of the 19 states. All citizens over the age of 18, some 47.5 million voters, were registered. A new system of local government was established and women in the north were allowed for the first time to vote and to stand for election. A site was chosen for a new federal capital at Abuja, near the geographical centre of the country. Some entities were reorganized, such as the trade unions, customary courts and marketing boards, and new procedures announced for land use. Murtala's assassins were tried and executed.

Elections unfolded at one-week intervals over a period of five weeks, for national bodies, then state and finally, presidential. On 1 October 1979, Nigeria returned to civilian rule, with the first president directly elected by the voters nation-wide, Shehu Shagari, from Shagari village near Sokoto in north-western Nigeria. Among urgent priorities were the overstretched public services infrastructure, stagnation of agriculture, and widespread violent crime. Soon after his installation, however, President Shagari found it necessary to warn one of his more vociferous political opponents: "in this country now, there are in the end only two parties; the civilians and the soldiers." (Williams)

The Anyaoku family continued to return home on their annual leave to Obosi, where their husband and father was actively involved in local government structures and in supporting the national transition to civilian rule. He was made Ndichie chief in 1980, as *Adazie Obosi*.

President Shagari was re-elected in 1983. He was sworn in for a second term on 1 October and when he announced a new cabinet in early November, the list included, as foreign minister, Chief Emeka Anyaoku, until then Deputy Secretary-General of the Commonwealth. Within two weeks of his appointment, he accompanied President Shagari to the Commonwealth Heads of Government Meeting in New Delhi.

Chief Anyaoku's host was P.V. Narasimha Rao, then foreign minister of India and later prime minister. He took the Commonwealth foreign ministers on a tour of Rajahstan where, after they had seen the sights, a correspondent of All India Radio was busy with a microphone collecting reactions. "I said, 'After viewing the cultural history of India, the history of Indian civilization that goes back thousands of years, for me, a Greek and Roman history scholar, the impact has been such that I wonder why colonization has not been the other way round! That was my true reaction, because the more I saw of India's historical background and cultural history, the age of it, for someone who thought on the basis of Greco-Roman history and philosophy that civilization began around 2,000 BC... visiting India made a very lasting impression on me."

A few weeks later on New Year's Eve, 31 December 1983, the military took power again and Nigerians woke up on the first morning of 1984 to find they had a new president, Maj Gen Muhammadu Buhari. The reasons given for the military action were familiar: mismanagement of the economy and deteriorating social conditions, corruption, indiscipline, and alleged rigging of the 1983 elections.

On New Year's Day, Chief Anyaoku heard the early morning news on the radio; he had been foreign minister for less than two months. While the military were searching the city for former cabinet ministers and broadcasting appeals for them to report their presence, and others were in hiding, Chief Anyaoku proceeded firmly and against most advice of family and friends, to report to the nearest police station, where he was greeted respectfully by name and title, and treated cordially, with the courtesy that accompanies cabinet rank. He returned home with no further ado. But contacts were soon made with the Commonwealth secretariat, and as word spread of the coup, Chief Anyaoku with the support of all Commonwealth governments returned to his Commonwealth post of Deputy Secretary-General.

His tenacious support for good governance was reinforced, though not initiated by this experience: "I, having gone through that, became even more convinced that democracy, which reflected the popular will, was the answer. But I was mindful of the fact also that a democratically elected government had an obligation to behave better, to avoid a situation where the populace would be led into believing that doing away with democracy could provide a welcome relief. I was disappointed at the fact that the thinking public-opinion-makers in Nigeria seemed to have accepted the coup. But my interpretation was that people had reacted to the record of the government, not to the new Shagari administration of which I was a member, but the record of the earlier administration.

"And what I particularly regretted was that I knew that Shagari was aware of the fact that his first administration had not performed anywhere near well enough. And indeed, when he invited me to join the government, he had told me that the reason he was asking me to join the government was that he was determined to do better than in his first administration. ...

"Being in Shagari's second administration gave me a direct personal stake in the democratic system in Nigeria, and put me in the position of understanding more fully that it was totally unnecessary to have that military coup d'etat. ...My reaction to that coup was the same way as I had reacted in 1966, because as you know I was a great critic of the first military coup in Nigeria. ...although Balewa's administration was making some mistakes, I never thought that those mistakes justified military intervention. So from day one, I have always been strongly against the unconstitutional change of government."

President General

The next military coup was two years later, on 27 August 1985 when the Chief of Army Staff, Gen. Ibrahim Babangida, took control with the support of leading officers of the SMC, who accused their colleagues of abuse of power. Unlike the previous military leaders who were designated Head of State, Babangida was proclaimed President. A popular soldier and senior officer of the majority group on the SMC, he promised a more liberal approach to the economy and human rights. Former president Shagari and his vice-president Alex Ekwueme were released from 30 months detention and restricted to their home areas. President Babangida announced that the military would relinquish power to a democratically elected civilian government on 1 October 1990.

Having seen the soldiers do this once before, Chief Anyaoku firmly believed that it could be achieved again, and he was active in encouraging it, sparing no opportunity to appraise those in power at the highest level of the importance of democracy to Nigeria's development as well as to its international standing. His fervent expectation was that within three months of his taking office as Commonwealth Secretary-General on 1 July 1990, his country would be ruled by an elected civilian government. He was acutely conscious of the impending conflict between a military regime in Nigeria and the Commonwealth commitment to good governance which he planned to pursue, and the impact this would have on his own position and credibility. He was deeply disappointed when the dates of Nigeria's return to democracy were set back.

The military government announced in April 1990 that it had foiled a coup by junior officers "backed by rich and powerful people". Some officers and soldiers were detained. While ethnic violence flared in the north in 1991, a new timetable was announced for a return to civilian rule. State elections held in mid-December resulted in the investiture of civilian governors in January 1992.

Speaking to the News Agency of Nigeria at the end of his annual Christmas holiday in Obosi, Chief Anyaoku accentuated the positive. He said it was a matter of great satisfaction that "for the first time in a long while, we have had relatively violence-free elections; that is an achievement of no mean proportion. We can all recall the days when elections in the country were characterized by violence; people were killed, whole houses were burnt and great damage was caused. It is a source of great satisfaction that we have recently had elections that were free from violence. They might not have been perfect elections, but they were very satisfactory elections in terms of allowing the people to express their choice of who should govern them in the states."

He went further in publicly proposing a new system of custodianship to prevent future military intervention in politics.

Council of Elders

Asked by the news agency for his suggestions on preventing intervention of the military in politics in Nigeria, Chief Anyaoku gave a carefully considered reply.

"I have always felt, looking around the world where the phenomenon of military intervention in national politics has existed, one common lesson is that it is always helpful to have safeguards against possible temptation on the part of the ranks of the military who were not immediately involved in the handover of power wanting to do what their predecessors did. And because you could never get any two exactly similar situations, each country has to think of its own safeguards.

"Speaking very much as a Nigerian... who is as fiercely attached to my country as I am in terms of its progress, I would say that perhaps we should think of arrangements for having an effective custodian of our constitution and our public code of conduct.

"We should have a national council of state which could consist of all ex-heads of state, representatives of the armed forces and police, some four or so traditional rulers, some two to four very experienced retired statesmen of proven integrity.

"If such a body were to exist, not as part of the government but as a custodian of the constitution and public code of conduct, then perhaps we could say that if any elected government were ever again in the future to abuse the constitution or to abuse the public code of conduct by becoming unacceptably unaccountable, corrupt or dictatorial, such a body can say 'enough is enough' and there could be national elections within three months of the sacking of the government that is guilty of such abuses."

Noting that democracy needs a "long gestation period", he said the concept of a "custodian"for the national constitution and national code of conduct would "obviate the need for the military feeling that they must perform the duty of providing a corrective regime... if we as a people recognize that we have long been too prone to the phenomenon of civilian/military/civilian/military governments, and that the reason why we have had these military interventions have always been given to be that the constitution and the code for public behaviour have been abused, we should want to stop it."

The proposal was widely covered in the media, headlined "Council of Elders". The newspapers on that Monday, 13 January 1992, also carried photographs of the social event of the weekend in Lagos at the Cathedral Church of Christ, where two former heads of state and a former vice-president (Gowon, Obasanjo, Ekwueme) spanning 17 years of national service, attended the wedding of Adiba Folashade Anyaoku and Ayodele Osadebaima Ighodaro.

Adiba's wedding

It was a buoyant season for the Chief. He had successfully completed his first Heads of Government Meeting as Secretary-General, in Harare in October, and got the mandate he wanted to visit South Africa and begin to explore possibilities for Commonwealth intervention, which he had done in November. State elections had been held in Nigeria in December, and the timetable to democracy seemed to be back on course. And now his daughter, his first born, a talented lawyer who had followed his early footsteps into the Commonwealth Development Corporation (CDC), had made a marriage match with Ayo Ighodaro, a trade and investment adviser.

Before Christmas, they had completed the negotiations and preparations for the traditional family marriage at Obosi. The wedding took place after a three-week interval and after much ceremony — first the traditional rites in the village on 21 December and then the white wedding in church on 11 January. Since the Anyaokus had returned to Obosi only in early December for their annual holiday, time was short before the wedding, and in Igbo tradition, the bridegroom's family had to visit the family of the bride three times, bringing drinks and kola nuts and gifts. Ayo came with his family, both men and women, for the first time on 15 December.

The visitors were presented with kola nuts, blessed by Mbidebe Ogalanya, an Ozo title-holder who is the Chief's representative and relative — "his grandfather and my father were cousins". He broke the first kola nut, and the visitors broke the second one, giving thanks that they had traveled safely, and praying for a safe return.

"We welcome you to Obosi, to *Adazie Obosi's* compound," said the Anyaoku family. "We have accepted that you will marry our daughter. The road to this marriage is like the road to fresh water, because the road to firewood can often be blocked and closed but the road to fresh water is always open. We pray God to guide and guard them, they are going to be blessed with the fruit of the womb."

The male visitors presented some cash, which was accepted as part of the marriage ritual but later returned. Then they went to sit outside the *iba* (the room with the seat of the chief), and the neighbours from the immediate vicinity, all related in some way, came into the compound to hear why the visitors had come, to have drinks and share in the festivities.

"On behalf of Chief Otabo Ade, head of our delegation today, and of the current head of Ighodaro family of Benin, we are no longer strangers, we are in-laws, and we thank you for that." They received kola nuts again, blessed, prayed, broke them and passed them around. And they were given two unbroken kola nuts to take with them, "so when it gets home you can tell of where it came from."

"May they be grandpa and grandma..."

On another occasion, from the mother's side came gifts in Yoruba tradition, presented by the women:

○ kola nuts, 42 altogether, for marriage, to carry away any evil in their lives;

○ bitter kola, remove the coating, it is one whole nut, may they remain whole together for their whole lives, and may they be grandpa and grandma;

○ alligator pepper, even the tiniest one is full of seeds, fruitful may they be, may they be blessed with children like their parents are, multiply in the house of Ayodele like the seeds of the alligator pepper;

○ honey, may their life be sweet as honey for ever more;

○ *shnap,* as important as the content of this is in any ceremony, may they both be very important at work, at home, among their friends, to remain on top forever;

○ sugar, to sweeten their lives together;

○ a wardrobe full of clothes and inside it is traditional Yoruba *oja* cloth for tying the baby, she will have twins, she will have boys, she will have girls, also *aso oke* cloth;

○ holy bible, the most important of all the presents, by the grace of God, they will be comforted by the book, and the word of God will guide them.

If there any doubts about the efficacy of these traditions to married life by those who may not have encountered them before, one has only to meet the results of the union: the lively, healthy and very attractive grandchildren — Irenne Ebelechukwu Babamayowa Ighodaro and Osita Osarogie Oluwatimilehin Ighodaro.

A "bitter disappointment"

National elections were held for a bicameral house in mid-1992, under a government decree that tried to break with past political polarization by allowing the formation of two new parties as the only contenders. Presidential primaries started in August, conducted state-by-state in the manner of the United States of America, and then were suspended only to be held in September; this was when Yar'Adua emerged the winner over 11 other candidates for the Social Democratic Party (SDP). The results were promptly cancelled and the handover to civilian rule delayed for a third time. Eventually, the two parties were allowed to select their presidential candidates although several potential nominees, including Yar'Adua, were banned from contesting.

The SDP selected the multi-millionaire media magnate Chief Moshood Abiola and the National Republican Convention (NRC) chose a leading industrialist Alhaji Bashir Tofa, both prominent Muslims and businessmen close to President Babangida. The election was finally held on 12 June 1993. The results were not announced, but leaked information indicated that Abiola had won comfortably, taking 19 of the now 30 states, including several in the north. The results were formally annulled on 23 June, and no further challenges allowed through the law courts. The National Election Commission, suspected of leaking the results, was suspended.

The following day, Chief Anyaoku spoke out strongly, saying the annulment was a "severe setback to the cause of democracy, particularly at a time when all Commonwealth governments have pledged themselves to promote democratic rule in their countries," and a "bitter disappointment" to all those who have been looking forward to the assumption of office of a democratically elected government.

"For eight years, Babangida made the world and me believe that we had a programme which would result in a democratically elected government at the end of it," Chief Anyaoku said later. "And when, in August 1992, I heard and read in the newspapers, statements by people like Obasanjo saying that Babangida was not going to hand over, I had gone home, and on 26 August 1992, I met with Babangida and asked him whether he had any hidden agenda, telling him that for me, my word was my greatest possession; and when governments asked me whether Nigeria was going to return to civilian rule, and if I told them that I believed the answer was yes, they took me seriously. And so I wanted to know if there was any hidden agenda. He had assured me there was not.

"And so when, at the end of it all, Babangida annulled the elections. I was concerned that Nigeria no longer had much credibility abroad."

Babangida stood down as promised on 26 August 1993 and appointed Chief Ernest Shonekan to head an interim government. But Shonekan, who attended the Commonwealth summit in Cyprus in October as "Head of State and Commander-in-Chief of the Armed Forces", remained a figurehead with real power vested in Gen. Sani Abacha, who had continued as minister of defence. In November, Gen. Abacha put pretense aside and took power. He abolished democratic institutions including the senate, national assembly, state councils and all political parties; reinstated rule by the military with a civilian cabinet at the centre and military governors in the states; and purged officers loyal to Babangida.

Chief Anyaoku was in Johannesburg attending the concluding proceedings of the South African constitutional negotiations leading to elections, and the irony of South Africa moving to democracy while Nigeria moved in the opposite direction was not lost on him. He issued a blunt statement.

"Any government that does not derive its legitimacy from the ballot box is never to be encouraged. Nigeria has been in political turmoil since June 1993 when the laudable democratization programme culminating in the presidential election was aborted. Since then, the central concern to all those who truly love Nigeria has been to ensure the reinstatement of that programme of democratization based on the true wishes of the people of Nigeria as expressed through its democratic institutions."

Abacha vs Abiola

Some weeks later, in early January 1994, after a family holiday in Obosi, Chief Anyaoku travelled to Abuja for a first meeting with Gen. Abacha since his takeover, but the General refused to give any timetable for a return to a democratically elected government. He said he would prepare for a constitutional conference, and "I told him I didn't think Nigeria's problem was a question of a faulty constitution."

The next time he met Abacha was in May, during the inauguration of Nelson Mandela in South Africa, and when he could not get a firm appointment through the ring of protective officials, he astounded them all by walking up and knocking on the door of Abacha's hotel room where he was waiting to receive his delegation of former heads of state. A short private meeting ensued which they agreed to continue in Abuja.

On 12 June 1994, the anniversary of the annulled election, Moshood Abiola declared himself president, pledged to set up a government of national unity, and went into hiding, amid public demonstrations demanding his inauguration. Abiola was arrested on 23 June. The oil and gas unions went on strike supported by others, local refineries stopped, and there were major shortages of petroleum and kerosene. Abiola refused to come out of prison under the strict conditions imposed by the military regime. Abacha responded with repression, sacking the heads of the unions and detaining more democratic activists, purging the army and closing the main opposition newspapers.

"In July, by the time I visited Nigeria, all the strikes were on. Nigeria was grinding to a halt. I felt that I owed the country the duty of making a public statement on my arrival, which I did. And the essence of that statement was to say that things were not at all well with the country."

His statement was lengthy and blunt: "By every index, Nigeria has become like a motor car with a capacity to run at 200 km per hour but which is moving only at 20 km per hour and showing signs of a possible total breakdown. ...There is therefore an urgent need for Nigeria's leaders to reach a truly national consensus on how to pull the country back from what seems to be an inexorable drift to national disaster.

"While every country has its own unique political circumstances, I believe that there are useful lessons for Nigeria from the experience of other pluralistic countries that have successfully tackled the challenge of finding durable democratic structures and good governance. I therefore hope that, in my discussions during this visit, I will be able to explore ways in which the Commonwealth can assist Nigeria's efforts to achieve democracy as it has now successfully done in no less than 11 of its member countries, including South Africa."

He noted in an earlier statement that Nigeria was one of only two remaining military regimes in the Commonwealth, the other being Sierra Leone. However, within days, as if to taunt the elusive nature of his objective, there were again three, after a military coup in The Gambia.

Meeting in detention

The Secretary-General proceeded to Abuja, where Gen. Abacha asked why he was hitting the country so hard. "I said to him, 'Did I say anything that was not true?' He didn't say more. But we had a conversation. And he agreed that I could go and see Abiola. I was the first outsider to go and visit Abiola, in his place of detention. ...When I had asked him, his first reaction was very negative and in that he was supported by Babagana Kingibe who was present. ...But I persuaded them in the end by making two points:

"One, was that if I was not allowed to see Abiola I would say so in public, that I had asked, and after all, in 1986, the Commonwealth Eminent Persons Group was allowed to see Mandela in prison. I would have to tell the world of my request and his refusal.

"And secondly, that I was getting representations as to the state of Abiola's health.

And if I didn't see him, I would not be in a position to comment objectively on the state of his health. Unless they were not themselves sure of his health, I would want to see for myself."

At a banquet that evening hosted by the Head of State, the Secretary-General was again blunt about his objectives. "I proceeded to tell him that I was sure I was singing tunes that were not usually sung in the environment there, and that I might appear over-concerned about the fate of my country and the affairs of the nation. But I hoped that he and everyone else would understand that this came from a total sincerity and commitment... And that I had lived long enough abroad to know that the most cruel thing that happens to Africans, to any African, is to grow old in the cold, European climate; that I would not ever want that to happen to me. And so I would continue to care deeply about the state of affairs in my own country, to which I have every mind to retire."

The following morning, Chief Anyaoku and his assistant, Chuks Ihekaibeya, were collected by the Commissioner of Police and driven around Abuja over a circuitous route to a compound full of state security and police personnel. When they entered the room where the detainee was seated, he was told he had a visitor, and it was clear that they had not informed him in advance. Two senior police officers remained firmly seated until Chief Anyaoku insisted they depart so he could discuss their presence with the prisoner, who agreed they could come back because he had no secrets from them. Chief Anyaoku also noted that Abiola was "moving in obvious pain; he told me his back had been injured. ...

"I put a number of questions to Abiola. I said I wanted to know his views about the state of affairs in the country; the possibility of talks; the people who would enjoy his confidence and so could take part in talks on his behalf. And then how he was being treated.

"On the first, he told me that he would never have stood for election if the military, Babangida and his group, had not assured him that they meant to leave politics. He said he would not have exerted himself to the extent that he did, spent his money to the extent that he did, if he had known that these fellows did not mean to hand over. He felt betrayed.

"Secondly, that he had the mandate of the people. And his views must be based on what the people want. He knows that all those who voted for him are sick and tired of military rule. And that Nigerians do not want military rule anymore. And that he, himself, is not going to bargain away the mandate that he has.

"Then thirdly, he gave me the names of those in whom he would have confidence for them to represent his interests in the talks I was proposing. If such people were selected, and they talked with him about how to return to the mandate of the people, he would be open to their views as he himself had no fixed ideas. He would accept any talks with which I would be involved.

"And finally, that they were not treating him very well. He had no access to radio or television or even newspapers. And his family were allowed to come only once in a while. And as far as his accommodation was concerned, I could see the house where he was being kept. One of the commissioners jumped in and said, Excellency, we are moving Chief Abiola today to a different and better accommodation. I said that would be good. We then concluded our discussion, I thanked him and said that I found the conversation valuable."

The Secretary-General thereafter issued a public statement confirming that, "At my request to the Federal Government, I have this morning met with Chief Moshood Abiola in his place of detention."

Before leaving the country, he wrote a letter to Abacha, hand delivered through his officials, urging on him "my thought that there should be carefully prepared private talks between representatives of his government and Abiola, to fashion out a consensus that would be the basis of returning Nigeria to democratic rule. And I repeated what I had told him by word of mouth, that the triumph of South Africa was the triumph of a national consensus on how to share power in a pluralistic state. And that I believed this was what Nigeria needed."

After a week, the officials admitted that they still had not delivered the letter. Abacha said he would reply after he had read it. When there was no response by September, the Secretary-General wrote another letter, longer than the first one, spelling out the reasons for his proposal. Finally, in November, a five-page reply arrived "that said, in effect, that I was too pessimistic, not taking adequate account of the extent to which

the structures associated with the constitutional conference were in fact
working out the national consensus I was advocating.

"I was in no way persuaded by that, because my point all along has
been that the annulment of the elections created within Nigeria two main
camps: those who were in favour of the annulment; and those who were
opposed to the annulment, in the name of democracy. And that a solution
could only come if the two sides were enabled through their trusted
representatives to work out a consensus.

"I therefore wanted, in December when I went to give the first Tafawa
Balewa memorial lecture to have an opportunity to develop the thought
further with Abacha. But of course, I didn't have the chance. And this was
in some ways an exasperating experience."

He delivered a courageous analysis of the national condition in The
First Sir Abubakar Tafawa Balewa Annual Memorial Lecture in Abuja on
19 December 1994, causing nervous foot-shuffling and shifting of limbs in
an audience of several hundred that included military hierarchy and federal government ministers, public servants, academics and the public; but
when he had finished, they gave him a standing ovation for his carefully
crafted message.

**The First Sir Abubakar Tafawa Balewa Annual Memorial Lecture,
Abuja, 19 December 1994**

Excerpts:

"Sir Abubakar saw that the content of his overriding message of unity had
to be given substance through the practical expression of his three other great
themes — of humanity, of integrity in government, and of democracy. ...The
glaring difference between such a Nigeria and the country we have had in
recent years must, I believe, remain both a scourge to the conscience of all
thinking Nigerians, and a challenge to all those who truly aspire to rebuild faith
in our unity.

"As a people, we Nigerians have many admirable traits. At the head of these
stands our great attachment to individual liberty. I do not know of any of our
constitutional documents in which the principle of the liberty of the individual
in Nigeria is not depicted as inviolate. Indeed by nature and disposition,
Nigerians will not want to wear dictatorship, whatever its stripe.

"It is this irrepressibility of the Nigerian sense of individual freedom which in
the final reckoning explains the fact that notwithstanding the protracted military
interventions in the nation's governance since 1966, manifestations of the people's attachment to the value of the liberty of the individual have throughout
remained evident often to the chagrin of the military Government in power. ...

"As for a free and democratic society, the facts about the present state of affairs in Nigeria speak for themselves loud and clear; and I mean objective facts, not subjective comments or explanations on which opinions would naturally differ.

"To mention just a few: at a time when in consonance with what has become a world-wide movement and in accordance with a commitment by all its membership to the fundamental political values of the Commonwealth, every other country with which Nigeria should be compared is practising credible democracy, we still have a military government; political parties are still not able to organise themselves legally; a number of our citizens are still either in detention or have their movements restricted for evident political reasons and the citizens can no longer expect the full protection of the universally recognised juridical principle of habeas corpus, or that all administrative decisions can if necessary be subjected to the discipline of an independent judiciary.

"...as I travel round the world in the course of my work, from West to East and North to South, I find that Nigeria is now frequently mentioned in the press as a country where the human rights of its citizens are not respected and press freedom is being progressively muzzled. ...

"In my Tom Mboya Lecture in Nairobi in November last year, I touched on the role which the army has played in contemporary African politics. I made the point then that the issue should never be one of a good military government versus a bad one. It is that the army should have no place in politics. Let me amplify the point.

"Experience in many parts of the world has clearly shown that there are inherent problems with the very nature of a military government itself. Neither by training, nor by professional ethos is the army designed for the task of governance. The primary and essential function of the army is to defend the state against external threats and internal subversion; their training and orientation are accordingly directed to this function. Ranking order within disciplined forces is intended to be almost inviolate. Consequently, in many instances a coup brings into government the additional strains arising from the fact that the discipline of the military ranking order has been broken. Thus the inherent instability in a military government is immeasurably increased.

"...There is also the fact that military rule, however benign or enlightened, is in the last resort rule by command or, as some would say, rule by the big stick."

"When you have the confidence of your support," Chief Anyaoku says, "you can be bolder, you can be more principled. ...We have a proverb in my place that says that, 'When you are challenged on your way to somewhere, you must stop and think of the number of people who would rally to your defense before you accept the challenge'."

A northern newspaper, *The Democratic*, had headlined a report on his earlier visit, "Anyaoku: Mediator or Meddler?" and he replied in a letter to the editor which was published, saying, "How could I, a national, be meddling in the affairs of my own country?"

The Federal High Court had ruled Abiola's detention illegal in October, but Abacha refused to release him. Instead, the national constitutional commission announced that there would be elections in 1996 leading to a new government in 1997, and that the ban on political activity would be lifted in March 1995.

Nineteen-ninety-five

In a New Year Statement issued from Accra, Ghana, where the Anyaoku family had spent the holiday in deference to security concerns about staying for any length of time in Nigeria, the Secretary-General spoke of "significant successes" in the Commonwealth during the previous year as well as "disappointing setbacks". In the first category was South Africa's conversion to a non-racial democracy, while the "setbacks" included Nigeria, where "it remains to be seen whether the various constitutional and other initiatives will prove to be an advance towards or a further retrogression from the much-desired objectives of national political regeneration and economic reconstruction. ...

"Happily," he said, "there are already signs that 1995 will bring new opportunities." But hopes were dashed before the first quarter was over. And there was plenty more to come.

The trial began in January of Ken Saro-Wiwa and 14 other Ogoni activists charged with complicity in the murder of four Ogoni chiefs who had opposed their campaign methodology. Chief Anyaoku continued to send messages to Abacha, trying to facilitate talks, with no response, only to hear that the military government had initiated talks with the National Democratic Coalition of Nigeria (NADECO), supporters of Abiola. "However, in the view of NADECO, government was not serious." NADECO wrote to Chief Anyaoku soon after, specifically thanking him for the views expressed in the Balewa lecture, as well as for the statements of a number of Commonwealth foreign ministers.

"I have sent yet another message, because I do believe that if it was possible for me to orchestrate the talks, that they might be able to reach a consensus. ...because I think the country is tired of military rule. The country is tired of the instability, it's paying dearly for the social and economic state of the nation. And Abiola would not want to remain in prison indefinitely. And I somehow hope that the prospect of Abacha being able to leave government in safety and be free to enjoy his wealth and whatever, would in the event of talks help the emergence of a consensual package.

"I know that the country, the government in particular, is not in favour of what Abacha told me to be 'internationalizing' Nigeria's internal affairs. So the people could not readily accept the UN or anybody else from outside brokering a national consensus. In my case, because I'm a Nigerian, they would latch onto my Nigerianness, and play down my being Commonwealth Secretary-General. And secondly, they know that I am not partisan and I have no political ambitions in Nigeria. They also know that I have accepted a second term of office in the Commonwealth which takes me to the year 2000. I therefore have the credentials for helping to create a consensus.

"The fact that the government has not replied to me positively, seems to strengthen the case of those who argue that the military government is not yet ready to hand over power. Such people would say that that was why the constitutional conference decision of last December to make 1 January 1996 as the departure date of the military was opposed by government. ...

But "they are managing to contain all of the pressures. ...if you read Nigerian newspapers, the allegations are that the government is buying its way through, settling those who seem to be potential sources of opposition and those they can't settle, they arrest and imprison."

In March, the Abacha regime claimed a coup attempt which the media dubbed "the coup that never was". This claim facilitated the detention of some 150 serving and former officers, including the pair who had handed over power to civilians in 1979: Obasanjo, the former head of state, and Yar'Adua, his former deputy.

Both were charged with the same offences, for which *Tell* magazine and other Nigerian media later revealed the details of a frame-up. The accused received different sentences from the military tribunal; the former was given life imprisonment, the latter was sentenced to death. The ruling military council, in the vortex of an international furore that they perhaps had not quite anticipated, commuted the sentences to 15 years and 25 years, but mental and physical harassment continued, with Yar'Adua being moved to five different prisons in the first year, amid rumours that the pair had been stripped of their military ranks. Within a year, both were reported to be in poor health. There were fears that their lives were in jeopardy, and this later proved true in the case of Yar'Adua, who died in prison almost three years later.

The regime withstood the fury of the international community, international organizations and the world's retired heads of state who regard Obasanjo with great respect, as an "elder statesman", after his orderly handover of power, his role in the Commonwealth Eminent Persons Group to South Africa, and establishment of the Africa Leadership Forum.

On 16 March, the day after the arrests, Chief Anyaoku sent another message to Abacha and made a public statement, saying that reports of a new wave of detentions "constitute a serious turn for the worse in the country's continuing drift towards a self-inflicted tragedy. International concern and disapproval has in this connection been heightened by the reported arrest and detention of General Olusegun Obasanjo, widely known as the only Nigerian military head of state to have relinquished power voluntarily and returned the country to a democratically elected government.

"These developments underscore the point that, unless and until the military government speedily returns the country to democratic rule, Nigeria's current ills, including instability and potential for disastrous conflict, will continue to worsen. I am therefore contacting the Nigerian Government to further explore ways in which the country can be assisted to hasten the return to democracy."

Chief Anyaoku telephoned Abacha and told him that the detentions were wrong, that it was a disastrous decision on his part. "That was the last time he spoke to me on the telephone; thereafter, he never took my calls."

The national constitutional council rescinded its timetable in April and further delays in the transition to civilian rule were announced later in the year; the inauguration date of a new president was set back to 1 October 1998.

In mid-1995, in South Africa again to discuss constitutional development, the Secretary-General said he continued to receive representations from Commonwealth members "expressing deep concern about reports of the arrests of pro-democracy campaigners, the continuing closure of newspapers, the suspension of *habeas corpus* and the secret trial by the Nigerian military government of military and civilian personnel, including the country's widely known former head of state, General Obasanjo.

"...the fact that these concerns are being conveyed to the Secretariat from all regions of the Commonwealth makes it inevitable that developments in Nigeria will receive particular attention by Commonwealth Heads of Government when they review the implementation of the association's core principles at their next summit meeting in November 1995 in Auckland.

"In the meantime, the depths of concern expressed suggest that Commonwealth governments will want to react strongly against any developments which they see as seriously worsening the already worrying situation in Nigeria."

In July while the Secretary-General was preparing to testify to the House of Commons select committee on foreign affairs, Michael Binyon wrote in *The Times,* under the headline, "Commonwealth chief issues threat to Nigeria":

"Chief Anyaoku, who has tried to exert public and private pressure on General Sani Abacha, is known to be appalled by the damage the military leader is inflicting on Nigeria, and believes the time for quiet diplomacy has ended. The former foreign minister will tell MPs about his own attempts to influence the general and the warnings he has delivered about the public outcry if General Obasanjo is executed."

On 1 October, the 35th anniversary of Nigeria's independence, the Secretary-General was in Jamaica attending the Commonwealth Finance Minister's Meeting when he learned with relief of the commutation of the death sentences for the detainees. His statement spoke of the need for consensus aimed at reconciling the internal divisions. However, by month-end there was more cause for alarm:

"I have learnt with deep concern that Mr Ken Saro-Wiwa has been sentenced to death by a military tribunal in Nigeria. I earnestly hope that this sentence will not be carried out and I appeal to the Nigerian authorities to spare his life. This step will be important in helping the process of reconciliation and the speedy return of Nigeria to democratic rule. I shall be conveying this appeal in appropriate terms to Abuja."

In a letter of 9 November 1995, addressed to HE General Sani Abacha, Head of State and Commander-in-Chief of the Armed Forces, The Villa, Aso Rock, State House, Abuja, Nigeria, the Secretary-General appealed for reason:

"From Auckland where your Commonwealth colleagues are gathering for their biennial meeting, I have this morning learnt that the Provisional Ruling Council has confirmed the death sentence on Mr Ken Saro-Wiwa and eight others. ...I write today to repeat my heartfelt appeal for clemency and do urge you, whatever the rights or wrongs of the case against Mr Saro-Wiwa and the others, to exercise your utmost humanitarian judgment and spare them their lives and their families and people the agony of avoidable bereavement. I believe that the cause of peace and stability in our country will be best served by this crucial exercise of mercy at this time. Chief E C Anyaoku, CON."

Auckland

Chief Anyaoku's patience had run out, as Binyon noted in *The Times*, despite the Igbo philosophy of *ndidi* (patience), and the proverbial warning of restraint that says, "he who volunteers to use his head to break the coconut will not eat from it." He was now more determined than ever that the Commonwealth Heads of Government Meeting in New Zealand in November 1995 would put teeth into implementation of the 1991 Harare Declaration, by approving a programme of action that would "translate words into deeds".

Commonwealth leaders went to Auckland prepared to talk frankly about the need for a persuasive course of action. The host government set the tone with a tough pre-summit statement from the foreign minister, Don McKinnon, saying that, although he could not stop Nigeria from attending a Commonwealth meeting, New Zealand would not offer its traditional warm welcome to the Nigerian representative. "Recent developments in Nigeria, particularly since the arrest of General Obsanjo, have been strongly criticized world-wide, including by Commonwealth governments. The Commonwealth Secretary-General himself, Chief Emeka Anyaoku, has added his voice to those criticisms, including in his statement of 16 March 1995."

Nigeria refused to take the hint, and Abacha's foreign minister, Chief Tom Ikimi, was bullish about his plans for CHOGM. "For the avoidance of doubt, let me state it here that Nigeria will be there and will participate fully in its work."

Chief Anayoku dismissed any suggestions that it might be difficult for him to remain objective: "In fact, being a Nigerian enables me to appreciate even more the importance of changing the situation there." (*Diplomat*, Sept/Oct 95) "But of course being a Nigerian, totally committed to my country, in its broadest sense, it is a source of personal distress to me that my country should be behaving so out of tune with the Commonwealth."

He refused to be drawn in advance of the meeting on what action should be taken, and declined to predict the outcome. "No secretary-general would consider it prudent to anticipate what heads of government would want to discuss or what conclusions they would want to reach." (news agencies) However, he did not deny speculation in The Times that the summit would press for Nigeria's suspension; "the article is not inconsistent with what I've been saying about Nigeria."

When the heads gathered for their first formal session after the official opening on 10 November, "the discussion encompassed concerns about

the continued existence of the military regime, and the continued detention of General Obasanjo and those who had been tried secretly for
alleged coup plots," Chief Anyaoku said later. "The discussion was
informed by... the general wish that Nigeria should be encouraged to
move quickly to democratic government." Some participants, such as
President Mugabe and President Mandela were frank, but language was
temperate, with the exception of Chief Ikimi who shocked the meeting,
by doing "what no one could ever recall happening", directly criticizing
the two heads of state in a manner that one senior official described as
"most impolite and discourteous."

Early the following morning, as 33 heads of government and high-
level representatives of 15 other member countries prepared to depart for
Queenstown for their traditional weekend retreat, international television broadcasts carried news of the execution of Saro-Wiwa and eight
others. The reports said the 54-year-old writer had been found guilty by
a special tribunal of murdering four Ogoni community leaders killed
during a clash at a political rally in Port Harcourt the previous year:
"Saro-Wiwa fought for the rights of his minority Ogoni ethnic group
through the Movement for the Survival of Ogoni Peoples. ...Ogoni is in
an oil-producing area of Nigeria."

Chief Anyaoku called his key Secretariat advisers. "When I heard the
news, I talked with some of my colleagues to make sure that they had
heard the same news.

"I didn't quite believe it, although when I sent my pleas to Abacha following the confirmation of the death sentences by the PRC, I had been
mindful of the fact that with Abacha having responded positively to
international pressure over the death sentence on the coup plotters and
the reduction in the sentence of Gen. Obasanjo, the hawks within his
regime were feeling that Nigeria must not, and his leadership in particular must not, be seen to be weakening. And so I feared then that he might
choose the Ken Saro-Wiwa case for showing that he was a strong and
determined man who was not to be pushed around or deflected by international opinion. But what I hadn't expected was that it should happen
during the time of CHOGM..."

He made a public statement immediately, on 11 November 1995: "I
have just heard the news of the execution of Ken Saro-Wiwa and eight
others with outrage and indignation. I am sure that anger will be shared
by a great many across the Commonwealth. This act confirms the need
for the Commonwealth summit not to be deflected from its purposes in
agreeing, among other things, an action programme to address instances

where member countries violate the Commonwealth's fundamental principles, including respect for human rights."

The assembled Commonwealth leaders were "horrified"; the British prime minister, John Major, called it "judicial murder" and Mandela, who had been an advocate of dialogue and quiet diplomacy and had sent a high-level delegation to Abuja to talk to Abacha, issued a strong statement calling for the expulsion of Nigeria from the Commonwealth. One of his senior officials explained why the executions had precipitated this change in his approach. " ...in his view, the brutality of it, that nine people were executed, who were perceived by him, and by the rest of the international community, not as murderers but as political activists, as environmental activists. And the international opinion was not at all impressed by the manner of the tribunal, their trial and sentencing."

Nigeria was thrust more boldly into the focus of the meeting, and at the retreat it was at first proposed to begin with a discussion of Nigeria. The Secretary-General advised, however, that since the Commonwealth had no agreed basis for dealing with cases like this, it would be more logical to first consider an Aide Memoire which contained procedures to deal with this eventuality. He had prepared the Aide Memoire with great care, consulting widely with a number of Commonwealth leaders in all regions of the world during the previous year, and had circulated it well before the meeting. Thus, the Aide Memoire was virtually an agreed document, and it was approved without further delay. Once the document was adopted, it provided a basis for dealing with member countries who violate the Harare Declaration, titled "The Millbrook Commonwealth Action Programme on the Harare Declaration".

"So from the point of view of the evolution of the Commonwealth, Auckland moved the association to the stage of becoming much more demonstrably concerned with translating its declarations from rhetoric into action," Chief Anyaoku said later. "The Commonwealth is now concentrating on its members states and putting its own house in order."

Paragraph 10 of The Auckland Communiqué says: "...Heads of Government, with the exception of The Gambia, agreed to suspend Nigeria from membership of the Commonwealth pending the return to compliance with the principles of the Harare Declaration. They urged the Nigerian Government to take immediate and concrete steps to adhere to these principles, and offered whatever practical assistance the Government might request in this respect. They called for the release of the 43 prisoners currently being held for involvement in an alleged coup attempt and the release of Chief Abiola.

"They further decided that if no demonstrable progress was made towards the fulfillment of these conditions within a timeframe to be stipulated, Nigeria would be expelled from the association."

CMAG

The approved mechanism for implementation was a Commonwealth Ministerial Action Group (CMAG) that was mandated to deal broadly with fulfillment of the Harare declaration, in two ways:
● to assist countries requiring assistance, to live up to the principles in the declaration; and
● to deal with countries who seriously or persistently violate those principles.

The group, to be convened by the Secretary-General would comprise eight foreign ministers, supplemented as necessary by one or two ministerial representatives from the region concerned. The group's task would be "to assess the nature of the infringement and recommend measures for collective Commonwealth action aimed at the speedy restoration of democracy and constitutional rule." It was subsequently announced that members for the first two years would be the foreign ministers of Britain, Canada, Ghana, Jamaica, Malaysia, New Zealand, South Africa and Zimbabwe.

The first CMAG meeting was held a month later, 19-20 December 1995, at Commonwealth headquarters, Marlborough House, in London. Zimbabwe was elected to chair the group with New Zealand as deputy. They reviewed developments in Nigeria, and decided to send a mission of five foreign ministers to pursue dialogue with the Nigerian government at the highest level. CMAG noted the establishment of three of the institutions required by the transition timetable, but added that there had been "no effort" to engage pro-democracy groups in a "genuine dialogue". And despite the specific appeal at Auckland, "Chief Moshood Abiola, General Obasanjo and others remained in prison; press restrictions had been tightened and other civil and political liberties eroded."

The group also noted that "the implications of Nigeria's suspension from the Commonwealth were to:
● exclude participation by representatives of the Government of Nigeria at all inter-governmental Commonwealth meetings and nominees of the Nigerian Government in other inter-governmental Commonwealth activities;
● preclude Nigeria from participation in Commonwealth sporting events;

- cease all Commonwealth technical assistance to Nigeria, with the exception of assistance aimed at facilitating the transition to democracy; and
- leave contact at professional and non-governmental levels with Nigerian agencies to the discretion of individual pan-Commonwealth organizations."

They welcomed measures taken by other members of the international community since the Commonwealth's decision at Auckland. These included:

- visa restrictions;
- interruption of sports contacts through denial of visas to official delegations and national teams;
- embargoes on the supply of arms and other forms of military co-operation, including the expulsion and withdrawal of military attaches; and restrictions on development assistance.

"The Group expressed the hope that the dialogue would achieve the desired results. However, in the event of failure, existing measures could be made more effective by better co-ordination and further measures would be necessary. The Group requested the Secretary-General to commission a study on possible further measures, to be applied on an incremental basis as the situation demands. These could include:

- a freeze on financial assets and bank accounts in foreign countries of members of the regime, their families and collaborators;
- action to prevent new investment including bank loans;
- action against export credits;
- a ban on the export of support equipment for the oil industry; and
- partial trade embargoes, for instance oil sanctions.

"The Group recognized the significance of the leadership which the Commonwealth had demonstrated at Auckland. It took the view that the Commonwealth should continue to play a leading role in a united international effort to help in the speedy restoration of democratic civilian rule in Nigeria."

At the time of the second meeting four months later, when the Abacha government had still not agreed to receive the ministerial mission, CMAG said that "notwithstanding the holding of non-party local government elections in March 1996 and other steps, the general human rights situation in the country had continued to deteriorate; not only had political and other detainees not been released but further political detentions had occurred.

"Accordingly, the Group reviewed measures which the Commonwealth could take in order to register continuing disapproval of

developments in Nigeria, as well as to encourage the Nigerian authorities to adhere to the Harare principles. In this context, they considered possible further measures and decided to recommend for implementation" the following:
- visa restrictions on members of the Nigerian regime and their families;
- withdrawal of military attaches;
- cessation of military training;
- embargo on the export of arms;
- denial of educational facilities to members of the Nigerian regime and their families;
- an immediate visa-based ban on all sporting contacts;
- a downgrading of cultural links;
- the downgrading of diplomatic missions.

"The Group further decided that a ban on airlinks with Nigeria and additional economic measures, including freezing the financial assets and bank accounts in foreign countries of members of the regime and their families, should be considered in consultation with the European Union (EU), the United States and other members of the international community with a view to their adoption as appropriate." The Secretary-General was mandated to undertake these and other consultations, and he continued to strategize for the group, but after the first two meetings, he encouraged direct contact between the chairman, Dr Stan Mudenge, and Ikimi.

"And I have spent a great deal of time speaking with a number of Nigerians with influence on Gen. Abacha; those that I am able to talk to in London when they visit, who have personal relationships with Abacha, trying to urge that Abacha should encourage the emergence of a national consensus from a serious dialogue between the 'pro-June 12 election' and the 'anti-June 12 election... I see such a national consensus, which will emerge from such a meeting, as crucial, because a great deal of the problem in Nigeria springs from divisions."

The government of Nigeria eventually offered to send a high-level delegation to hold discussions with CMAG. Specific dates were set for June, and after their meeting, the two sides issued a joint statement welcoming the dialogue and stating their positions, which were widely divergent. In August, CMAG decided to send a team of senior secretariat officials, led by the Deputy Secretary-General, to Abuja to discuss the modalities for a visit by CMAG ministers, which eventually took place in November.

Increasingly, the secretary-general found that his main challenge was holding together the group, because of sharp differences of strategy that emerged, with three on one side and five on the other side "in relation to... sanctions against Nigeria. ...so this was becoming more complicated because I believe very strongly that, if the Commonwealth is seen to compromise with Nigeria's actions that are in violation of the Harare declaration, the Commonwealth will lose credibility, and will return itself to a position... where it was vulnerable to charges of hypocrisy.

"I was very keen that the credibility of the Commonwealth should be sustained, but at the same time, I have to face the reality that there are three members of the group who would want to limit the extent to which Nigeria is isolated from the Commonwealth. So it is coping with this divergence of opinion within the group that constitutes my greatest challenge. ..."

Furthermore, while "South Africa was vulnerable to international sanctions; Nigeria is not. ...if there was an effective international sports sanction against Nigeria, that would work, that would make a difference, but I doubt if we can, because Nigeria is not without clout in Africa. ...You cannot isolate Nigeria from Africa; and you also have, outside Africa, countries waiting to grab Nigeria's oil."

As if to underline the point about Nigeria's "clout", he received top-level representation from both the UN and the OAU urging against sanctions on Nigeria. "And that is why I worry about the Commonwealth, because the Commonwealth would then be reduced to a situation where Nigeria could laugh at the Commonwealth and say, you're inconsequential."

Edinburgh 1997

The CMAG delegation that visited Nigeria was well appraised of the government position, but unable to meet with opposition or pro-democracy groups, or detainees. So they decided to hear their representatives in London in July, who made three main points:

"First, they painted the picture of a worsening human rights situation in Nigeria, that things were not changing since Auckland; if anything, at the human rights level, they were worse. Second, they alleged that the democratization process being proclaimed by Nigeria was not credible, that it was not to be trusted. And third, they claimed that Abacha's regime was doing all it could to ensure that he, Abacha, succeeded Abacha, and so the process would not be credible."

CMAG had agreed that the main points would be conveyed to the government of Nigeria for their response, and the letter to Ikimi made these points, in diplomatic terms. The foreign minister did not reply to the points, saying that the letter arrived rather late; and instead he pro-

duced a different sort of reply. He wrote a letter demanding the right of
Nigeria to be in Edinburgh during the Heads of Government meeting in
October. The letter was highly personalized and claimed credit for the
Nigerian government for the election of the Secretary-General in
Malaysia in 1989 and his re-election in Cyprus in 1993, a matter upon
which there was a lengthy list of willing campaigners, including not only
the then Nigerian foreign minister, Gen. Ike Nwachukwu, but also a
number of foreign ministers and heads of state from Africa, Asia, the
Mediterranean and the Caribbean. This was couched in courteous language, and the Secretary-General replied courteously that allowing
Nigeria to come to Edinburgh CHOGM would require a decision of the
heads of government.

Just before CHOGM, three delegations from Nigeria arrived to meet
with Chief Anyaoku, two groups of traditional leaders and the third, a
former foreign minister. All came with the message that the breach
between Nigeria and the Commonwealth should be arrested. Another
former foreign minister was stationed in Glasgow to be near, but not at,
the CHOGM.

Heads of Government had agreed in Auckland that they would
review the composition, terms of reference and operation of CMAG every
two years. This they did when they met in Edinburgh in October 1997,
and took another unprecedented step by giving CMAG power to act, in
certain circumstances, without reference to heads of government.

They "empowered CMAG to invoke, in the period before 1 October
1998, Commonwealth-wide implementation of any or all of the measures
recommended by CMAG if, in CMAG's view, these would serve to
encourage greater integrity of the process of transition and respect for
human rights in Nigeria."

They further agreed that, after the 1 October 1998 date set by Nigeria
for handover to civilian rule, "CMAG should assess whether Nigeria had
satisfactorily completed a credible programme for the restoration of
democracy and civilian government. ...if in that assessment, Nigeria had
completed a credible transition to democratic government and to obser-
vance of the Harare principles, then the suspension will be lifted; but if it
remained in serious violation of the Harare principles, Heads of
Government would consider Nigeria's expulsion from the association
and the introduction of further measures in consultation with other members of the international community as recommended by CMAG."

They expressed concern about the continued detention and imprisonment of many Nigerians, including Chief Abiola and Gen. Obasanjo, and

decided — despite many attempts at lobbying to the contrary — that Nigeria should remain suspended from Commonwealth activities. They noted the positive contribution Nigeria was making to the efforts through the Economic Community of West African States (ECOWAS) to support democratic government in the region, and expressed the hope that this reflected "a determination to comply with the Harare principles in its domestic policies."

The Nigerian government chose to put a positive spin on this, with Ikimi "applauding" the Commonwealth decision which maintained the suspension of Nigeria, and saying that because there would be no further action until 1 October the following year, the Commonwealth had by implication accepted Nigeria's own programme of democratization. In reality, there was nothing much they could do to change it, only apply pressure to ensure that it was credible and democratic.

At the end of 1997, the Anyaoku family spent their fifth Christmas away from their beloved Obosi, and holidayed in the Serengeti national park at the invitation of the government of the United Republic of Tanzania.

Nigerian attendance at CHOGM

1966 Brig B A O Ogundipe, Leader of Delegation
1969 Chief O Awolowo, Deputy Chairman, Federal Executive Council
1971 Dr the Hon. Okoi Arikpo, Commissioner for External Affairs
1973 Gen. Y Gowon, Head of the Federal Military Government and .
      C-in-C of Armed Forces
1975 Gen. Y Gowon, Head of the Federal Military Government and
      C-in-C of Armed Forces
1977 Gen. Shehu Yar'Adua, Chief of General Staff, Supreme
      Headquarters
1979 Maj Gen. H E O Adefope, Commissioner for External Affairs
1981 Alhaji S Shagari, President,
1983 Alhaji S Shagari, Presidet
1985 Commodore O E Ukiwe, Chief of General Staff
1987 Vice-Admiral A Aikhomu, Chief of General Staff
1989 Vice-Admiral A Aikhomu, Chief of General Staff
1991 HE Gen. I Babangida, President
1993 HE Chief Ernest Shonekan, Head of State and C-in-C of Armed
      Forces
1995 The Hon. Chief Tom Ikimi, Minister of Foreign Affairs
1997 suspended

Times change

As the 1 August date for presidential elections in Nigeria drew nearer, and Abacha secured the presidential nomination of all five authorized political parties, it became increasingly clear that he intended that the new president would be himself.

"I have heard news reports," Chief Anyaoku said in a statement in April 1998, "that the scheduled 1 August 1998 presidential election in Nigeria may be replaced by a referendum on the candidate now nominated by all five registered political parties, General Abacha." The Secretary-General said he would bring these developments to the attention of CMAG, noting that the transition process, to be credible, "must command the support of the Nigerian people."

Just over a week later, he had to issue another statement condemning the conviction of yet another group of alleged "coup plotters" who were sentenced to death, and appealing to Abacha's government to "exercise the utmost restraint and humanitarianism."

On Monday, 8 June 1998, late afternoon, Chief Anyaoku arrived in Harare from his first visit to Mozambique since it had formally joined the Commonwealth. He had just checked into his hotel room at 6pm, when BBC flashed the news that Sani Abacha's residence in Abuja was surrounded by troops, amid unconfirmed reports of his death. The secretary-general's private office staff at Marlborough House in London had been frantically trying to contact him, while he was still in the air, after a two-hour delay in departure. He switched on the television in his hotel room, and picked up the cordless phone to call London, but before he was connected, BBC radio confirmed that the Nigerian head of state was dead.

He listened briefly and then cut short his call to London, to try to call Lagos, but it seemed that the rest of the world was calling at the same time and the tone sounded particularly busy, adding somehow to the drama of the moment. He issued a statement conveying condolences to members of the family, and adding, "I have no doubt that all Nigerians would wish to ensure that peace prevails and that the succession arrangements are based on genuine national consensus."

He didn't reach Nigeria by telephone until later that night, to hear the news firsthand from colleagues and friends. They had heard the name of, but knew little about, the burly, soft-spoken military man who had been chief of staff and who now announced that he was, reluctantly, the new head of state — Abdusalami Abubakar. At the time of his announcement, he was just another Nigerian head of state in a military uniform, received with some trepidation, but in the days that followed, he became much more than that: a central figure in the Nigeria's transitional ruling council.

It was a moment of suspended animation for Nigerians within and outside their country as they waited to see and hear if the new head of state would maintain the policies and personnel of the old one, or would change the course of the nation, and how boldly. Would he maintain the timetable to elections and handover to civilian rule on 1 October 1998? Or would he bow to the demands of the opposition which, having had the courage to oppose Abacha under threat of detention or worse, were now demanding that elections be delayed while they prepared themselves?

Chief Anyaoku remained glued to the phone, fax and television as events unfolded in Nigeria and he watched Abubakar take office on CNN. He received a few close friends, including a Zimbabwean government minister who was a previous High Commissioner to London, but with characteristic initiative, he was already weighing up the need to go immediately to Abuja and the potential for positive influence on the events at home.

"You will want to see many people," one visitor said, rather vaguely, commenting on his delayed departure. He replied, in his now familiar manner of making a frank assessment of his role in relation to others, with self-assuredness but little hint of arrogance — "Yes, and I think many people will want to see me."

The twinkle in his eye grew into laughter at that rejoinder, and then reflected pain, as the talk wavered over the length of time that had passed since he had visited his beloved home country, due in part to the fact of Abacha's appalling human rights record and that it had become impossible to contact or communicate with him, but also in reluctant deference to strong warnings of the threat to his own personal security.

"Nigeria's reclusive leader, Sani Abacha, died as he had lived," said the *Daily Telegraph* in London, "sealed off inside the tightly guarded Aso Rock, the presidential palace in the capital, Abuja." *The Times* added, "Even in the unhappy history of Nigeria over the past few decades, the four-year presidency of Sani Abacha stands out as a dark and blood-stained page...."

Homecoming

Within 24 hours, Chief Anyaoku had spoken by telephone to Gen. Abubakar, who invited him to visit Nigeria. One week later, Chief Anyaoku welcomed the release of Gen. Obasanjo and eight others, noting that further "equally resolute steps" are needed. And just over two weeks later, he was on his way to Abuja, saying the positive steps taken so far by Nigeria's new head of state were a promising start. He welcomed this in his official capacity, and as a Nigerian. "An opportunity has emerged in Nigeria for dialogue and national reconciliation."

During a four-day visit to Nigeria at the end of June, he had three meetings with the new head of state, a long meeting with the still-detained Abiola, an emotional reunion with the recently released Obasanjo, and a number of contacts with representatives of Nigeria's vibrant civil society.

It was an emotional moment when he drove to the sprawling farm at Ota near Abeokuta to pay a call on the man who calls himself a "prison post-graduate" because he was detained post-independence, and they raced toward each other into a welcoming embrace. One of them, Chief Anyaoku, had been outside the country for four years, unable to come home although he would never use the term "exile"; and the other had been inside for three years, as a prisoner, often in poor conditions amid concern for his life. Their experience reflected the situation of many Nigerians who had been in prison or exile during Abacha's tenure. The two men spent almost an hour in private conversation, which Obasanjo characterized for the media as "catching up on old times... You see after, three years in prison, I have been slightly out of circulation. The Secretary-General came to brief me about the goings-on in the country and the world."

The Nigerian media burst out with its characteristic vigour after years of repression under Abacha, and every detail of the transition and the visitors who came to call was scrutinized. Chief Anyaoku in a lengthy interview with *Champion* that ranged across the return of exiles and the attitude of the international community to his feelings on returning home, said his message to Nigerians was one of hope.

"Hope that this new administration is aware of what needs to be done to restore confidence. First, genuine national reconciliation. Secondly, the dignity and self-respect of Nigerians. Thirdly, the sense of security of Nigerians. Finally, Nigeria's place in the international community."

Gen. Abubakar opened up a channel of regular contact with the Secretary-General, telephoning him often for advice on specific matters, such as how to build bridges with the international community. Although a quiet man and rather shy, he was encouraged by Chief Anyaoku to get out and make contact with people, both at home and abroad, that he had the personal opportunity, in his own behaviour as head of state, to build confidence in the future of the country and the transitional process. As a result, he traveled to Britain and France, the United States and South Africa, and met often with the media, winning them over with his relaxed manner. "His calm mood, witticisms and friendly banter with the press calmed the stressed nation," Pini Jason wrote in *New African*. "Nigerians could laugh again alongside their leader. Abubakar is healing the wounds of a fractured nation."

In his many conversations with Gen. Abubakar, Chief Anyaoku shared the benefits of his years of diplomatic and democratic experience, urging him to scrap all the structures that Abacha had created "because they had no credibility within and outside the country", and to proceed with a speedy handover to a democratically elected government. He suggested the setting up of an independent electoral commission, and proposed names of people who would ensure its impartiality and credibility. "And I urged for the credibility of the exercise that international organizations such as the Commonwealth and the UN might be involved."

The sensitive matter of the imprisoned Abiola was fraught with pitfalls as the regime was of the opinion that if he reclaimed the presidency on his release, this could spark unrest in what was already a volatile and expectant transition. However, international visitors were allowed access to Abiola in detention, and some made the diplomatic faux pas of revealing contents of their discussions, saying he would renounce his claim to the presidency if he was released. Chief Anyaoku did not do this. He noted that Chief Abiola "was surprisingly alert mentally for a person who had remained imprisoned, incommunicado over long periods, for four years", but he was very well aware from his many years of dealing with South Africa and Mandela, that prisoners could not be expected to state their case from prison, only after release. And he was very careful to say that Abiola must speak for himself when he was free.

"I am not surprised that Chief Emeka Anyaoku was more careful," said Uncle Bola's column in Nigeria's *Sunday Tribune* of 5 July 1998. "I am very proud of this brilliant Classics scholar of the University of Ibadan. ...Chief Anyaoku rightly said that only Chief Abiola could speak about his mandate and his future. That is the truth, the whole truth, and nothing but the truth."

Three days later, Chief Abiola collapsed during a meeting with a high-ranking United States delegation led by the Under Secretary of State for Political Affairs, Thomas Pickering with the Assistant Secretary of State for Africa, Susan Rice and the US ambassador Nigeria, and died.

"...and then my shock at the news of the death of Chief Abiola," Chief Anyaoku said later, "the telephone call I had the day he died from Gen. Abubakar to tell me of Chief Abiola's death, and assure me that there was no foul play. And we discussed the question of foreign pathologists coming to take part in the autopsy. And my belief that the pathologists have now confirmed this, that Abiola died of natural causes."

Nigeria at the crossroads

The Secretary-General reported back to CMAG that he believed Gen. Abubakar was sincere in his commitment to restore a credible democracy and hand over power as soon as possible. He added that the change in the political atmosphere in Nigeria was "nothing short of dramatic" and that the "sense of fear and foreboding which characterized the Abacha regime has largely dissipated."

He said Gen. Abubakar was consulting widely with different sections of the community over the fate of the existing transitional structures, the nature of new transitional arrangements, and a target date for the handover; and that he had impressed upon him the importance of a handover by the military to a "credibly elected government" before 1 January 1999.

In the event, after wide consultations, a firm timetable was put in place, and an Independent National Election Commission (INEC) was established, chaired by Justice E O I Akpata, who wrote to express gratitude for the Commonwealth's technical assistance in the planning and conduct of the local government elections on 5 December 1998, which they said contributed in no small way to the success of the elections. Chief Anyaoku commended the INEC for working closely with political parties "to facilitate an inclusive and transparent electoral process" and said he was delighted at "the evident enthusiasm of Nigerians at this first election in the transition to democratic civilian rule." He said the Commonwealth had been engaged with the transition programme in Nigeria by providing technical assistance and experts to INEC in the areas of logistics, training and advice, and that they would continue to do so.

State elections took place in January 1999, and elections to the national assembly and presidency followed in February. Commonwealth election observers expressed satisfaction with the process, saying technical and logistical problems had been addressed, and that the elections represented another important step in Nigeria's transition to democracy.

Following the elections, CMAG immediately recommended to Commonwealth heads of government, who accepted, that Nigeria's sus-

pension should be lifted, and that Nigeria should return to full membership on the date of assumption of office of the newly elected government.

The Secretary-General said lifting of the suspension would enable the
new President to attend the next Commonwealth CHOGM in South
Africa in November 1999, where "he could expect a very warm welcome
from his colleagues. ...There is a real expectation that Nigeria will quickly take up its traditional leadership role as a major player within the organization. ...Above all it is a new beginning, laden with great opportunities and challenges for the future:

• to heal the wounds of the past;
• to provide all the people with a share in the national prosperity and
each of them with a sense of belonging;
• to exercise utmost vigilance in order to secure their fundamental freedoms; and
• to build a strong, stable and democratic future in a country forever
united in its diversity."

The Peoples Democratic Party (PDP) had swept to victory in the polls,
including the presidential election. And on 29 May 1999, an expectant
nation heard the promise of its first democratically elected civilian president in over 15 years:

"I, Olusegun Obasanjo, do solemnly swear that I will be faithful and
bear true allegiance to the Federal Republic of Nigeria and that I will preserve, protect and defend the Constitution of the Federal Republic of
Nigeria. So Help Me God."

8

CHALLENGES

Chief Emeka Anyaoku has spent his long career transforming the ideals of freedom,
peace and democracy into workable realities.
(University of New Brunswick, Fredericton, Canada, Doctor of Laws degree, 1995)

Emeka Anyaoku is a man who, with his quiet determination,
has changed lives and changed countries.
(South Bank University, London, Doctor of Laws degree, 1994)

CHIEF ANYAOKU set himself a number of goals when he decided to seek the post of Commonwealth Secretary-General in 1989, and he honed them into a set of specific priorities during a six-month retreat in his home village of Obosi before he took office in July 1990. A decade later, it can be stated without fear of contradiction that he has achieved the specific objectives he set for himself and a few more, as shown in this book. He would not claim solitary victory in his achievements; one of his strengths has been in working with others. But he has played a key role, often, in identifying, guiding and pursuing the processes, and consulting and advising heads of government; and it is not only praise-singing for South Bank University to say that he has "changed lives and changed countries".

With the same single-mindedness with which he has carried out his mandate, he made preparations to consolidate the foundation for the future at his last Commonwealth Heads of Government Meeting (CHOGM) as Secretary-General, in Durban, South Africa; and to hand over a vibrant and relevant association to his successor. There is an Igbo proverb that says, "What we are remembered by is the work we have done."

It could be argued in some cases that his objectives were not inclusive enough, particularly in the goals of democratization, which could have cast their net further. But his analysis showed a clear understanding of what was possible and what may not have been possible and why; and he chose, deliberately, to tackle those situations in which he could make a difference. That the major successes were in Africa is therefore not surprising, as the arena gave him a comparative edge.

There were other times when his reach exceeded his grasp, as when he failed to get a consensus on his proposal for a global humanitarian order midway through his first term, and faced a north-south alliance of influential member countries lined up against the idea. This experience helped to temper his vision of what was possible, and he was more precise at putting together the blocks for a firm foundation on most initiatives thereafter. He didn't abandon his objective, but proceeded to redesign it. This is not to say that everything he touched turned to gold, but if it turned out to be tin, then he didn't throw it away, he retooled it. And he often tempered his impatience in favour of a sustainable, consensual foundation stone, deliberately laid and firmly placed.

Nonetheless, there will be those who say that this biography of the man and his work is not a critical or academic analysis, that it is too positive a presentation, that it doesn't dig out the contents of his closets and reveal his warts. There are several reasons for this.

The author set out to tell a story, as noted in the Preface, not to undertake a comparative study of the degree of impact on each Commonwealth country since the Secretary-General took office. This book is about Eleazar Chukwuemeka Anyaoku; it is not intended to be an assessment of all achievements of the Commonwealth during his tenure, rather how he operated and how he influenced the agenda. The story related in the previous chapters contains plenty of violence and bloodshed, plenty of pain and anguish — but he didn't cause it. Rather, he has contributed to healing it, where possible. He was fully aware of the rare mantle of opportunity he had in leading an international association with fundamental values similar to his own, with no block votes and no vetoes, and with direct access to the head of the association and over 50 heads of government.

That his contribution should be the subject of academic analyses and debate is not in doubt; perhaps this book and his volume of selected speeches, *The Missing Headlines*, offers a starting point for others.

When *The Missing Headlines* was published in 1997, a prominent reviewer said of the content, that it "offers informative insights into a highly interesting and influential international figure. ...The rationale of the book's title lies in his belief that, while much of the Commonwealth's consultation and activities necessarily has to be hidden from the media, much too goes unreported or rarely attracts media interest. Anyaoku's hope is that by revealing some of those 'missing headlines', greater public debate on the work of the Commonwealth will be encouraged. ... From such a diplomatic eminence, his views would naturally attract international attention.

"In Anyaoku's case, his speeches also command intellectual admiration. ...For this reviewer [Anthony Kirk-Greene of St Anthony's College, Oxford]... the bonus of this collection is to be found in Anyaoku's brilliant extra-mural — as it were — contributions, for example 'The Image of Africa' presentation, 'Africa and its Diaspora: From Political to Intellectual Emancipation', and 'Tackling the Legacy of Africa's Slavery'. Here we have sound, reflective scholarship as well as deep diplomacy. ...

"Anyaoku's patently unpretentious intellectualism (how often in his speeches does he neatly invoke the classics as well as quoting pertinently from lesser known sources) is matched in its scope by the number of countries and the variety of occasions on which he has been invited to speak. ... *The Missing Headlines* shares a merit with the best volumes of selected speeches, namely that of inspiring the reader to wish he could meet the man behind the speeches and the headlines."

The subject is a positive person by nature, who seeks the best in people, who tries to build achievements not empires, who builds up rather than tears down, and who has devoted his life to improving the human condition, and combating racism and apartheid. His vision was clearly reflected in the title of his second report as Commonwealth Secretary-General, prepared for the summit in Limassol, Cyprus in 1993: *The Commonwealth — A Growing Force for Good.*

Of himself, he says, "...it doesn't come easily to me to think uncharitably of others. And I'm glad of that."

His closets? Well, the trouble with his closets is that they are open to scrutiny, and contain no skeletons; no dirty laundry, no drugs, mistresses, political skullduggery or whiff of corruption. If that (an honest person, happily married and devoted to his family) is considered odd in the human condition at the beginning of a new millennium then perhaps we should take a good look at our judgmental responses.

"Argue don't shout"

There were sceptics when he took office, for all sorts of reasons, among those who did not know him well: because he is a technocrat, because he is an African, because he is a Nigerian, because he has a quiet way of getting results, in the manner of the advice given by the late Mwalimu Julius

Nyerere to his nation, "argue don't shout"; or the Igbo proverb, "do not separate your mind from your tongue". Some colleagues and officials felt superior to him, or thought they could manipulate him and were disappointed. He gained in confidence and stature as he proceeded into his second term in 1995, and faced fewer challenges of this nature.

His outright critics are few, and their criticism based on personal differences in approach rather than shortcomings: a senior official who erected bureaucratic barriers which he dismantled; another who, unfamiliar with his goals and objectives, and his manner of achieving them, looked upon him as an African upstart. Others perhaps who disagree with his vision of a common humanity with equality of race, religion and gender.

The most valid criticism comes from those closest to him, who find themselves running to keep up, his exacting standards difficult to reach. He does not always see the demands he makes on those around him (at home and office) through his formidable vision and workload, but they seldom complain because they know he pushes himself the hardest. This is not unusual in a statesman of his calibre.

An interesting aspect of analysis of Chief Anyaoku is that his critics tend to highlight the same traits as his praise-singers: the single-mindedness and determination, which leaves colleagues standing and wearies his staff; his belief in people and devotion to principle which leads him to put aside cynicism; and his personal attention to detail, which keeps others on the hop. Many who work with him do not understand what motivates him.

Critics are fewer in number than when he took office; at that time, the main critique, other than those unstated which were racial in nature, was that he was a technocrat, could he provide the necessary leadership? Would he inspire, and speak out as necessary? He would not have been the first leader of an international organization to have been selected with those credentials; the second Secretary-General of the United Nations, Dag Hammarskjöld from Sweden was "virtually unknown" when he took office and was "generally believed to be a non-political technocrat". (Urquhart and Childers)

A sense of self-worth

It is fair to say now as Chief Anyaoku's term draws to a close that some former critics have become reluctant converts or at least acknowledge that he has succeeded in his mission to make the Commonwealth a relevant and active force in the world, toward the goals of good governance, sustainable development, and common humanity. As is often the case, scepticism fades under the glow of positive results.

Another aspect that should be openly explored is the contribution he has made as a role model, to changing racial stereotypes, particularly in the so-called "old" countries of the Commonwealth which used to be seen as "white", and to changing the image of Africa through his own personal style and intellect. This was deliberate on his part, always an element of his actions and never far from his vision. But never presented as a confrontation or in a manner to offend, rather thoughtful though pointed. The attitudes he has changed in this regard cannot be measured easily, but the many that have become obvious to this writer over a period of time are clearly the "tip of the iceberg". That he lives his ideals and his aspirations in his daily life is a given, cliché thought it may appear in words. He "is" his principles and they are unbendable.

Ego, yes he has one, though it could be called a sense of self-worth. If this were not a part of his make-up, he perhaps could not talk with confidence to heads of state and government, and senior officials, and win them over to his point of view or reach common ground. It does not manifest itself in arrogance, rather it is rooted in a lifetime of awareness of racial politics, in which the measure of an individual is often taken as judgment for an entire race. He is not unaware in his human contact that his interlocutor is judging his race and the continent of Africa, as well as his person. His achievement in that sphere is perhaps his most significant, and he has not flinched from it no matter how harsh the gaze.

It could be said that his achievement is reflected in the eyes of the beholder, for a decade ago, those who crossed his threshold saw a black man, an African, with impeccable dress and manners, taking up a position of international influence. One quite bizarre description in a patronizingly positive article in *Country Life*, described him as colour-coordinated: "a quiet study in brown, his shoes, suit, striped shirt, belt, polka dot tie and dark skin all in matching shades." Now, that attitude has changed, and he is seen for what he is — the Secretary-General of the Commonwealth.

He has achieved that, too, through perseverance and determination, a sensitivity to attitudes, and often through sheer force of will, under cover of his lively sense of humour. In his home area in eastern Nigeria, they say, "Laughter is the same anywhere in the world" or, "A good humoured person has no enemy."

I once asked Chief Anyaoku to tell me some proverbs, and he replied, "a thing must happen to necessitate a proverb." I later learned through study what he had not enlightened me about, ie ignorance had blinded me to the recognition that what he had said was, in fact, an Igbo proverb. "It depends, you see, our proverbs are not just recited by themselves, they are part of our means of expressing thoughts and philosophies in the course of conversations."

On route to Auckland for a pre-CHOGM consultation at the end of June 1995, his particular brand of initiative made good copy for a columnist of the London newspaper, the *Evening Standard*, who wrote: "I have a new hero. He is Chief Emeka Anyaoku, Secretary-General of the Commonwealth, and he has scored a mighty victory over the American bureaucracy. The Chief was at Los Angeles airport the other day, en route to Auckland. His New Zealand visa, however, was elsewhere. Airline staff refused to let him fly without it. All seemed hopeless. Then he had a brilliant idea. He pulled out a photograph of three men. 'Do you recognize this man?' he asked, pointing to the left. 'That's President Clinton,' came the reply. 'And what about him?' said Anyaoku, pointing to the right. 'That's that Mandela guy,' answered the minion. 'And what about the one in the middle?' asked the Chief. 'Why, that's you!' gasped the official, hugely impressed. There were no further delays."

Renaissance

He has already contributed to the African renaissance, by laying a firm foundation through his person and his work. The most substantive chapters in this book reflect his major achievements, in contributing to the successful transitions in South Africa and Nigeria. He is keenly aware that these are Africa's giants and that the African renaissance depends on their strength and their health, their vision and their leadership. He also retains a strong admiration for the principles and achievements of other, smaller countries in the neighbourhood.

Tackling the leaders of apartheid and building bridges across racial barriers, which would seem to have required both a positive attitude and formidable courage, were easy when compared to the cuts administered by the military regime and some of its media in his own country; ultimately suggesting that he should resign his post if he did not approve of his home government, arguing that "he was morally bound to resign his position immediately the country was thrown out of the club."

However, Nigeria was suspended, not "thrown out"; and there are a number of precedents to protect international civil servants from the vagaries of changes in government. An article in *The Guardian* in Lagos on

25 January 1997, said, "holding on to the argument that... all member countries are his constituency, Anyaoku shrugged aside his critics and stayed put. Instead of calling it quits with an organization he has been serving for the past 30 years, he remained neutral and focused his energy and guts on how the country could be re-absorbed."

And there were other opinions from at home and abroad: "It is one of the truths of life that we can do nothing to change the past, while what we do with the present and the future is limited only by our own determination," said the oration at one of over 20 universities that have conferred honorary degrees. "Today we welcome to the University of New Brunswick a man who lives by that precept. His Excellency, Chief Emeka Anyaoku... is living proof of the power of the individual human spirit.

"The problems that Chief Anyaoku has confronted in his lifetime are never far from us, even in Canada. When evidence of ethnic, racial and religious intolerance can be found in our own society, it is difficult to imagine how the world can ever be free of them. Yet, it is also clear that one man can make a difference. Your Excellency…You remind us that our common humanity transcends the injustices of history, and that whatever we do to build a better future we must do together. Your principles and your achievements inspire us all."

A transparent integrity

At home in Nigeria, a journalist for the *Sunday* newspaper wrote in September 1996 that, Chief Anyaoku can be described in the same words as he himself used to describe the late Prime Minister, Sir Abubakar Tafawa Balewa, whom he said "brought a transparent integrity to bear in public service; and in keeping with his own character he stood for a gentle, tolerant and humane Nigeria, and for democracy."

"And," the journalist Chiemeka Iwuoha added, "where more temperamental chief executive officers would rant and rave about the iniquities of military misrule or race-ridden international relations, the Secretary-General has chosen the lecture circuit, books, and occasional interviews to pass across his ideal of a successful Commonwealth, which are: multi-partyism; humane international dealings, and a quiet pride for being an African."

A High Commissioner from Asia said, "I find him even better than his reputation."

This is a Secretary-General who believes in consensus rather than confrontation, in persuasion rather than force, and in the power of morality over corruption; and yet has fulfilled the expectation of his ancestral name:

Anya=Eye O*ku*=Fire, the Eye of Fire or fiery eye, a name earned in combat, associated with chivalry and courage on the battlefield, at a time when commanders led from the front not the rear, when the warrior's appearance and demeanour was part of his strength, and when a determined and well-prepared opponent could win over his adversary, even before the blows began.

"There is a saying in my place, 'If a person loves peace, it does not make that person a coward'."

The vision and the objectives

The first African Secretary-General of the Commonwealth decided on taking office that his main institutional goals were the removal of South Africa as a barrier to relations within the Commonwealth; definition of the future strategic role of the Commonwealth; renewed confidence in the role of the Commonwealth; and restructuring the Secretariat in order to restore confidence and raise the level of services to member states. In addition, he identified three areas of political focus: apartheid in South Africa; democratization and human rights; and interventionist attempts to resolve conflicts or to assist in pursuing democratic development.

Clearly, as shown in previous chapters, he achieved his primary goals. This does not suggest that every Commonwealth country is democratic or that all democratic systems are perfect. Nor does it suggest that every country in which he initiated a process has completed it. Nor that sustainable development, gender equality and economic progress can be completed in a decade.

But firm foundations have been laid, with the Harare, Millbrook and Edinburgh declarations giving clear definition to the future strategic role of the Commonwealth. South Africans have elected their second post apartheid government and are facing the challenges of the 21st century together with their Commonwealth colleagues. The bad old days of the 1980s confrontations that saw the Commonwealth acting "with the exception of Britain" on most things to do with southern Africa have been replaced with frank discussions by heads of government on issues such as globalization, that have set the tone for other discussions between governments and private sector, civil society, and international financial institutions. After Durban, the Commonwealth chairperson has a stronger role, that of presenting the views of the association in international fora such as the United Nations.

Renewed confidence in the role of the Commonwealth can be seen in political, economic, social and technical spheres; and at all levels, from the non-governmental sector which meets at a biennial NGO Forum to heads of government and ministerial meetings. As well as democracy and governance, debt relief and the particular problems of small states, the Commonwealth has been playing an increasingly influential role in gender policy and practical implementation, environmental issues, financial management, equity investment, and information technology. One barometer of progress is the substance and focus of the Secretary-General's comprehensive biennial reports:

A Commonwealth of New Dimensions, 1991
The Commonwealth — A Growing Force for Good, 1993
Development and Good Governance — Local Action, Global Reach, 1995
The Commonwealth — In Pursuit of the Millbrook Action Plan, 1997
From Kuala Lumpur to Durban, 1999.

In his introduction to the latter, which was his last report as secretary-general to heads of state and government of the Commonwealth, he characterizes himself as its "principal servant".

The most difficult challenge in many ways was restructuring of the secretariat to re-tune the engine of the Commonwealth, improve efficiency and resource management in an organization already cost-effective by any comparative international measure, and raise the level of services to member states. Restructuring the secretariat was perhaps a more difficult challenge than that of restoring confidence in the Commonwealth itself.

Cyprus, 1993

The heady success of the Edinburgh economic declaration "back in Britain" in 1997 was some distance from Limassol, Cyprus just four years earlier when Commonwealth leaders reaffirmed the urgent need for "a substantial outcome" to the Uruguay Round of Multilateral Trade Negotiations, and when some leaders from the "old" Commonwealth begrudged the Secretary-General his second term. This had its roots in two confrontations, one political, the other bureaucratic. The political strand was his proposal for and pursuance of a Global Humanitarian Order to guide the international community's handling of conflicts and crises; and the bureaucratic intervention was his determined stance not to allow British and Canadian officials to dictate the terms and consultants for streamlining the secretariat. His determination to pursue reorganization of the secretariat into a "leaner, fitter" structure did not cloud his insistence on retaining the essential aspects of its multi-cultural character.

An establishment of 431 staff was trimmed down to 320, and 17 divisions were streamlined into 12. "I wanted to ensure that we have effective, responsive administrative machinery and get the best value for the limited funds we have." At the top, replacing the secretary-general's two deputies and two assistants, he now has three deputies – political, economic/social and development cooperation.

"We are running a multi-cultural, multi-national secretariat, in the context of the legacies of the Empire and colonialism. If we do not have a hierarchy, we'll have a situation where an assistant director will be accorded more recognition and more respect than an assistant secretary-general or his or her director, for reasons of historical legacies. I didn't want to be less subtle than that, but they all got my message. ...it's important in this multi-cultural, multi-national setting that offices should be acknowledged and their holders acknowledged.

"The cultural aspect is important, and one of the things that excites me most about the Commonwealth and the job I'm doing, is this blending of cultures. I have become thoroughly convinced that the differences do not inhibit the ability to work together. ...we have had one or two who have shown signs of, not quite arrogance but, over-confidence in their own system, not mindful that there is a lot in others."

That reorganization of the secretariat to modernize and make it more efficient, almost cost him his second term, so offended were some of the host country's senior officials who believed they should make the decisions about how this would be done, rather than the Secretary-General. To say that it almost cost him his second term is perhaps too strong because it was never put to the test and there were many supporters willing if necessary to stand his guard. But the British government was put in a position of begrudging him a second term, despite his excellent personal relations with John Major, then Prime Minister. Such was the remorse of the politicians, that two warmly congratulatory letters were received by the Secretary-General immediately after the meeting of Commonwealth leaders in Cyprus in late 1993:

- one was from external affairs minister Barbara McDougall who had represented the Canadian prime minister at CHOGM: "your skilful management, professionalism and sense of humour have been key ingredients in the smooth operation of this meeting"; and

- the other was from Major: "I felt that the meeting both sustained the family atmosphere of the Commonwealth and demonstrated the practical role which it can play in areas appropriate to this unique organization."

The Cyprus CHOGM began with 40,000 Greek Cypriot women joining hands and lining the highway for almost 70 km from the conference venue in Limassol to the conference opening in Nicosia, chanting "Freedom for Cyprus". It ended with a final communiqué that stated sparsely, "Heads of Government decided to offer Chief Emeka Anyaoku a further five-year term of office, commencing on 1 July 1995." This was immediately posted on notice boards in the secretariat by a senior British official, as "Commonwealth Secretariat Official Notice 39/93", with the full text of paragraph 73, concluding, "from 1 January 2000, the term of office for any subsequent Secretary-General would be four years, with a maximum of two terms for any one incumbent." The "official notice" neglected to mention that two terms, though not the extent, was the recommendation of the secretary-general as part of the restructuring exercise. He also got agreement on his proposal that deputies should be hired on the basis of skills employed, not elected by heads of government.

During this period, he did not have an administratively strong deputy of the calibre that he had provided to his predecessor. "The things I used to do for my predecessor were not done for me. So I had to do them. But in the end it was a very happy relationship, and I think the servicing of the meeting was very, very good."

A weakness as well as a strength has been his unyielding belief in the positive nature of the human spirit; he was not always successful in recruiting staff who shared his ideals of equality, although he did improve the gender balance of senior professional staff with the addition of some competent women. He insisted on vetting senior staff appointments, but too often took the advice of others rather than relying on his own good judgement, with the result that some of the old racial attitudes crept back into the senior echelons of the Commonwealth Secretariat.

"The Secretary-General believes in running a very tight ship," said an influential British magazine. "Chosen partly for his uncontroversial approach, he did not flinch from making cuts where necessary. ...While making sure there is adequate geographical balance (there are about 30 different nationalities in the staff at the moment), Chief Anyaoku is determined to maintain a 'merit-based recruitment policy'." (*Diplomat*, Sept/Oct 95)

The quiet man

The tone of the reference to the secretary-general in the 1993 communiqué was in sharp contrast to Harare two years earlier, which praised "the record of action" contained in his report; and Auckland two years later, which "commended the Secretary-General for the leadership he had continued to provide in the affairs of the Commonwealth."

The 1993 reference reflected the perceptions of some senior officials who had been involved in the institutional review, specifically they had their favourite candidate for the management audit and the Secretary-General had been very firm in his insistence on another, smaller firm that presented a more multi-cultural and diverse approach. It was a bruising battle, and the vanquished used the Cyprus CHOGM to seek their revenge.

"For a number of people, that was their first lesson. Somebody called me and said, 'I didn't know you were as tough as that.' What would I say to that?"

"The quiet man at Marlborough House," wrote Robert Mauthner in the *Financial Times* shortly after his election in October 1989, "who is liked by everyone but has, not so far, shown his teeth, may yet surprise the sceptics. That, at least he announced yesterday, is his firm intention."

"Polished, accomplished, distinguished, charming," *Gemini*'s Derek Ingram wrote in *Malaysian Business* in August 1990, just after the Secretary-General took office. "A number of adjectives recur when people write about the diplomat in Emeka Anyaoku. He is all of those things, and quite a lot more – determined, tenacious, energetic and tough. Above all, as you get to see when you have known him a few years, he is his own man."

While the institutional review was being concluded, a process of physical renewal was completed for the Commonwealth's stately home, Marlborough House. The refurbishment had been underway for six years, from 1987 through 1992 and, at one of the first occasions after returning from temporary offices in Carleton Gardens, the Secretary-General spoke of these dual processes:

"With all the changes taking place in the Secretariat at present, being back in Marlborough House provides both reassurance and continuity — but in a context of renewal and change. Just as this building has been strengthened and renewed, so also has the Commonwealth Secretariat as an organization. A new direction has been established; the structure has been modernized; the management style has been reviewed and the image that we are presenting to the world is being updated.

"In all the years of my long association with the Secretariat I cannot remember a period of more intense and critical self-examination dedicated to bring about a more efficient and effective organization. You will understand that this has been no easy task," he told the Commonwealth Youth Programme management committee in April 1993.

"Changing an organization such as the Secretariat requires the handling of a range of different agendas, sectoral interests, constituencies and a variety of perspectives."

The Secretary-General's office is on the first floor, up a sweeping staircase, past life-size murals of the Duke of Marlborough on horseback, in battle. The office itself, once described by a weary correspondent for *Country Life* who "trekked cross the pale acreage of his office carpet", has one wall occupied by a very large bookcase, as one would expect, and other walls hung with paintings from different parts of the Commonwealth, a small table and a few African artifacts. Various royalty occupied Marlborough House over the centuries, and this room was once Queen Mary's bedroom; she moved to Marlborough House on the death of King George V in 1936, and died there in 1953. The same *Country Life* correspondent who trekked across the carpet, claimed that the Secretary-General's "affectionate personal staff let slip a favourite joke", in which the current occupant is said to wonder what Queen Mary would make of finding him there if she came back to haunt it!

A different world

A more insightful article in the respected British magazine, *Diplomat*, in mid-1995, just after the Secretary-General completed his first five-year term of office, captured the relaxed mood of confidence that accompanied him into his second term.

"A hot day in July," began the article by Shaen Catherwood and James Robertson. "On Pall Mall, British Muslims are demonstrating against the UN Secretary-General Boutros Boutros-Ghali. The boys in blue stand by watching them exhaust themselves shouting. We retreat from the heat into the shadows, from the clamour of impotence into the deep hush of power — Marlborough House, home of the Commonwealth Secretariat. Soft carpets, softly closing doors and softly spoken security staff are all that lie between the Commonwealth Secretary-General Chief Emeka Anyaoku and the traffic. But what a different world. ...

"Chief Anyaoku seems unfazed by the splendour of his surroundings: he fills the room not with pomposity or self-adulation, but with a quiet dignity and impeccable courtesy.

"When asked about the interior decoration, he — characteristically — understates his influence. 'They were kind enough to consult with us and I had a hand in choosing the colour scheme. The original colour was much heavier than this – much more royal.' Offered the pick of Her Majesty's gallery, he chose a light, fresh, modern abstract painting that seemed 'custom-made for the new colour scheme'. More significantly, a painting devoid of imperial associations. ...

"Decades of political and administrative experience have not stolen the youth of this suave Nigerian, while his unflappable demeanour conveys a natural authority. Such a dignified public face must be a distinct advantage to the Commonwealth in 1995, when many parts of the global establishment are losing the automatic respect they once commanded." (*Diplomat*, Sept/Oct 95)

In growing recognition of his influence and public presence, he graced the cover of *Diplomat* as well as, among others, *World Statesman* and *Leadership*, to popular inflight magazines *High Life* (British Airways) and *Hemispheres* (United Airlines), from *Africa Today* and *West Africa* to *African Expatriate*, and the special edition of *First* magazine on globalization, published for the Durban summit. The international president of the latter, Sir Patrick Cormack, FSA, MP, said in his introduction: "The Commonwealth's position as a unique inter-regional international organization has been strengthened and enhanced by the wise, patient, statesmanship of the Secretary-General."

International stability and intermestic issues

The controversial proposal for a global humanitarian order, sidelined at Cyprus into the hands of a high-level group on international stability which met during 1994, was reconsidered after presentation of their report. A main theme was how the international community could best deal with actual and potential conflicts in a changing world following the end of the great power confrontation.

The 1995 summit welcomed the recommendations of this intergovernmental group, and commended the Secretary-General's efforts to "foster peace and stability" through his "good offices" role.

Chief Anyaoku's analysis of the changing world order was contained in a word he coined early in his tenure — *intermestic* — to define "issues that are essentially domestic but have international repercussions", and vice versa.

"Intermestic does not exist in the dictionary but, in my view, it conforms with all laws of English philology. ...when I put forward this idea I had a great deal of explaining and reassuring to do, that my concept of a Commonwealth role in dealing with *intermestic* issues was never intended to be against the wishes of the governments concerned. I made the point that any such role must be at the behest, or certainly with the agreement or acquiescence, of all the parties concerned with the conflict.

"One of the lessons of the post-Cold War era is that it is becoming untenable to defend what happens in individual nations against interference or intervention from outside on the basis of Article 2 of the United Nations charter. The notion of sovereignty is being progressively eroded. ...The trend is toward greater internationalism. And so it becomes easier for individual countries to accept assistance from fellow members of a regional grouping. But, regional organizations must handle this in a way that is sensitive...

"I wouldn't want to say it is an intervention... the expression should be a "more active involvement" in the resolution of actual or threatened conflicts in member states. ...

"Lesotho and Kenya were 'good offices' roles which strictly, under Article 2 of the UN charter, would be unacceptable because these are internal affairs."

And yet, for his "intervention" in Lesotho, he drew perhaps the highest accolade a Commonwealth citizen can aspire to, in being awarded an honour usually reserved for nationals. Prime Minister Pakalitha Mosisili awarded the highest civilian honour, "in recognition of his outstanding contribution, not only to the Commonwealth nations generally, but in particular, to the well-being of Lesotho and her people by his tireless and selfless interventions to restore the rule of law, democracy and constitutionality, as well as the dignity of Lesotho as a sovereign nation and member of the Commonwealth."

Recalling the Secretary-General's pivotal role in negotiating the 1992 return from exile and reinstatement of the late king, His Majesty Moshoeshoe II, and the transition from military rule to democratic governance, the prime minister turned from his distinguished audience to look at Chief Anyaoku and, in a tone filled with emotion, said to him: "You are one of us."

He also received the highest national honours from Cameroon, Namibia, and Trinidad & Tobago. In accepting the Trinity Cross, "on behalf of my fellow Nigerians ...linked by history and ties of kinship... and on behalf of the larger Commonwealth family for whom multicultural and multiracial Trinidad & Tobago is an exemplar," Chief Anyaoku gave the islands his highest accolade in return: "...may you continue to be a powerful inspiration to humanity in an age where one of the key challenges is the management of diversity."

Democracy's enemies within

The Secretary-General has characterized the main threats to international stability as divisive pluralism or "the tensions and conflicts spawned by differences of race, ethnicity or religion"; failure to consolidate good governance; unacceptable levels of poverty; and finally, "problems which are not constrained by national boundaries, such as environmental degradation, drug trafficking and commercial crime."

Democracy's "enemies within" include specifically — as well as poverty — racism, fundamentalist nationalism, and ethnic and religious fundamentalism.

"They exploit all democracy's resources — free press, free speech, the ballot — not to strengthen democracy but to deny it to others," Chief Anyaoku told the Commonwealth Parliamentary Association (CPA) in Bahamas in 1992. "They are democracy's enemies within."

In his first report as secretary-general in1991, Chief Anyaoku had said, "The Commonwealth can offer itself as an exemplary force for the containment of the divisive trends latent in pluralism because it is an association which itself operates on the basis of full respect for all racial, religious, cultural and ethnic differences within its diverse membership."

"In a world where internal conflicts seem to have largely replaced inter-state conflict, the Commonwealth has not been immune, " he said in his final report in 1999, "and increasingly Commonwealth governments are using help from the Secretariat to resolve domestic conflicts or defuse tensions. My response has usually been either to send an emissary or to go myself when the situation necessitates it and my other commitments allow. In the period since 1991, the Commonwealth has helped to resolve conflicts or defuse conflict situations, in [as well as South Africa and Nigeria] Bangladesh, Guyana, Kenya, Lesotho, Papua New Guinea, Sierra Leone, Solomon Islands and Tanzania, to name only some.

"The involvement of the Secretariat in what are essentially domestic affairs is a tribute to the Commonwealth connection. It needs to be ensured that nothing is done to diminish that confidence which governments are increasingly reposing in the Secretary-General and the Secretariat."

Testing principles against practice

South Africa and Fiji returned to the Commonwealth during Chief Anyaoku's tenure, and three new members joined: Namibia, Cameroon and Mozambique. The South Pacific island of Nauru (population 8,000) became a full member in 1999. There are 54 Commonwealth countries, and no shortage of new applications, including Palestine, Rwanda and Yemen. A future returnee may be the Republic of Ireland, which left the Commonwealth in 1949, just eight days before the "Nehru formula" enabled India and other republics to retain full membership.

Chief Anyaoku wanted to acknowledge the role of Her Majesty, Queen Elizabeth II, as head of the Commonwealth, and he chose the occasion of her 50th wedding anniversary when, for the first time ever, she addressed the opening session of the heads of government meeting in Edinburgh. "The Queen is a great asset... In the days gone by, when people like Margaret Thatcher would have jettisoned the Commonwealth, the Queen's attachment to the Commonwealth was very important."

"I believe in testing principles against practice," the Secretary-General told *Diplomat* magazine, "and in practice, the Queen's role as head of the Commonwealth has been immeasurably beneficial to the association, bringing an undoubted sense of continuity and stability both through symbolism and benign influence. Her role is not perceived in terms of an ex-colonial master or madam continuing a neo-colonial role — absolutely not. Today's Commonwealth is an association of sovereign nations each responsible for its own policies, freely electing to work together for mutual benefit."

Chief Anyaoku spoke often and with pride of "the people's Commonwealth ...a very active and relevant non-governmental [NGO] sector, which sets us apart from many international organizations." Pru Scarlett, who has worked in this sector for many years, gives full credit to Chief Anyaoku: "We had been pushing for greater NGO involvement in CHOGM for many years, and we got as far as a special NGO accreditation and an NGO desk. It happened when he took over, and we got full exposure at the Edinburgh summit. Some officials didn't want it, but thanks to his work behind the scenes, about 20 heads of state came to see for themselves. ... Edinburgh was a turning point in NGO involvement."

The Secretary-General pursued an active agenda to strengthen the role and participation of women, including a process for engendering the secretariat. He addressed the Fourth World Conference on Women in 1995 in Beijing, China, and encouraged the definition of a Commonwealth

Plan of Action on Gender and Development (2000-2005), which seeks to accelerate the empowerment of women. "Without the full participation of women, societies in both developed and developing countries are working towards their goals with one hand tied behind their backs. ...Women are the world's great untapped human resource for the future."

The Commonwealth resource

On the day that he made his acceptance speech to heads of government in Kuala Lumpur, 24 October 1989, Chief Anyaoku pledged to use "all the energy and resources available to me". His energy was boundless but the resources pledged by member countries were meagre and shrinking. "We are expected to do more and more with less and less." He sees the mobilization of resources as a major challenge for his successor, elected by heads of government at Durban in 1999: the former deputy prime minister and minister of foreign affairs and trade of New Zealand, and former vice-chairman of the Commonwealth Ministerial Action Group (CMAG), Don McKinnon.

Heads of government agreed in New Zealand in 1995 to strengthen the secretariat's capacity for developmental work by restoring resources of the Commonwealth Fund for Technical Co-operation (CFTC) to 1991/92 levels in real terms. That commitment is yet to become reality. In Edinburgh in 1997, heads of government agreed to "sustain and where possible increase" the flow of resources to the secretariat and its various funds, especially the CFTC; to the Commonwealth Foundation, Commonwealth of Learning (COL) and the Commonwealth Partnership for Technology Management (CPTM).

A review of CFTC-funded programmes concluded that it has provided technical cooperation of a high quality delivered more cost-effectively than other multilateral aide programmes. Yet, only 2.1 percent of the multilateral aid from the four developed countries of the Commonwealth finds it way into the CFTC and other Commonwealth multilateral programmes and agencies. By any standards, this is disproportionately small."

The challenge for the major contributors is to channel a higher proportion of their existing multilateral budgets through Commonwealth programmes, Chief Anyaoku says. For developing countries whose economies have progressed, the challenge is to increase their financial contributions. "A desirable target would be to seek, by the year 2000, to double in real terms the resources available for development co-operation through the CFTC and other Commonwealth multilateral programmes."

From Kuala Lumpur to Durban

Harare, Limassol, Auckland, Edinburgh summits were about meeting the challenges of the 1990s for good governance, human rights and sustainable development; while Durban focused on the agenda for the 21st century, especially the opportunities and challenges of globalization.

"We have not taken as seriously as I think we can and should, the role of the Commonwealth consensus, and the role it plays in informing the global consensus. In other words, we have adopted the Edinburgh declaration, but there is no firm plan for Commonwealth members of ASEAN, OAU, OAS, G8 or European Union, taking that declaration back to these regional organizations. ...

"Consensus is a seminal concept in the Commonwealth. The association lives by consensus, because there is no better way of reconciling the diversity within it or of ensuring that its decisions are implementable. ...But the focus is not only on consensus-building *within* the Commonwealth, but on *global* consensus-building, on how the Commonwealth could be a catalyst and facilitator of larger international consensus on issues that concern the world community." This puts in place the third plank of his vision of the Commonwealth:

- as a force for democracy, human rights and good governance;
- as an instrument for economic development of its member states; and
- as a builder of global consensus.

With his last summit, as he had planned it, returning to the continent of Africa, to the country of the African renaissance, and with the satisfaction of knowing that the Commonwealth was now remodelled for the 21st century, that he was not leaving it as he had found it, the Chief could begin to extend his vision further into the future. He could look back on that time of reflection before he took office, on what he had planned to achieve, and what had been achieved. And project his vision forward.

"Looking into the new millennium," he said in a Foreword to *The Commonwealth Ministers Reference Book 1999*, "I believe that there are two particular challenges for which the Commonwealth will become even more important to its members and to the wider international community. One is the management of diversity. Diversity or pluralism is, of course, normally a positive phenomenon. But, as the post-Cold War period illustrates, when cultural, ethnic, religious and other differences are not managed effectively, they also create division, even armed conflict. ...

"The other issue which is bound to have an important place on the Commonwealth agenda for the 21st century is how the risk inherent in globalization can be managed more effectively and humanely so that the benefits of the process can be shared by all. ...The wealth of the few cannot be sustained amidst the impoverishment of the many. ...

"I am convinced that alongside our current concerns of democracy, development, consensus-building and conflict resolution, these two issues will be key elements on the Commonwealth agenda in the years ahead. It is also certain that the highest priority will continue to be attached to the cross-cutting issue of promoting gender equality. ...

"The initial vision of the 1990s as a decade of hope must not be allowed to dim, but must inevitably now be tempered with greater realism."

A common humanity

Finally, who is this book for, and who wants to know about Chief Anyaoku and what he has achieved? During his career, he has visited all member countries except one (Tuvalu, which air connections deprived him twice of the chance of visiting) and he has friends and colleagues in all regions of the world, as well as in professional organizations whom he has addressed and encouraged as a firm supporter of the non-governmental Commonwealth; and the media who have largely ignored the achievements, as noted in the title of his volume of speeches, *The Missing Headlines*. Like many people, he inhabits more than one world, and those who know him in his international role may not have had a window to his traditional role, and vice versa.

Africa and the diaspora have a range of role models to which this person can be added, and cited as one of the heirs to the legacy of Marcus Garvey for his international crusade for human values and equality, a common humanity — and his understanding of the role of socio-economic development of the African continent in changing racial perspectives, which have their roots in underdevelopment and the trade in African slaves. This explains the high priority he placed on democracy in South Africa and Nigeria, and his personal attention to both of those transitions, toward leadership for the continent in the next millennium.

But mostly, throughout the research and writing, my target audience has numbered four (now seven) people: his children and grandchildren, the next generation, who know what he does but not all that he has achieved, at home and abroad. They are among the youth in whom he places his faith to continue the work for a common humanity and a better world.

SELECTED REFERENCES

Achebe, Chinua, *Things Fall Apart*, William Heinemann Ltd., London 1958; African Writers Series, HEB, 1962

Achebe, Chinua, *No Longer At Ease*, William Heinemann Ltd., London 1960; African Writers Series, HEB, 1963

Achebe, Chinua, *Morning Yet on Creation Day*, Heinemann Educational Books, London/Nairobi/Lusaka, 1975

Ademoyega, A., *Why We Struck: the story of the first Nigerian coup*, Evans Bros. (Nigeria), Lagos, 1981

Aguwa, Jude C.U., *The Agwu Deity in Igbo Religion*, Fourth Dimension Publishing, Enugu, 1995

Akwanya, Amechi, *Orimili: One Man's Struggle for Power in Pre-Colonial Nigeria*, Heinemann International, Oxford, 1991

Amadiume, Chief Soloman, *Ilu Ndi Igbo: A Study of Igbo Proverbs*, Vol. 2, Fourth Dimension Publishing, Enugu, 1995

Anyaoku, Emeka, *Tackling the Legacy of Africa's Slavery*, Commonwealth Secretariat, London, 1991

Anyaoku, Emeka, *The Image of Africa*, Commonwealth Secretariat and Channel 4, 1992

Anyaoku, Emeka, *Report of the Commonwealth Secretary-General*, Commonwealth Secretariat, London, 1991, 1993, 1995, 1997, 1999

Anyaoku, Emeka, *The Missing Headlines: Selected Speeches*, Liverpool University Press, Liverpool, 1997

APIC — Africa Policy Information Centre, *Nigeria: Country Profile*, Washington DC, 1996

Arnold, Guy, *Modern Nigeria*, Longman, London, 1977

Carrington, Lord Peter, *Reflect on Things Past: The Memoirs of Lord Carrington*, Collins, London, 1988

Clarke, John D., *Yakubu Gowon: Faith in a United Nigeria*, Frank Cass, London and New Jersey, 1987

Collins, Larry and Dominique LaPierre, *Freedom at Midnight: The epic drama of India's struggle for independence*, HarperCollins, London, 1975, new edition 1997

Derbyshire, J Denis and Ian Derbyshire, *Political Systems of the World*, Helicon, Oxford, revised 1996

De St. Jorre, John, *The Nigerian Civil War*, Hodder & Stoughton, London, 1972

Dike, K. Onwuka, *Trade and Politics in the Niger Delta 1830-1885: An Introduction to the Economic and Political History of Nigeria*, Oxford at the Clarendon Press, London, 1956

Doxey, Margaret P., *The Commonwealth Secretariat and The Contemporary Commonwealth*, Macmillan, Basingstoke, 1989

Du Bois, W.E.B., *The World and Africa: An Inquiry into the Part which Africa has played in World History*, New York, 1946

Dyson, Sally (ed.), *Nigeria: The Birth of Africa's Greatest Country, From the pages of Drum magazine*, Vol. One & Vol. Two, Spectrum Books, Ibadan, 1998

Ejizu, C.I., "The Taxonomy, Provenance and Functions of Ofo, A Dominant Igbo Ritual and Political Symbol", *Anthropos* 82 (1987): 547-567.

Ekwensi, Cyprian, *Divided We Stand*, Fourth Dimension Publishing, Enugu, 1980

Ekwensi, Cyprian, *Survive the Peace*, Heinemann Educational Books, London, 1976

Ekwuno, Olu-Uda, *The Life of Olaudah Equiano*, Longman African Classics, Hounslow, 1988

Eleazu, Uma O., *Federalism and Nation Building: The Nigerian Experience 1954-64*, Arthur H. Stockwell Ltd., Devon, 1977

Eminent Persons Group, Commonwealth Secretariat, *Mission to South Africa: The Commonwealth Report*, Penguin, Harmondsworth, 1986

Financial Sanctions: Banking on Apartheid, Commonwealth Secretariat and James Currey, London, 1990

Gunthorp, Dale (ed.), *The Commonwealth Yearbook*, published by Hanson Cooke Ltd. for The Commonwealth Secretariat, London, 1996, 1997

Hanlon, Joe et al, *South Africa: The Sanctions Report,* Commonwealth Secretariat and Penguin, London, 1989

Hanlon, Joe (ed.), *South Africa: The Sanctions Report: Documents and Statistics,* Commonwealth Secretariat and James Currey, London, 1990

Hazlewood, Arthur (ed.), *African Integration and Disintegration: Studies in Economic and Political Union,* Royal Institute of International Affairs and Oxford University Press, London, 1967

Ibekwe, Patrick, *Wit & Wisdom of Africa: Proverbs from Africa & the Caribbean,* Africa World Press, Trenton, New Jersey, 1998

Isichei, Elizabeth, *The Ibo People and the Europeans: The Genesis of a Relationship — to 1906,* Faber and Faber, 1973

Isichei, Elizabeth, *A History of Nigeria,* Longman, Hounslow, 1983

Iweka-Nuno, I.E. (translator), *The History of Obosi and of Ibo-Land in Brief,* partially translated from the Ibo [sic]* copy, 1923

Johnson, Phyllis and David Martin, *Apartheid Terrorism: The Destabilisation Report,* Commonwealth Secretariat and James Currey, London, 1989

King, Martin Luther, *Letter from Birmingham Jail,* April 1963

Mandela, N., *Long Walk to Freedom: The Autobiography of Nelson Mandela,* Macdonald Purnell, Randburg, 1994

Manning, Patrick, *Slavery and African Life: Occidental, Oriental, and African Slave Trades,* Cambridge University Press, 1990

Mazrui, Ali, *The Trial of Christopher Okigbo,* Heinemann African Writers Series, 1971

Mbeki, Thabo, *Africa: the time has come,* Mafube and Tafelburg, Johannesburg and Cape Town, 1998

McIntyre, W. David, *The Significance of the Commonwealth 1965-1990,* Macmillan, Basingstoke, 1991

Nwankwo, Arthur A., *Nigeria: The Challenge of Biafra,* Rex Collings, London, 1972

Obasanjo, Olusegun, *Nzeogwu,* Spectrum Books, Ibadan, 1987

Ojigbo, Okion, *Nigeria Returns to Civilian Rule*

Ojukwu, Chukwuemeka Odumegwu, *Biafra: Selected Speeches and Random Thoughts of C. Odumegwu Ojukwu, General of the People's Army,* Harper & Row, New York/Evanston/London, 1969

Ojukwu, Chukwuemeka Odumegwu, *Because I am Involved,* Spectrum Book, Ibadan, 1989

Okri, Ben, *The Famished Road,* Jonathan Cape, London 1991, Vintage edition, London, 1992

Omotoso, Kole, *Just Before Dawn,* Spectrum Books, Ibadan, 1988

Rake, Alan (ed.), *New African Yearbook 1999/2000,* 12th edition, IC Publications, London, 1999

Sadiq Ali, Shanti (ed.), *Ghandi & South Africa,* Hind Pocket Books, Delhi, 1994

Smaldone, Joseph P., *Warfare in the Sokoto Caliphate: Historical and Sociological Perspectives,* Cambridge University Press, 1990

Smith, Arnold with Clyde Sanger, *Stitches in Time: The Commonwealth in World Politics,* André Deutsch, London, 1981

Ubahakwe, E, *Igbo Names: Their Structure and Meanings,* Day Star Press, Ibadan, 1981

Urquhart, Brian and Erskine Childers, *A World in Need of Leadership: Tomorrow's United Nations,* Dag Hammarskjöld Foundation, Uppsala, 1990

Usman, Yusufu Bala, *For the Liberation of Nigeria,* New Beacon Books, London, 1979

Waldmeir, Patti, *Anatomy of a Miracle,* Penguin, London, 1997

West Africa magazine, 1990 — 1999, London

Williams, David, *President and Power in Nigeria: The Life of Shehu Shagari,* Frank Cass, London, 1982

* Ibo was the accepted orthography during the colonial period and most books written pre-independence within and outside Nigeria used this spelling. The correct orthography is Igbo, and this was reintroduced soon after independence. However, for proper pronunciation you would have to listen to an Igbo-speaker, who can swallow the g, because it is not pronounced as Ig-bo, rather more like 'Ee [pause] bo', with emphasis on the pause.

PROFILE OF THE SECRETARY-GENERAL
AND THE COMMONWEATLH

Biographical note

HE Chief Emeka Anyaoku, CON
Ichie Adazie Obosi, Ugwumba Idemili
Commonwealth Secretary-General

ELEAZAR CHUKWUEMEKA ANYAOKU was elected third
Secretary-General of the Commonwealth by Heads of
Government at their meeting in Kuala Lumpur in 1989 and took
office in July 1990; he was re-elected for a second term beginning
in July 1995 and relinquishes office in the year 2000. He is a
Nigerian national, born at Obosi in 1933 and educated at
University College, Ibadan, where he studied Classics, graduating
with a London University Honours Degree, as a college scholar, in
1959. After two years with the Commonwealth Development
Corporation, and four years in the Nigerian Foreign Service
including a period at the United Nations, he joined the
Commonwealth Secretariat in 1966, just after its inception. He was
appointed Director for International Affairs in 1971 and Assistant
Secretary-General in 1975, and was elected Deputy Secretary-
General in 1978. He has worked with the Commonwealth for over
30 years, except for a short stint as Nigeria's Foreign Minister in
1983, and has been a keen observer and player in many of the
issues in which the Commonwealth was involved in Africa, Asia,
the Caribbean, Europe and the Pacific, as well as other major
international events during that period. He is/has been a member
of the International Board of the United World Colleges and the
Governing Council of the International Institute for Strategic
Studies in London, and a trustee of the Rajiv Ghandi foundation,
the Malaysian Commonwealth Studies Centre at Cambridge and
the World Commission on Forestry, as well as vice-president of
the Commonwealth Trust. He holds over 20 honorary university
degrees and other decorations, and was awarded Commander of
the Order of the Niger (CON) by the elected President of Nigeria,
Alhaji Shehu Shagari, in 1982. He was installed as Ndichie Chief,
Ichie Adazie Obosi, at Obosi, in December 1980, and invested with
the title *Ugwumda Idemili*, at Ogidi, in January 1990. He married
Olubunmi Solanke in 1962; they have three sons, a daughter and
son-in-law, and two grandchildren.

Honorary Degrees

1990   University of Ibadan, Nigeria, D.Litt
1991   Ahmadu Bello University, Zaria, Nigeria, D.Phil
        University of Nigeria, Nsukka, Nigeria, LL.D
1992   University of Aberdeen, UK, LL.D
        University of Redding, UK, LL.D
1993   University of Bristol, UK, LL.D
        Oxford Brookes University, UK, LL.D
        University of Birmingham, UK, LL.D
1994   University of Buckingham, UK, D.Litt
        Institute of Education, Univ. London, Hon.Fellow
        University of Leeds, UK, LL.D
        South Bank University, UK, LL.D
1995   University of New Brunswick, Canada, LL.D
        University of Bradford, UK, D.Litt
        University of North London, UK, LL.D
1997   University of Liverpool, UK, LL.D
        University of London, UK, LL.D
1998   University of Nottingham, UK, LL.D
1999   University of Dublin, Trinity College, LL.D
        University of Zimbabwe, D.Litt

Other Decorations

Commander of the Order of the Niger, Nigeria, 1982
Livingstone Medal, (Royal Scottish Geographical Society), 1996
Hon. Fellow of the College of Perceptors, UK, 1998
Freedom of the City of London, 1998
Trinity Cross, highest national honour of Trinidad & Tobago, 1999
Commander of the Most Courteous Order of Lesotho, highest civilian honour, 1999
Grand Officer of the National Order of Valour, Cameroon 1999
Order of the Welwitchia (First Class), highest national honour, Namibia, 2000

The Commonwealth

The Commonwealth is the second largest global association of independent states, after the United Nations. Today it has 54 member states of which 19 are in Africa; 19 in Asia and the Pacific; 13 in the Americas; and three in Europe. It has a total population of 1.7 billion people, and spans every major political grouping, regional bloc and economic zone. More than one in four people in the world lives in a Commonwealth country; its membership includes some of the world's fastest growing economies, as well as the richest and the poorest. The Commonwealth has no charter, its members voluntarily consult and cooperate; they subscribe to a number of declarations and uphold a set of fundamental principles, enshrined in the 1971 Singapore Declaration and the 1991 Harare Declaration. These principles include the equality of all people, as well as democracy and good governance, respect for human rights and the rule of law, and sustainable economic and social development. The leaders meet every two years at Commonwealth Heads of Government Meetings (CHOGM); the last one before the new millennium was in Durban, South Africa in November 1999. There are regular meetings of ministers, ie education, finance, health, law, women affairs, youth, and of parliamentary, media and other associations, including non-governmental organizations and private sector. Virtually all English-speaking countries belong to the Commonwealth, except the United States of America and the Irish Republic.

List of Commonwealth members, 1999

COUNTRY (CAPITAL)
1   Antigua & Barbuda (St John's)
2   Australia (Canberra)
3   The Bahamas (Nassau)
4   Bangladesh (Dhaka)
5   Barbados (Bridgetown)
6   Belize (Belmopan)
7   Botswana (Gaborone)
8   Britain (London)
9   Brunei Darussalam (Bandar Seri Begawan)
10 Cameroon (Yaounde)
11 Canada (Ottawa)
12 Cyprus (Nicosia)
13 Dominica (Roseau)

14 Fiji (Suva)
15 The Gambia (Banjul)
16 Ghana (Accra)
17 Grenada (St George's)
18 Guyana (Georgetown)
19 India (New Delhi)
20 Jamaica (Kingston)
21 Kenya (Nairobi)
22 Kiribati (Tarawa)
23 Lesotho (Maseru)
24 Malawi (Lilongwe)
25 Malaysia (Kuala Lumpur)
26 Maldives (Malé)
27 Malta (Valletta)

28 Mauritius (Port Louis)
29 Mozambique (Maputo)
30 Namibia (Windhoek)
31 Nauru (Nauru)
32 New Zealand (Wellington)
33 Nigeria (Abuja)
34 Pakistan (Islamabad)
35 Papua New Guinea (Port Moresby)
36 St Kitts & Nevis (Basseterre)
37 St Lucia (Castries)
38 St Vincent & The Grenadines (Kingstown)
39 Seychelles (Victoria)
40 Sierra Leone (Freetown)
41 Singapore (Singapore)

42 Solomon Islands (Honiara)
43 South Africa (Pretoria)
44 Sri Lanka (Colombo)
45 Swaziland (Mbabane)
46 Tanzania (Dar es Salaam)
47 Tonga (Nuku'alofa)
48 Trinidad & Tobago (Port of Spain)
49 Tuvalu (Funafuti)
50 Uganda (Kampala)
51 Vanuatu (Port Vila)
52 Western Samoa (Apia)
53 Zambia (Lusaka)
54 Zimbabwe (Harare)

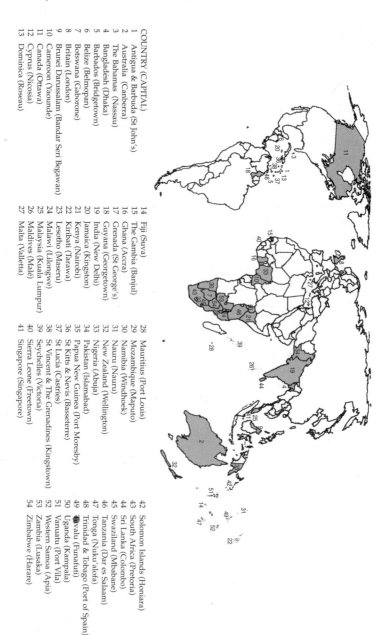